D0983650

Open the Door

Open the Door

The Life and Music of Betty Carter

by

William R. Bauer

Ann Arbor

The University of Michigan Press

Published in the United States of America by
The University of Michigan Press
Manufactured in the United States of America
⊗ Printed on acid-free paper

2005 2004 2003 2002 4 3 2 1

A CIP catalog record for this book is available from the British Library.

Library of Congress Cataloging-in-Publication Data

Bauer, William R. (William Roy), 1957–
Open the door : the life and music of Betty Carter / by William R. Bauer.
p. cm.
Includes bibliographical references (p.), discography (p.), videography (p.), and index.
ISBN 0-472-09791-1 (cloth : acid-free paper)
1. Carter, Betty, 1930– 2. Jazz singers—United States—Biography. I. Title.
ML420.C2584 B38 2002
782.42165'092—dc21 2001005504

Jacket photograph by Patrick Sylvain. Patrick Sylvain, poet, writer, visual artist, and teacher received his M.Ed. from Harvard University. Mr. Sylvain currently teaches at the Boston Public Schools and is also a PEN-New England board member. He has works published in several journals, revues, and anthologies.

To Betty Carter (1929–98)
in memory and in celebration

Contents

Preface and Acknowledgments

Betty Carter was many things to many people, but to her colleagues on the bandstand she was first and foremost a musician. This observation may seem obvious; yet, in light of the assumption many people make that singers are not musicians, it sums up Carter's most telling achievement. Several years after having worked with her, bassist Buster Williams expressed it best: "Betty is a real musician. You can play with her just like you would with any other strong musician. You don't have to hold back or add flowers to the changes [the chords]. Whatever you know and hear you can use."[1] Miles Davis described her as "a helluva musician."[2] Carter won her fellow musicians' respect because, more than any other singer, she applied the principles of bebop and postbop to the jazz vocal. It was her profound commitment to these principles that fueled her lifelong mission to expand the singer's role. As she herself put it: "When it's all over for me, I would like it said that Betty Carter was not just a singer, but a jazz musician *and* a singer."[3]

Carter challenged the prevailing view by upending a notion—implicit in much of the writing about jazz—that vocalists have few significant musical ideas of their own. Urging us to reevaluate the contribution singers make, her music beckons us to look deeper into the ways all singers craft their interpretations. Studying the work of singers has intrinsic merits, but it is also crucial to a general understanding of jazz because instrumental jazz often draws upon a vocal model for its expressiveness. Several musicians have echoed bassist Ira Coleman's sentiment that working with a singer is important to a player's musical development.[4] Having to place music within a singer's range can force players into difficult keys, for example, leading them to develop their musicianship. More important, in weaving interpretations out of the lyric's narrative, vocalists can inspire players to relate their sounds to the music's emotional message. Freddie Hubbard told Norman Provizer: "I love singers. They teach you how to phrase, especially on ballads."[5] Several instrumentalists sing as well as play, and when practicing a melodic passage a player may scat it to feel its precise phrasing.[6] In an idiom that places such a strong emphasis upon asserting one's individualism, the exhortation to "find your own voice" takes on near literal significance.

Betty Carter's accomplishments can best be understood from carefully considering her musical methods. This I have done within the context of her own personal aesthetic and approach, about which she often spoke eloquently. Describing her thought process on the bandstand, she once revealed to drummer Art Taylor how conscious she was of organizing pitch in an instrumental way: "When you're scatting, you can almost see the notes. You can see your half-tones and you know how they're supposed to sound because you see the keyboard in your head."[7] An artist in the best sense of the word, Carter had a vivid idea of what she wanted to say and she used every means available to give birth to her musical vision. This is one reason why her work had such a compelling immediacy in performance and is so rewarding to return to again and again on recordings. Clearly her singing warrants serious study on its own terms, as music.

To explore her approach in depth is consistent with Carter's own feeling that jazz deserves the kind of intensive study that other music receives. She once told interviewer Art Roberts: "Just to decipher what Supersax did with Charlie Parker's solo, for a musician just to break it apart on a score sheet, is very educational."[8] In this spirit, I have translated fifteen of Carter's performances into music notation. In addition, I have included phonetic transcriptions to illustrate her approach to singing lyrics and scat syllables, shedding light on her characteristic phrasing and articulation.[9] These transcriptions may appear difficult at first glance, but reading musical and phonetic notation of Carter's recordings while listening to them helps render key aspects of her artistry apparent. The analyses are designed so listeners may experience the music "through her ears," so to speak. To this end I have used musicians' terminology in my discussion of the music. Because it is useful at times to conduct musical analysis without reference to music notation, I have referred to musical passages by timing as well as by measure number so readers may locate them on a CD player using the digital timer. For this reason I have also not restricted my musical analyses to transcribed examples.

A warning must precede any reference to music notation, for as with the writing of spoken language it necessarily leaves out much in order to convey much. Simply to arrange words on a page flattens out a significant element of their meaning and expression known to linguists as *suprasegmentals*, belying the remarkable variety of melodic shapes that result when those same words are spoken. To produce a meaningful reading, we automatically supply missing information. So it is with music. If the notes on the page are to make sense, we must breathe into them the remembered life of performed sound. Even then, several aspects of music cannot be written down and must be transmitted orally. This is especially true in the case of jazz, where the music's aesthetic leads musicians to take elements that standard notation most easily sets down in writing—the alignment of rhythm with the beat, for example, or the tuning of pitch according to a tempered scale—and manipulate them in such a way as to take them beyond notatable form. The bending of time and tone that results is a distinguishing feature of jazz. This intentionally unmeasured plasticity has ramifications for the transcriber, for it lies in the spaces between what is considered "correct" in European classical music, the source of standard notation. In those moments when a musician breaks the "rules," she reveals that *she* is in utter command of *them,* and not the other way around. Furthermore, by transgressing the uniformity that can sometimes result from performances of music notation, she also asserts her own distinctive approach to sound. At times I have notated such moments too precisely, setting their awkwardness on the page against their naturalness in sound. Most other times, however, I have used less concrete notation for such moments. My usage should not be taken to indicate any carelessness on Betty Carter's part, for it is the notation that is unsound and must be jury-rigged in order to suggest the ways she outstrips its limitations.

I therefore urge the reader to listen to the recordings while studying the music examples, for the latter are not meant to stand on their own. Rather than discourage readers from finding out how the music actually sounds, the transcriptions should spur readers to listen more closely to what Carter actually did. All musicians, instrumentalists and vocalists, composers and improvisers, can benefit from studying her phrasing and her concept. But Carter's music was obviously not intended only for musicians: having come of age musically when the complex style of bebop was in ascendance, she felt that the style had a direct appeal for all. Nevertheless, she realistically acknowledged that jazz challenged listeners, and by connecting the music to words and images she gave her audience a variety of ways to gain access to its intricacies.

Betty Carter's relatively small recorded output has in some ways dictated my approach to this study. The "alternate takes" from her session reels—a key tool for exploring an artist's approach—have yet to be issued, but several tunes in her repertoire recur throughout her career. By comparing these renditions I have shown that the defining features of Carter's style remained consistent even as her approach kept changing.[10] Private recordings are also mentioned in the text, but only those that are commercially available have been transcribed. Recordings are only part of the story, however, for Betty Carter lived to perform. In performance she became a physical incarnation of the music—bending, turning, twisting, abruptly freezing in tableau, conducting her rhythm section with the drop of a hand or the stamp of a heel. Her recordings necessarily omit the visual designs that helped her audiences grasp her sonic abstractions. For this and other reasons, Carter handled the recording process with a different kind of care than she did her live work. In addition to the greater scrutiny listeners can give to recordings, the high costs of recording can also affect the process in subtle ways, say, limiting the degree of risk an artist will take. Selecting one of several takes for commercial issue is one of the ways an artist exercises control over these factors, and Carter had strong ideas about what material warranted release. Nor was she averse to using the available technology—rerecording the vocal tracks, for example—to exploit the medium's distinctive possibilities. Although she treated recording with greater deliberation than she did her work before an audience, she always worked for a "live vibe" in the studio.[11]

Furthermore, Carter did not exaggerate the value of the product that resulted from the recording process. To the contrary, she tended to view the commercial release of her music largely as a tool for marketing her live work. She once berated a critic who raved about a recording for not bothering to come out and catch her live show.[12] She had learned early on that, for a jazz musician, recording was not what paid the rent: "Over time you can make money if you realize that people are the most important thing: if you depend on a record you're in trouble, you've got to depend on your [live] audience."[13] In many respects, each of Carter's performances was a single instance of an ongoing and fluid musical process that reached no particular conclusion in a definitive version of the tune. As with transcription, one hazard of studying a recording is that it can lend a fixed, immutable character to an improvisation that took shape as it was emerging from the musician's imagination. With all of the above factors in mind we can experience Carter's recordings in their proper perspective.

My analysis of Carter's musical work has been framed within the story of her career's unfolding, for many features of her work cannot be understood without referring to events in her life, as well as in the music world she inhabited. In order to survive as an artist, for example, Carter filled many roles in the music business at one time or other, and often all at once. Not only was she a singer, entertainer, lyricist, actress, storyteller, improviser, composer, arranger, and band leader, but she also involved herself at various times in producing, distributing, marketing, and publicizing her own recordings, booking her own gigs, contracting her own sidemen, and handling contractual and legal issues that arose in her dealings with people in the business. In areas that she herself did not take on, such as sound engineering and postproduction, she educated herself enough to convey her wishes precisely to others who had the technical expertise to bring her vision to life. Amid all of these activities she taught herself to be a shrewd businesswoman as well. All of these roles influenced the choices she made as a musician.

Despite her suspicions of formal jazz education Carter was also a teacher. In the latter half of her career she generously shared the wisdom she had accumulated from a long life in the music world. It helped that she was so articulate and that she had worked hard to acquire the skills she displayed with such ease. Her words and her example rang with an authority that can only come from having lived the jazz life. She taught not so much by giving instruction or recommending imitation, as many teachers do, but by giving musicians the opportunity to perform and by urging them to develop their own voice. Her teaching approach, as it were, has much to recommend to jazz educators. Yet, as much as Carter's work as an educator enduringly changed the landscape of the jazz world by unearthing much of the talent that drives the current scene, it should not be viewed as more significant than her own musical work, but rather all of a piece with it.

Carter felt that the decline of jazz as a cultural force in the 1960s grew from a fragmentation of the community that sustained it, and she battled this decline mightily, both in word and in deed. Since then, the way the music is transmitted from older to younger musicians has slowly but steadily shifted from the street to the university. Carter was dubious. I suspect she feared, as I do, that the institutionalization of jazz education could cause the music's practitioners to lose touch with the oral culture that lies at its roots. The story of her career argues for the continued vitality of the oral tradition that she herself embodied. In order to celebrate and preserve this culture, I have drawn from it, building the following narrative not only from the usual documentary sources, but also from my interviews with Carter and with those who knew and worked with her, as well as from interviews she gave to the many journalists who spoke with her over the years. As a result, her outlook on the events of her life, as well as her own inimitable voice, emerges from these pages.

Betty Carter lived in the fullest sense. Armed with strong opinions and a hungry passion for life, she seized every opportunity she was given to expand her horizons. When opportunities were not forthcoming, she created them. She was a quick study, making good use of everything she learned, and she adapted to the needs of each new situation as it arose. Because of her innate curiosity, life provided raw material for her art, and her work has the gritty texture and sharp tang of the real world. Hers was not a pretty, rarefied artistry, but the kind that hit you with the directness and freshness of a splash of cold water. When you were in her presence, you knew you were alive. A person with a sharply etched character, Carter was hardly a saint, yet she was heroic in the face of the chaotic events that beset her. She liked being in control. Rather than drift aimlessly, she took charge of situations as they arose. She navigated troubled waters with a sureness and a resilience that one can only marvel at. Above all else she was faithful to her muse and happiest when she was making music. She rarely compromised her professional goals on behalf of her personal life, and she trusted very few people deeply or for any length of time. In many ways a secretive person, she drew a firm line between her private self and her public persona, a line that I have largely respected in this book. Yet in spite of this division, her work was a direct expression of who she was. As composer David Amram has noted: "Everything she did, she did as she felt at the moment."[14]

The myriad events of Carter's fifty-year career unfolded during a critical period in American musical life, a period that has left a deep imprint on the present. By reliving these events through her eyes, not only can we note Carter's contribution to American culture, but we can also learn about the forces that have molded, and continue to mold, jazz's history and meaning. To take one example, during the 1960s most vocalists were eager to shed the jazz designation in order to survive the steady erosion of the music's audience. By the end of that decade, it was not unusual to encounter the view expressed by vocalist Ann Richards, who said: "I grew up surrounded by jazz, but right now I'm trying to break that stigma."[15] Instead of avoiding this label, Carter courageously deepened her commitment to the bebop ideal, fully aware that doing so would damage her opportunities as a performer. Rather than view the slamming shut of music industry doors as the end of her career, she redefined the role of the jazz singer. To the casual observer, as Carter steadily expanded the boundaries typically placed around the jazz vocalist's realm, she sounded more and more "out." But to those who understood the jazz process, her work was the fulfillment of everything that a jazz singer should do, and more "in" than that of many instrumentalists. Paradoxically, Carter embodied and enriched the jazz tradition even as she challenged its assumptions about the singer's place in it. She was so steeped in the idiom and sensibility that Carmen McRae once told *Down Beat* writer Harvey Siders that "there's really only one jazz singer—only one: Betty Carter."[16] Anyone seeking a definition of jazz singing could do no better than look at Carter's career and her work. This book illustrates just how rich such a definition needs to be in order to convey the complexity of the role that one vocalist filled in the jazz world. Still, it merely scratches the surface.

Carter was an African American woman, and she identified passionately with her roots in black culture. These roots informed her view of the world, even as she forged her own aggressively unique personal vision. Although she had a large white following, to this day Carter remains best known in the black community. She viewed jazz as a distinctly black music, one that grew out of the experience of black Americans exiled in their own country. Any frank recounting of her life in the music business could hardly argue for a color-blind history of jazz. Carter did not yield ground in order to cross over to a white audience, but demanded recognition for her artistry on her own terms. This stance hindered her success in the entertainment world and kept her from attaining the stature of her colleagues—Ella Fitzgerald, Sarah Vaughan, Billie Holiday, Carmen McRae, and Dinah Washington—singers who made their mark when jazz was America's popular music. Midway through her career, Betty Carter abandoned her hopes for widespread recognition and instead secured a place of honor in the jazz underground. She believed that her highest calling was to produce a music of depth and soul, one that reminds us of our complexity as individuals, with all our strengths and frailties. Her message continues to have an urgency that transcends the historical reality through which she lived.

In the course of living her life and doing her work, Betty Carter left a profound mark on the lives of others, transforming whatever and whomever she touched: tunes, musicians, audiences. She once described her self-appointed mission to bassist Chris White: "I always thought whenever I got on the stage, before an audience, that I had a job to do. And that was to see to it that that audience went out of this club, or this concert hall, or whatever, with a little piece of me on their minds. I set out to do this."[17] Few people remained the same when Betty Carter was finished with them; her impact produced a fresh perspective. In her hands, songs you thought you knew well evoked wonderfully exotic worlds made palpable by the clarity of her artistic vision. Listeners emerged from these worlds with a renewed vision of life, love, and music. For musicians a gig with Carter was never routine. Habits brought onto the bandstand got retooled into fresh strategies for shaping the listener's attention, strategies to be used long after leaving the band.

During the past few years, Carter's distinctive sound has been used in a variety of settings to convey a hip insider quality. You can hear her behind the closing scene of an episode of the television series *ER* singing the bridge to "I Don't Want to Set the World on Fire," her voice wafting from an apartment's half-opened door into the lonely night outside.[18] Close to the beginning of the 1999 film *American Beauty,* Carter's voice can be heard offering an oblique commentary on one character's muddled attempt to reach out to another, with her own composition, "Open the Door." To those who treasure her characteristic approach to the jazz vocal, hearing the sound of Betty Carter's voice will provide an invitation to come through the door she held open to that miraculous world where sounds become music, where singing becomes artistry, where life and jazz meet.

Acknowledgments

This is not the book I embarked upon writing in 1998. That July, I met with Betty Carter in Brooklyn to tell her the news of the book contract. After discussing the need to assemble photographs and my wish to conduct an interview to follow up the ones I had already conducted, she and I parted with the expectation that we would meet up again in the fall. This meeting was not meant to be. On 26 September Betty Carter died of pancreatic cancer. I found out later that her illness had only been diagnosed in mid-August. The disease took her life so swiftly that her death left everyone in the jazz world stunned. That so vibrant a figure was no longer present to work her magic was incomprehensible. I now felt that my original study, which had depended largely upon Betty's own perspective on the events of her life, needed to be opened up. I turned to the vast network of people who had known and worked with her to flesh out the story of her life and to address gaps that remained in my research. It is a tribute to Betty that nearly everyone I spoke to was eager to contribute. Most welcomed the opportunity to revisit their memories of her. This book bears the traces of the love they had for her. I regret that time constraints kept me from speaking to others who wanted to contribute.

Several people went beyond the pale, not only spending several hours responding to my inquiries, but also opening up their datebooks, file cabinets, and lives to add significant bits of data. This book has benefited greatly from the help of David Amram, Dwayne Burno, Bruce Flowers, Beverly Harris, Jim Harrison, JoAnne Jimenez, Grachan Moncur III, and Kenny Washington. Matthew Yaple deserves many thanks for his groundbreaking research on Betty, which places this book on very firm footing indeed. His enthusiasm for my project has been a huge source of encouragement.

Many of the musicians and music business professionals who knew Betty reached deep into their memories to provide important details about her life, including Clifford Barbaro, Cameron Brown, Ira Coleman, Jimmy Cleveland, Peven Everett, Craig Handy, John Hicks, Javon Jackson, Cecil McBee, Harold McKinney, Daniel Mixon, Khalid Moss, Lewis Nash, and Janet Thurlow, as well as Arnold Jay Smith, studio manager Lynn Berry, producer Sid Feller, and sound engineer Joe Ferla. Over the course of several talks, producer Joel Dorn clarified many uncertainties. Some members of Betty's family, her brother James Taylor Jones III, and her sons, Kagle and Myles Redding, also took time to help with my research, with Kagle providing many of the photographs.

Several people provided—either in short interviews or conversations—answers to questions crucial to the book's accuracy, including Lyle Atkinson, Danny Bank, Todd Barkan, George Benson (from Detroit), Andy Bey, Irene

Meadows Blanding, Willie Boler, Gail Boyd, Don Braden, Ray Bryant, Lodi Carr, Michael Carvin, Noal Cohen, Michael Cuscuna, Johnny Gary, Gail Goldstein, Derek Gordon, Tommy Gryce, Slide Hampton, Barry Harris, Joey Helguera, Stephen Horelick, Michael Kantor, John Levy, Danny Michael, James Romeo Redding, Tanya Reed, Larry Ridley, Ernie Rogers, Louise Ryles, Jimmy Scott, Richard Schultz, John Screiber, Kevin Struthers, and Lois Sheely. Danielle Walker translated several French sources.

Many of my former teachers have helped develop my musical understanding, but two in particular, Robert Abramson and Jack Beeson, indelibly formed my thinking about the relationship between music theory and performance, the unique contribution of singers to music, and the rhythms inherent in the English language. As a teacher and as a scholar, Patricia Carpenter gave me a powerful model of excellence. Advisement given to me by Howard Brofsky, Leo Treitler, and John Graziano established the scholarly standard I set out to meet. At an early stage in the process, concrete advice on how to organize my research—a large part of writing a book—came from author Walter Lord. Music copyist Tom Bencivengo prepared the music examples on Finale 2000. My former student Anand Pathuri transcribed several interviews, including one between Betty and me that ran over three hours; my son Conrad Bauer transcribed my long interview with Kenny Washington; Karen Streech provided essential typing. Both of my sons, Conrad and Isaac, alerted me to Betty's status in the hip-hop scene.

Many people offered invaluable nuggets of information or came up with a valuable primary source, guided my research in a fruitful path, read parts of the manuscript, gave encouragement when I most needed it, or provided some form of intangible support, including Bonnie Berchielli, Joshua Berrett, Kevin LaVine of the Library of Congress, Francis Davis, Luann Dragone, Jacqui Drechsler, Dorothy Earley, Charles Estus, Dorothy Ferabee (from *Fresh Air*), Edward Fertik, Patricia Gesell, Ben Goldstein, Allen Grundy, Ora Harris, Darryl Jordan, Marshall Hornblower, Alex Jaekel, David Kagan, Orrin Keepnews, Sara Kiesel, Wolfram Kauer, Alan Kuras, Joel Lester, Howard Mandel, Jeff McMillan, Jim and Mary McGuire, Karen Monroe, Esq., Anthony Nevins, Joe Petrucelli, Becca Pulliam, Heidi Reigler, David Lionel Smith, Mark Stryker of the *Detroit Free Press*, Dr. Billy Taylor, and Mike Whitney. Authors of unpublished writing about aspects of Betty's work, Karen A. Scheiber, Jane Manners, Jemilla Mulvihill, have undoubtedly influenced my thinking. Selma Porter helped me get out of my own way, so I could proceed with the business of writing and living. Nancy Stout commiserated with me in writerly ways, helping to get me through some of the more challenging times. Stuart and Sandella Walker shared the glories of black music with me when I most needed to receive its message. Singer Melba Joyce has championed my work on Betty for a long time and has inspired me with her own outstanding, but sadly neglected, jazz vocalizations.

Many thanks to the Institute of Jazz Studies and its staff for opening its remarkable collection to me. In particular, my colleague and friend Vincent Pelote helped to jump-start my research with his own enthusiasm for Betty and with his encyclopedic knowledge of the Institute. He also read portions of the manuscript. The Jazz Research Roundtable and its corollary listserv on the Internet have been a steady source of information and encouragement among like-minded souls. In a similar vein I am grateful for the countless conversations I have had with jazz scholar, radio host, friend, and stepson Evan Spring, who has helped with the research, commented on the manuscript, and provoked my thinking about the world of jazz and Betty's place in it.

I would like to thank Rutgers-Newark for providing the opportunity for me to spend time writing this book, including a leave of absence in fall 1998 to pursue my research. A grant from the Rutgers Research Council helped defray the cost of preparing the music examples. The students who studied in the university's master's degree program in jazz history and research during the past three years have pushed me to articulate my thinking. Sage counsel about the perils of perfectionism from my department chair, Annette Juliano, kept this book from remaining merely a promising manuscript.

Sometimes saying *thank you* doesn't come close to acknowledging the magnitude of the help that was given. Such is the case with the contribution of my good friend and colleague Lewis Porter. I cannot possibly thank him enough. His unstinting attention to this project from its very beginnings, his sharing of vital primary source material from his enormous personal jazz archive, ranging from African American newspaper clippings to rare video footage and recordings, as well as his thoughtful guidance and idealism, have helped make this book a reality. The model of his scholarship has influenced my work on this book in countless ways.

My family has grounded me during the writing, freeing me to become absorbed in the process of researching and writing without feeling disconnected from them. The Bauer clan has been supportive and understanding of my total immersion in this project. Conrad and Isaac quickly learned to assess whether or not the author had had a good writing day and to respond accordingly. Evan, mentioned earlier, his brother Declan, and Declan's wife, Robin, have all added their spirit to the cause. Most important, my wife Marjorie's belief in this project has been crucial to its completion. During the prolonged journey this book represents she kept many aspects of our lives humming and balanced. In addition, every one of these pages is graced with her editorial wisdom.

All books inevitably stem from their author's understanding of its subject and this one is no exception. As much as my understanding has grown from an evolving interaction with the materials available to me, the recordings, the documents, as well as the people who participated in Betty's life, I take sole responsibility for any of this book's defects. I urge readers who have information or corrections to contact me through the publisher. Data concerning unissued audio and video recordings would be especially useful in compiling a comprehensive discography and videography. I apologize to any contributors I have neglected to mention.

This book bears a dedication to Betty Carter. Implicitly, however, it honors the people of all generations who continue to actively support jazz—the musicians, the teachers, the audience, the entire network of concert promoters, club owners, recording industry executives, writers, radio and television personalities, everyone who is working to advance the music. As Betty used to sing about one of her heroes: "Don't weep for the lady, she wouldn't want it that way."

Acknowledgments for musical examples

Introduction

On a summer day in 1948, a nineteen-year-old singer named Lillie Mae Jones left her hometown of Detroit, Michigan, and headed for Toledo, Ohio, to join up with the Lionel Hampton big band. After a relatively short time in the business she was already embarking upon a journey that few performers ever make, a journey that takes them out of their local scene and onto the national stage. Present at Detroit's awakening to bebop, and now passionately devoted to the gospel of John Birks "Dizzy" Gillespie and Charlie "Yardbird" Parker, the singer was the epitome of "cool." Almost in spite of this devotion—yet also because of it—she was going out on the road with a dance band.

In a gesture of self-definition, Jones assumed the name Lorene Carter.[1] This simple act put a reassuring distance between past and present: shedding her given name and taking a new one, she declared her independence from her family and embraced her new persona as a performer. Her name would eventually evolve into the one by which we knew her, and the process that led her to it sheds light on the principal characters involved and the historical forces that guided their actions.

This process actually began several weeks before the singer left home, on 19 June 1948. It was on that day that the young singer informally auditioned for Lionel Hampton when his busy touring schedule led him to the Forest Club at the corner of Hastings and Forest in Detroit.[2] Dressed in an outfit and cap that flaunted her allegiance to bebop,[3] Lillie Mae stood out from the crowd of "jitterbugs" who had come to dance and enjoy an evening of big-band entertainment. Because of her avid loyalty to bebop, she had only come at the urging of friends, especially her boyfriend, Thomas Daniels. At first she could barely hide her disdain for the swing-era style.

For a small but growing number of young people, bebop was all the rage.

The first stirrings of the style—also known as modern, or progressive, jazz—had been heard some years before, mainly in Harlem. Only during the preceding year or so had it begun to catch on in Detroit. Before long the city would produce a generation of musicians schooled in the new style, but for most of those assembled at the Forest Club that night bebop was still somewhat fresh. Fancying herself on the cutting edge of musical style, the young hipster was too sophisticated to take interest in such old-fashioned music as Hampton's. For her, big-band music was history.

Once in the presence of the musicians, however, Jones and her friends could barely resist the temptation to join the listeners crowding the bandstand, absorbing the explosive power of Hampton's music. Some soloists in the band were experimenting with the new idiom, and the influence of bebop in some of the band's arrangements may even have earned her begrudging approval. The driving rhythmic impulse behind the band's music, along with Hampton's crowd-pleasing antics and his charismatic engagement with the audience, had a way of driving crowds to a frenzy.

Standing on the sidelines, the rookie entertainer was gradually drawn into the spirit of the occasion. She started to sing along with the band for her own entertainment, exploring various harmonic possibilities against the impromptu backup the music provided for her. She stood close enough for the band leader to hear her, and he later recalled that with every chord the band hit "she would insert a phrase, such as 'shoo-bop-a-daa,' singing on the thirteenth or the flatted fifth, or a flatted seventh."[4] Along with her habit of answering the band's phrases with a bebop comment, the singer's stylish outfit and beguiling looks caught the band leader's eye. Hampton didn't need much goading from Jones's friends to invite her onto the bandstand: "Hamp looked at me and said: 'Can you sing, Gates?' So, I looked at him like he was crazy, like, 'What do you mean, can I sing?' Like, 'Sure I can sing.' And he called me up and I sang."[5] Hampton's way of addressing Jones was not unusual for him, as it turned out. "Hamp called everybody 'Gates.' If he [didn't] know your name, your name was 'Gates,' . . . and everybody in the band calls everybody 'Gates.'"[6]

Encouraged by her friends and armed with a cocky attitude, the aspiring vocalist took to the stage. She initially intended to stick to the melody of the tune Hampton called, probably "Oh, Lady Be Good,"[7] but the urge to show off her skill at improvising was too strong to resist. Using the wordless vocalizing known as scat, which Ella Fitzgerald had helped popularize on the same tune, Jones invented an entirely new melody to George Gershwin's popular song.[8] Hampton vividly recalled that "she came on up and started to scat and I was just amused, everybody in the band was thrilled and the crowd—she knocked the crowd out."[9] In her brief time on stage, Jones's scatting, her self-assurance, and her stage presence convinced Hampton of her potential.[10] Two weeks later he sent a telegram to her booking agent offering her a job.

The above reconstruction of Carter's and Hampton's meeting is based on several descriptions they gave more than twenty-five years later.[11] Key differences in their sensibilities come out in the subtle ways their descriptions diverge. Carter's versions emphasize factors that were beyond her control: her friends' pressuring her to come to the dance and their urging her to sit in with the band. Hampton's versions stress Carter's interest in getting a start in the business and his willingness to help her do so. The discrepancies remind us that, while they both experienced a single event, each of them brought a different outlook to it and came away with different ideas about its significance.

When Hampton added Carter to his roster, bebop was making its impact felt on big bands and on popular music in several ways. Eager to please his audience, Hampton wisely kept his ear to the ground for the latest craze. Even before bebop had proven its commercial potential at the national level, he began to show an interest in it. By implying that he had discovered Dizzy Gillespie in 1939 when he featured the trumpeter on "Hot Mallets," for example, he sought to link himself to one of the music's master builders.[12] Nor did Hampton shrink from promoting himself as an insider to the new scene, going so far as to represent himself as one of its innovators.

Hampton may have exaggerated his involvement in the creation of the new music, but he took a sincere interest in the next generation of musicians. Several of the players he employed during the late 1940s and early 1950s were associated with bebop, most prominently trumpeter McKinley Howard "Kenny" Dorham, bassist Charles Mingus Jr.—who provided some arrangements as well—and guitarist John Leslie "Wes" Montgomery.[13] In this light, Hampton's offer to hire an unknown singer after hearing her only once does not seem so extraordinary. Not to be outdone by his young colleagues, Hampton also explored the music's expanded harmonic vocabulary in his own work on the vibraphone, albeit in an offhanded way. During the late 1940s one can hear bebop mannerisms and occasional references to bebop players' solos crop up in his playing. Hampton showed greater receptiveness to the innovations of younger players than many from his own generation, and he could reasonably take some credit for having given the new style exposure.[14]

While bebop was predominantly an instrumental idiom, bop vocals played a significant role in the new music's popularization.[15] Scat was hardly new. Singers had been putting nonsense syllables to comic effect for years by the time Don Redman and Louis Armstrong produced its first recorded examples in the late 1920s.[16] Dizzy Gillespie's scat solos, with their playful imitation of bebop players' phrasing and articulation, increased the complex style's accessibility for nonmusicians. In 1947, when Ella Fitzgerald brilliantly rendered "Oh, Lady Be Good" and "How High the Moon" in scat, she sounded a bebop fanfare to the nation, and the music's popularity surged. Clearly Lionel Hampton was looking to broaden his band's appeal when he hired the resourceful young bebop singer from Detroit who had made a specialty of scatting.[17]

Hamp's playfulness with people's names, and his wish to exploit the novelty of Lorene Carter's modern sound and manner, led him to dub her "Betty Bebop."[18] If she had hoped to make a name for herself by joining the band, this was not what she had in mind. Carter hated the name and claimed Hampton introduced it because he had difficulty pronouncing "Lorene." While he may have had humorous intentions, Carter was not amused. But calling his new singer Betty Bebop gave Hampton an obvious way to signal to his audiences that she was his vocal representative of the modern style. For better or worse, the name did give Carter a clear sense of her place in the band. "I could scat and I had a good ear, so he used me for that. He couldn't have Charlie Parker or Dizzy Gillespie, so he got me!"[19] Members of the band took to calling Carter "the Kid," a nickname she accepted and would use throughout her life. It suggests the protective attitude they came to hold toward her. Although she grew in confidence and skill during her time with Hampton, this nickname lingered as a vestige of her original role as the band's resident novice.

During Carter's tenure with the band she became increasingly impatient with the restrictions Hampton and his nickname placed upon her. Early in 1951, after two and a half years of performing in Hampton's band and eager to leave behind the pigeonhole he had fashioned for her, she flew the coop. With her musical apprenticeship now behind her, Carter set about proving she was a full-fledged singer who could not only sing scat, but could also "turn a lyric." The time had once again come to shed her name and reinvent herself. But to do so now posed a problem: a new name would render her unrecognizable to the national audience she had reached thanks to the promotion Hampton had given her.[20] She later recalled that: "even though I complained about being called Betty Bebop, it was the name itself which kept people. It was easy for people to say. I got mileage out of it. When I came back to the city [New York] . . . the first thing that hit me was 'Ol Betty Bebop is back in town.'"[21]

By this time it was clear that the bebop craze had begun to wane. Mainstream listeners who had enjoyed the style at the end of the 1940s had already moved on, reinforcing the idea that many had been attracted by the "ephemeral lure of the incidental trappings rather than by the quality of the music itself."[22] In addition, the public had begun to associate the term *bebop* with drug use. In Carter's words, people felt that "if you had anything to do with jazz, bebop jazz, you had to be an addict and were not to be trusted, not dependable."[23] Carter had a keen eye for how to manage herself, even this early in her career. "I knew I was going to have trouble later. You know, you have foresight. Here's a word that everybody's talking about 'down with!' Which has nothing really to do with the music. Out of that dope crazy world came the most creative music."[24] Carter had what we now might call a marketing problem. How could Betty Bebop capitalize upon the exposure she had gained from her time on the road, while freeing herself from the stylistic limitations and negative connotations that came with the term *bebop*? The solution seemed simple enough: combine the *Betty* from Betty Bebop with the *Carter* from Lorene Carter. But over a decade later Carter still had not entirely escaped Hampton's legacy, even after making two records without a single scat solo. As late as 1966 she complained to Bill McLarney that the name Betty Bebop detracted from her image by suggesting a more limited singer than she had become. During this period Carter grew increasingly sensitive about the issue of style as the pop music market steadily drifted away from jazz. When a club owner would put the name Betty Bebop in parentheses underneath her name on the marquee, she objected, insisting he bill her *only* as Betty Carter: "I was fighting mad, you see, trying to get that name established in people's heads."[25] She even nixed a sign billing her as "The Bebop Girl." The lengths to which she had to go to establish her new name suggest that Betty Bebop had attained considerable renown in jazz circles as Hampton's scat-singing prodigy. They also reveal several character traits for which she would later become known: her hardheaded integrity; her stubborn defiance of the men who controlled her work options; her proud reluctance to acknowledge her debt to people who gave her a leg up in the business; and her idealistic insistence that people judge her solely on the merits of her talent. Carter cast herself in the mold of the rugged individualist, the loner, the self-made woman who would stand on the outside looking in, rather than sacrifice her autonomy to gain acceptance. Success would come on her terms or not at all. This is both a heroic and a lonely image, and not surprisingly, an oversimplification. Beneath her street-smart veneer, Carter had a tender, vulnerable side that shone through in her ballad renditions. Much of the complexity of her art lies in her willingness to reveal weakness where in life she sought to convey strength.

As Carter began to surface from the depths of obscurity in the mid-1970s, her attitude about her name relaxed a bit.

> I don't dislike the "Betty Bebop" nickname anymore; I've been converted again. I realized bebop was valuable, but I didn't realize *how* valuable until 1975, when I hear young kids come up to me and ask what the

> bebop era was all about. I came up in that world and loved that music. The musicians had a great influence on me, and I lived and worked with that music. And I still live it. So I don't care about the name now—you can call me "Betty Anything-you-wanna."[26]

During this time, Carter's growing concern for sustaining a jazz tradition that took bebop as its stylistic and cultural point of reference mitigated her earlier fear of being reduced to a single stylistic niche.[27] The wish to transmit her conception of jazz to the up-and-coming generation of young musicians placed bebop in a historical frame of reference, as a heritage to be preserved rather than as a new movement on the cutting edge of style. Although it was thirty years since the music had been on the forefront of stylistic innovation, to her it was ever fresh, ever giving birth to new possibilities.

The story of Betty Carter's various names has a curious twist to it. The singer mused wistfully in 1994 about having forsaken her given name, Lillie Mae Jones, or at least *Lillie.* She had not entirely done so, in fact, having absorbed it briefly into the name of her production company, Liljay Productions, in the early 1980s.[28] But in her misgivings about having abandoned her given name, she betrayed a note of remorse about the way she had broken off her association with her family when she left home. Significantly, after 1994 she prominently displayed photographs of her parents and other family members on the kitchen wall of her Brooklyn home in place of the pictures of her with the Lionel Hampton band that had been there earlier. Long before, in the late 1970s, Carter had begun to take time to rekindle family connections with the network of siblings and cousins that remained in the Detroit area. In renewing these connections and recovering lost memories, she began the slow process of healing wounds inflicted long before.

1

Childhood

In her singing, Betty Carter could wring as much feeling from a well-placed silence as she could from a song's lyrics. So it is with the impression she has left us of her childhood: from the hollow spaces carved out by her words echoes a sadness associated with her family. When she spoke of her childhood, for example, Carter didn't dwell much on her family life: "The family wasn't close enough where you passed around pictures and did the birthday bit."[1] As a child, Carter received more independence than nurturing from her parents.[2] Later, they did little to encourage their daughter's efforts to excel musically because they opposed her choice of career. Nearly thirty years after leaving home Carter recalled:

> I have been far removed from my immediate family. There's been no real contact or phone calls home every week to find out how everybody is. . . . As far as family is concerned, it's been a lonesome trek. . . . It's probably just as much my fault as it is theirs, and I can't blame anybody for it. But there was . . . no real closeness, where the family urged me on, or said . . . "We're proud" . . . and all that. No, no . . . none of that happened.[3]

From her family experience Carter forged an image of herself as a self-reliant fighter, and it was important to her that people recognize her independence: behind many anecdotes she recounted about her career lies the implicit message that she was not beholden to anyone. "Everything I did, I did pretty much by myself, without any help from people in the business other than musicians and club owners and stuff like that. But if you meant having somebody really close to you like a mother or father, or an aunt or uncle . . .

that wasn't there for me."[4] Carter's brother James challenged this view, stating that "she resented Mom's philosophy about life, but she didn't hesitate to ask her for money."[5]

Carter did retain a link to her family throughout her career, albeit a tenuous one. Visits with her relatives occurred when she returned periodically to work in Detroit after leaving home for good in the early 1950s.[6] A particular source of bitterness was her recollection that family members did not come out to hear her perform, not even when she had finally gained recognition for her work.

Bertha Jones's eldest child had an especially antagonistic relationship with her mother. Reflecting back on it gave Carter a deep sense of loss; yet it sounds as if Carter's own willfulness may have influenced her mother's reaction to her, especially during her adolescence. Her brother recalled, "She gave my mother, really gave her the blues, to put it mildly," adding that when she was fourteen or fifteen years old, "she was very outspoken. . . . I never could understand why she was resentful of her mother."[7] In contrast, Carter's younger sister, Vivian, "loved Mother, and they were close, very, very close," according to James. "Just opposite of Betty. Betty and Mother were always bickering back and forth."[8]

As she got older, Carter felt she understood her mother better, but the distance between the two women never closed.[9] Bertha Jones died in the early 1970s, when the jazz scene had reached its lowest ebb. This ultimate separation denied Carter the chance to vindicate herself in her mother's eyes and justify her career choice. Even as she expressed regret about her mother's death, there was a hint of rebelliousness in her wish to say, "I did not completely lose," as her mother predicted she would.[10] The schism between Carter and her immediate family must have been all the more painful because she came from a close-knit extended family that maintains a strong sense of continuity to this day. Strong-willed, self-determined people, her extended family taught her from her earliest years to strive for success.

Our knowledge of Betty Carter's paternal side of the family reaches back to before the Emancipation Proclamation, when her great-great-grandfather, Dennis Edgerson, was born a slave.[11] Soon after 1863, "Grandpa" Edgerson left Maryland and moved his family, including his daughter Martha to Louisiana. While there, Carter's great-grandmother Martha married Richard Dixon of Virginia and give birth to Carter's paternal grandmother, Elmira "Ain'tie" Dixon.[12] A pivotal figure, Elmira would go on to have seven children, including Carter's father, James Taylor Jones II; seventeen grandchildren, including Carter (née Lillie Mae Jones), her siblings Cheza B., Louise, James III, and Vivian, and her cousins; as well as forty-four great-grandchildren. By all accounts a powerful individual, Elmira reigned as the family matriarch, and for the Jones women particularly she was a paragon of strength.

When Reconstruction ended in 1877, Grandpa Edgerson moved his extended family to Auburn Township in southeast Arkansas, where they met Carter's great-grandfather, Richard Jones—who was originally from Tennessee—and his family. One of four siblings, Jones's only son, James Taylor Jones, was born in Varner, Arkansas.[13] While living at Grandpa Edgerson's farm in Dumas, a cotton town located eighty-five miles southeast of Little Rock,[14] Betty Carter's grandparents, James Taylor Jones and Elmira Dixon, had their first child on 22 May 1901. Unlike his younger siblings, Carter's father, James Taylor Jones II, did not attend school, but he could read and write.[15]

In the early 1920s, James Jones II fathered two daughters, Louise and Cheza B.—Betty Carter's half sisters—and shortly after moved his family to Pine Bluff. The seat of Jefferson County, Pine Bluff was an urban center on the Arkansas River midway between Dumas and Little Rock. Most of the city's black residents lived to the northwest and had their own stores, churches, cemetery, and schools.[16] Around 1926, Jones II, his two daughters, his new wife, Bertha Cox—also born in Arkansas—and his sister Alberta, joined a large wave of black emigration to the north, leading them to Detroit. During the first decades of the century, Detroit's black population had grown rapidly, indeed, almost exponentially.[17] Among other reasons, Henry Ford's application of the assembly line to automobile manufacture and his offer of a guaranteed minimum wage drew workers from all over the country, especially from the South. At a Ford plant a man could earn as much as six dollars a day, a good sum for factory workers in the late-1920s. At the Ford Motor Company's River Rouge plant James Jones II got a job as a press operator. Not long after the boll weevil blight in early fall of 1927, his father came to Detroit to work at Rouge as well, bringing Elmira and their remaining children. They settled at 2512 Brush, in the St. Antoine district of Detroit's largest black enclave, Paradise Valley.

The year 1929 was an eventful one for James Jones II. In February his sister Irene died at age fourteen, and in September his father also died. Between these two losses he had a daughter on 16 May, whom he and Bertha named Lillie Mae.[18] That October, the stock market crashed, sending the country reeling into the Great Depression. In Detroit, a large proportion of black workers lost their jobs, and soup lines formed at such places as Bishop's Theater. Nevertheless, Carter's parents were doing well enough to have two other children—Vivian Omera, born on 1 February 1931, and James Taylor III, born on 28 October 1933.[19] By the mid-1930s, James Jones II was earning enough to move his family from Paradise Valley to 1029 Stanley, on the fringe of Detroit's West Side, where many upwardly mobile black people lived. He and his brothers were among a growing number of African Americans who were achieving greater economic stability, and by 1940 all of the Jones clan had moved out of the ghetto. Elmira herself was living at 9598 Delmar then, in a "checkerboard," or racially mixed, neighborhood just a few blocks outside of Hamtramck. The economy continued to improve, and by the first years of the 1940s the ranks of the unemployed in Detroit had fallen dramatically. Along with Los Angeles, San Francisco, and Chicago, Motor Town was helping to bring the nation out of the depression, largely because of lucrative defense contracts.[20]

Hardship struck the Jones family again in 1946, when Elmira witnessed her son James die of kidney failure on 8 June and then succumbed to the effects of high blood pressure on 13 September. But the legacy of middle-class values they transmitted to succeeding generations survived them: James Jones III worked as a deputy for the Wayne County Sheriff's Department and in 1962 was among the first black people to move their families to northwest Detroit. His son, James Jones IV, would become a journalist. Having progressed from being farmers to factory workers to civil and medical workers to college graduates, the Jones family took pride in its members' accomplishments. All of them expected to attain improved social conditions, improved living conditions, improved prospects for work, and they struggled to achieve these goals.

Betty Carter's mother insisted that her children call on their relatives. James Jones III vividly recalled visits with his grandmother: "Ain'tie used to chew snuff and spit it in spittoons."[21] Bertha Jones, however, apparently remained aloof from her in-laws. In filling out her husband's death certificate, for example, she listed Ain'tie's name and place of birth as unknown.[22] Bertha's indifference to her husband's family seems to have grown from a general tendency toward autonomy—a value she stressed with her own children. Carter's brother recalled, "Mom taught us to be self-sufficient, to do your own thing. She said we could remain under her roof until we were 18. Then we had one choice: Leave."[23] The Cox branch of the family tree, which was situated in Flint, is therefore less well represented in the family's oral history.[24] Carter recalled that Bertha's sisters, Aunt Litha and Aunt Patsie, were both married to ministers, and that her mother's brothers were both ministers: Reverend Earnest Cox and Reverend James Cox.[25] When Bertha was expecting her first child, she turned to her own family, staying with one of her sisters at 1004 Baltimore Boulevard in Flint.[26] "She was afraid to have me by herself and not to have the family around. . . . We stayed there long enough to, maybe, stop nursing, and then she came back up to Detroit."[27]

Carter's half sisters, Louise Ryles and Cheza B. Rogers—C.B. for short—lived at home during her infancy, but while she was growing up they did not play a significant role in her life.[28] Both left home early, with C.B. marrying young and Louise moving initially to Washington, D.C. But C.B. came to play a greater role in her younger sister's life after their father died in 1946. Carter's reluctance to discuss her relationships with her siblings and her cousins, especially her cousin Irene, is surprising. Born 9 October 1929 and named after her deceased aunt, Irene Jones Meadows-Blanding described herself as Betty's "cousin-mate" because their birth dates were so close together.[29] She recalled spending much time with Carter as a child and disputed the claim that Carter's relatives didn't attend her performances. As children Lillie Mae and Irene would recite a chant that reveals just how deeply into the soil of the singer's youth stretch the roots of her outspokenness: "We chew gum, we eat popcorn, we don't lie." Irene's recollections of Elmira, who raised many of her grandchildren and instilled in them a sense of pride—teaching them that black is beautiful, for example, before it became a slogan—suggest that, as much as Lillie Mae had a mind of her own, she must have benefited from her Ain'tie's influence.[30] Irene cited Elmira's stance on color as an instance of her character: "You're white, so what; you're black, so what. The same God that made you made me."[31] Strong women in the Jones family, and Ain'tie was the inspiration for them all.

Carter's father had a strong personality as well, and he apparently felt a special bond with his daughter Lillie Mae. His son described him as "a very temperamental, difficult individual. . . . Betty and Dad were similar in their outlook to a certain extent. . . . She always had that temperament."[32] Passionate and full of life, father and daughter both knew what they wanted and expected to get it. Irene recalled that her parents' generation was strict with children, saying, "We were raised the biblical way."[33] The punishment might take a physical turn. Carter once told her nephew, "We had to mind my parents or they would get the strap to your behind."[34] Carter's brother put it more bluntly, recalling that their father "was a battering type of father. He liked physical violence. [He nailed] me, my mother, anybody else he could get a hold of,"[35] adding that "it's really traumatic for a kid to see the father beat up the mother, especially at a young age like that."[36]

Strangely, Carter did not mention her grandmother Elmira's death, and she spoke of her father's death without much emotion.[37] "So he was out of the picture. My mother was then struggling by herself to deal with two kids, my younger sister and my brother."[38] In many ways, by the time she was seventeen Carter had already written *herself* out of the picture. James II's death left the family without a breadwinner and Carter without an advocate in the household, so from her perspective at least, it spelled the dissolution of the family. The family stayed together for a short time after he died, but before long Carter's mother and siblings went off in different directions: Bertha apparently married again and joined her siblings in Flint; Vivian married and stayed in Detroit; James went to Korea when the war began.[39] After her mother remarried, the singer rarely saw her, but at various times in her life Carter was in touch with other family members. After her career turned the corner in 1979, for example, she enjoyed warmer relations with her siblings.[40] As of this writing James and C.B. both continue to live in Detroit. While they occasionally saw her when she appeared on television, Carter's family did not understand her importance in the jazz world. James had a short career as a singer before he joined the sheriff's force, and he apparently loves jazz, but not Carter's "concept," as she put it.[41] In James IV's work as a journalist, he took a special interest in musicians, occasionally writing features on his aunt Betty. Louise Ryles now lives in Oakland, California. On 23 November 1987, Vivian died of pancreatic cancer.

Betty Carter spent her childhood years growing up on the West Side of Detroit, with church and school acting as important points of reference. Her experience in church did not leave an obvious mark on her musical approach—she rejected the passionate delivery and the highly ornamented melismatic style of gospel, for example—but it did play a key role in the formation of her character and helped spark her early interest in music. The devoutness of Carter's home came largely from her mother's side of the family, but her father also had strong religious convictions, and she described both parents as "strictly Baptist church people."[42] It was their religious convictions, in fact, that later led them to disapprove of her career choice. Before she was eleven years old, Carter worshiped at Chapel Hill Baptist Church, which she attended with her family.[43] Any interest James Jones II took in music found expression in the worship of God, for he directed the church choir, at least for a part of Carter's childhood.[44] His musical contribution to church was apparently not a prominent feature of her upbringing, for Carter said nothing to suggest that he played a role in her musical development.

At church, Lillie Mae did not stand out as a soloist, but singing was an important part of her experience there, and the church in turn nurtured her musical growth. In addition to having a low vocal range, her ability to hear harmonic relationships and resist drifting to the melody line made her a valuable member of the alto section.[45] As with other jazz musicians who grew up attending church, the experience presented her with musical raw materials that she drew upon in oblique ways, and traces of the singer's worship experience later emerged in her approach to performing, albeit in transmuted form.[46] The range of vocal timbres she encountered there, which ran the gamut from warmly resonant to coarsely raspy, sensitized her to the coloristic potential of the voice. Singers' free rendering of hymns' tunes showed how an established melody could become a vehicle for personal expression. She also encountered the use of nontempered intonation and the bending of pitch there. The freedom of movement typical of African American worship helped her become comfortable with using her body as an expressive instrument. Furthermore, she was exposed to a musicalized speech and a mode of interaction that would become an integral part of her sound image. The use of call-and-response between the preacher and the congregation inculcated in her an appreciation of how such interaction can unite people around a single emotional core. Carter's powerful stage presence, as well as the fervor with which she dedicated herself to making the music communicate, derived partly from the model of performance/participation presented by worship. Many of these features are not unique to black church music and can be found in other African American musical expressions. But while Carter pointedly disclaimed any direct musical influence from the gospel style, her absorption of church music's aesthetic foundation rooted her later musical work in a set of distinctly African American cultural values. In church the youthful singer also got some early experience playing piano.[47]

Carter has implied that she did not pursue the role of soloist because of her distance from the religious aspects of church.[48] Neither she nor her younger siblings identified with church as a religious experience. As her brother put it: "I was never too enthusiastic about going to the Baptist church anyway, so I was in and out as fast as possible. Vivian was in the same category."[49] Lillie Mae found various ways to set herself apart from the church community, using whatever financial resources she acquired as she got older to dress distinctively, for example. "I was always trying, even at that time, to do something different, to wear something different. . . . I always seemed to think differently, when I look back now, about the way I went to church."[50]

At the age of eleven or twelve, she asserted her difference even more strongly by leaving her family's congregation and joining a church of her own choosing.[51] Musical dissimilarities between the two churches were not a factor in this decision. The Hartford Avenue Baptist Church was closer to her house than the Chapel Hill Church, and Carter was going to school with the minister's daughter.[52] Friendships she had developed at school were already becoming more important to her than her family. Carter's schoolmate, pianist Harold McKinney, who attended both churches as well, described Chapel Hill's music as rougher, more primitive than Hartford Avenue's music. Both churches made use of the haunting intonations of "plainchant," however, which suffused hymn tunes with a blueslike wailing quality.[53] According to Carter, no conflict arose with her parents concerning her leaving their church. "My mother didn't care what church I went to, as long as I went."[54] Carter felt strongly enough about her new congregation to be baptized there.[55]

Located at the intersection of Hartford and Milford in the McGraw–West Grand Boulevard section of Detroit, the Hartford Avenue Baptist Church housed the first black congregation established on the West Side. The church catered to the neighborhood's affluent black population, which included many professionals and business owners, and by 1945 its membership exceeded one thousand. Its congregation was growing so rapidly that its facilities were renovated and enlarged that year to the tune of ninety thousand dollars.

The pastor of the Hartford Avenue Church, Reverend Charles A. Hill, was a key figure in Detroit's early struggle for civil rights. Having come to the church shortly after it was founded in 1920, he had built it into a center for social activism by the early 1940s. Hill promoted the cause of unionism by opening the church to the United Auto Workers (UAW) for meetings and was instrumental in the formation of UAW Local 600. Around the time Carter joined the church, Hill was working with Coleman Young, who would become Detroit's mayor some thirty years hence, to reorganize the local chapter of the National Negro Congress (NNC). During this same period the Detroit chapter of the National Association for the Advancement of Colored People (NAACP) elected Hill as its president. His leadership led to his appointment to the Mayor's Interracial Commission in the wake of the 1943 race riot. Hill fought aggressively to obtain better housing, better jobs, and equal protection under the law for all black people, not only for those in his congregation.

Hill stirred controversy by inviting Paul Robeson to appear at the church when the singer was castigated for supporting the Soviet Union's platform on minorities. In the anticommunist frenzy after World War II, Hill's progressive politics led his detractors to label him "Red" in an effort to undermine his political strength, and by the end of the 1940s a more moderate NAACP had distanced itself from him. Despite his obvious radical sympathies, when called before the House Un-American Activities Committee in 1952, Hill cited the Fifth Amendment, stating that "the Bible is my only guide."[56] It is difficult to gauge how much of an impact Hill had on Carter's thinking. His successor, Reverend Charles Adams, recalled that Hill's preaching was not much different from that of other Baptist preachers. Nor was it noticeably "tilted in the direction of his ideological commitment."[57] But as a family friend it would have been hard for her to remain untouched by his dynamic personality.

Betty Carter's church experience deepened her feelings of racial solidarity. Thus while she did not sing in the gospel style herself, she treasured the style's sovereignty as a strictly African American expression. Toward the end of the 1950s, when recording artists fused the sacred style with secular lyrics to assemble a pop sound that crossed over to a white audience, she viewed the musical synthesis as a transgression of racial boundaries. Speaking of this in 1979, she said: "We thought the sound of the gospel was never going to become a commercial art form. Everybody was taken aback when Ray Charles made that music a commercial form. . . . [I]t was like blasphemy to take it out of the church and put it in the street. But now it's in the street selling Coca Cola and everything else."[58] Her indignation on the matter bore a subtle resemblance to her parents' designation of jazz as "the devil's music." She related her parents' strict views on jazz not only to their religious beliefs but also to their middle-class aspirations. "There were a lot of black people at this time who weren't into anything that had a reputation of bringing the race down. Alcohol and the bars were involved with that sort of living. The church was a separate thing. You were a sinner if you were involved in something like that."[59] As a result, Lillie Mae received little exposure to jazz as a child. "We are talking about 1940–41, and when we listened to the radio, we listened to 'Superman' and we listened to 'Amos and Andy.' That was what you were listening to on the radio, because it was all that was available to you: 'Dinah Shore and the Hit Parade.' When your family is involved and your church, you naturally listen to this music and you're not going out to night clubs at an early age."[60]

Early on, Carter's parents restricted her exposure to jazz by not owning a record player: records were expensive, and besides, James and Bertha Jones wanted to barricade the doors to such influences.[61] The singer described her extended family on both parents' sides as not only disparaging of the lifestyle associated with jazz, but entirely ignorant about the music as well.[62] Even after Betty Carter had made a name for herself, she felt her relatives continued to disapprove of her career choice.

Although Carter denied that her siblings had much influence over her, there is one way in which her older sister, Cheza B., did play a role in her musical development. At times during her adolescence the singer would stay with her sister's family in northern Detroit. Being away from her parents, she could follow her curiosity where it led, and while there she had her first encounters with the music of such masters as Coleman Hawkins and Ben Webster. Her earliest exposure to jazz came from C.B.'s husband, Ellis Rogers,[63] who owned a record player. Rogers loved jazz, especially the music of Duke Ellington, and he shared his love with Carter. She recalled how her brother in-law "came on the scene with his whole vast catalog of Duke Ellington records."[64] In the singer's early high school years, around 1943 or 1944,

Rogers enabled Carter to experience Ellington's work, going all the way back to his earliest music.[65] She always knew when Ellington played in Detroit because Rogers would go hear him perform.[66] Later, after moving in with C.B., Carter was able to listen to jazz on the radio to her heart's content, and radio programming was beginning to include more and more black artists, including Louis Armstrong, Billie Holiday, and Ella Fitzgerald.[67] Fitzgerald and the Delta Rhythm Boys had had a hit in 1945 with "It's Only a Paper Moon,"[68] but judging from Carter's first recorded efforts it was the legendary singer's later work that had the profoundest impact on the young singer.

Carter spoke admiringly of the great singers that preceded her, and she viewed her own work within the context of a jazz vocal tradition. Paradoxically she also insisted that she did not look to these singers as a source of musical inspiration. Her portrayal of herself as self-reliant led her to disavow having absorbed stylistic elements from any particular singer. She was quick to point out, for example, that it was not her exposure to singers that gave her the idea to get into the business.[69] Her feelings about the importance of individuality and the hazards of imitation ultimately led her to draw more heavily upon the work of instrumentalists for inspiration, but even there she disclaimed receiving direct influence from any specific player.

Originality was therefore a central concern of Carter's from early on. Inevitably, however, her first recorded efforts betray an awareness of what other singers were doing at the time. Perhaps this is one reason why she hated to hear her old recordings. Sarah Vaughan was certainly a formative influence, to take one example, and several features of her style may be heard in Carter's earliest recordings. Five years younger than her idol, Carter probably did not yet know much about Vaughan when the latter appeared in Earl Hines's band, both singing and playing the piano, as early as mid-March 1943.[70] By early 1945, however, Carter was aware of Vaughan's first sides as a leader, recorded the preceding December. Dizzy Gillespie was at that session, and Vaughan would soon record with him again, this time under his leadership. Carter has described listening to Gillespie, Vaughan, and other artists on the jukebox at the malt shop across from her high school in 1945–46, well before Gillespie and his band created a stir in Detroit early in 1947, with Vaughan on the bill. Vaughan appeared at the Frolic Show Bar in March 1947,[71] by which time Carter was hearing music in clubs. The younger singer made a point of meeting her heroine then or soon after, and they remained friends throughout their careers.

Besides church, school was another place Lillie Mae Jones had always sung.[72] From an early age she felt comfortable in the spotlight and yearned for the attention she received there. "I think I probably was born with wanting to get out front, wanting to be on the stage."[73] Once up in front of people, she found she had an immediate rapport with them. Only later did she view singing as something she might pursue seriously.[74] In an interview with Christopher Kuhl for *Cadence* in 1982, Carter said: "I wasn't a singer at the age of five, six, or seven. I was about fifteen before I realized that I could hold my own on the stage."[75] In her reflections on her early musical development, Carter revealed that she did not take the matter of a professional career in music lightly. She used the term *singer* as though it were a title she had to earn and viewed singing as a discipline she had to master. "I had to develop it into something. It took time."[76]

When Carter was fifteen, she also received some piano lessons at the Detroit Conservatory, but she did not progress beyond a modest level. "I was learning the easy scales, the regular, C, D, E, F; the early books."[77] She did not bring the same intensity to her piano studies that she brought to her singing, and she never developed the proficiency that Sarah Vaughan or Carmen McRae attained at the keyboard. Carter used the experience to build upon piano skills she had begun to acquire in church and music-reading skills she was acquiring in school.[78] By 1944, then, music had begun to draw Carter in, providing a separate space for her to enter. It gave her a sense of her own uniqueness and became a way of setting herself apart from her family. As she put it: "I discovered I had something different. My father thought I had something different."[79]

Carter's experience in high school was what gave her the strongest impetus to pursue a career in music. At a critical time in the formation of her identity, Carter's schoolmates encouraged her, giving her important feedback and a greater sense of belonging than she received at home. From them she found support for her musical interests and abilities.[80] Unlike church, where Carter held her enthusiasm for music in check, school gave her a forum for getting attention, and in many ways she blossomed there.[81] While she did not excel academically, early on she demonstrated aptitudes for music and sports.[82]

Living on the West Side enabled Carter to attend Northwestern High School. Bounded approximately on the east by Grand River Avenue, on the south by Buchanan, on the north by Tireman, and the west by Epworth, the West Side of Detroit owed its open character partly to its architecture. The prevalence of one- and two-story single-family detached homes that had basements and backyards helped create a "feeling of closeness between neighbors . . . [that] made for a cohesive community striving for common goals."[83] Unlike the poor black section of the city, the homes were usually owner-occupied and housed a suitable number of residents. Located on the corner of West Grand Boulevard and Grand River Avenue, Northwestern—the fifth oldest high school in Detroit—was a short walk from the Jones's home. Its distinguishing landmark, standing in front of the building, was a cannon presented to the school in 1920, six years after it had opened for classes.[84]

While Northwestern had no black faculty, its student body was integrated, and Carter had white and black friends.[85] African Americans could not attend the senior prom because it was held at facilities that barred blacks. Most soda shops in the neighborhood would not seat black students, and the Fisher YMCA located across the street denied them admission. By the time Carter attended the school, however, black students were allowed to participate in contact sports, join the cheering squad, or be class officers.[86] Having grown up on the outskirts of the West Side, and therefore in a transitional region between the West Side's largely black enclave and the outlying white neighborhoods, Carter described her neighborhood as racially mixed. Yet, as much as Detroit had a reputation for being the "Arsenal of Democracy," the city's whites generally offered vehement resistance to blacks settling among them.[87]

Carter's experience stood in stark contrast to that of the denizens of Paradise Valley, however, which housed the city's highest concentration of poor blacks. While Carter was hardly insulated from the effects of racial inequality, living in her neighborhood protected her from racism's worst manifestations. When rioting tore through the downtown area in June 1943, for example, it did not spread far beyond Paradise Valley.[88] Significantly for the aspiring singer, the music scene was a front for progress in race relations: by 1947, around the time Carter was making her start in the profession, Detroit and New York were the two cities in America with integrated musicians' unions.[89]

Carter took pride in her school and emerged from it with a respect for education.[90] Her recollection of Ruth Harley, a pianist hired to accompany the school choral groups, suggests that Harley may have been the singer's first musical role model at school. Carter spoke of her with intense admiration, remembering her as the first black pianist who worked in Northwestern: "She was a young, really beautiful woman. . . . She also liked my personality."[91] I imagine the fifteen-year-old Lillie Mae Jones taking up the piano in emulation of Ruth Harley. The music faculty of Northwestern received the eager student warmly, and the music department became a safe haven for her.

Encouragement she received from her music teachers, especially one of the school's choral directors, Miss Wagner, gave Carter a positive outlook toward herself. As a woman in a leadership role, Wagner made a strong impression on her student: "She was classically trained. All [music] teachers were in those days."[92] Under Miss Wagner's direction, Carter's music-reading skills improved, and she had ample opportunities to perform. She learned the school songs, sang in assemblies and at commencement, and if the school was giving a dinner or some other special event, the chorus and the a cappella chorus would perform. “I happened to be an alto in this group. Fortunately, for me, this is what gave me my first ego trip.”[93]

Carter impressed the choir director enough to gain an early opportunity: “She hurt her back, and we had a commencement to do, and she couldn’t raise her arms. . . . She liked my personality and my whole attitude toward the music. . . . She tried out a couple girls to see what they could do, and I was able to handle it.”[94] The singer’s ability to model her conducting on her teacher’s suggests that Wagner was also an early influence: “By what I was doing, she knew that I had been watching her.”[95] Thrilled by her first taste of leading an ensemble in performance, the young conductor was primed to take charge: “There I am in front of the commencement class waving my arms about with the pianist accompanying us. . . . After that they pat me on the back and gave me plenty of smiles.”[96]

In high school, many of Carter’s friends shared her love of music, and they did musical activities together. Most of them had studied classical music and thus exposed her to it as well. Carter admired a set of twins named Lavinia and Lacinia Martin, who had perfect pitch. She also was friends with Harold McKinney, whose whole family was musical.[97] McKinney had begun his piano studies with his mother at the age of four. At Northwestern he was active musically as a member of the Radio Club, the Dance Band, and chairman of the entertainment committee.[98] Few of Carter’s high school friends matched her zeal for bebop, especially as early as she did, but they kept an open mind.[99]

Carter became aware of the sounds of bebop first from recordings, and she immediately formed a liking for the music of Charlie Parker.[100] Her brother recalled his first exposure to the startling new music and his sister’s ardor: “One day, Betty brought these records home by Dizzy and Charlie for me to listen to. When I first heard it, I didn’t like it. I thought it was crazy music, like Chinese.”[101] Her earliest experience of bebop occurred largely at the local hangout. “I’m only hearing dribs and drabs of bebop through neighbors and in school, and on the jukebox. There was a jukebox right across the street at the sweet shoppe or the malt shoppe outside of school. . . . We had bebop records on the jukebox, Charlie Parker, Stan Kenton, Woody Herman, Dizzy Gillespie, Sarah Vaughan, Billy Eckstine.”[102] Hearing bebop on the jukebox gave Carter and her friends a chance to absorb the characteristic sounds and licks of the day. Playing hooky from school, they would “sit around and learn the solos.”[103]

Bebop utterly captivated Betty Carter. Its rigorous standards gave it an appeal for her that popular music lacked. Given her religious upbringing and her parent’s attitude toward the entertainment world, perhaps Carter felt she could justify her devotion to the music—which grew to missionary proportions—because the musicians had such lofty aesthetic ideals. The music's virtuosity made an obvious distinction between musician and nonmusician, and this may have appealed to her need to set herself apart from the crowd. Its assertion of African American "otherness" made it both an expression of Carter's ethnic pride and, paradoxically, a foreign language to the older generation of African Americans who were striving to assimilate into American society. In fact, the subversion of mainstream social conventions that bebop embodied was sure to shock her conservative parents.[104] Finally, musicians' success—and that of Dizzy Gillespie in particular—demonstrated that a musician could not only survive while playing an aesthetically superior music, but actually make a living at it. All of these features shaped the expectations forming in Lillie Mae's mind as she contemplated the possibility of embarking on the radical path of a jazz career. Looking back on this time almost forty years later, Carter recalled how all encompassing was her involvement with bebop: "Along with bebop came a fad, a look, an attitude, an approach to the language. The whole language that we talk now, 'hip,' 'groove' and 'pad'; 'cat' and slapping of the hands; you know how they say 'howdy do?' . . . Bebop had that long before anybody or you all [i.e. whites] got it."[105] Carter adopted the hip mannerisms that went along with the music and took her first steps into the world of bebop as a groupie.

While school gave the singer an environment in which to explore the role of performer, it did not provide many opportunities to perform in the new, largely instrumental, idiom: "In my school, I was active more in singing commercial music, the music that was heard on the radio every day. That's how I got into the business, by doing assemblies and singing in school, by being on the stage there."[106] Classmates such as saxophonist George Benson recalled Lillie Mae Jones participating in after-school jam sessions.[107] Partly due to her innate abilities, but mostly because of her enthusiasm, she was steadily honing her craft without feeling that any special effort went into it.

Coming of age musically when many opportunities existed for a young artist to get her start, the young singer soon sought ways to test the waters: "When I came up there were a lot of theaters across the country that had an amateur show night—the Apollo [in Harlem], the Paradise in Detroit, the Howard in Washington, the Royal in Baltimore, [the Strand Ballroom in] Philadelphia, and the Regal in Chicago . . . a lot of theaters for young people to try out their wares."[108] The Paradise Theater on Woodward Avenue near Mack was where the seventeen-year-old singer first received the attention of the professional music world. A friend of hers had entered her name into the talent contest at the theater, which gave amateur shows every Tuesday night.[109] Among other things, the story illustrates the tangible kind of support Carter received from her friends at Northwestern. "It was one of the girls in the music department that got the audition papers; a young white girl. I didn't do it myself, because I didn't even think about it. . . . I never had gone to the Paradise."[110] The theater had instituted amateur nights in April 1946.[111]

As Carter tells it, she got involved in this process accidentally. Once she got started, however, she showed remarkable tenacity. First, she needed to audition for the amateur show. Telling her parents she was going somewhere else, she sneaked out of the house the preceding Saturday afternoon. Then, after she passed the audition, she had to lie again to get to the theater on the night of the performance.[112] Accompanying herself at the piano as she sang Gershwin's "The Man I Love," Carter felt right at home in front of the audience.[113] According to her, she won first prize, and it was the audience's endorsement of her "coming out" that gave her the confidence to strike out on her own and become a singer. Once she did, she never looked back.[114]

With this auspicious beginning the singer gained a foot in the door. A local talent agent named Chester Rentie took her on as a client, approaching her mother to ask if he could book her.[115] "I was going to get paid for it, so naturally the money soothed any doubts that my mother had about me going to this Sunday afternoon cabaret. The money cooled her out."[116] After that she started getting local jobs here and there at other Sunday afternoon cabarets and fashion shows where no alcohol was served.[117] Chester A. Rentie had opened his booking agency at 2010 St. Antoine in January 1945.[118] He handled such local acts as boy wonder Frank "Sugar Child" Robinson (who upstaged Lionel Hampton's band when it appeared at the Paradise in September, 1945), pianist Willie Hawkins—whose keyboard wizardry "attracted considerable comment and attention from Art Tatum when he came to Detroit"[119]—Ethel Strickland and her educated dog Curly, ventriloquist Freddie Robinson and his dummy, Connie, and song-and-dance man Playboy Williams.[120] Around this time Rentie was serving as the "Mayor of Paradise Valley."[121] According to Forest Club owner Sunnie Wilson, newspaperman Rollo Vest had come up with the idea of having Paradise Valley's inhabitants elect a businessman via newspaper poll as the unofficial mayor for a term of two or three years. It was designed initially to sell newspapers, but the idea caught on and became a way of promoting a sense of community in Paradise Valley.[122]

Curiously, in later descriptions Betty Carter chose not to elaborate on Chester Rentie's role in her early professional life. But at the time she must have entertained hopes of bigger things ahead, for Rentie's charges did occasionally move out of the local fold. In May 1946, for example, singer Mildred McIver left Detroit for Chicago to join the all-female big band International Sweethearts of Rhythm and was supposedly being groomed to replace the conductor Anna Mae Winburn, who was getting married.[123] Carter was still too young to sing in bars, but this did not keep her out of them for long. She used a forged birth certificate to slip through their doors into Detroit's nightlife: "I just defied my mother and took off to do gigs other places and everywhere else."[124] The novice singer increasingly turned to the musical scene in Detroit for a sense of belonging. As it happens, Detroit was the right place to be at the time, for a fresh approach to jazz was beginning to gain momentum there, sweeping the city's bright, young minds along with it.

2

Bebopping in Detroit

To most listeners of the 1940s bebop seemed to come out of nowhere. As its innovations were absorbed by each successive jazz style, however, they have come to lose much of their novelty. Time's passage has smoothed the music's hard edges, inevitably softening its astonishing impact. It is easy now to forget the initial impression bebop gave and hear the music simply as an extension of the swing-era style. Such a hearing is encouraged by the fact that the upstart style built upon rhythmic, melodic, and harmonic elements drawn from the established one, as well as by the coexistence of the two approaches after bebop emerged. Judging from its initial reception, however, these connections were lost on bebop's first audiences.

Two passages from David Meltzer's sourcebook, *Reading Jazz,* give us an idea of what people thought of bebop when it emerged.[1] In 1948, at the height of the bebop craze, critic Weldon Kees wrote: "Although bebop's defenders reserve as their trump card this music's 'element of the unexpected,' it is precisely bebop's undeviating pattern of incoherence and limitation that makes it predictable in the extreme."[2] Kees aligned himself with critic Rudi Blesh, who had written in the *New York Herald Tribune* that bebop "comes perilously close to complete nonsense as a musical expression." Both critics' experience of the music as strange and disorganized typifies the reaction of so-called squares who did not speak the avant-garde's musical language.

The second passage, by Dave Brubeck—written in 1951 as the initial fervor over bebop had begun to subside—articulates the high aesthetic ideals to which musicians aspired, while also illustrating the snobbery that often went with these ideals:

> Ignoring the original melody (which the initiated knew without reiteration), [bop] musicians improvised their own themes based upon

> their own alteration of standard tunes. They demanded that audiences listen. Tempos were set for instrumental performance, not for dancing. This music . . . was a radical protest, not only against a world in war, but against the growing commercialism that threatened the extinction of an American art form.
>
> For its audience, bop attracted a comparatively small, but fanatically loyal, group of intellectuals, artists, and malcontents, who felt in the tense new music some of their own revolt from a society that had betrayed them. While the general public sought to *escape* in popular vocalists, hill-billy tunes, novelty tunes and vulgarized interpretations of rhythm and blues, the restless protest fringe was seeking *expression* of its discontentment. . . . Bop, and later, "cool jazz" were extreme reactions against the vulgar escape music that thrived on the hysteria of the times.[3]

Both of the above passages reinforce the idea that many listeners, both pro and con, initially heard bop as a counterreaction to swing and not as its stylistic outgrowth. In part it was the assertive attitude projected by the music that made it stand out from what came before. Using musical raw materials that had an ingratiating gregariousness in the hands of big-band players, bebop musicians gave their music a confrontational quality. Through their music, they manipulated the day's cultural codes, wryly commenting on the stylistic gestures of the prior generation's sound, exaggerating them to the point of distortion and, in the process, forming an incisive caricature of popular music. In its extreme tempos and its freer treatment of dissonance; in the rhythmic complexity that interwove the soloist's unpredictably phrased line with an intricately grooved accompaniment; in its often harsh timbres arranged in a rich web of sound; and, in the technical skill required to play it, which excluded all but a few virtuosi, bebop gave voice to urban black musicians who refused to accept the role of outsider in silence. In the process, an elite culture crystallized around the music, with the experience of alienation from American society and the rejection of mainstream social conventions as defining qualities. Armed with the sounds of modern or progressive jazz, bebop musicians assailed musical conventions as well. Calling this music modern or progressive instantly set it apart from the music that preceded it, relegating swing to the history books.

With the rise of this new approach and the decline of the social dancing that had supported the large ensembles, more and more instrumentalists were playing jazz in small groups.[4] No longer placed in service of an extramusical function, jazz performance became increasingly music-centered, and musicians consciously sought to produce sounds worthy of listeners' undivided attention. Initially the players may not have deliberately distanced themselves from mass appeal or set themselves above commercial motives, as Dave Brubeck's description suggests. They needed to make a living, after all. But neither did they devise the music with visions of crossing over. Almost in spite of this, the music attracted a substantial white following.[5] Nevertheless, bebop was expressive of a process of social redefinition that a new generation of African Americans was initiating. Mixed in with a color-blind notion of racial progress was a fresh strain, more aggressive than before, that conveyed a growing sense of black solidarity.

Betty Carter herself described bebop as though it had been some kind of invasion:

> It wasn't anything they could stop, because they tried in the beginning. They said, "oh, the crazy music. Where is it coming from?" It got all the bad reviews and everything; nobody liked it; "too fast, too this, and too that." Suddenly it just started to move and seep into the way composers wrote, the way arrangers wrote arrangements, the way piano players played accompanying other musicians, attitudes, language, style, walk, everything. It just had an effect on everything at that time.[6]

As her description makes clear, bebop was not simply a new approach to music but a new mode of being as well, "a swing about your body," and "a gait in your walk," that generated a sense of collective identity for insiders.[7] The ardor with which she defended bebop throughout her life stemmed as much from the music's social significance as it did from her fascination with its sounds. Carter spoke nostalgically of the time in her life when she became involved with bebop and of the thriving musical scene in her hometown.[8] Each Detroit neighborhood did not receive the new music with the same enthusiasm, and hers was the first to show signs of interest. The bebop craze began to make inroads on the West Side as early as 1945–46, during her junior year in high school, when the first examples of the style became available on records. People there accepted bebop more readily than those on Detroit's East Side, Carter recalled, "because the East Side was more or less the blues territory. . . . The West Side was more sophisticated, you might say, because there was a mixture of people over there."[9] To many upwardly mobile black people, the blues conjured up images of the southern rural conditions and the flagrant racial injustice they had fled. While bebop absorbed the standard blues progression into its repertoire, the musicians modified it, giving it an urban hipness that distanced it from these images and placed the older idiom's black signification into a modern context.

The clubs were in Paradise Valley, concentrated in the city's musical entertainment center on the East Side known as "Black Bottom." Many of these clubs, especially the so-called black-and-tan cabarets, had been drawing "slumming" white audiences since the mid-1920s.[10] Observing that the city's major bands could be heard in clubs located around the intersection of St. Antoine and Adams, historian Lars Björn has described bebop's impact on the neighborhood: "The new style . . . developed in the musician's subculture of Paradise Valley, which became known as a place for 'after-hours' spots, a place to play after the night's work in a ballroom or black-and-tan. In nightly 'jam sessions' innovative musical ideas were exchanged in an environment without commercial pressures."[11] From the outset, then, the bebop audience in Detroit had a large white component, but anyone who wanted to hear modern jazz had to go to Black Bottom.[12]

After her talent night triumph, Lillie Mae Jones increasingly sought out opportunities to hear musicians play. With her false identification she got into clubs in Black Bottom, although she claimed it was not really necessary, as people did not seem to care much that she was a minor.[13] A novice bebopper could hardly have wished for a more welcoming environment, and the direction the teenager's life took owes much to the auspicious circumstance in which she found herself. Summarizing the reminiscences of a number of musicians, musicologist Paul Berliner has described the nurturing environment Detroit offered young musicians and the easy access they had to the sounds of jazz: "Sympathetic club owners in Detroit left their back doors open so that passersby and underage audiences who congregated in the alleyways could sample the music of featured artists."[14] Pianist Barry Harris recalled that he would slip into the Bluebird Inn and play a few numbers while the house pianist took a break: "The bandstand was in the window. I'd knock on the window and the pianist, a cat named Phil Hill, would turn and look at me. When he finished a song I'd run in and play a couple of tunes and run back out."[15]

In the late 1940s, nightclubs such as the Bluebird, Club Sudan, Freddie Guignard's, the Graystone Ballroom, the Paradise Club, and the West End Hotel on the far side of the railroad tracks near the Fleetwood Cadillac plant all embraced the new music.[16] These and a host of others gave local and visiting musicians an environment in which to explore and develop the sounds of bebop, both in formal performances and in jam sessions that often went until dawn. By the time Carter had embarked upon her career, there were several young musicians in Detroit learning bebop.[17] The list includes many who would gain national acclaim: saxophonist Sonny Stitt, trombonist Charles Greenlee,[18] reed and flute player Bill "Yusef Lateef" Evans, and others who never left Detroit, including drummer Leon Rice and pianist Theodore Sheely.[19] Barry Harris admitted that Theodore Sheely surpassed not only him but also Berry Gordy—who later founded Motown records—as the best boogie-woogie piano player in their circle, and he also admired Sheely's ability to improvise.[20]

Betty Carter did not speak much of her early musical activities in her hometown, and few of her fellow Detroit natives recalled her being an active presence in the bebop scene at this early stage, perhaps because the idiom's instrumental focus limited the impact a vocalist could then have. Furthermore, the singer's ambitions of achieving national fame may have led her to resist identifying with the local scene. Nevertheless, as a teenager she surrounded herself with up-and-coming jazz talents and drew upon their growing expertise and musicianship. As she recalled: "It was all sit-in, chances you take, and around town we had a lot of piano players like Barry Harris, Tommy Flanagan. . . . I came up with these guys you know; Kenny Burrell, and [others who] had gigs around town. . . . There were other local piano players that were very good. Jazz was like a fever in Detroit at that time. All we were doing around town was 'scatting' and 'turning the corner,' 'catting.' "[21] At first she sat in with her peers who played in jam sessions after school and at local dances. Showing her characteristic boldness, she did not let her inexperience deter her from joining musicians on the bandstand. Harris, who also attended Northwestern High School and was about seven months her junior, said that she would sit in when he and his friends played at informal affairs. She would do "her Sarah Vaughan thing," singing "Mean to Me" and other songs associated with her idol.[22] In addition to her appreciation for famous singers, the budding vocalist was attuned to those who worked in the local scene, singers who had no national reputation or recordings, but who were excellent performers.[23] Throughout this time she was increasing her grasp of the principles of bebop performance and expanding her repertoire.

By developing the ability to improvise using the bebop vocabulary, Lillie Mae Jones made her own niche and distinguished herself from pop singers: "The field was open if you wanted to scat. If you were interested in bebop you had to have a knowledge of improvising and be quick and fast. Otherwise you would just be ordinary."[24] An essential component of the jazz process, if not of the music itself, improvisation operates by degrees. Even in a relatively straight rendering of a melody, the spirit of improvisation can and should be present, informing the musician's rhythmic and melodic nuancing, phrasing and articulation, accentuation, dynamics, and timbre, making a familiar tune feel altogether fresh. Paraphrasing the melody, a performer might stay fairly close to it and make only subtle modifications, as most vocalists tend to do when singing lyrics. At the other extreme, a performer might abandon the melody entirely in favor of a newly conceived line spun out of the tune's harmonic thread. For singers this approach typically entailed scatting—inventing nonsense syllables; but, even before the advent of bebop, Louis Armstrong and Billie Holiday had taken familiar pop songs such as "All of Me" way beyond their original form. Obviously, then, improvisation was not unique to bebop. Many big-band musicians improvised in addition to playing fixed arrangements, and it was in big bands that the earliest beboppers became known to the public as soloists. In small combos, however, bebop players pushed improvisation to the forefront, and, as in Dave Brubeck's description above, defied listeners to follow them along the winding paths their thought process took. Erupting like molten lava from a player's horn, sounds coalesced into a crystalline structure that, for the initiated, had its own unique logic and beauty. It was this approach to improvisation that enthralled the young singer.

As jazz changed, the vocalist's role inevitably changed as well. Most dance bands had at least one singer who performed a crucial function: providing listeners with images with which to associate the music's nonverbal meanings. Even so, as historian David Stowe has pointed out, many musicians considered singers somewhat ornamental—"unfortunate concessions to commercial taste."[25] With the new style's emphasis upon instrumental virtuosity, most beboppers neglected to capitalize upon the direct appeal of vocalists, reinforcing the idea that their groups had a less commercial orientation than big bands.[26] Nevertheless, singers continued to have an oblique impact on jazz musicians. The sound ideal many instrumentalists aspire to, for instance, reflects the significance of vocal expression. Players routinely emulate singers by employing vocal gestures—especially when riffing or playing blues licks. Pianist Walter Bishop Jr. recalled that Charlie Parker urged him to learn the lyrics to a song "so you know what you're saying when you solo."[27] As with a person's speaking voice, which has inherently recognizable qualities—dynamic, rhythmic, and melodic, but particularly timbral, ones—jazz players are expected to contribute their own "voice" to the group so as to make the resultant combination unique. While a musician's timbre is not the only element of her sound that makes it recognizable, it is the most tangible one. Forging a distinctive sound is therefore an essential feature of a jazz musician's training, and Carter spoke passionately about the importance of sounding like no one else. Developing a technique entails the thorough investigation of one's instrument, for singers as much as for players, in order to exploit all of its unique timbral resources.[28]

A characteristic breathiness was an integral feature of Carter's vocal timbre throughout her career. Especially evident in her middle and high registers, it added complexity to her sound.[29] Because Sarah Vaughan's timbre exuded the rounded warmth of a trained voice, Carter may have cultivated this breathiness to set herself apart from one of her idols. Combined with a sparing use of vibrato, it gave her sound a cool, remote quality at times—part of her hipness. When Carter did use vibrato, most often on long notes at the end of phrases, it noticeably warmed her tone and contributed to the vocal line's sense of movement.[30] Adding to her breathy quality, she sometimes used a sudden exhalation of air for rhythmic effect.

It is when scatting that a singer displays her timbral virtuosity most. Statements Carter made to Leonard Lyons in 1975 reveal how her ideas about scatting had evolved: "I do everything I can, when I scat, to not, say, start a phrase as most scat singers do with shababa*doo* [/ša/ba/ba/*duw*/], or shababadoo-*wa* [/ša/ba/ba/duw/*a*/] or -*wee* [/*wiy*/]. A lot of scat singers start a phrase off with that sh (/š/) sound."[31] Elaborating on these thoughts, she reflected back on early choices she made: "If you're listening to a lot of scat singers . . . you hear them starting a phrase like that. I probably was guilty of that also in the beginning of the bebop era because . . . when you started to scat that was one of the sounds [you used]. . . . Since everybody did that, I tried to avoid that particular sound. By avoiding sounds that I thought were typical scat sounds, I had to create other sounds."[32] She also decided early on to refrain from copying instrumental timbres in her scatting, as other singers often do:

> I'm not a trumpet and I wasn't about to imitate one, sound-like. I have a tiny sound in the first place, it's not mellow, except when I sing ballads. When I sing fast and brassy my sound has a tang in it, anyway; there ain't nothing I can do about it. . . . I may simulate an instrument without really trying to do that. But because I avoid certain sounds that are typically voice sounds . . . like shoobeedoobee [/šuw/biy/duw/biy/], I may remind you of what a trumpet may do.[33]

Furthermore, unlike many singers from her generation, Carter did not view scatting as a novelty routine, to be used largely for entertainment value: "I'm serious about my scat, I'm dead serious about it. Some people play with it, they use it as a throwaway."[34]

Early in her training she integrated into her own approach essential elements of the jazz process that keep the music fresh—to listen intently and adjust spontaneously to one's fellow musicians, for example, and to incorporate their ideas into one's spur-of-the-moment decisions: "Different piano players had different approaches to certain songs and a different way of playing it, and you had to adjust to that. This made you think this way today, and think this way yesterday, and tomorrow, and whatever. It was never the same."[35] During this time she educated herself in ways instrumentalists adjust to singers, such as transposing music into a suitable vocal range.[36] Many features of Carter's growth necessarily remain a mystery because, without heavy reliance upon music notation, much of a jazz singer's musical development happens on an intuitive level. There is no doubt, however, that the fledgling singer took advantage of the opportunities afforded her by bebop's arrival in her hometown, especially as she became better versed in the idiom. She understood that she was in the midst of something important—"among giants," as she later put it.[37]

Fairly soon she felt confident enough to reach out beyond the local scene and sit in with musicians who stopped in town on road trips. With its thriving club scene in Paradise Valley, Detroit was an ideal place to be booked, and many jazz greats passed through on their midwestern tours. Dizzy Gillespie first came to Detroit as a leader in July 1946, shortly after he had made his first recordings for the Musicraft label. According to critic Leonard Feather the band "laid an egg" on this occasion.[38] Detroit's African American newspaper, the *Michigan Chronicle,* offers no record of that visit, but it does document Gillespie's appearance with Ella Fitzgerald later that year at the Forest Club on 18 November.[39] Apparently the earlier performance did not make enough of an impression to be included in the paper's year-end summation of highlights, reinforcing the idea that Gillespie was not yet hot in Detroit.[40] The trumpeter appeared next in Detroit at the Paradise Theater from 14 to 20 February 1947 with Sarah Vaughan and Illinois Jacquet on the bill.[41] On the second day of this run, the Paradise presented an all-star jam session in the afternoon featuring Jacquet and members of Gillespie's orchestra.[42] Feather wrote that, on this occasion, "police had to be called out to keep the crowds from getting out of hand."[43] Recalling the event, saxophonist James Moody crowed: "Oh man; people, boy, they'd be wild. Lines would be all everywhere . . . Just lines, crowded, coming in to see Dizzy."[44] In fact, a throng of nearly six hundred adults and teenagers got impatient when the audience for the preceding show refused to leave and nearly rioted, smashing the box office windows and unhinging the doors. Amazed by bebop's surge in popularity, theater owner Lou Cohen remarked: "We never expected such a crowd as this."[45] Clearly, by 1947 Gillespie was starting to gain broad appeal outside of New York City.[46]

It was not until later in the year that Lillie Mae Jones first heard Dizzy Gillespie perform live, when she snuck in to hear his band at El Sino Club at 1730 St. Antoine on the corner of Beacon. Bill Malone and Bill Pierce had opened the club on 11 April 1947, partly in response to the increasing public demand for the new music.[47] To great fanfare, Gillespie's big band performed at the club starting on Friday, 6 June. As was typical then, this was not just an evening of modern jazz but a show with several different kinds of entertainment on the bill, including singer Alex "Muddy Water" Thomas and a brother-sister dance team, Antonio and Bedelia, which performed an exotic dance routine entitled "Temptation Nocturne."[48] The public's response was so positive that Gillespie's engagement was extended for an additional week. The band had several jazz greats in it, including James Moody, pianist John Lewis, bassist Ray Brown, as well as Detroit natives vibraphonist Milt Jackson and vocalist Kenny "Pancho" Hagood.[49] Betty Carter later recalled hearing such Latin-tinged charts as "Manteca," as well as "Cubana Be" and "Cubana Bop," which Gillespie would record that December.[50] She liked the way the group's arrangements made a big band sound new and fresh, and the bold harmonies of such tunes as "Things to Come," "Emanon," and "Good Bait" would continue to ring in her ears many years later.[51]

The young singer was such a fan of the trumpeter, who had become the most visible icon for modern jazz, that she had visions of joining his band. Realizing her dream would have immersed her in the bebop idiom she loved so well, while also giving her the exposure that came from singing with a touring band. She could entertain such fancies because, unlike most of his colleagues, Gillespie took an interest in vocal music and used it to please audiences. The trumpeter took pride in having introduced several singers, including Johnny Hartman, Austin Cromer, Tiny Irvin, Betty Sinclair, and Alice Roberts.[52] He generally preferred female vocalists to male, but during this period he showcased such male vocalists as Pancho Hagood, Joe "Bebop" Carroll, and Johnny Hartman.[53] Lillie Mae Jones especially envied the latter because he was making his start at about the same time she was. Her jealously is intriguing, for unlike the former two—who specialized in scat vocals—Hartman was a crooner who modeled his sound after Sarah Vaughan's erstwhile partner, Billy Eckstine.

Dizzy Gillespie's own scat singing played a key role in his rise to fame. As Barry McRae pointed out: "The eccentricity of dress, the deliberate exploitation of bebop's giddiness, and most particularly, the use of the leader's consciously frivolous singing were major factors in selling the band to the public."[54] Gillespie's playful approach to singing had ample precedent: before the emergence of modern jazz, Cab Calloway, Bulee "Slim" Gaillard, and Leo Watson had each developed distinctively giddy versions of scatting. Alyn Shipton has suggested that Gillespie's stage persona may have benefited from his work opposite Gaillard at Billy Berg's in Hollywood over a year before his El Sino run.[55] Although Carter took her scatting seriously, her earliest recorded efforts reveal some debt to the trumpeter's approach. She undoubtedly had female models as well—most prominently Ella Fitzgerald. Fitzgerald had made limited use of scat before the bebop craze, in such songs as "Mr. Paganini" and "The Dipsy Doodle." After bebop caught on, however, scatting became an important feature of her act, and she brought the art of vocal improvisation to dazzling heights.[56] Few singers have exploited the license that scatting grants, or met the challenge it poses, as virtuosically as Ella Fitzgerald did.

In liberating singers from a song's text as well as from its melody, scatting frees them from the role of storyteller. But there is a price: in return for this freedom, the singer must invent convincing vocables—nonsense syllables that effectively capture the line's phrasing—as well as satisfying melodic ideas. This bargain enables scat singers to use sound in much the way jazz players do: as a vehicle for the expression of feelings and ideas that are not directly linked to words. Unlike singing lyrics, in which a musical setting typically reinforces the song's verbal meaning, ideally enhancing it as well, scatting makes singing into a music-centered activity. This distinction is not absolute, however, for certain singers collapsed it, conversely, by bringing a music-centered orientation to their delivery of lyrics. As a result, the ability to phrase like an instrumentalist has become so crucial to jazz singing that it may be considered a defining feature. By treating the phones of the English language almost as though they were scat syllables, jazz singers manifest a fascination with the sonic properties of speech that may also be found in other African American—as well as West African—cultural expressions. In jazz, the singer must not only express the lyrics' verbal meaning; she must create a musically satisfying statement as well. Perhaps this is one reason Billie Holiday did not scat, for, as has often been noted, her renderings of popular songs often had the character of instrumental solos. Unlike Sarah Vaughan, whose manipulation of musical elements for their own sake sometimes buried the lyrics' verbal content in affectation—being perhaps carried away by the sheer beauty of her own vocal timbre, Holiday's musical stylizations generally heightened the words' dramatic impact, even when they cut across the lyrics' meaning with biting irony. Each singer in her own way explored the musical and narrative effect an improvised vocal line can have on the delivery of lyrics. The expressive possibilities Holiday and Vaughan opened up were not wasted on the young singer from Detroit.

The jazz vocal tradition was therefore already well established by the time Dizzy Gillespie began to sing, so it is an exaggeration to suggest, as Barry McRae has done, that he "changed the rules of the jazz vocal."[57] Nor was the basic idea behind scatting especially new. People have sung vocables in Western and non-Western cultures for centuries. Such singing has served a variety of purposes: to copy natural and man-made noises, for example, or to encode meanings, as in the sexual innuendo of many madrigals' "fa-la-las." Some scatting brings to mind the playful way a child toys with vocal sounds before she discovers their semantic function. Bobby McFerrin has sometimes evoked the unformed speech of an infant to humorous effect.[58] Aping the behavior of the possessed, Joe Carroll sometimes gave his scatting the character of uttering the unspeakable: a bebop "speaking in tongues." Although scat lyrics are nonsensical, scatting does not altogether lack meaning, for an array of nonverbal and pseudoverbal associations can shape the vocal line, as Clark "Mumbles" Terry has shown. Gillespie and Carroll exploited these associations when singing together, to create scat conversations delivered in some hip foreign language. In various ways, then, the complex sounds of bebop did infuse the jazz vocal with a fresh intensity, bringing along an array of methods for imitating the new idiom's distinctive phrasing and articulation.

Lillie Mae Jones responded enthusiastically to Gillespie's wacky stage presence, as well as to his scat singing.[59] Not content merely to sit out on the sidelines, she had to sit in with the musicians, and she went to the club on several nights during that run in June 1947 to create the opportunity. Jeri Grey, a dancer in the chorus line at El Sino, knew Gillespie and his wife, and she let him know that the awestruck young girl was a singer. Later in the evening, Gillespie called Lillie Mae up onto the stage. She may have exuded confidence, but she was "boiling inside" with trepidation.[60] Doing a song she knew well and relying on her "big ears"—her ability to grasp the music quickly—helped her stay focused.

> With Dizzy I did "Mean To Me." I remember doing that, because he had an arrangement on that tune that Sarah Vaughan used when she had a job with the band. He still had the arrangement. . . . I remember doing the first chorus, and then the band came in, the interlude, and then he looked at me and said, 'We're going to change keys.' . . . I heard the music change keys and when I went along with it, he looked at me and he winked, like my ears were on.[61]

Betty Carter has suggested that she sat in on other occasions Gillespie came to Detroit. While it is doubtful this included Gillespie's appearance with Ella Fitzgerald at the Paradise the following November, which would have been too conspicuous an occasion, a more opportune time would have been an engagement at El Sino starting 21 November featuring Chano Pozo. She may also have done so later on, during the 1950s, when she periodically returned to sing in Detroit.[62] Speaking to drummer Art Taylor in 1972 she pointed out that on later occasions Gillespie asked *her* to sing, thus endorsing her talents: "He didn't have to, so he must have dug something I was doing."[63] Gillespie's acceptance of Carter gave her encouragement at an important stage in her development.

Although she wanted more than anything to join Gillespie's band, her pride kept her from asking him: she wanted *him* to approach her.[64] Looking back much later, Carter felt that it was probably all for the best that she did not end up in the group.[65] In particular, she felt that the drug use prevalent among many of his musicians could have posed a serious risk to her career, and she was glad that she had averted that possibility.[66] Gillespie's band broke up early in 1950, so Carter would have had less than two years in it.

While Dizzy Gillespie was enjoying the attention of the growing bebop audience, the music's other important innovator, Charlie Parker, had been receiving psychiatric care at Camarillo State Hospital in California. On 7 April 1947, Parker finished his treatment and returned to New York. By July, he had put together his classic quintet and embarked upon an exceptionally productive phase of his career. From December 1947 to March 1948, Parker took his newly formed quintet on the road, booked to perform mostly in the Midwest. In *Bird Lives,* Ross Russell states that after the famous "Klactoveesedstene" session of 4 November the quintet left New York City and headed for Detroit for two weeks at El Sino, adding that the band had a return engagement at El Sino in December.[67] While there is no record of the first engagement, two short items in the *Michigan Chronicle* quietly note Bird's presence in town in late 1947 and early 1948.[68] Ken Vail has confirmed that Bird played a two-week stretch at El Sino starting Friday, 19 December 1947, opposite Sarah Vaughan. At this engagement they sold out the house.[69]

Carter has described Parker, who became her guiding light for the rest of her career, in almost mythic terms. She was fond of recalling how being in his presence led musicians to reach for higher levels of creativity. For Carter, Parker was an "introduction to something new . . . a push to strive for something different."[70] Of course the young bebopper made it her business to hear his band when it came to Detroit. At that time Bird had Miles Davis, pianist Duke Jordan, bassist Tommy Potter, and drummer Max Roach with him.[71] From the tone of Carter's recollections, we can easily imagine the thrill she must have felt to be in the presence of musicians she idolized: "I had to have the experience of sitting in with Charlie Parker and those guys. When they came to town, I'd be the first one there, standing in line—a real fan."[72] According to Brian Priestley, Parker's book at that time—his active repertoire—was largely made up of such tunes as "Night in Tunisia," "Dizzy Atmosphere," and "Shaw Nuff," tunes that had already become established as bebop showpieces during the preceding few years.[73]

According to Carter, she first met Bird when she and her friends went to El Sino to hear the group rehearse. He showed up four hours late for the rehearsal, looking for something to eat. Leading him to a nearby restaurant, the teenager had his ear and told him she was a singer. Rather than risk being perceived as overly aggressive, she waited to be approached by him. After Bird and she had struck up a relationship, he asked her if she wanted to sit in.[74] "I just improvised at that time, because that's what everybody was doing anyway. I think I sang 'When I Fall In Love' and 'The Man I Love'"[75] Thereafter, according to Carter, whenever she came to see him, he invited her to join him. "When you can sit in with someone *that* great and then the next time you go to see him, he says to you, 'Do you want to sing?' . . . you know you kind of impressed him."[76] By handling the matter indirectly, she could mask her ambitions behind a cool veneer so as not to come on too strong.

An incident Carter observed at the club illustrates that Parker, in striving to achieve ever greater heights of virtuosity, had distanced his music from the world of show business: "You can imagine what it was like to be in Larry Steele's chorus line . . . all those beautiful dolls wearing long dresses, and then, later on, when they do their masterpiece, they have short skirts on and everybody is kicking high. Charlie Parker was rehearsing them with "Hot House," "Confirmation" and all his fast things. Those poor girls were kickin', and it was really something to see. . . . Tempos were lightning fast."[77] Carter's recollection provides evidence that people did dance, or at least tried to dance, to bebop. But it also suggests that Parker was not especially interested in suiting his music to the dancers' needs. For him, the dancers played an ornamental role: the primary activity was performed by the musicians.

The encouragement Betty Carter received from Dizzy Gillespie and Charlie Parker came at an important time in her life and gave her strong reason to believe in herself: "When Dizzy Gillespie and Charlie Parker say you can sing, who says you can't. . . . They gave me the go-ahead power . . . that made me bold enough to say 'I can do that.'"[78] She made use of their endorsements to make inroads on the Detroit jazz scene and beyond: "That's pretty good credentials for a young girl. That's what I lived on in Detroit for a while."[79] After working with some local bands, including one called Sax Carry, Carter expanded her reach to clubs in the Midwest, performing at such venues as the Cotton Club in Cincinnati.[80] She also worked in Dayton, Ohio, and has described a job at the Classic Gardens there with Eugene Edward "Snooky" Young as her first professional gig.[81] This description would place her first paying job sometime in 1947, when Young began leading his own group in Dayton after a two-year stint with Count Basie's band. Other remarks to the effect that she was already getting paid for singing after Chester Rentie began booking her suggest that she was working professionally before that gig. During this time she traveled as far as Pittsburgh.

Carter has spoken passionately on several occasions about the values musicians from that world shared: "I was fortunate at the time I started out, because individualism was very important. At that time money wasn't the thing you thought about. We thought about trying to get our 'thing' together.

We thought about being different, because . . . it was like a sin to sound like somebody else."[82] From the fondness with which Carter recalled her initiation into the jazz world, it is clear that bebop gave her a sense of belonging she had never known, while also permitting her to express her individuality. The warm reception Carter received from fellow devotees stood in stark relief to the chill breeze that blew in the void between her and her mother.

3

Apprenticeship

Even as the swing era was waning at the end of the 1940s, a jazz performer's primary vehicle for career advancement was still the big band. In addition to providing steady work and the essential experience that comes with it, big bands offered an education in life on the road and gave an ambitious young person one of very few avenues out of a local scene. Performing as a featured soloist in an actively touring big band was the customary method of achieving nationwide exposure. With the name recognition gained from such exposure, a musician could later tour as a single backed by the hosting club's house band or form her own ensemble.

Life on the road looked glamorous from the outside, and it did have its rewards, but for singers especially it was laced with an array of hardships. The pay—notoriously low, especially for someone breaking into the business—was quickly absorbed by hidden expenses, including room and board, and a wardrobe, which was, as always, a costly affair. Travel could be a grind. Long bus rides between jobs were the norm, and sometimes tightly scheduled gigs entailed driving all night. For black bands in particular, lodgings were generally less than ideal. If the black neighborhood did not have a hotel, local residents welcomed band members into their often already overtaxed homes.

For singers, the stresses of being on the road were exacerbated by an inherent tension in the vocalist-instrumentalist alliance. Upon joining a big band a singer immediately attained the status of soloist, giving him greater visibility than rank-and-file band members. For this and other reasons singers enjoyed a direct rapport with the general public that only a handful of players ever achieved. Singers, however, were rarely judged on their musical merits alone. When compared to the years of practice required to master an instrument, singing seemed to require no technical expertise, so players found it difficult to take vocalists' musical contribution seriously—even as they worked to emulate singers' lyricism. Instrumentalists, who had been subject to rigorous peer review, often resented singers' easier route to celebrity. Their tightly knit society left singers, who were generally viewed as inferiors, decidedly on the outside. In addition to these tensions, there was also the issue of gender. The role of vocalist was virtually the only one a woman could realistically aspire to fill in the music business because, aside from some notable exceptions, most instrumentalists were men. Gender inevitably complicated the situation by bringing nonmusical considerations such as physical appearance and sex appeal into play.

The tense dynamic between players and singers would only get worse as the decline of social dancing eroded the market for instrumental music. Gradually strengthening singers' position in the music industry, this circumstance would make sidemen increasingly dependent upon vocalists for work. For female vocalists especially, then, touring with a big band was in many ways an arduous experience. Many simply quit singing after leaving a band, sometimes marrying a band member in the process. As with other commercial enterprises, it was the careers of those rare few who went on to win prominence, such as Lena Horne, that fueled the hopes of many a budding talent.[1]

After the end of World War II, opportunities for a singer to join a big band began to disappear. Partly due to wartime rationing and travel restrictions, dance bands became increasingly costly to maintain, and by the end of 1946 some of the most famous ones had broken up. In fact, the collapse of the big-band industry was probably the main reason why bebop became commercially viable at the end of the 1940s. While some large groups continued to do well, the ones that prospered were not as oriented toward jazz as those from the swing era had been. The increasing popularity of singers backed by orchestras and by small groups also hurt the big bands.

As the fortunes of most dance bands fell, however, Lionel Hampton's seemed to defy gravity. When Carter joined his band in 1948, she was signing on to the organization at the peak of its popularity. Hampton himself had gained national attention over a decade earlier, when the addition of his vibraphone rounded out the Benny Goodman quartet from 1936 to 1940. That was during the big band's heyday and the clarinetist was at the top of a heap of highly successful band leaders. Goodman's racially mixed group, which included pianist Teddy Wilson and drummer Gene Krupa, gave its black members a prominence with white audiences they could not have achieved on their own.

In the early 1940s Hampton capitalized upon his fame by forming his own group. After a series of hits in the mid-1940s that included "Flying Home," "Hamp's Boogie Woogie," and "Hey! Ba-Ba-Re-Bop"—which, despite its title, had little to do with bebop—Hampton's band toured virtually nonstop, was heard on the radio, and generated records at a steady rate. The band's capacity to draw crowds made it an attractive act for promoters. Benefiting from the marketing acumen of Joe Glaser's Associated Booking agency, Hampton's name seemed inescapable. His activities were heavily publicized in the African American papers, including Detroit's *Michigan Chronicle,* with concert announcements, various promotional campaigns, such as a "Hey! Ba-Ba-Re-Bop" lyric writing competition, and a steady barrage of feature articles. The band leader's crusades to discourage juvenile delinquency and encourage young talent, and his opinions on various musical matters, were all received with interest.[2]

Among the many musicians to whom Lionel Hampton gave early breaks were two of Betty Carter's favorite singers—one well remembered, the other largely forgotten—Ruth "Dinah Washington" Jones and Wini Brown. Over thirty years after joining the group, Carter would recall Brown's voice with obvious affection: "She had a veiled voice, a powerful voice. . . . She's an unknown singer that I put together with Sarah Vaughan, Ella Fitzgerald, or Billie Holiday. These are singers who had a great influence on us all before we knew what success was or when we were just trying to get better."[3] Wini Brown made one record with Hampton, "Gone Again," which stayed on Billboard's race-record charts for two weeks and reached number 13 after Decca released it in July 1948.[4] Carter reminisced about it with Gil Noble in 1993, and about the singer whose deep alto tones formed the basis for her own sound in her lowest register, saying that she was a "beautiful woman . . . round, beautiful face, you know, and big eyes."[5] Carter recalled that this singer with the "unique, husky" voice had taken Madeline Green's or Dinah Washington's place in Hampton's band. While with Hampton, Washington had recorded a few blues numbers that made the race-record charts. But her greatest fame dates from the years after her time with his band, when her voice rang out from jukeboxes in black neighborhoods across the country singing such R&B hits as "Baby, Get Lost." Carter later crossed paths with her when they were both working in New York in the 1950s,[6] and in 1960 Washington produced several pop hits, including "Baby (You've Got What It Takes)," "A Rockin' Good Way (to Mess Around and Fall in Love)," and "This Bitter Earth."

Given that Hampton had employed two of Carter's favorite singers, with one still in the band, it seems unlikely that her attendance at that fateful dance in the summer of 1948 was entirely due to pressure from friends. The singer may have sensed that working with Hampton could well be her last chance to involve herself with a nationally touring organization. But admitting she had designs for getting into the band when she auditioned for Hampton would have seemed "unladylike" by the day's standards—and unhip in bebop circles—and this may have led her to downplay her ambitions. As Carter later recalled, she left the Forest Club never thinking she would hear from Hampton. But Chester Rentie had kept in touch with him, and two weeks later, the band leader contacted her agent, who then informed her that Lionel Hampton wanted her in his band.[7] Carter later recalled her disbelief: "I went to his [Rentie's] office to see the telegram. At that time, I probably was more stunned than anything else that he actually called me, and that I really got this job. . . . I knew it was a working band. I really had no idea that Lionel Hampton would ever call me for the job. . . . I just *knew* that he wasn't interested in somebody like me, you know. Wini Brown wasn't a bebopper. She's a nice singer."[8] Around the time Carter auditioned for Hampton, Wini Brown had given her boss two weeks' notice because she was marrying the band's baritone saxophone player, Charles Baker Fowlkes.[9] With his new wife, Fowlkes left Hampton that summer to join Arnette Cleophus "Arnett Cobb" Cobbs, who had left Hampton's band in 1947 to form his own combo, and Ben Kynard moved from the alto section to fill the baritone chair.

While Hampton has confirmed that Toledo was indeed the place Carter met up with the band, the city did not appear in the band's itinerary. Given the band's relentless touring schedule, however, there may have been gigs inserted into the schedule in early July, and one of these could easily have been in Toledo. The band spent the six weeks after the dance at the Forest Club touring Ohio, West Virginia, Pennsylvania, and western New York, before heading west to Akron on 30 July, Gary, Indiana, on 31 July, and Peoria, Illinois, on 4 August. As Toledo lies somewhat on the way from Akron to Gary, it seems likely that Carter went to Toledo to meet up with the band as it made its way west. This would place the date of her joining the band roughly two weeks before Wini Brown and Fowlkes left the band. A week after playing in Peoria the band broadcast from Denver and then continued on to Los Angeles.[10] It spent the period from mid-August to mid-October mostly in California—Hampton's old stomping grounds—with occasional forays up and down the coast. While there, the band made several Armed Forces Radio Service (AFRS) Jubilee recordings on which the voice of Hampton's newest vocalist may be heard.[11] Carter reported that in California the band played mostly at dances, working in theaters rather than nightclubs.[12] Her apprenticeship was in full swing then, for as she later recalled, "The theaters were the places that we really learned our craft, because we still had four shows to do a day."[13] While in Seattle Hampton encountered a fifteen-year-old trumpeter named Quincy Jones who would later join the band.[14]

In October the band made its way back east, and by 10 December it was in Harlem for a weeklong run of performances at the Apollo Theater. In addition to the Hampton band, the program included several comedy acts, Mantan Moreland and Kitty Murray, Red and Curley, and Shorts Davis. Moreland was well known for his role as Birmingham Brown in the Charlie Chan movie series. In 1946 he had starred in two race films, *Mantan Messes Up* and *Mantan Runs for Mayor.* That December he was a big draw, as his recent film *Tall, Tan, and Terrific* had just been released. Carter worked opposite Moreland on other occasions, both with Hampton and when she went single. Lionel Hampton recalled, "If you were a black entertainer of any kind—musician, singer, comedian—being a headliner at the Apollo was your proudest achievement."[15] The savvy New York audience did not make it easy: it was famous for "booing folks off the stage—and throwing eggs and tomatoes and whatever else was handy."[16] The theater held special significance for Betty Carter because she knew the importance it had played in the careers of Ella Fitzgerald and Sarah Vaughan. Carter's recollection of her first performance there remained vivid many years later: "I was scared, on the road, going to the Apollo Theater in New York City. When I arrived, I jumped on that stage and that audience went crazy. With a little bit of scatting, they went crazy and ever since then, it was like that all the time."[17] Jack Schiffman, son of the late Apollo Theater owner, Frank Schiffman, has given us a listener's perspective on Carter's early performances: "Lionel Hampton introduced a small girl, hair bobbed short, eyes seemingly larger than her face, [who] burst out on stage, took a deep breath, and sang bebop riffs, a whole machine-gun load of them, that turned the house upside down. I never saw an audience turned on so quickly to a new sound."[18]

Hampton's schedule followed an annual routine of movements between coasts. In the first half of 1949 the band shuttled back and forth between New York City—where it also recorded for Decca—and other mid-Atlantic and midwestern cities, frequently appearing in Chicago. By June it had begun its tour west, traveling from Buffalo through the stretch of Canada between Niagara Falls and Detroit, dipping south to Kentucky and then playing a series of dates leading to California. From July to October the band stayed on the West Coast and, echoing the pattern of the preceding year, returned to New York City for the end of the fall season. 1950 followed a similar course, with the first half spent in Manhattan recording for Decca and using the Big Apple as a base of operations for excursions into outlying areas on the East Coast and Midwest. A southern tour in the summer would again lead the group out to California and back to the East Coast at the end of autumn.

Initially Carter took Wini Brown's place in the Hamptones, a vocal harmony group. Doing so enabled the young singer to get her feet wet without being thrust in the role of soloist too early. Very soon, however, Hampton was promoting her in her own right. By 15 April 1949, when the band played at the Strand Cinema in New York City, the name Lorene Carter appeared in newspaper advertisements. For a late December run at the Apollo Theater that same year Hampton publicized Carter as Betty Bebop, and in forthcoming announcements her name appeared either way. Soon it also began to appear as Betty Bebop Carter, suggesting that by her twenty-first birthday she had arrived at the stage name by which she later became known.

Hampton's invitation to join the band brought Carter into the company of several phenomenal musicians. Milton Brent "Milt" Buckner had been playing piano and arranging for the band since 1941. Having grown up performing in Detroit in the 1920s, he was known for introducing the "locked hands" approach to voicing chords. Buckner left around the time Carter joined the band, only to rejoin it in 1950.[19] Charles Mingus stayed with Hampton during 1947 and 1948, and Wes Montgomery toured and recorded with Hampton from 1948 to early 1950. Mingus and Montgomery were not the only band members associated with modern jazz. The presence in the band of such players as trumpeter Ernest Harold "Benny" Bailey, who was coming from a stint in Gillespie's band, and trombonist Albert Thornton "Al" Grey, who would go on to play with Gillespie in 1956, demonstrates that Hampton had a true interest in the new music and was not simply jumping on the bebop bandwagon.[20] Both Bailey and Grey were with Hampton from 1948 until around 1953. There were several singers in the band while Carter was there, including—at various times—Irma Curry, Jeanette Franklin, blues singer Sonny Parker, Jimmy Scott, and Jackie "Skylark" Paris. In March 1949 the group had LurLean Harris, Sonny Freeman, and Roland Burton, "a tall, handsome, debonair type, who sang all the male ballads for the ladies,"[21] who also sang with Herman McCoy in the Hamptones.[22] The fact that Hampton had so many singers set his band apart from others and serves as another indicator of the band's success.[23] At first, Carter kept her distance from most of the other band members, feeling that her bebop pedigree put her above these musicians. She admitted to being a snob, saying, "I probably went through that critical bag. Young, too, and a bebopper, you know, I probably put up an attitude about 'she's all right, and he's okay.'"[24] Long bus rides and performing together soon eroded her aloof manner, however, and as she warmed up to her coworkers, they came to feel like family, while to them she became "the Kid."

Joining such a well-known organization so early in her career fueled the Kid's self-confidence. In 1976 Carter told bassist Chris White: "You can get pretty cocky after being out from about '46 to '48 and get with Lionel Hampton. You know, as a kid, you can think you're pretty together. That ain't no time to pay no dues, really."[25] As confident as she was, however, she had a realistic appraisal of her selling points: "I had a pretty good ear, was a pretty good singer, but most of all, I had a good rapport with people."[26] She could also assess her weaknesses with ruthless objectivity. She knew, for example, that she lacked the instrument Sarah Vaughan had: "I had the ear, the knack, the personality, and everything else, but I didn't have the voice. The voice had to become mature. It takes time to develop a sound."[27]

The brash, young performer's flamboyance undoubtedly suited Hampton's taste for showing off, but her independence led her to resist his direction.[28] He in turn had a notoriously short fuse. It was only a matter of time before friction arose between such strong-willed individuals. Ironically, while Hampton gladly used her bebop allegiance to widen the band's appeal, he found her open rejection of his swing aesthetic maddening, and her outspokenness caused him to lose his cool on more than one occasion.[29] She loved to recall how he impulsively fired her several times because she refused to play along when he asked such provocative questions as, "Whose band do you like best, mine or Dizzy's?"[30] One such occasion took place shortly after the band arrived at the Apollo. Being pulled from the lineup during the first show of a run was a severe punishment: because it served as a showcase for critics, who would then get word out about the band's appearance and draw audiences for following shows, this show was a crucial source of exposure for the ambitious singer. Shocked to discover her absence, Frank Schiffman and Hampton's wife Gladys confronted the band leader, and by the time the band got onstage for the next show, Carter was there.[31] She later recalled: "It was Gladys who saved me when he got angry enough to fire me. She wouldn't let him fire me," adding that "if it had not been for her, I don't think I would have stayed with the band that long."[32]

Gladys Hampton, née Riddle, had worked as a dressmaker and designer when Hampton met her in Los Angeles. They married on 11 November 1936 shortly before Hampton joined Benny Goodman's band. Gladys became Hampton's personal manager and, later, the band's business manager. Armed with a reputation for being tough, she ruled with an iron hand.[33] Her penchant for "economizing," as tenor saxophonist Dexter Gordon put it, led her to pay notoriously low wages, which contributed to the band's high rate of turnover.[34] She also managed the band's publishing company, Swing and Tempo Music, and its record label, Hampton Records.[35] Gladys had superb financial instincts and a remarkable ability to hold the line in business negotiations. When she saw that the band caused crowds to circle the block at the Apollo, she cut a deal with Jack Schiffman to receive a percentage of the gross box office receipts, instead of a straight fee. Then, rather than play the usual four shows a day, the band would play as many as it could.[36]

Gladys Hampton's encouragement came at a critical time in Betty Carter's development, and she did more than mediate disputes between Hamp and the singer. Gladys had achieved a prosperity few African American women of that time enjoyed.[37] Lionel Hampton proudly recalled in his autobiography that "Gladys was wearing diamonds and fur coats and driving a little sports car to meet us, or flying in to meet us. In 1949, she was named 'Most Outstanding Woman of 1948' by Mary McLeod Bethune, commander-in-chief of the Woman's Army of National Defense (the WANDS)."[38] Her affluence, as well as the clear example she provided of a female running an organization, gave Carter an image of what she could strive for: "I had this role model of Gladys Hampton to emulate. She took care of the band, saw to it that everything ran smoothly, that everybody got paid and such. That was the first time I'd ever experienced dealing with a woman who was the boss."[39] She also demonstrated to Carter that, although men dominated the jazz world, a woman could stand up to them. Hampton recalled that Gladys "taught her [Carter] a lot about being a woman in the music world. Betty says the main reason the guys didn't like her was because she was a female. She also said that the one thing she had in her favor was that Gladys controlled the band."[40]

When Carter joined the band, she put her family behind her.[41] The Hampton band took on the role in her life she wished her family had taken, nurturing her talent and acknowledging her worth. The pictures that later hung on the wall of her Brooklyn apartment displayed images that evoke a time when Carter felt appreciated—the tour bus, Gladys Hampton's Cadillac convertible, a surprise birthday party for Carter, a birthday cake, and a briefcase given as a birthday present. In light of Carter's strained relations with Bertha Jones, Gladys was a welcome ally who in many ways functioned as the singer's surrogate mother. As Lionel Hampton noted: "She taught her a lot about dressing and would pass some of her clothes on to Betty."[42] Such generosity takes on added meaning when we consider that gowns went for anywhere from $120 to $150 apiece, much more than a starting singer's weekly salary.[43] The maternal role Gladys filled in Carter's life was not unusual: she took the band's other female singers under her wing as well, including Dinah Washington.[44]

In one matter, however, Gladys Hampton would not intercede—Carter's role in the band. "Everything I did with the band was bebop. . . . I never really got a chance to sing any songs."[45] By using Carter exclusively for improvised scat choruses, Hampton could avoid having to create new arrangements for her: "He'd stick me into songs they were already doing, so I was singing a chorus here, a chorus there."[46] Given her dedication to bebop, her irritation at being cast in this mold is surprising and reminiscent of the saying: "Be careful what you wish for—you may get it." Having developed her scatting to set herself apart from the crowd, why did she want to sing ballads—unless she were fashioning herself after Sarah Vaughan? As time wore on, Carter expressed increasing ambivalence about this matter: "I went to him one time and said, 'I want to sing a ballad.' He said, 'no, no, no, . . . you stick with that bebop.' "[47] That Hampton had such a narrow use for so enterprising a singer eventually led to problems between the two. Emblematic of this conflict, the name he had given her only made matters worse. Gladys urged her to go along with Hampton, and because Carter knew she needed the experience, she initially saw the wisdom in this advice.[48] But as the singer's expertise and self-assurance grew, she became less and less tolerant. Gladys's reluctance to get involved in this issue reinforces the impression that, while she took care of the business end of the organization, she left the musical decisions to her husband.[49]

Due to Carter's resourcefulness and her drive to improve herself, the time she spent in the band proved invaluable to her growth in many ways. In addition to benefiting from the experience she gained in front of audiences, she made good use of idle hours between gigs by gaining a better understanding of music theory.[50] Carter had an innate curiosity about how music is put together, but she also had other motivations for educating herself musically. After encountering men's patronizing attitudes toward singers, she sought to distance herself from the stereotype. As she put it: "I didn't want to be *dumb!*"[51] She recognized as well that mastery over music's technical aspects would give her greater control over her work, allowing her to take an active role in music making. The informal schooling she received while in the band later enabled her to run her own rehearsals.[52] Her arguments with Hampton often spurred her on, motivating her to improve herself.[53] Speaking in 1979 she recalled: "I learned something about chord structure, putting an arrangement together, writing notes on a staff, seeing music, and transposing. I learned that from a fellow who is now playing first chair with Count Basie, Bobby Plater. I bugged him to death to show me this and that."[54]

Of all the musicians in the band, saxophonist and flutist Bobby Plater took the most interest in "the Kid." Originally from Newark, Plater had joined the band in 1945 as part of Hampton's push to update its sound.[55] By 1948 he had become a principal soloist and, after Arnett Cobb left, the band's "straw boss" or foreman. In addition to a boplike approach to soloing, he provided some of the band's arrangements, specifically those for the blues singer, Sonny Parker. As Carter's seat partner, he turned tedious bus rides into ear-training lessons: "Bobby Plater taught me how to write arrangements on the bus, without the piano."[56]

Given the impact instrumentalists have had on Carter's concept, her early interest in arranging seems reasonable:

> My first big band arrangement was on *Good Night Irene.* I just wanted to see if I could voice [chords]. I used the old Glenn Miller sound, with the clarinet playing top. We played it at the Clique in Philadelphia just to see how it sounded, because I had written it on the band bus. I wrote my score out traveling back and forth, then I wrote out the parts, and at rehearsal we passed the parts out and I heard it for the first time.[57]

The choice of tune is startling unless we consider that Pete Seeger's group, the Weavers, had made Leadbelly's song a huge popular hit in 1950. As an arranger, Carter was not quite ready to employ the modern idiom: "I screamed, 'Oh, this isn't me.' But I felt great because I *did it.*"[58]

The obstinate singer had other, ulterior, motives for learning to arrange: "Then I decided to write one for myself to go into the Apollo."[59] Carter next arranged "Orange Colored Sky," a tune Nat King Cole and the Stan Kenton band had made into a hit that year.[60] Its cool feel and surreal lyrics about being love struck, literally, would have been a fantastic vehicle for her, but the band leader stood his ground: "Lionel Hampton wanted me to do another tune which I had been singing for years, every time I came to the Apollo. It was a song where the band plays a real hip arrangement he's got in his book and I come out and do four or five choruses of scat on it. Well, I was ready to sing a few words, to let people know that I not only could scat, but that I also could sing a ballad."[61]

This incident was a turning point for Carter: "That was it! It didn't make any kind of sense for me to continue. I had been on the road for two and a half years, and I had been exposed. It was time for me to step out there on my own."[62] According to Janet Thurlow, who took Carter's place in the band, Carter's appearances at the Apollo from 28 December 1950 to 3 January 1951 were her last ones as a member of the band.[63] Carter later recalled that Hampton remained angry at her for "a long time."[64] Only much later did she acknowledge the unique training she had received while with Hampton, which gave her the means to strike out on her own.[65]

The bulk of Hampton's recorded output from this time consists of instrumental numbers, but there is some documentation of Betty Carter's work with the band.[66] In addition to appearing on some broadcasts, recordings of which are often called *air checks* or *air shots,* and a film short, Carter was included on two studio recordings. The first recorded examples of her singing, which come from four AFRS Jubilee broadcasts recorded in the fall of 1948 and perhaps the following winter, show that by the time she joined the band Carter had integrated the elements of bebop into a viable expressive language and could also effectively sing vocal harmony. She and Roland Burton provide backup vocals for Herman McCoy's opening statement of "Confess," and then the trio repeats the tune in rhythmic unison and close harmony.[67] On "I'll Dance at Your Wedding," Carter sings the lead vocal followed by a well-formed scat solo on the first sixteen measures of the form.[68] Atypically, Carter quotes two Gillespie titles: "Ool-Ya-Koo" and "Oop-Pop-a-Da." Two distinct male voices trade scat phrases on the bridge before the group reconvenes to sing the lyrics of the final A section, complete with the twist ending, "at *your* wedding and mine."

The next recording of Carter is a scat chorus on trombonist Jay Jay Johnson's "Jay Bird" from an air check made late in 1948.[69] Another, presumably later, performance of the same tune—but with no vocal—was recorded for an AFRS Jubilee broadcast (no. 327).[70] The tune came from Johnson's first session as a leader on 26 June 1946, when the trombonist presented it in the standard bebop format: a unison head followed by a series of solos, in this case by saxophonist Cecil Payne, Johnson, and pianist Bud Powell.[71] Its origins made it a logical vehicle for Hampton's bebop vocalist. The big-band arrangement Hampton used began with a four-measure introduction played by the whole band, but on the air check the vibraphonist led into this with a pseudomodernistic solo. The chart then proceeds with a statement of the theme. Musical example 1 shows the head of the air check, followed by Carter's scat chorus. (All of the musical examples follow the Appendix.)

While "Jay Bird" uses the AABA′ harmonic structure of George Gershwin's "I Got Rhythm"—the "rhythm changes" beboppers used most often, aside from the blues, as a template for their compositions—the melody follows an unusual ABCA format. The fresh melodic material in measures 9–16, with its embedded descending chromatic line, generates a sense of movement across the repeat of the chord changes. Repressing the standard melodic repeat here heightens the impact of the return to A after the bridge, at the pickup to measure 25. On the AFRS version instrumental solos follow, whereas on the air check Carter takes the first chorus after the head, an example of how she was simply inserted into instrumental charts. The entire trombone section then performs a transcription of Jay Jay Johnson's solo from the original recording![72] Ben Kynard and Benny Bailey then each take half-chorus solos, now postponed in the chart due to Carter's scat chorus, followed by Hampton's solo (on the AFRS broadcast Wes Montgomery takes the first half of this chorus). Driven by heavy backbeat drumming, the chart closes with a wild out-chorus that culminates in a quote from Gershwin's "Who's Got the Last Laugh Now."

Both performances illustrate by omission how crucial the contribution of the rhythm section was to modern jazz. Hampton's band swings hard, but the melodic lines lose their bebop quality when the rhythm section comps—complements or accompanies the horns—in the swing-era style. While drummer Earl Walker plays kicks—offbeat accents on the bass drum—behind the solos, especially apparent in the AFRS version, his heavy beating out of a four-to-the-bar feel cannot match Max Roach's groove on the original, and he drains rhythmic buoyancy from the lines.[73] The general mood is showy, lacking the subtle, withheld quality of the original, chamber version. Comparing Hampton's ersatz bebop with Gillespie's big-band charts from the same period reveals why Carter felt Hamp was simply not hip enough for her.

A close listen to Carter's solo on "Jay Bird" reveals that by the time she joined Hampton's band she had already developed a range of musical means to create interest, even within the constraints of an inserted scat chorus. As early as this solo, for example, Carter demonstrated in her choice of scat syllables that she could effectively use vocal timbre to create rhythmic momentum, as well as to reinforce the memorability of her musical ideas.

When discussing the elusive element of timbre, theorists typically are reduced to using the synaesthetic language of the wine taster, speaking of a player's tone as smoky, or wispy. In such discussions it is hard to go beyond rough distinctions between light and dark tone colors because, unlike other musical parameters such as pitch, there is no agreed-upon scale with which to calibrate degrees of timbral change. In the case of singers, however, it is possible to gauge nuances of timbral difference through the use of phonemes. The following sequence of vowels produced in front of the mouth, for example, gradually decreases in brightness: /iy/, /i/, /ey/, /e/, /æ/, /ay/ (as in the words peat, pit, pay, pet, pat, pie); on the other hand, the following sequence, produced in back of the mouth, gradually increases in brightness: /uw/, /u/, /ow/, /oh/, /æw/, /a/ (as in pool, put, boat, ball, pout, pot). Similarly, aspirated consonants—created with a sudden release of the breath—such as /p/, /t/, /k/, /f/, and /s/ produce stronger accents than their unaspirated counterparts—/b/, /d/, /g/, /v/, /z/, respectively—partly by emphasizing higher partials of the harmonic series. Of interest in their own right, phonemes also give us a precise way to analyze the ways a vocalist coordinates timbre with other musical elements. (For a detailed explanation of the phonetic symbols see the appendix.) For lack of a suitable analytic vocabulary, timbre's importance in the work of instrumentalists is often neglected; yet, in their tonguing, phrasing, and articulation, many players approach the timbral subtlety singers achieve with vowels and consonants—James Wesley "Bubber" Miley and Joseph "Tricky Sam Nanton" Irish were famous for using "growl and plunger" techniques to do so.

Betty Carter's solo on "Jay Bird" reveals how she used timbre to produce a wide variety of accents. On the most basic level, she generally correlates long note values with long vowels—indicated in the transcription by the semivowels /y/ or /w/ after, say, the short vowels /i/ or /u/ respectively. Conversely, she tends to use short vowels to clip the rhythm of short note values, as in the staccato sequence of /du/du/du/ sounds leading up to the /diy/ə/ in the fourth measure of the form (m. 36). The net result of this usage is that vowel lengths often reinforce agogic accents, which result from rhythmic duration.[74]

In "Jay Bird," Carter shows that timbre can also be used to increase a pitch contour's definition or movement. At the end of the first eight-measure phrase, in measure 39, she creates groupings of four quarter note triplets through a four-syllable phonemic pattern (biy/dn/dwiy/ow/-/biy/dn/dwiy/a/), emphasizing the higher pitches of the melodic contour with the brighter /iy/ sound, which reinforces the half note triplet feel these pitches generate. The rhythmic delay she introduces here—indicated by the arrow above the staff—is an illustration of intentionally unmeasured plasticity. While the alternative notation shown in the NB may seem more accurate, it does not convey the ease with which Carter flows while clashing so boldly against the time. Later, when she comes out of the bridge at measures 57–60, Carter lends a repeated melodic idea a sense of growth by altering its syllables.

Perhaps the most striking use of timbre occurs at measure 63 when, in the final measures of her solo, Carter hammers home an idea that had occurred in shorter bursts at measure 51. Using a sequence of alternating /n/ and /d/ sounds, a sequence she may have learned from Ella Fitzgerald, she energizes the repeated eighth note figure here with two different kinds of accent. Both phones are formed toward the front of the mouth, but the closed sound of the /n/ places weight *on* the beat, while the /d/ gives the offbeat a staccato accent. Carter uses timbre here to group the repeated pitches into pairs, strongly articulating each separate beat in the process. There is nothing inevitable about this choice, for she could have phrased across the beat by reversing the alternation (/dn/dn/dn/dn/), or undercut the pairings with a sequence of different vocables, or used the same syllable—/di/, say—on each eighth note; but the passage would have lost much of what makes it so hip.

The care Carter showed in her correlation of syllables to other musical elements was not new: other scat singers have expressed a sensitivity to the relationship between phonemes and melody. Regarding pitch, trumpeter-singer Clark "Mumbles" Terry has stated: "You see, it's not 'ooooo' [/uw/] up there . . . but 'eeeee.' [/iy/]. You use certain vowels in certain areas [of your vocal range]. 'Aaaaa' [/a/] is higher than 'ooooo' [/uw/]. Whatever fits the material."[75] Referring to rhythm he adds: "We teach young singers not to use the same syllables. Not 'oooodoooshibeeeedoooo' [/uw/duw/ši/biy/duw/] all the time. We teach them there are twenty-six letters. Use whatever the rhythm and tempo are suited for."[76] In "Jay Bird" Carter places many of her melodic peaks at the top of her chest voice, just below her break, which adds intensity to them. Following the example of Charlie Parker, she also accents her melodic peaks, brightening the sound of all but a few of them (mm. 33, 36, 38, 39, etc.) with the phoneme /iy/. For closure she often relies on the sound of the phoneme /a/, with an added /t/ (/dat/ in m. 37), or /p/ (/bap/ or /dap/ in mm. 45 and 47, respectively), or without a final consonant (/a/ in mm. 40, 42, 50, and 65). This approach gives her phrase endings the truncated quality typical of bebop articulation.

This solo also illustrates that Carter conceived of her ideas whole, not in fragments—as analysis would seem to indicate. The solo's impact as music results from the accumulation of diverse elements—timbres, rhythms, pitches—which are wedded to each other to reinforce their individual contribution. Being conversant with her raw materials, Carter did not labor over the decisions she made as she performed, but made them spontaneously. Yet while the control she exercised over her materials was largely intuitive, it operated at a high level, even in her earliest recordings. Carter chose not to elaborate much upon her methods, feeling that listeners' musical understanding was equally intuitive. But close listening can give us fresh insights into her work, especially as the passage of time weakens our connection to its original context.

Two songs from other AFRS broadcasts, presumably from early in 1949, give us a sense of Carter's continued growth as a singer. One is the ballad "Nothing in View," which was written by Bobby Plater to feature Roland Burton and perhaps Plater's eager pupil. Aside from a boppish passage in the trumpet section that occurs almost as an afterthought, however, little about the tune exploits Carter's modernistic idiosyncrasies. In several brief passages she hangs back slightly behind the beat, and in her last solo passage she swoops and bends pitches, two tendencies that would later become more pronounced. The other song is a modern-sounding rhythm-changes tune called "Gladys' Idea."[77] Misled by the title, announcer Bud Widom identifies the singer as Gladys Hampton; but it is clearly Betty Bebop. A comparison of the scat chorus on "Gladys' Idea" with Carter's solo on "Jay Bird" discloses key resemblances: in both solos she uses an almost identical melodic idea at measures 4–6 of the form, for example, and she begins the second A section of each with a similar phrase. This recurrence of licks notwithstanding, Carter's solo on "Gladys' Idea," with its imaginative phrasing and treatment of dissonance, is highly original. This broadcast documents the highest level of scatting she had thus far achieved.

In addition to the broadcasts we have from this time, Hampton recorded Carter twice on the Decca label while in New York in 1949. On 24 January she scatted on a tune called "Benson Boogie," a blues with a boogie-woogie feel. This recording gives us a relatively unusual instance of Carter scatting on the time-honored blues progression. Sonny Parker sings the lyrics, and Carter takes an offbeat scat solo that ends tartly on the bebopper's trademark flatted fifth. The other recording, a vocal rendition of Charlie Parker's "Now's the Time," better known as "The Hucklebuck," was cut later that year, on 10 May. Bird had recorded the tune in the famous "Ko-Ko" session on 26 November 1945. Early in 1949, Tommy Dorsey recorded the song in a version that virtually stripped it of any bebop characteristics. Soon after Dorsey's version, saxophonist Paul Williams had a hit with the song on Savoy in February that was on Billboard's race-record chart for thirty-two weeks, holding first place for fourteen of them.[78] No doubt inspired by the success of the latter version, drummer-vocalist Roy Milton covered the tune for the Specialty label, which released the record in April.[79] Perhaps it was the tune's modernistic associations that prompted Hampton to let his resident bebop vocal specialist sing the lyrics.[80] In a more progressive sounding version than Dorsey's, Betty Carter sings the song's lyrics and a short solo scat break toward the end of the performance. Taken somewhat slower than Parker's version, the rendition has a shuffle feel, and Carter later remarked, "You won't believe that 'Hucklebuck.' I used to do it calm."[81] Released by the Decca label on 13 August 1949, the tune spent a week at number 12 on Billboard's Juke Box chart.[82] Long since forgotten, the two recordings Lionel Hampton made with Betty Bebop were the only ones from 1949 listed by critic Roger Kinkle as representative jazz sides.[83]

According to Carter, some people from Universal Studios in Hollywood heard Hampton's band when it played at a dance in Newark, and shortly before she left the band, they brought the band out to California to shoot a series of short performances.[84] The Snader telefilms provide rare footage of Carter as she scats on a modified rhythm-changes tune called "Cobb's Idea," which was originally conceived of as a feature number for Arnett Cobb before he left the band. In the film Hampton ushers the singer, stunningly attired in a shoulderless black dress, to the microphone at the end of the second complete chorus, and she proceeds to scat the first sixteen measures of the next chorus over the rhythm section's support with the horns in the band adding a hand-clapping pattern behind her.[85] In a short time Carter conveys a high degree of self-assurance and stage presence, while Hampton looks on with obvious pride.[86]

Carter's experience with Hampton had lasting consequences for many aspects of her life. She formed several important personal connections that provided a social and professional network for her over the next two decades and beyond. In addition, many of her later attitudes bore the mark of Hampton's own philosophy, such as his openness to the latest developments in recording technology.[87] Most important, she was one of the last jazz singers to have her roots in the big bands.

4

On Her Own

Lionel Hampton's band had been a surrogate family for the Kid, a community that had nurtured her growth and acknowledged aspects of her personality she herself valued. Not content with the security it offered her, she asserted her independence yet again. The singer later recalled that "once you had done a big band you don't want to do it anymore. That's it! It's time to get out of that unless you're forever gonna be a band singer and you want to stay with a big band for ten years."[1] Upon leaving the band at the start of 1951, Betty Carter gravitated to her hometown, "to regroup and get over this. When you are with something for two and one-half years, you have to realize 'now what do I do? Do I take a shot at going to New York or stay in Detroit at home?' I stayed there about six months and had to get out."[2] Any hopes she may have brought home with her that she and her mother might feel differently about each other did not come to fruition. Bertha was now in Flint, apparently remarried, and her daughter had already established a separate existence. In the singer's life story, her mother remains an enigmatic figure about whom family members have little to say. Carter's return to Michigan only confirmed that the two women had nothing in common.[3]

So when the summer came, she left home again. Having become familiar with New York City over the preceding three years, it seemed a logical place to go. She did not have any family there, however, and she would have to fend for herself.[4] Carter did return to Detroit now and then while on road trips to the Midwest and no doubt often visited with family while there. But after her second departure her family ties remained tenuous for a long time. As late as 1976 she was saying, "My family right now does not know a thing about what I'm doing."[5]

The challenge of trying to make it in the "Big Apple" appealed to Carter, showing how much she believed in herself:

> New York City. That's it. That's where it works. . . . There are other places to go; but still, if you want to take some chances and really learn at the same time, especially with the energy level that it [has], that's the place to go if you really have something. There is something about New York and what it does to you to make you do your thing. You won't get laid back. You got to fight if you are to survive. That is so necessary in jazz because it makes you think all the time.[6]

She moved into a hotel on Forty-seventh Street, where "it looked like the world in show business lived."[7] Carter recalled that, during the early 1950s, Sammy Davis Jr. and Will Maston's trio, whom she had met while working with Hampton, the Mills Brothers, and various "interpretive dancers" and instrumentalists, including Miles Davis, all lived near Forty-seventh Street and Broadway. At the time the trumpeter was staying at the University Hotel on Twentieth Street and in and out of the Hotel America on Forty-eighth Street.[8] Carter remembered, "There were about three hotels that accommodated all the musicians. We stayed in the hotels and didn't pay our rent. The hotel managers kind of knew that we weren't going to pay our rent on time, but they seemed to go along with it and understand."[9]

As a performer making her way in Manhattan, Carter lined up work the way most starting performers did: by word of mouth. Around the corner from where she lived was a bar called the Turf, downstairs in the Brill building on Broadway and Fiftieth, "where everybody hung out in the daytime. This is where the work sifted through and came in."[10] As she came to deal with the people who controlled the various channels of communication between an artist and her audience, from clubs and other venues to record labels and radio stations, the young hopeful discovered that her commercial success depended upon the good graces of businessmen who were generally not as interested in musical excellence as they were in cashing in. Situated on the fault line between art and capitalism, the alliance between musicians and businessmen—especially agents—is a notoriously strained one. With the agent handling the business end so the client can focus on making music, the relationship often acquires patriarchal overtones. Joe Glaser's relationship with Louis Armstrong is perhaps the most prominent example of this dynamic. Haunted by the sense that they are earning only a fraction of the yield generated from their work, many musicians nevertheless remain in the dark about the industry's inner workings, either by deception or by choice.

In her earliest efforts to promote herself as a single, Betty Carter also encountered the effect racial inequality had on the music industry, for the industry's power structure mirrored the segregation that divided neighborhoods along color lines. Shortly before she had moved to New York, the music industry had adopted the term *rhythm & blues* as a euphemism for "race music," which had designated music marketed specifically to African Americans;[11] but, initially at least, the new term did little to bridge the gap between black and white listeners. When Carter began coming to the Brill building, the people who decided whether a song would be bought, a performer hired, a record made, a career advanced, were all men, and the majority of them were white. Working with these people, who were positioned to market a black artist's music to white listeners, was the only way to achieve national celebrity. As a result, many excellent black artists were barely known outside the African American community, because they lacked access to nationwide channels of distribution. Carter would later come to resent the way her career had suffered during the 1950s because of the split between white and black music.[12] In an interview with Leslie Gourse in 1982, she described how, even in New York City where the effects of racism were felt less than in other cities, WEVD played black jazz and WNEW played Frank Sinatra and Peggy Lee;[13] how "black entertainers couldn't stay in the Las Vegas hotels where they were working;"[14] how in 1955 a black artist such as LaVern Baker could have a commercial hit with "Tweedle Dee" only to have Georgia Gibbs cover it and produce a popular success,[15] and how Elvis Presley did not publicly acknowledge his debt to black music. She also recalled that "when Billie Holiday got busted in the 1940s and went to jail, it made headlines; but when Anita O'Day used drugs you didn't hear about it or about how many times she did get busted," adding that "no rehabilitation places existed for black people—only prison."[16] Yet, as much as Carter resented this state of affairs, she also came to feel that musical segregation benefited African Americans because it enabled them to retain a degree of control over their music.[17] She discovered an informal guild of black performers who would assemble at the Turf, where a promoter would go if he wanted to find a singer or a dancer for the next weekend, and she soon insinuated herself into the social network there: "We got a lot of work hanging out in the bar. . . . I did very well."[18] There were many places for performers to work, including many low-profile venues—small clubs, tent shows, and the like—so, for a young artist breaking into the business, the opportunities seemed unlimited.

Starting in January 1952, for about six months Carter worked at the Apollo Bar in Harlem, located down the street from the Apollo Theater, at 303 125th Street on the corner of Eighth Ave.[19] The club had featured other bebop artists such as Charlie Parker and Max Roach.[20] Carter worked with pianist Freddy Washington's "All-Star Band" with Jimmy Butts on bass.[21] During her run there the club featured Jimmie "Chickie" Horne, the singing emcee, and other now-forgotten performers such as Ray Sneed and Margurita Lopez. One job led to another, and she went from the Apollo Bar to the Paradise at 110th Street and Eighth Avenue, operated by the same owners who rotated Carter from one bar to the other.[22] A later appearance at the Apollo Bar, in October 1952, was written up in *Variety.* Many features of her style were apparently already in place: "Betty Carter has an interesting idea. She takes standards and musical comedy tunes and strays far from the melodic line into a swing and bop form. Some of the Negro singer's stuff is ingenious, but much shows little imagination. Her major number is 'Perfidia,' which has moments of delicacy and charm. Her bop excursions are strong enough to warrant an encore in this house."[23]

Carter recalled that once, when she played the Paradise, Charlie Parker came into the bar, sat in front, and asked if he could play.[24] One of the club's co-owners, the tenor saxophonist George "Big Nick" Nicholas, remembered hiring Carter for eight straight months. Known for a boisterous singing style, Nicholas, who led jam sessions at the Paradise in the first years of the 1950s, had played with Dizzy Gillespie at the end of 1947.[25] Carter got to work opposite such jazz greats as pianists Thelonious Monk and Horace Silver, tenor saxophonists Ben Webster and Sonny Rollins, and drummers Max Roach and Art Blakey: "The whole world came through musically at that time. I worked there a lot."[26] According to Carter, Billie Holiday used to come in to catch her working and would ask her to sing "Moonlight in Vermont," which Carter described as "her [Holiday's] favorite tune at that time. . . . She would always ask me to sing that."[27] Shortly before Holiday died she would tell Max Jones: "I love her. She's really got something. . . . Betty's five years ahead of her time."[28]

The work consisted of "just going in with the house bands and singing standards," such songs as "Thou Swell," "Perfidia," "Gone with the Wind," "I Could Write a Book," and "Can't We Be Friends."[29] Finally she was getting a chance to sing the love songs Hampton had denied her, and her musical ideas grew more sophisticated as her skills increased.[30] From early on Carter had strong ideas about how she wanted her music to sound, ideas about putting together arrangements and programming sets so they would be interesting to her and her musicians, as well as to the audience. Her commitment to meet the interwoven demands of these three distinct parties determined the course of her stylistic development. Rather than rely solely upon the songs' words to get over, she used what she had learned from scatting, and from Billie Holiday and Sarah Vaughan, to make her performances musically engaging. In addition to her concern for the quality of her music making, Carter cultivated a certain look. Encouraged by Gladys Hampton, her interest in fashion had advanced well beyond her childhood wish to stand out at church. Dancer Tina Pratt, who described Betty "Bebop" Carter as a favorite at the Rendezvous Club in Detroit, recalled the singer's "famous skin-tight, backless dresses with the hemline trimmed in fur."[31] Living on a limited budget, Carter made many of her own clothes at this time, as well as such accessories as the trademark bebop cap she wore.[32]

During the early 1950s Carter worked "all over the city,"[33] and she soon developed a reputation in the New York scene. She began to appear at better rooms, such as the Onyx, in May 1953, and at Baby Grand in August 1955 on the same bill as comedian Nipsey Russell, stripper Betty Brisbane, and Big Miller, who was billed as "Rock and Roll Blues straight from Detroit."[34] She recalled working at Roseland as well. Having already begun to build up a following in African American neighborhoods in cities on the East Coast and in the Midwest while with Hampton's band, she continued to do so as her solo career progressed. She appeared at the Showboat in Philadelphia in March 1953 and the Beige Room and the Regal Theater in Chicago in 1954. "It was the thing to do. You had occasional trips outside [New York City], to Atlantic City, or maybe Philadelphia, Washington, Baltimore, or Detroit, but you lived here—you would take all the gigs that came your way."[35] Other locales included Boston[36] and Asbury Park.[37] Owned by Herb Keller, the Showboat was the main jazz club in Philadelphia at that time.[38] Pianist Sam Dockery recalled working there with Carter after he left Art Blakey, when he was in the club's house band.[39] Carter was involved with the Philadelphia scene in the mid-1950s and formed many important associations there. The press announcements from this time give us only a glimpse of her performing activity because many clubs did not advertise, but relied upon word of mouth.

Soon after Carter left Lionel Hampton she also went on a road trip through the South. Organized by promoter Spizzy Canfield, the tour consisted of a succession of "camp shows" that took her as far as Biloxi, Mississippi. She worked "across the tracks, staying in the little hotels."[40] The tour featured Mantan Moreland and included comedians Bud Harris and Kitty Murray. On her numbers Carter was backed by the Hampton family band out of Indianapolis, which was run by trombonist Locksley Wellington "Slide" Hampton's brother Don, and which included several other Hampton siblings. The tour probably took place before the trombonist joined Buddy Johnson's band in 1955.[41] There was also a shake dancer and a tap dancer, "a little bit of everything."[42] Aware of Gillespie's southern excursions, Carter made no adjustments in her style or repertoire. She was gratified, and a bit taken aback, that southerners could take in her modernistic brand of jazz: "I was scatting down there even, and people got quiet and listened."[43]

None of this work paid especially well, but Carter viewed the experience as an essential part of her training as an entertainer—"dues paying." She would always value the fact that she had been given the freedom to experiment and the time to develop: "There were places where we could go and try out our thing and find out what we could do. It wasn't instant. . . . We were working in all kinds of strange places; living conditions were not the best. We still worked hard. . . . Who cared about the living expenses?"[44] For Carter, an essential aspect of this experience was working in front of a black audience, the final arbiter of quality in her eyes. "So we moved among our people. That was the only way we could do it."[45]

Working mostly in small clubs—the ordinary "bar around the corner"—Carter had to contend with the big names in her field who worked the "bigger rooms." As much as she yearned for a breakthrough, she accepted the reality that she was not quite ready for their level of celebrity: "Well I'm going through the '50s. . . . I'm the youngest of a crop of singers with Vaughan, Holiday, Washington. And these are giants—they've got it covered."[46] She was pleased with her niche on the New York scene, however, and perhaps because of her relatively quick success with Lionel Hampton she felt her prospects for success were good: "I was, like, on the cusp. I was the jazz singer that they could touch, because Sarah Vaughan was still a star. Ella Fitzgerald was a star at that point. Nobody could really touch these girls. . . . I was the local jazz singer in New York for awhile. That was my thing."[47] Nevertheless, she was making steady inroads.

Carter's growing network of connections led to an opportunity to record relatively soon after her arrival in New York, on 12 December 1952, in a cameo appearance on a record made by King Pleasure for the Prestige label.[48] This recording earned her some recognition in jazz circles: "That was when I first got to New York and King Pleasure had had 'Moody's Mood for Love' out, and his shot was 'Red Top,' which was Gene Ammons' tune."[49] Carter already knew the song well by the time she recorded it. She noted that Ammons, who had recorded the song on 2 September 1947 for the EmArcy label, had dedicated it to his wife.[50] The popular tenor saxophonist had produced two versions, one instrumental and one with the vocal refrain on which Pleasure based his version. While it is conceivable that Carter heard the song when Ammons appeared in Detroit the October after he recorded it,[51] she certainly encountered it on jukeboxes all over the city. A month later, Lionel Hampton covered it, and it was probably still in the book when Carter joined the band the following summer. Ammons's solo soon become so well known that other musicians quoted it, such as when Big Nick Nicholas launches into his solo on "Ool-Ya-Koo" recorded with Dizzy Gillespie's band that December.

King Pleasure, also known as Clarence Beeks, had made a name for himself by writing and singing vocalese, or adding lyrics to a well-known instrumental solo. Eddie Jefferson had developed the approach, transforming such classic jazz solos as Coleman Hawkins's tenor saxophone version of "Body and Soul," which the singer had recorded as early as July 1952, into clever vocal numbers. Later in the 1950s, vocalese caught on with Lambert, Hendricks, and Ross, who enshrined many a jazz solo in words, including their sly commentary on psychoanalysis set to Wardell Gray's "Twisted."[52] By faithfully reproducing famous players' solos, vocalese specialists acknowledged the canonic status these performances had acquired in the jazz community. King Pleasure had recently enjoyed a big success with another vocalese number, "Moody's Mood for Love," in which he sang Eddie Jefferson's lyrics to James Moody's famous solo on "I'm in the Mood for Love." Shortly after making "Red Top," Pleasure went on to have a hit based upon Charlie Parker's famous solo on "Parker's Mood."[53] Carter undoubtedly knew of Pleasure's work from the well-received performances he gave at the Apollo Theater during this time.

Ammons's tune is built upon a modified twelve-bar blues progression. After Pleasure and Carter sing the original lyrics in octaves, Pleasure then proceeds to render Gene Ammons's tenor saxophone solo in vocalese, followed by Carter singing Gail Brockman's trumpet solo.[54] The key Pleasure chose for "Red Top" may have suited his range, but it brought Carter's voice into her squeaky head voice, which she had not yet mastered. Much of her line was therefore set in an uncomfortable tessitura, or portion of her vocal range—right around the break—and made it difficult to enunciate Pleasure's lyrics.[55] In addition, vocalese placed severe limits on improvisation, and this kept her from leaving her mark on the material.[56] Carter did not have these stumbling blocks in mind she when left Hampton to sing lyrics, and she was less than enthusiastic about the result. She did find a way to sneak in an embellishment or two of her own, an upper-neighboring-tone figure, or inverted mordent, that instrumentalists commonly use. Alice Roberts was one of few singers who employed this ornament, and Carter probably knew the recordings she made with Dizzy Gillespie on Musicraft in 1946. For Carter this melodic figure, especially used in up-tempo numbers when she tended to sing it on a single syllable, became a distinguishing feature of her sound.

Working at the Apollo was an important opportunity, and performing there contributed to Carter's hope for imminent success, for the theater provided many artists with a springboard for leaping into the national arena: "Every time you went into the Apollo, you thought somebody was going to see you and make you a big star. That was the big thing. I did that theater, maybe two or three times a year."[57] The brothers who ran the venue, Frank and Bobby Schiffman, admired her work,[58] and her prior association with them smoothed her entry on the New York scene. Bobby Schiffman loved having singers on the bill, and he claimed that Carter often gave him the key ingredient for a successful show.[59] She presented herself with assurance there, telling arrangers how she wanted her music to sound and insisting that the conductor get his time from her.[60]

One of her earliest gigs as a single at the Apollo Theater took place on Friday, 13 February 1953, when she appeared in a show that included the Orioles, Paul Williams, the Five Dancing Dyerettes, and comedian Anita "Pigmeat" Echols.[61] A huge variety of acts crossed the theater's stage, and the bebop vocals specialist found herself sharing it with such acts as the Temptations, Bo Diddley, John Lee Hooker, Julian Edwin "Cannonball" Adderley, Thelonious Monk, James Moody, and many others. "I was there in the '50s with the Flamingos, . . . the Moonglows, the Isley Brothers, Ike and Tina Turner, all the people."[62] With an implicit boast, Carter recalled that "it didn't matter what you did; you just had to be good at it. At the Apollo, you could play classical music if you did it well. I remember a dancer who worked on her toes. She couldn't get into a big ballet company because they didn't take black dancers. But she was brilliant, and they loved her at the Apollo."[63] She continued to work there into the 1960s, appearing as late as 1966, opposite several blues acts. Carter had been dubious when one of the Schiffmans approached her about that gig: "Now what does he need with me on that show with Muddy Waters and T-Bone Walker?" but he persisted: "He said to me, 'You'll be the difference. We'll put you right in the middle. We'll have blues on this side of you and blues on that side of you!'"[64] From doing that performance—the last she did at the Apollo—she concluded that, since she did not have to adjust her music to be on *that* program, she would never have to compromise her aesthetic ideals.[65] The wide range of styles Carter encountered at the Apollo was striking. She recalled working with Sonny Till's "doo wop" group, the Orioles, as early as 1950, while she was still with Hampton, when "our music was played on the lower part of the dial."[66] Although audience tastes changed during the 1950s and 1960s, the Schiffmans would continue to seek out Carter's distinctive sound and her ability to appeal directly to the crowd.

In some ways, performing at the venue solidified Carter's sense of membership in the community of performing artists. Confronting the exacting standards of the Apollo audience allowed her to gauge her ability as a performer: "We always had a challenge going for us when we were at the Apollo. It was our job to go in there and kill them."[67] The schedule at the theater, while often grueling, allowed Carter to measure her growth: "We worked five shows a day sometimes, one right after the other. So you kept grading yourself: the morning show was better than the second show, or vice versa."[68]

Carter fondly recalled the collaborative environment at the Apollo. "No one had to dominate. We liked each other. I'd hang around clubs with Sarah Vaughan or Ruth Brown."[69] Without in any way damaging this sense of community, however, ambitious young performers who had something to prove also competed against the other acts. The showcase format carried an implicit competitive tone reminiscent of cutting sessions—musicians' informal peer review system—and in some ways they served a similar function. Such shows put performers to a public test, and left it to the highly vocal audience to separate the wheat from the chaff: "You'd have to follow this act, and you'd have to know *how* to follow it. And then you'd have to close your act, and make sure that the next act *couldn't* come on after you, or at least had a hard time coming on after you."[70] Clearly, rising to the challenge posed by the Apollo audience also galvanized Carter's sensibilities as an entertainer.

In the course of living and working in New York, Carter acquired her first manager.[71] John Levy had been George Shearing's bassist for three years when, in 1951, he stopped performing to manage the pianist. At thirty-nine years old, he was a seasoned performer, having worked with such musicians as Billie Holiday and Lennie Tristano, but he was quite new to managing acts. Not long after Shearing made him his road manager, Levy began to add other acts to his roster, and he was also managing pianist Ray Bryant when he took on Carter. Associated with the Shaw Agency, he later added singer Nancy Wilson, saxophonist Cannonball Adderley, and Wes Montgomery to his roster. Carter already had strong ideas about how to present herself, and felt she knew too much about the business to be taking advice from a manager: "He [Levy] didn't realize that you couldn't manage people on the road, that you had to have an office so that people could get in touch with you. When he finally figured that out I was gone."[72]

Neither Carter nor Levy could recall when they joined forces or when they parted company, but between May 1955 and April 1956 he arranged a few recording dates for her with the Epic label. In her first session as a leader she recorded with a small ensemble that included Ray Bryant on piano. Levy wanted to use the recording to introduce his new artists, and Columbia/Epic released it under the title *Meet Betty Carter and Ray Bryant.*[73] Roughly Carter's age, Bryant came from Philadelphia, where he had established himself as a solid bebop player. The session had other fine musicians in it: Joseph Rudolph "Philly Joe" Jones on drums, who soon went on to work with Miles Davis, Jerome Richardson on flute, and Wendell Marshall on bass. Carter had worked with Jones in Atlantic City two years earlier, where he had played and recorded with Tadd Dameron when trumpeter Clifford Brown was with the group.[74] Quincy Jones received arranger credit, but Bryant was largely in charge of putting the charts together.

The recording's twelve cuts included six standards from Carter's book and six instrumental numbers, presented in alternation.[75] On these early tracks Carter treads a fine line between hip coolness and earnest warmth that lend the performances an engaging richness. Among the standards, "I Could Write a Book" stands out as one she would later record several times. To place the tune comfortably in her vocal range, it is set a perfect fourth lower than its original key of C major. She would perform it in G major throughout her career, but she would never stick so closely to Richard Rodgers's melody (example 2).

There are several interpretive touches that set Carter's line apart from the one Rodgers composed. Listen to the way she hangs back a bit, keeping many of her words from landing squarely on the first beat of each measure. This delay, an essential feature of Carter's swing that she most likely absorbed from Billie Holiday, as well as from Jimmy Scott, generates complexity by adding a conflicting rhythmic layer to the metric impulse, rather than simply reinforcing it with corresponding attacks. Even when note values are not tied across the barline, the placement of an unaccented syllable or word, such as "a (book)" in measure 7 [0:14], or "could (write)" in measure 13 [0:27], often creates a subtle conflict with the time laid down by the rhythm section. At such moments it sounds as if her barline falls a half-beat later than the band's; but Carter knows precisely where she is, for at other times words fall securely into the groove.

Carter's bending of pitch obviously affects her reading's melodic shape, giving it a playful elusiveness, but it also contributes to her swing by delaying her arrival at scale degrees. Her laid-back phrasing and pitch bending are good examples of intentionally unmeasured plasticity, for just as her rhythmic choices often resist exact measurement in relation to the meter, as in measure 6 [0:12], her choice of pitch often eludes description in terms of the tempered scale. This approach has its dangers, for at times she sounds out of tune. Risky, too, is her sparing use of vibrato, a tool that often gives singers a margin for error, albeit a slight one, or buys them time to hone in on their intended pitch. She acknowledged that she was taking chances: "In the early days I had the swinging ability, the ears and the ideas, but I was overextending myself, and I wasn't the most in-tune singer in the world. I was paying attention to being exciting and surprising, rather than to the quality of my pipes."[76]

In addition to helping her enunciate the lyrics, Carter's ingenious treatment of phones in "I Could Write a Book" has musical implications. She is careful about her placement of certain words' final consonants, for example, occasionally using them to mark the beat, as she does on the /s/ of "just" in measure 25 [0:52]. By musicalizing phones Carter injects the song's semantic content with nonverbal meaning. At the end of her opening statement of the melody, measures 33–36 [1:09–1:17], for example, she stretches out the line "how to make two lovers of friends" over four measures, taking twice the time to deliver these words as is prescribed by the sheet music. To get the most warmth out of the word "lovers," she elongates the initial consonant in measure 34 [1:11], exploiting its ability to carry pitch. Here her pronunciation of the word and her back phrasing conspire to create a luxuriant lingering over the song's central idea.

Carter's scat solo on "Thou Swell" (example 3), also on her Epic recording with Ray Bryant, shows that her technique, vocal range, and daring had increased since her time with Hampton. The broad melodic gestures of Carter's solo in "Thou Swell" also reveal her sure instinct for pacing melodic events. In the span of the solo's opening measure [1:03] she ascends a twelfth to a smeared A-flat, the flat seventh of the tune's key of B-flat major, before spending the next five measures [1:04–1:08] elaborating upon a motive built out of a chromatic descent from A-natural, the leading tone, to G-natural. A skip up to B-flat in measure 6 [1:08] releases the tension Carter had created by dwelling on these pitches, after which the line plunges back to the bottom of her range, all within the span of a measure [1:08–1:09]. After rising to a C-natural, the solo's highest pitch, and then outlining the original tune's falling tonic pentachord (F-natural, E-flat, D-natural, C-natural, B-flat) with agogically stressed pitches, Carter closes with an inverted dominant pedal-point that prepares for the return of the A section, where she returns to singing lyrics for the second half of the chorus. Her choice of syllables in measures 12–13 [1:14], /duw/əm/ba/bə/də/šiy/ra/, illustrates her continued exploration of the phonetic raw materials available to her. Here her striking choice of syllables, /šiy/ra/, draws attention to her reference to the descending major-second motive from measures 2–6.

Meet Betty Carter and Ray Bryant reveals Betty Carter's debt to Sarah Vaughan, Ella Fitzgerald, and Dinah Washington, as well as Billie Holiday, for she was still absorbing their impact at the time she made the record. Showing the younger singer drawing upon her various influences, it gives us an important window onto her early style development—one that establishes a frame of reference for what was to come. The record's reception upon its release is also revealing. The critic who reviewed it in *Down Beat* had nothing but praise for Bryant and his sidemen. Largely on the basis of Carter's singing, however, he went on to give the record two stars out of a possible five, noting that "Bryant alone would get four." Discussing Carter, he went on to add: "Her singing frequently lacks taste. Her style is so affected that it often comes close to sounding like a caricature. Her phrasing is sometimes grotesque; she has little consistency of line and often does somersaults instead of flowing.

Miss Carter is the reductio ad trauma of the use of the voice in jazz as an instrument."[77] Elaborating upon his philosophy of jazz singing, the reviewer allowed that the jazz voice must be "instrumentalized, but not to the extent that the essential nature and capacity of the voice itself is overlooked and becomes instead a contorted gimmick."[78] In closing he advised Carter to "learn the values of simplicity and naturalness."[79]

In her entire oeuvre, Betty Carter's work with Ray Bryant stands out because she was still staying relatively close to the melodies; yet, ironically, even this early in her career she was criticized for her imaginative departures from the tune. Rooted as it was in the bebop sensibility, with its emphasis on improvisation, Carter's unquestionably stylized approach was apparently a bit too clever for certain listeners. While some were intrigued by the offbeat intelligence her singing conveyed, many could not brook the degree to which she abandoned the familiar outlines of their favorite songs. Other jazz singers also took expressive liberties with their material, but they tended to assert their concept surreptitiously by following the melody's broad outlines and the lyrics' original prosody. In contrast, Carter brazenly drew attention to her interpretations, at times inverting a song's melodic shapes and breaking its sentences into smaller sense units.

A double standard seems at work here, perhaps two. The same listeners who did not mind if an instrumentalist took off on a melody, or even ignored it completely, as Coleman Hawkins did in his famous rendition of "Body and Soul"—listeners who in fact counted upon such inventiveness—expected a vocalist to hew closely to the melody's outlines. The presence of words undoubtedly intensifies the impact of a singer's melodic variations, which—unlike the license a player may take—confront listeners with an interpretation of the lyrics that may cut powerfully against theirs. Those who enjoyed humming along with a singer found Carter's rephrasing of tunes disruptive. But as much as she sought to connect with her listeners, Carter was not interested in coddling them. Carter's crime against composers was all the more outrageous. Over her career Carter defied the accepted role of female vocalist, expanding it from that of interpreter to bold improviser. Her earliest recordings barely hint at where her sensibility would ultimately lead her, yet already she was disturbing the status quo. Significantly, when asked once whether she had to be stronger in the business because she was a woman, she spoke only about the job she had set out to do as a musician: "to see to it that that audience went out of this club, or this concert hall, or whatever, with a little piece of me on their minds."[80] She added that, in some of the dives where she worked, it was a challenge to get the bar quiet, and she worked to seize the bartender midgesture with the beauty of a moment she had created. For one who sought to exert that kind of power over the listener, there could be no pacifying her audience with predictable readings.

Carter has portrayed this time in her life as a happy one. She was a young artist living and learning within the network of musicians who peopled the Manhattan jazz scene. She was a hip insider, welcomed into an extended family of like-minded souls.[81] Her description of the ethos that prevailed among her and her colleagues contrasts sharply with remarks she made about her family: "There was love. . . . It existed; it was just there, it was expressed for each other. There was that natural respect of each other's music and each other's being there. There was no fighting and fussin' and feuding over the music. It was cooperating time at that time, 'cause everybody wanted to play, everybody wanted to learn, everybody wanted to listen, everybody wanted to be an individual."[82] This idealism spurred her belief that she could adhere to her principles and still achieve the fame her heroines had achieved.

As early as 1954, however, changes had begun to occur in the music industry and in the world outside it, and the commercial viability of jazz had almost imperceptibly begun to erode. Bill Haley's "Shake Rattle and Roll" hit the charts in late fall of that year, signaling the emergence of rock and roll as a viable style. The following year, with "Rock around the Clock," Haley would produce the first rock-and-roll single to top the pop charts. As Betty Carter persisted in her efforts to make it as a jazz singer, the forces behind these changes gradually made themselves felt on the music world and beyond.

5

Early Successes

By the latter half of the 1950s Betty Carter had made enough of a name for herself to break through in the recording industry. More important, musicians knew her as a creative singer who could participate convincingly in the musical give-and-take on the bandstand. Her next recording dates came about as a result of connections both professional and personal that she had made in New York and Philadelphia. Less than a year after she recorded with Ray Bryant, she went into the studio again. In addition to arranging all the music, alto saxophonist Gigi Gryce assembled and conducted the session's small band. Carter recalled that the record date came about largely because of her friendship with Gryce.[1] The two shared several attitudes, and he became an important figure for her in several ways.

Having received an undergraduate degree in composition at Boston Conservatory, Gigi Gryce had acquired a reputation among musicians as a "professor" who generously shared his musical knowledge. Gryce was also on a personal crusade to correct injustice in the recording industry. To this end he cofounded two music-publishing companies with saxophonist Benny Golson: Melotone and Totem, in 1955 and 1958 respectively.[2] While not unprecedented, it was still somewhat unusual then for musicians to form publishing companies to hold the copyrights for their own music. Gryce, however, urged musicians to exploit the copyright law to get a larger slice of the pie they themselves had made. From an artistic standpoint, the recording process served to document and disseminate the creative work of musicians; other industry personnel were there to usher the music into the world at large. But commercial forces tended to reverse industry roles, making musicians—even many who achieved star status—into little more than hired hands. Rarely partaking of the profits from their record sales, musicians typically received only a fee for sessions. Granted, revenue from instrumental jazz records was usually negligible compared to earnings from pop records, a discrepancy that became more and more the rule as the decade wore on; but there were enough examples of musicians being ripped off to justify their mistrust of label executives. Herman Lubinsky of Newark's Savoy Records was notorious for underpaying his artists and denying them royalties. Given the peer-review system that operated within the jazz community, which demanded a high level of musicianship from insiders, the control that a non-musician could exert over an artist's fate was also irksome to musicians. In this context, getting composer *and* publisher credit for a recorded track was an important way for musicians to earn the income they deserved. Even so, the copyright law only protected those who wrote their music down, not the improvisors who were responsible for much of the best recorded work from this time.

Racial inequality intensified this dynamic, for the division of labor in the industry predictably fell along racial lines. Echoing the sentiments of certain segments in the black middle class—as well as the Black Muslim movement, which lobbied for a separate black economy—Gryce encouraged black musicians to seize the means of production by starting their own publishing and recording companies.[3] Business ownership became a key means for keeping capital generated from African American labor within the black community. Such ideas were not new to Betty Carter. Her exposure to Reverend Charles A. Hill's socialist leanings no doubt familiarized her with such strategies for attaining fairer employment practices for blacks. Furthermore, Gladys Hampton's ownership of Hamptone and Glad-Hamp Records had already given Carter an appreciation for the importance of controlling one's commercial interests as well as one's artistic ones. Nevertheless, Gryce's tutelage helped Carter extend her grasp of the industry's inner workings in practical terms. Through Melotone Publishing, for example, he held the copyright for Carter's first composition, "I Can't Help It." Gryce would also lead the session at which Carter recorded this song, but it was not among those they took into the studio on 25 April 1956.

The band for their first date consisted of several musicians Gryce was working with then. In addition to a complement of horns, the group included Carter's fellow Detroiter Hank Jones on piano, Milt Hinton on bass, and Osie Johnson on drums. Carter sang four titles, including Gryce's "Social Call," which vocalist Ernestine Anderson had recorded the preceding October.[4] While the material from this session was well executed, it was not immediately released because there was not enough for a twelve-inch LP.[5] On these cuts, especially Harold Arlen's "Let's Fall in Love," Carter already shows signs of striking out from her models. In her rendering of that song, for example, she further explored having the vocal line grow from her own speech rhythms, yet her delivery was now more stylized, as she toyed with the lyrics' sense units to create subtle delays in the arrival of syntactical closure. In addition to tantalizing the listener's ear in its quest for verbal meaning, this approach also freed Carter to create a high degree of unpredictability via rhythmic displacement.

Gryce's charts enhance Carter's delivery by highlighting her unique abilities. In "Let's Fall in Love" a lone walking bass punctuated occasionally by horns supports her line during much of the tune. This bold arranging gesture marks the first appearance of a feature that Carter later used often in her own arrangements. Her one scat solo from the session, on "Frenesi," a tour de force lasting two choruses, indicates even greater ambitiousness in this area than she exhibited while with Hampton. By giving her horn figures to play off of in the second chorus, Gryce enabled Carter to show off her improvisational skills. In addition to revealing that she was growing musically, these recordings also show what she was capable of when she had an effective vehicle for her talents. The material was not released until 1980 with the title *Social Call*, along with a reissue of Carter's collaboration with Ray Bryant. By then Carter could acknowledge the growth that had taken place in her youthful explorations. "Really, you could hear me trying to get better, slicker or sharper or something."[6] At the time, however, executives at Epic must have felt otherwise, for in addition to dropping any further plans to record Carter, they released her from the label's roster in October 1956.[7]

It was around this time that Carter moved into a two-story house at 125 N. Seventeenth Street in East Orange, New Jersey, in the Newark metropolitan area. She was approaching thirty, and renting a hotel room in the city had lost its charm. Then, as now, Newark provided easy access to Manhattan while enabling musicians to escape the high cost of living there. Carter had first visited the city when she performed there with Hampton. Several musicians she knew and admired, including Bobby Plater and Sarah Vaughan, had grown up there, so it seemed a logical place for her to make a home. The city had a vibrant nightlife of its own, but aside from an occasional gig at such night spots as the Cadillac Club, Sparky J's, or Club 83 (also known as Lynn and Lynn's), or sitting in for a number or two at other clubs, Carter did not actively pursue connections to the Newark jazz scene.[8] She took up tennis at around this time, perhaps inspired by the tournament victories of Althea Gibson.[9]

In February 1958, Carter had another chance to record with Gryce, this time for the Peacock label. The label's owner, Don Robey, had plans to reactivate its subsidiary, the Progressive Jazz label, with a new album by Carter and one by alto saxophonist Sonny Criss.[10] Robey was one of the most powerful black entrepreneurs in the South after World War II, and he had a hand in virtually every aspect of show business there. He got into the business by booking various acts at his Bronze Peacock Dinner Club in Houston, including Louis Jordan, T-Bone Walker, and Lionel Hampton. This activity led Robey to organize southern tours on the one-nighter "chitlin circuit," and Carter probably met him when Hampton's band toured the South in 1950. Robey formed Duke/Peacock records in 1949 in order to promote the career of Clarence "Gatemouth" Brown, whom he managed.[11] Through his Buffalo Booking Agency, first operated out of a record store he owned, Robey launched the careers of the blues and gospel singers Bobby Bland, Little Junior Parker, B. B. King, Big Mama Thornton, and the Original Five Blind Boys. While his claim that he was the first to put a rhythm section behind a gospel act may be an exaggeration, Robey did have an impact on popular music by paving the way for gospel to emerge into the commercial marketplace.[12]

Robey had all but abandoned his Progressive Jazz label not long after he had launched it in 1953 with a lone Phineas Newborn Jr. recording.[13] According to Carter, the record she made for Robey also grew from her personal association with someone at the label: "the A&R [artist and repertoire] man was a friend of mine. He cut it for his own kicks."[14] Gigi Gryce chose the musicians for the recording, which was done in two sessions, and contributed several of the arrangements, as well as securing arrangements from trombonist Melba Liston, Benny Golson, and others.[15] On six cuts a smaller group was used that included Jerome Richardson, who had played flute on Carter's recording with Ray Bryant, now also playing tenor saxophone and bass clarinet. On the other six, Gryce employed a larger contingent. Solos by Golson, Ray Copeland, and Kenny Dorham, and expert comping by pianist Wynton Kelly, gave Carter the surroundings and the impetus she needed to swing hard, and she did. There was no rehearsal prior to the sessions; the band simply ran through the numbers and then recorded them.[16] The record was released in December 1958 with the title *Out There with Betty Carter.* Capitalizing on current events, the record cover featured a photograph of a sputnik and a USAF missile, presumably to illustrate just how far "out there" Carter actually was.[17] In April 1959, Peacock released two cuts, "On the Isle of May" and "But Beautiful," on alternate sides of a single.[18] Enthusiastic about the results, Carter later told Bill McLarney in 1966: "It was weak on engineering and rehearsals, but it had the best jazz ideas of any record I've done."[19]

The scat solo on "You're Driving Me Crazy" brings Carter's lightning quick changes of vocal register to a virtuosic zenith, in addition to showing off her bold harmonic "chops," or skill at negotiating the song's changes (example 4). Starting on a smeared D-flat, she plunges to the solo's lowest pitch, a thirteenth below, all in the span of two measures [0:38–0:40]. This attention-grabbing gesture, which outlines a descending $I^7(\sharp 9)$ chord, features Carter's trademark inverted mordent and a novel choice of syllables. In measure 3 [0:40–0:41] she leaps up a minor tenth from a low F-natural to bring the line into her middle register. Outlining the ii^7 harmony in measure 13 [0:51–0:52], Carter traverses a minor ninth to arrive on a high D-flat against the D7(♯9) harmony that starts the following measure. Using quarter note triplets and shortening her vowels, /də/dow/wow/wu/wu/wu/, she brakes her ascent to the next downbeat, where she suddenly brightens the timbre with the syllables /wiy/ba/ to reinforce the agogic accent there. Later in the solo she echoes this gesture, sweeping climactically up a twelfth to a high G-natural in measures 31–32 [1:11–1:12]. Her use of the syllable /ba/ on this ascent, and quarter notes shifted to the offbeats, gives this passage a more open character than the earlier one, which helps her build intensity to the solo's climax. In the context of the song's lyrics, all of this movement through extreme registers coupled with Carter's ingenious use of scat syllables serves to enact the craziness to which the song's narrator is driven. Speaking about some of the risks she took on that record, she has said, "'You're Driving Me Crazy'; no, you don't do that instantly with anybody. . . . Those were my ambitious years."[20]

Although the character of Carter's solo on "You're Driving Me Crazy" contrasts sharply with that of her solo on "Jay Bird" (example 1), both solos share certain key features. As in that solo, she here uses the highest pitches of the first half of the solo, at measures 7–8, to emphasize the natural-3 and flat-3 of the scale (in this case D-natural and D-flat). She also uses the lower part of her range for anchoring the closure before the bridge, at measure 18 [0:56–0:57]. Soon after the beginning of the bridge, in measure 20, Carter returns to her upper register, reinterpreting the third degree of the scale as the tonic of D major. While her ensuing melodic line moves freely within the range of an eleventh below this pitch, the peaks of each phrase descend from 3 (in m. 20 [0:59]) to 2 (in m. 24 [1:03]), to reach 1 in measure 27 [1:06–1:07] along with the tonic harmony's return. As a reminder, Carter begins the phrase starting in measure 26 [1:06] by compressing these pitches into the gesture that leads into measure 27. The descent that has taken place over the preceding eight measures has helped to release the harmonic tension of the bridge, which had tonicized the III, D major, as the tonal progression brings us back around to B-flat major via the key of D minor. The strategy Carter used in "Jay Bird" to build her solo's broad melodic shape is strikingly similar. Unlike that solo, however, in "You're Driving Me Crazy" a 9–8 appoggiatura resolves over the A section's return to the tonic, reinforcing the importance of the C-natural we had heard in measures 24 and 26. Also in contrast to "Jay Bird," Carter closes the solo on the 2 of the scale (the ninth of the tonic chord), heard here as the raised ninth of a sustained A7(♯9) chord [1:15–1:17] that precipitates an unexpected return to the D major of the bridge. Occurring as it does on the heels of a rhythmically disorienting passage [1:13–1:14], this moment adds to the arrangement's feeling of giddy insanity.

Although she later modified her way of molding lines when scatting, Carter revealed some consistency of approach in her early solos. In "Thou Swell" and "You're Driving Me Crazy" she grabs the listener's attention by traversing a wide stretch of her entire vocal compass with an opening gesture that moves in a single direction. The ensuing lull in melodic activity that results from the alternation of two pitches sets up the next directional move. Using low pitches at important points of articulation—such as the end of the second A section—allows Carter to build to subsequent peaks, and possibly end the solo with a flourish. Compared with her later work, these early examples reflect the telescoping of a solo's movement into the shorter time span in which Carter had to solo.

Of necessity Carter's repertoire was expanding during this time, and the album introduced several tunes which she would continue to use for some time, including "By the Bend in the River," "But Beautiful," "All I've Got," "Make It Last," and her own composition, "I Can't Help It," which opens the album. "I Can't Help It" stands as an anthem of Carter's attitude toward life and music (example 5).

In her interview with Leonard Lyons, Carter described how she conceived of "I Can't Help It" while walking under a railroad bridge in East Orange on her way to the train to Manhattan, in response to pressure she was feeling to make her approach more pop oriented. She had Melba Liston write it down for her as soon as she got to New York City.[21] In some ways the song's unusual structure mirrors its message. With no introduction, Carter sings the first two words a capella and in free time, an original enough way to begin. Because the tune is built on a standard chord progression (V^7/V–V^7–I–vi), and because it incorporates a good amount of repetition, she wisely breaks with tradition and omits the customary restatement of the eight-bar A section. This first part of the song, at measures 1–8 [0:00–0:35], creates its own miniature AABA′ form harmonically, with a move to the subdominant in measure 5 [0:19] to mark the contrasting b phrase. The song's characteristic melodic gesture is a move from the minor-ninth to the major-ninth of the V^7/V [0:04–0:07], melodically stressing the flatted third degree of the scale moving to the natural 3—a favorite melodic idea of hers from this time, here reharmonized. The tune's bridge, or B section, at measure 9 [0:35–0:41], briefly tonicizes the iii before bringing us to the dominant, G major, all in the span of four measures, rather than the usual eight. A comparison of the song, as notated, with Carter's highly stylized rendition of it—shown in example 7—illustrates in graphic terms where the job of the composer ended and that of the performer began, in her mind. Throughout the song Carter back phrases, often delaying passages by more than a beat. Sometimes she arrives at cadences on time, catching up by compressing her rhythms after she has stretched them out, as she does in measures 6–8. At other times the delayed material spills over into the cadence, as in measure 12.

After the customary return to the A section, the form is reiterated; but unlike "I Could Write a Book," Carter uses the form's repetition to sustain the music's sense of growth until the end by inventing more elaborate variations on the original line. Starting at measure 21 in example 5, the melody is repeated in the upper staff to show how much the singer departs from the song in this chorus. At the start, in measures 21–24 [1:21–1:36], a call-and-response passage between Jerome Richardson on tenor and the vocalist makes use of recording technology to produce a timbral contrast by adding a touch of reverb to the voice, lending it a strangely distant quality. This effect was also used on the coda to Norman Mapp's "Foul Play," from the same record. When Carter returns to the bridge of "I Can't Help It," at measure 29 [1:51–2:05], her subtle modifications of the melody are made partly in response to pianist Wynton Kelly's own variations here. With the return of the A section at the pickup to measure 33 [2:06], a whole new melodic shape bursts forth, in a higher, more penetrating register than before. Carter's use of melodic variation here seems itself to embody the song's injunction to be spontaneous. But as impromptu as it sounds, it is likely that Carter had a good idea of what she was going to sing before she set foot in the studio. The performance ends almost inconclusively on a $IV^7(\sharp 11)$ [2:39], keeping the question open as to whether the lyric here is an invitation for the listener to give the song's philosophy, or Carter herself, a try. With the touch of sexual innuendo in the words "so try me and maybe you'll love me," the ending suggests that the singer is offering herself because "[she] can't help it." In addition to Carter's composition, two other tunes on the record were published by Gryce's publishing company, Melotone: "Foul Play" and "Make It Last." Initially produced and distributed by African Americans, *Out There* reflected the collaborators' solidarity with the black community.

Betty Carter's circle of associates was steadily expanding, and several other musicians became important to her artistic development and career at this time. Her association with Miles Davis, for example, was important to her on many levels and became more so as the decade progressed. Regarding her first encounter with Davis, which dated back to 1947 when he was working with Charlie Parker, Carter stated condescendingly: "I sat in with him in Detroit before he had even learned to play the trumpet—when his notes were really tit for tat."[22] She got to know him better when she came to Manhattan with Hampton, possibly as early as 1949 or 1950. Davis had returned to New York City around then and was staying in the Hotel America on Forty-eighth street.[23] Shortly after, when she left Hampton and came to New York, Carter became good friends with Davis. "I became very close with his family—his kids, his wife, and him; personally in touch with them . . . in our striving to get through the New York scene."[24] Her involvement with Davis extended to his family of origin, with personal ties to his mother and his sister.[25] Davis credited Carter with looking after his wife when he left her: "If it hadn't been for Betty Carter I don't know what Irene would have done. Because of the way I treated Irene back in those days, I think Betty Carter, even today, don't like me much."[26]

Davis also played a crucial role in Carter's professional life. While living in Detroit for about five months at the end of 1953 and the beginning of 1954 he would encounter her at gigs: "Betty Carter used to come and sit in with Yusef Lateef, Barry Harris, Thad Jones, Curtis Fuller and Donald Byrd. It was a really hip city for music."[27] Carter did not speak of being in Detroit during this period, other than passing through on occasional road trips. Perhaps she spent more time there than she cared to remember. Later, Davis included Carter in theater dates he did in the late 1950s, although she did not sing with his quintet. She recalled being backed by a pianist known simply as A.C. and bassist Teddy Smith; she could not recall the drummer's name.[28] From December 1958 to December 1959, Davis presented Carter at various theaters, including the Howard in Washington, Loew's Valencia in New York, and the Regal in Chicago.[29] Working with a front line of Cannonball Adderley on alto saxophone—until September 1959—and John Coltrane on tenor saxophone, as well as several superb rhythm section players, Davis was then enjoying a surge in popularity. He won the *Down Beat* Readers' Poll in 1958 with more than three times the votes of the second-place winner, Dizzy Gillespie. It was also one of his most creative periods, in which he produced some of his best-loved work, on *Porgy and Bess, Kind of Blue,* and *Sketches of Spain.* Nevertheless, while Carter's appearances with such a recognized artist inevitably boosted her career, they also were useful to Davis, offsetting the austere brand of showmanship he had cultivated. Indicating that the market for instrumental jazz was dwindling, Bobby Schiffman suggested that the only way he could draw crowds to the Apollo Theater was by featuring the vocalist who was on the bill: "If you had Betty 'Bebop' Carter and you had Miles Davis as the headliner, it was no good. She had to be the headliner. At least that was the pattern."[30]

Davis had a profound impact on Carter musically. The breathiness in vocal timbre, present in her sound at the outset, became more pronounced as her rhythmic concept broke out of the original bebop mold. Coupled with her sparing use of vibrato, her tone was often reminiscent of that characteristic sound the trumpeter produced with a Harmon mute minus the stem. Although Carter never acknowledged his influence directly, over the course of her career, as the trumpeter himself evolved, several other features that were suggestive of Davis's ongoing impact on her emerged. Around this time, for example, elements of the cool aesthetic that he was exploring while she was appearing with him were already seeping into her own personal vocabulary.

Sometime during this period, perhaps in early 1960, Carter was performing at Walter Dawkins's Key Club in Newark, on the corner of Williams and Halsey, when she met the man who would become her common-law husband, James Romeo Redding.[31] After work, at around one or two o'clock in the morning, she and a group of people had gone to the Owl, an after-hours club on Quitman Street in Newark that had once been known as the Afro Club.[32] Redding, who had grown up on a farm in North Carolina and just finished four years in the military, was working as a bartender there. He had come to Newark only months before, and he didn't know much about music. When his fellow bartender came over to him and said: "Betty Carter wants to meet you," his initial response was "Who?"[33] He was somewhat younger and much less cosmopolitan than Carter, but they were drawn to one another and became close. By the summer she was pregnant with their first child.

Carter began to appear on the same bills as Ray Charles shortly after she met James Redding, in the spring of 1960. Charles had first heard Betty Carter at the Uptown Theater in Philadelphia when she was with Lionel Hampton, so he had been aware of her work for almost a decade.[34] It was not until she had worked opposite Miles Davis, however, that he expressed an interest in having her appear on the same bill as him.[35] Davis's agent, Jack Whittemore, and Charles's agent, Larry Myers, both worked for the Shaw Agency, run by Billy and Milt Shaw.[36] Carter's work with Davis led the agency to represent her, which in turn led to her meeting Ray Charles. Carter had added to her act some tunes that were associated with Billie Holiday, who had died on 17 July 1959, as a tribute to the deceased singer.

This was around the time when Ray Charles's fortunes had begun to spiral dramatically upward. For several years he had been forging a distinctive blend of R&B and gospel that appealed largely to black audiences. In the mid-1950s Charles had had a string of hits starting with "I've Got a Woman" that the Atlantic label had released in 1955. "A Fool for You" and "Drown in My Tears" had also made it to number 1 on *Billboard*'s R&B charts in 1955 and 1956 respectively. His infusion of the ecstatic sounds of black worship into popular music shocked some people because of its blatant exploitation of religious feeling and its use of actual church melodies for entertainment.

However, by 1957 Charles had already begun to reach the mainstream audience with three of his preceding four R&B hits, which also surfaced on the pop charts. In 1959 he had his first top-ten hit with "What'd I Say (Part I)," and the following year he appeared at the Apollo billed as the "Soul Genius."[37]

By November 1959, Charles had made a major career move by leaving Atlantic Records and signing with ABC-Paramount. His new label, which was spawned by the huge entertainment corporation American Broadcasting Company–Paramount Theaters, gave Charles greater access to mainstream listeners than Atlantic had.[38] Perhaps the most significant aspect of his contract with ABC-Paramount was that Charles would be the producer of his own records. In addition to allowing him complete artistic freedom, this arrangement also gave him a much larger portion of the profits and probably the largest advance received by a black recording artist to date.[39] A stipulation unheard of at that time, and still quite rare, was built into the contract requiring that the masters from Charles's sessions revert to him after five years.[40] Charles also formed his own publishing company, Tangerine Music, at this time.[41]

Betty Carter appeared with Ray Charles at the McCormick Theater in Chicago in April 1960 as part of a short tour of the Midwest only days after he had been in the studio recording his first album for ABC-Paramount, *The Genius Hits the Road.*[42] Later that month they spent a week at the Apollo, with Cannonball Adderley and comedian Redd Foxx also on the bill. Commenting on the 27 April show, critics Jack Bradley and Jeann Failows wrote in *Coda* that Carter "looked as if she could swing, and did," adding that "the audience was with her from the second she appeared. With no attempt at imitation of Billie, she offered a tribute and sang 'Foolin' Myself,' 'God Bless the Child,' 'What A Little Moonlight Can Do,' and a lovely new one titled 'Don't Weep for the Lady' which was done with much feeling. This was very well received."[43] Carter's appearances with Charles during a week in July, at Chicago's Regal Theater—on the same bill as Art Blakey and the Coasters—may have taken place in conjunction with the Shaw Agency's "Hitmakers of 1960" tour that Charles headlined opposite Ruth Brown, the Drifters, and Redd Foxx. Later that month Carter was back in New York for a week at the Apollo, billed with Miles Davis, Sonny Stitt, James Moody, and Moms Mabley.[44]

In three sessions during the latter half of August, Carter recorded for ABC-Paramount. The label released the outcome of her sessions under the title *The Modern Sound of Betty Carter.*[45] For the charts, the record's producer, Sid Feller, turned to arranger Richard Wess, who had recently worked effectively for singer Bobby Darin. Feller attributed the success of the enterprise to Carter's brilliance and to the top-notch session musicians they used, however, rather than to any contribution from the arrangements, saying: "It's the first time where the vocalist made an arranger sound good."[46] Initially Feller worked just with Carter to lay out the album, in a process known as routining. During routining, the producer takes note of how the vocalist approaches the song and then makes decisions about where the arranger will put interludes, or how the arranger might elaborate on the ending with tempo, meter, or key changes.[47] Feller, who often taped his routining sessions on a portable recorder, paid special attention to when Carter "ad libbed" and when she wanted to scat, so Wess would leave space in the arrangements. From the routining a blueprint emerged that enabled Wess to fit the charts around what Carter would sing.

As with most of ABC-Paramount's records from this time, *Modern Sound* was recorded at Bell Sound Studios on West Fifty-fourth Street.[48] The set of twelve numbers, which included Harry Woods's "What a Little Moonlight Can Do" and Darshan Singh's "Don't Weep for the Lady"[49] from her Holiday tribute, reflected what Carter was currently presenting in her live performances. The recording included several standards as well as other less well known tunes.[50] Carter strayed quite far from the melodies, especially in her second choruses of such familiar songs as "I Don't Want to Set the World on Fire," "Mean to Me"—which listeners strongly associated with Sarah Vaughan—and "Stormy Weather," Lena Horne's signature tune from the 1943 all-black Hollywood musical of the same name. Although her digressions sound extemporaneous, aside from several expressive nuances her interpretation of each tune was somewhat formed before she went into the studio.

Carter's vocal on "What a Little Moonlight Can Do" seems to float over the wildly fast tempo of 288 beats per minute by way of the rhythmic trick of long meter, a feature that is built into this sixty four-bar tune. In long meter, the rhythm section plays two measures of time for each measure of the form, in effect making the eighth note the beat. Concomitantly, the harmonic rhythm seems to unfold twice as slowly in relation to the time. When Carter began doing her own arrangements, the technique would later crop up in several of her charts. To place the tune's tessitura within Carter's range, Richard Wess set it in B-flat major, rather than the usual key of G (example 6).

Listen to how Carter's phrasing exploits certain features of the words for rhythmic effect. In the title phrase (at mm. 3, 11, 35, and 59), for example, she uses the short vowel and crisp final consonant of the word "what," which she places off the beat, in order to clip it rhythmically and accentuate its syncopated position. In releasing the long /uw/ sound in a staccato /wət/, exploiting the transitional rounding of the lips between the two phones, Carter applies bebop phrasing drawn from her scatting to the singing of lyrics. The break this introduces between "ooh, what" and "a little moonlight can do" causes a momentary semantic disruption, but musical considerations can override verbal ones here because the title phrase is so recognizable. Instead of repeating three cutsey "oohs," as dictated by the sheet music, Carter sings a single, hip "ooh" across three descending pitches. This revision frees her to modify the pitches of the title phrase when it recurs later in the arrangement so she can explore the possibilities implied by her melismatic approach. She takes this exploration to an extreme degree when she prepares for the return of the title phrase, starting in measure 37. Over the mounting tension of the dominant harmony, she back phrases here, as indicated by the arrow above the staff, singing the key phrase "I love you" (/ay/ləv/yuw/) so late that the word "you" elides into the following "ooh" (/uw/). She comes out of these rhythmic acrobatics on a dime with the staccato "what" in measure 35 as though nothing had happened. This passage exemplifies the expressive power of intentionally unmeasured plasticity, for the emotional surge Carter creates here—enacting the effect love's chaotic force can have on one's ability to utter the words "I love you—would not have resulted if she had remained in lockstep with the band. In other passages her back phrasing gives her room to enunciate the lyrics, as in the passage at measures 27–28, "your hearts a-flutterin'" (/yə/ha/tsə/flə/də/rin/), where clusters of consonants crowd together. The song's closing gesture shows off the command Carter had gained of her head voice.

On *The Modern Sound of Betty Carter,* it is a pleasure to hear Carter stretch out and develop her ideas on several of the titles that feature her scatting, where she shows much greater rhythmic variety than she had yet displayed, as well as a terrific command of the changes, arpeggiating chords across wide stretches of her vocal range. Significantly, some of the arrangements incorporated strings. The choice to use strings in one of the sessions may have grown from the Holiday memorial concept, for the late singer had recorded *Lady in Satin* with Ray Ellis eighteen months before her death. Ray Charles may also have influenced the decision, for, not long after appearing with Billie Holiday at Carnegie Hall on 6 May 1959, he recorded with strings.[51] He used this sound in other recordings from this time as well, most prominently, in *Genius Hits the Road,* which included "Georgia on My Mind."

ABC-Paramount recorded *The Modern Sound* about nine months after Ray Charles had signed with the organization, and critic Bob Porter has suggested that Carter's association with Charles led to this recording.[52] Will Friedwald states this more strongly, asserting that Charles "pushed" his current label to let her do a solo disc.[53] But in none of her accounts does Carter attribute the album to her connection with Charles, and she neglected to mention the shows she had done with him prior to the making of *The Mod-*

ern Sound.[54] Similarly, Charles recalled learning that Carter was with ABC-Paramount only *after* he had signed on with the label.[55] It is unclear why they both would have disavowed Charles's connection to this project, if indeed there was one.

Listening to *The Modern Sound of Betty Carter*, however, one can easily hear why Charles loved Carter's sound: "Her voice impressed the shit out of me. It was a free jazz voice; she had this floating quality that haunted me."[56] On the surface one might think Carter's style would be out of place at a Ray Charles concert. But Charles himself had roots in the bebop idiom, and it is clear that, despite the growing success of his soul material, he had no intention of leaving this part of himself behind.[57] In fact, he had gone into the studio the preceding December to cut *Genius + Soul = Jazz*, which featured Count Basie's band playing instrumental arrangements made by Quincy Jones and Ralph Burns, with the singer himself on a Hammond B3 electric organ. At the time, Charles traveled with a collection of superb jazz players, several of whom were former Basie and Ellington players. When his band did instrumentals, it played in the jazz idiom, performing such numbers as Horace Silver's "Doodlin'" and Sonny Rollins's "St. Thomas." This provided a foil for Charles's vocal performances, which were saved for the latter portion of his shows.[58] The group featured Marcus Belgrave on trumpet—later Phil Guilbeau—and saxophonist David "Fathead" Newman. Backed by members of this group, Carter was right at home, and the band's numerous jazz numbers created a fitting context for her bop vocals.

In September 1960, "Georgia on My Mind," which Charles had recorded in March, began its historic rise on the *Billboard* charts. At the end of that month Carter began a weeklong engagement at the Apollo, her third appearance there in six months, this time with Charles, the Coasters, and organist Jimmy Smith.[59] Charles's touring show took the same bill to sellout crowds at the Howard Theater in Washington, D.C.[60] By mid-November "Georgia" was number 1 on *Billboard*'s pop chart. At this point in Charles's career, fans flocked to his shows, and Carter appreciated the opportunity this gave her to perform for large audiences without having to alter her style.[61] From Charles's standpoint, there was never a question of her adapting to him, because the two singers did not perform together; but she did have to contend with the expectations of an audience primed to hear the Genius of Soul. This was the same theater circuit she had been working for several years, but now, Charles's presence electrified the house.[62] Not since her days with Hampton had she enjoyed this kind of energy. Finally, after nearly a decade, she was receiving the kind of attention that vindicated her departure from that band; attention that would surely lead to a breakthrough in her own right.

6

Making Progress

Backstage at the Royal Theater in Baltimore one night, Ray Charles suggested to Carter that they team up on a record. She recalled the moment vividly: "After he asked me, it got silent; I mean, he had . . . a *big* hit record, he didn't need me. I was talking on the telephone; I said to the lady I was talking to, 'Excuse me, I'll talk to you later.' And everybody stuck their heads out of their dressing rooms. So I said, 'What did you say Ray?' And he said, 'Let's do an album together.' I was just in shock; I didn't want to believe it, I thought he'd just forget all about it."[1] Given his greater fame and entirely different style, Carter was understandably stunned. The label was also taken aback: "I think the people at ABC were more confused about me than anything else; they knew what Ray Charles was going to do, but I think they were trying to figure out what in the world he wanted to record with me for."[2] The sessions were scheduled to take place in Hollywood in June.

Before this, however, Charles's troupe was on the road, appearing at San Francisco's Longshore Hall in March. Carter was not at that performance, for she had another kind of engagement. Back in Newark, at Presbyterian Hospital, she was giving birth to her first son, Myles Kevin James Redding, on 14 March 1961. The name obviously recalls Miles Davis, but it also was in the Jones family, with a distant cousin, Miles Ward, who was born around 1922—he was still in Dumas, Arkansas as of 1987—bearing it as well. After getting permission from her doctor, Carter joined Charles on the road ten days after Myles's birth, leaving the infant in the care of her husband and friends.[3] Meanwhile, Charles's recent release from *Genius + Soul = Jazz,* "One Mint Julep," an instrumental, was rising in the charts. It would stay there for twelve weeks, peaking at number 1 on the R&B chart, making *Billboard*'s pop chart as well. Not long after, "Georgia" received the Grammy Award for the preceding year's best pop single.

Charles's recent successes coincided with a string of twenty one-nighters arranged by promoter Hal Zeiger.[4] His first national tour took him and his entourage through the Midwest, including performances in St. Louis, Detroit (at Masonic Auditorium), Cleveland, and Chicago, before returning to New York.[5] It culminated in two performances at Carnegie Hall on 30 April, one in the afternoon and another later in the evening. In addition to the Raelets, Charles's backup vocal quartet, and Betty Carter, the concert featured Charles's band augmented to include fifteen pieces. Much of the concert presented these musicians in different configurations, with Charles's most popular material coming in the final forty-five minutes.[6]

Frustrated that the program was dedicated to "elements that should have served as appetizers," the *New York Times* reviewer John Wilson was less than complimentary about Carter's contribution to the bill, dismissing her as an "overemphatic, strident singer."[7] The *Herald Tribune*'s reviewer was somewhat more positive, describing Carter as "a Charles discovery . . . who sang impressively in her lower register, forced notes flagrantly in her upper register, and closed the first half of the show with a touching tribute to the late Billie Holiday, plus some wordless swinging of 'Frenesi.'"[8]

When Charles returned home to Los Angeles after the tour, Carter was with him. They spent the first two weeks of June rehearsing the vocals before setting foot into the recording studio, which gave her time to calm her fears: "I went to his house to work on the tunes, and then went back to the hotel numb because I was really gonna do it."[9] Carter did not appear to mind having less artistic control over the project than usual: "He picked out most of the tunes—I think I picked out only one. He already had my key picked out; it was a little high for me, but I managed to deal with it at that point [*laughs*]. I sounded like a little teeny baby singing some of that stuff."[10] Consisting entirely of standards, the project served to expand Carter's book. Charles was hardly new to this type of material, having already demonstrated his ability to deal effectively with it, most recently on *The Genius of Ray Charles.*

Sid Feller, who was working closely with Charles at the time, flew out to Hollywood to produce the record. Charles, Feller, and the record's arranger, Marty Paich, collaborated on the charts, which were scored for a rhythm section of Charles on piano, Bill Pittman on guitar, Edgar Willis on bass, and Mel Lewis on drums, plus a twenty-two-piece string orchestra and backup vocals from the Jack Halloran Singers.[11] For some of the arrangements Charles's own traveling band of two trumpets, three saxophones, and rhythm section functioned as a separate unit within the larger ensemble, the balance of which consisted of Hollywood studio musicians.[12] The arrangements allowed Carter room to use her own sound rather than force her to adapt to the Genius of Soul, with the strings acting as a glue that made their two distinct approaches cohere. As he had done with his recent instrumental album, Charles took himself out of his usual context, perhaps to shore up his credibility among jazz musicians and cognoscenti while still directing most of his efforts to the mainstream.[13] The backup vocals were a concession to popular taste, but they do not significantly detract from the lead vocals, which take center stage.

On 13 and 14 June they laid down twelve tracks at ABC studios. Charles was known to spend hours in the studio, accepting nothing less than a perfect take. As was his general practice, for each tune he reserved a single reel, which might end up having as many as twenty takes on it, continuing to add to that reel until they had an "A," or master, take. Feller reported that, during one of the sessions, word got out to the surrounding movie studio that Charles was recording. An ad hoc audience of curious onlookers, including celebrities from the motion picture and music worlds, trickled into the control room. When Charles found out, however, he dispersed the crowd. Having spectators may have actually helped Carter relax and enjoy working in a studio, an environment she typically found cold and uninspiring.[14] Working efficiently, Charles and Feller recorded the twelve tracks in three three-hour sessions.[15] Performing such classic tunes as "Every Time We Say Good-Bye," "Alone Together," "Just You, Just Me," and "People Will Say We're in Love," Carter and Charles attained a chemistry that belies the speed at which they worked. When they walked out of the studio, the album was virtually ready for pressing and distribution.[16] In accordance with his contract, Charles retained possession of the session reels and thus has all of the out takes.

At the time, the opportunity seemed more than Carter could have wished for: "To have recorded with Ray Charles was an honor because he could have had anyone he wanted."[17] The record resulted in a minor hit with Frank Loesser's duet "Baby, It's Cold Outside," from the film *Neptune's Daughter.* This song, with a more innocent approach than Charles took, had given Margaret Whiting and Johnny Mercer a hit thirteen years earlier.[18] Charles and Carter were no doubt also familiar with the version done by Ella Fitzgerald and Louis Jordan,[19] which had made it into the top ten of the race charts for a few weeks in 1949. For the week between 3 and 10 March 1962, the Charles-Carter single peaked at ninety-one on *Billboard* magazine's "Top 100 Singles" chart, giving Carter more radio exposure and introducing her to a larger audience than she had so far enjoyed.[20] Since it was first released, the duet has been sporadically reissued on Ray Charles compilations, and the complete album became something of a cult classic for Betty Carter insiders, many of whom had been following her career from the time they first heard her with Hampton.

To be sure, Carter valued the measure of fame the record gave her, but later some resentments surfaced: "The Ray Charles record is what gets me the slow pop [of recognition, from listeners]. . . . I have no regrets making that record. . . . What I regret is that we never performed it in public."[21] In fact, Carter and Charles had several opportunities to do so, one within days of making the record, when they shared a two-week engagement at the Apollo with the Coasters, Benny Golson and Art Farmer's Jazztet, Jimmy Scott, and comedian Willie Lewis.[22] In July, the two appeared at Chicago's Regal Theater with the same aggregation,[23] but they were soon to go their separate ways, with Charles heading to France to perform at the Antibes Jazz Festival.[24] That September, Betty Carter appeared at the Apollo Theater opposite Brook Benton, the Drifters (billed as "Ray Charles Favorite"), dancer Bobby Ephriam, comedian Willie Lewis, and music director Ruben Phillips.[25] Charles's "Hit the Road Jack" came out in the following weeks and rapidly rose to number 1 on both R&B and pop charts. He was now commanding between thirty-five hundred and forty-five hundred dollars for a one-nighter.[26]

Unimpeded by financial considerations, Charles was allowing his drug habit to affect his reliability more and more, and he sometimes appeared late for shows or not at all. In the fall of 1961 he was in Europe again, performing in France, Holland, and Germany, and then returned to the States for a tour that brought him from Troy, New York, to Denver.[27] While on this road trip he was arrested in Indianapolis on drug charges that were ultimately dropped because the police had entered and searched without a warrant, even though the singer admitted to using heroin since he was fifteen years old.[28] Carter must have been aware of Charles's habit, but after these revelations the space between them grew, for she may have wanted to distance herself from the negative publicity he was receiving. On 14 November, she recorded three songs for ABC-Paramount, "Frenesi"—one of her specialties—"Rock-a-Bye-Baby," and "I Cry Alone." The first two were released as a single, and the third was never issued.[29]

In February 1962, around the time Ray Charles made his next record, *Modern Sounds in Country and Western,* Carter appeared at the Jazz Gallery in New York City opposite the Art Farmer/Benny Golson Jazztet and other jazz groups.[30] Charles and Carter performed on the same bill in March at Newark's Mosque Theater with Charles's twenty-one-piece orchestra along with comedian Nipsey Russell. Spurred on by the popularity of his crossover single "I Can't Stop Loving You," which was on the charts for sixteen weeks, and in first place for ten, *Modern Sounds in Country and Western* became

ABC-Paramount's first million-selling album.[31] By this time Monte Kay, who co-owned the Royal Roost with Morris Levy and who also booked the Modern Jazz Quartet, was handling Carter's bookings. She would retain him until at least 1965.[32] Carter's collaboration with Ray Charles gradually came to an end during the course of 1962. She worked with him in April, at the McCormick Theater in Chicago, and appeared with him in Chicago again, in what was probably their last gig together, at the Regal the following July.

Much later, in the shadow of developments in the music business during the late 1960s and early 1970s, Carter would come to feel that her work with Ray Charles, both on stage and in the studio, had little lasting impact on her career, that it was "nothing phenomenal."[33] By the mid-1970s it had lost its significance as a milestone: "It's okay, but it's a survival album in a sense."[34] Eventually, she would come to feel bitter about the way Charles had handled the matter. In 1976 poet Ted Joans, writing in *Coda*, described Carter as "peeved at the bad deal that Ray Charles gave her after they cut their album, because the album was no longer being distributed and Ray Charles didn't mention it in his interviews."[35] Carter felt that the record deserved to be reissued and took it as a personal snub that Charles had not pursued this course.[36] Ray Charles finally did get around to reissuing it on Dunhill in 1988, around the time Carter was achieving celebrity. In retrospect, the record had not given Carter's career the boost she had hoped it would. When she had finally established herself in her own right, she could afford to be more sanguine about the whole matter, telling Bob Weinberg in 1994: "I never expected to climb to the top of the heap because I recorded with Ray Charles. . . . If I was going to make it, I was going to have to make it on my own. That's the way life is, especially in this business. The most important thing is what you do on-stage in front of people."[37]

Ray Charles continued to admire Carter's sound long after the record was made, and significantly, he likened it to the sound of one of his favorite instrumentalists. Early on in his autobiography, which was penned in 1978 with the help of David Ritz, Charles stated his preference for Artie Shaw over Benny Goodman, placing Shaw in a whole different category.[38] Later, speaking about his admiration for Betty Carter, he says: "She's a hell of a singer. I like to compare her to Sarah Vaughan, which is like comparing Benny Goodman to Artie Shaw. Sarah's like Benny. She has unbelievable technique and deserves all the praise she's gotten. She's a master. But Betty's like Artie. She's a marvelous technical singer, but she's also got that old feeling—that raw feeling—that destroys me."[39] He then reminisced about his work with Carter: "I know people still ask for that album and I believe there was something special about the music we made together."[40]

Ray Charles had once been close friends with record producers Jerry Wexler and Nesuhi Ertegun, before his defection from Atlantic Records, which they ran. In signing with ABC-Paramount, however, he had burned his bridges with his former label.[41] Perhaps it was with some degree of irony, then, that Carter moved to Atlantic's subsidiary, Atco, through her association with Monte Kay.[42] This would be her third LP in two years, but Carter's experience with Atco was not a happy one. The dramatic influx of revenue from new pop styles during the late 1950s and early 1960s meant that singers had to deal more and more with demands from recording industry executives to orient their approach toward proven pop formulas. Producers who could not get pop singers to adapt their sound to rock and roll steered them into an "easy listening" format. Carter encountered this attitude in 1962 in her association with Atco Records: "Atlantic at that time was trying to change me without telling me, trying to make me conform. I think Nesuhi Ertegun and Jerry Wexler will know they were trying to do that to me because they really can't talk to me now. I mean I got this record *'Round Midnight,* Atco, and they don't know what to do with it."[43]

Ahmet Ertegun had founded Atlantic Records in 1947 with Herb Abramson. In 1953, Abramson left the label for military service, to be replaced by Jerry Wexler, whose orientation toward R&B greatly enhanced the label's success. Two years later Atlantic Records spawned Atco, and Abramson briefly returned to Atlantic in order to run the subsidiary with Ertegun's brother, Nesuhi. In addition to running Atco, Nesuhi Ertegun, along with Gary Kramer, produced records for the label. Their philosophy toward artists and repertory—generally referred to simply as A&R—led them to focus the bulk of the label's production on pop music, but they intermittently recorded some jazz on Atco as well.

In a series of four sessions on 10 August, 7 November, 6 December 1962 and 15 January 1963, Carter recorded seventeen songs for Atco. Atco quickly issued a single of "Shine on Harvest Moon" and "One Note Samba" in October 1962, clearly in the hope of producing a hit in the wake of "Baby, It's Cold Outside." By February 1963 Ertegun and Wexler had put together an album out of eleven tracks from these sessions and released it under the title *'Round Midnight.* At the time of the album's release, Carter's reading of Sasha Distel and Jack Reardon's "The Good Life" was also released as a single, on the flip side of "Nothing More to Look Forward To,"[44] which suggests that the producers believed these songs also had the potential to become hits. They never did release the four tunes recorded in November 1962.[45]

In 1975 Carter told Mark Jacobsen that she "froze and couldn't concentrate at all" when she sang with Claus Ogerman's arrangements, and she described the record as "one of the worst things [she had] ever done."[46] The album's first cut, entitled "Nothing More to Look Forward To," gives us a good idea of what Carter meant when she accused Atco of trying to change her. She sounds out of place trying to fit into the song's pop format. She hated the album so much, in fact, that she brutally defaced her personal copy, ripping the dust jacket with a pen or sharp object.[47] Nevertheless, she would later clarify that, while she hated the approach on the album, the material she recorded appealed to her, describing it as "more or less a soft album, a very sweet album. A lot of tunes that nobody ever sings, and nobody . . . ever thinks about doing."[48] When introducing "The Good Life" (example 7) in her performances, Carter, who had recorded it before Tony Bennett, would wryly comment, "Guess who made all the money." The tune remained in her active repertoire throughout much of her lifetime, and she recorded it again in the mid-1980s.

"The Good Life" provides Carter with a gorgeous, wistful vehicle for her flair for the dramatic. Jack Reardon's ironic lyric takes a fresh look at a stock situation in ballads: the moment when the song's narrator is being left by her lover. The lyricist ingeniously suppresses almost all overt indications of the narrator's pain at being cast aside, giving us only a glimpse of her emotion in the song's final lines. Instead, the narrator delivers an emotionally remote philosophical treatise on the shallow life her departing lover is headed for. Cast as a dramatic monologue, the song's oblique expression forces the listener to read between the lines to infer the narrator's emotion.

Betty Carter had a bona fide fondness, even a certain proprietary feeling, for this song. As much as the vocalist sang of love, she rarely performed tunes about vulnerable or helpless women who beg their men to stay. I imagine that she found the pride and intelligence of the song's narrator, as well as the irony in her manner, appealing. Tellingly, Carter modified the final words of the original lyric, which read, "Please remember I still love you, and in case you didn't know, Well just wake up, Kiss THE GOOD LIFE hello." Omitting the song's punny twist ending in favor of a more logical reading, Carter sings, instead: "Please remember, I still want you, and in case you wonder why, well just wake up, kiss the good life good-bye." In addition to the song's complex layers of story and subtext, the song's dense harmonies and restless use of secondary tonal areas would have been hard for the bebop-schooled singer to resist.

The deceptive harmonic moves that Sasha Distel has choreographed in this song—not identical to those shown in example 7, which contains Ogerman's chord substitutions—create a vague sense of instability that mirrors the illusory character of "the good life." Although the song starts on the tonic harmony, its first harmonic move—a $ii^7(\flat 5)$–V^7 progression to the relative minor—leads one to wonder in retrospect if the opening chord was not really a III chord in the new minor key. The next chords strengthen this doubt, echoing the first tonal gesture by preparing to move to the minor key a fifth higher, in effect tonicizing the iii of the opening tonality. This $ii^7(\flat 5)$–V^7 of the iii does not resolve, however, but leads instead to the ii^7 of the song's first chord. A listener familiar with the pushes and pulls of tonality might expect a dominant harmony to follow this last chord, but the songwriter inserts a ♭VII here, softening the return to the tonic in measure 11. Only when the following phrase leads to the dominant in measures 15–16, in preparation for the return of the A section, do we sense that the first chord we heard was in fact the song's tonic harmony. The second half of the song unfurls into a parallel period structure, or ABAB′ form, with a compelling turn of harmony in the last bars, a $ii^7(\flat 5)$/ii–V^7/ii at the words "(in case) you wonder why," to spur the melody to its climax. This climax is all the more gratifying because it sets up a ii–V–I cadence in the home key, the only authentic cadence in the entire song. Despite the song's urbane veneer, which superficially conceals its labyrinthine harmonic structure, Distel has cleverly contrived a harmonic pathway designed to lead attentive listeners, and perhaps even the jilting lover, to conclude that there truly is no place like home.

Tailoring the chart to Betty Carter's needs, Claus Ogerman transposed "The Good Life" down a fifth from its original key of A-flat major, in order to take full advantage of the singer's deep "chalumeau" register. The arrangement effectively sets Carter's dark tone color in relief against the lush harmonies in the strings and horns. Ogerman retained the essentials of the tune's harmonic structure, but added a few coloristic touches. In the $ii^7(\flat 5)$/iii–V^7/iii progressions mentioned earlier, at measures 7–8 and later in measures 23–24, the arranger substitutes a G minor^7 chord borrowed from F major in place of the half-diminished seventh chord that usually occurs there, lending the passages a startling harmonic brightness. A more dramatic alteration occurs at measure 9, where Ogerman interrupts this ii–V progression—which now appears headed for the parallel major of F minor—with a deceptive cadence to the IV (G-flat major), instead of the ii^7 (E-flat minor7) that Distel had used in the same location. This change allows Ogerman to proceed from the IV chord down the cycle of fifths to the original tune's striking ♭VII (a C-flat dominant seventh chord in this transposition) in measure 10, which had weakened the return to the tonic harmony in measure 11 by approaching it modally. Later in the chart, after this progression recurs in the second half of the tune at measures 25–26, Ogerman amplifies its effect, proceeding from Distel's $ii^7(\flat 5)$/ii–V^7/ii–ii^7 progression to the ♭VII, rather than the original version's V^7, echoing the earlier modal move to the tonic. The following tag reiterates the preceding four measures, further emphasizing this haunting modal cadence. By avoiding authentic cadences altogether, and the strong tonal pull they create, Ogerman enhances the fluidity of the song's harmonic movement.

Delving more deeply into an approach to ballads that she had used before, Carter contributes to the accumulated efforts of Reardon, Distel, and Ogerman by recasting the melody so it emanates from her own speech rhythms and from her instinct for dramatic timing.[49] In measure 9, at the line "You won't really fall in love" [0:34–0:42], she emphasizes the words "You won't really" by singing "won't" on the downbeat and bending up to the stressed syllables of the first three words. Later on in the song, in measure 25 [1:40–1:44], at the moment in the form parallel to measure 9, Carter adds urgency to the words "Please remember" by singing a grace note leading up to "please" and stretching out the long /iy/ vowel, as well as by dragging the word across the barline.

In the song's first eight measures Carter makes use of Distel's pitches, but beginning at the pickup to measure 9 [0:34–0:42], she starts to create her own melodic shape. In measures 9 and 10, on the words "you won't really fall in love," she retains the original melody's structural pitches—D-flat and E-flat—but approaches the words that occur with these pitches, "(real)ly" and "love," respectively, from above rather than below, matching the melodic contour of spoken intonation more closely than Distel's original line does. When she does rise, in measure 11 [0:43–0:49], at the phrase "for you can't take the chance," she stresses the word "can't"—instead of "take" as Distel does—by taking it a third higher than the original line, clarifying the crucial negation of the verb and letting emotion seep out from under the narrator's cool manner. In the next phrase, in measures 12–16 [0:50–0:58], at the words "So be honest with yourself, don't try to fake romance," Carter builds to a climax at one of the song's most harmonically tense moments by placing the words "so" and "with" on the highest pitches we have heard thus far and extending them across the barlines of measures 13 and 14, respectively. She also increases the phrase's drama by falling through a B-flat minor arpeggio on these words, instead of through Distel's gentle stepwise descent. In light of the personal philosophy Carter expressed in "I Can't Help It," it is not surprising that these words would hold special meaning for her. Her alterations in the line's timing, melodic shape, and accentuation all conspire to conceal the rhyme between "take" and "fake," further investing the lyrics with the rhythms of everyday speech. Carter proceeds to apply similar techniques to the song's second half.

In addition to "The Good Life" there are other songs from *'Round Midnight* that Carter liked, two of which she continued to keep in her repertoire at least until the end of the 1970s: the record's title song and "Heart and

Soul." In 1994 she even expressed a certain fondness for "Nothing More to Look Forward To," taking special pride in the arrangement's use of overdubbing, which enabled her to sing harmony with herself.[50] The album also includes Carter's second foray into songwriting, "Who, What, Why, Where or When." As with "I Can't Help It," the lyrics to this song create a first-person narrative that allows its singer to enter the narrator's persona and act out the words vocally, a feature that Carter wrote into many of her lyrics and one that she sought out in material by other lyricists.

Some of Carter's feelings about *'Round Midnight* resulted from a power struggle that arose with her producers concerning the choice of arranger. Carter had already picked Oliver Nelson when she found out that Wexler and Ertegun had lined up Claus Ogerman.[51] This was still fairly early in the American phase of the German composer's career. Ogerman had arrived in the States in 1959, and he had not yet done the charts for Antonio Carlos Jobim, Bill Evans, and Oscar Peterson for which he would become known. Although Nelson was relatively unknown, he suited Carter for several reasons: "I liked his voicing, what he did with the horns, the way he put them together—it was different—he had a different sound."[52] Nelson's sound had most recently come to light on the now classic recording, *Blues and the Abstract Truth,* as had his idealistic personal agenda: "I would have to be true to myself, to play and write what *I* think is vital and, most of all, to find my own personality and identity."[53] For Carter, race was also a factor in her choice of arrangers: "When I approached Atlantic with Oliver Nelson, they said 'like what do I mean?' In the end they got Claus Ogerman; he's not bad, but he was also young and new and a foreigner, and here's Oliver Nelson who's young and black."[54] At Carter's insistence, Nelson did eventually arrange eight of the thirteen tunes on the album. Carter reported that Nelson also got pressured by the producers to modify his approach: "They tried to tell him how to write for me. That was not what I wanted. I wanted him to feel free."[55] Carter did not scat on either the Ray Charles duets or *'Round Midnight,* leading me to suspect that her greatest efforts to shed her Betty "Bebop" image come from around this time.

Amid these recording projects, Carter was still gigging, both locally and on the road, and as with any single, she was often backed by an unfamiliar rhythm section.[56] Sometimes the quality of her accompaniment left much to be desired. "It was gigging time, so you just worked with what they had."[57] Frequently a player she worked with locally served as an anchor for the groups she assembled on excursions out of Manhattan. At the beginning of the 1960s, for example, bass player Teddy Smith filled this role. Smith's car rack enabled them to haul his instrument atop her 1960 Pontiac, except when it rained and the bass became another passenger in the cramped car.[58]

Carter's bane on the road was musicians who couldn't read well, which limited what she could do with her charts. Although she would often get into a town in the afternoon and rehearse with the musicians until they got on the bandstand, many still did not understand what she was looking for. As anyone who worked with her knows, if she felt a player was not competent she had no problem telling him so. It was during this time that she developed a way of looking at her sidemen, almost through them, to make them think twice about what they were doing.

The summer following her last Atco sessions, early in 1963, Carter headlined an extended engagement at Birdland, opposite the Philly Joe Jones Quintet and the Jaki Byard trio. For that date she had Sam Dockery on piano, Buster Williams on bass, and Bruno Carr, who had played drums with Ray Charles on the tour in early 1961. While this was not a regular trio, Dockery recalls going on road trips with Carter, working in Philadelphia and Atlantic City as well as in New York.[59] In the middle of the Birdland engagement Williams left to join Sarah Vaughan and Carter asked Philly Joe Jones's bassist Larry Ridley to fill in, so he doubled up, working both sets.[60] In July, Carter also participated in a weeklong engagement at the Apollo.

In September Carter had a unique opportunity to perform internationally with Sonny Rollins, on a three-week tour of Japan sponsored by the Art Friends Association.[61] The tenor saxophonist was reemerging after a self-imposed exile from performing, and he had trumpeter Reshid Kmal Ali, pianist Paul Bley, bassist Henry Grimes, and drummer Roy McCurdy with him. When they arrived at Tokyo International Airport, they were met by a television crew from the Nippon Broadcasting Company as well as a crowd of about three hundred fans, critics, and reporters.[62] Staying in the Tokyo Ginza, the entourage was given the royal treatment. Sporting a Mohican haircut, Rollins was interviewed at a press conference in the hotel's ballroom the day after the group arrived. He and the rest of the musicians met with "thunderous applause" from the 450 or so critics and reporters in attendance. With the civil rights movement escalating its activities the preceding summer, and television footage of the violent events in Birmingham, Alabama broadcast globally, the racial situation in the United States was in the minds of the reporters who interviewed Rollins. In response to their inquiries, the saxophonist claimed that, while he obviously had feelings about the matter, his primary concern was to make music.[63]

There was a large jazz audience in Japan, and Carter had a Nipponese following, for her records were available in Japan and many of them had been reviewed there. The singer appreciated the positive response she received from the Japanese audiences: "If the audiences everywhere were like they are in Japan, I'd be a star. I'd be what I want to be. The audiences there made musicians from the States feel like being jazz musicians was something to be proud of. And the p.a. [public address] systems were always perfect."[64] A private recording from this tour reveals how much disparity there was between Carter's highly arranged recordings from the early 1960s and her live work from the same period, showing that her commercially available material from this time does not come close to capturing the spontaneity of her live dates.[65] The tape consists of an up-tempo reading of "Just the Way You Look Tonight," which she had recorded in 1955, and the ballad "When I Fall in Love," which she had done on her recent Atco recording. It provides our earliest examples of the kind of fluid interaction with a rhythm section for which she later became famous, and one could easily mistake it for her live recordings from later in the decade. Her rendition of "When I Fall in Love" ends with a lengthy a capella passage in which nuances of melodic movement intimate the complex harmonic concept she had developed. After returning to the States, Carter toured the Midwest with pianist John Malachi, bassist Buster Williams, and drummer Billy Hart.[66] Flush with her recent success in Japan, she looked to the future expectantly.

7

Paying Dues

The year 1964 marked a turning point in Betty Carter's life. With five records to her name, and tours with such important figures as Lionel Hampton, Miles Davis, Ray Charles, and Sonny Rollins to her credit, she could at this stage in her career count on bookings in African American urban communities on the East Coast and in the Midwest, in addition to the greater New York area, where she had established audiences for herself. The former Detroiter could also rely upon musicians and club owners to welcome her home, and she worked there periodically at such places as Baker's Keyboard Lounge and the Flame Show Bar. While she was steadily employed, however, she still sang mostly in "small rooms." In the hierarchy of the performing musician this meant that she had not yet made it and was still working her way up through the ranks. But in 1964 she was earning a decent living in music and seemed on her way to bigger things.

The intermittent airplay Carter was getting on the East Coast was an encouraging sign. Radio had been an important factor in a musician's success since the early days of jazz, but with the rise of the modern disk jockey, such success depended even more upon radio promotion. Recognizing this, record companies developed various methods for exploiting the medium to market their products, even going so far as to bribe disk jockeys or hire independent promoters to do this for them.[1] Without a major label behind her to bring its influence to bear on radio stations, a lone performer did not have much access to the medium. There were a few idealistic deejays who were hip to the sounds of black music, however, and some of them championed Carter's cause. If you happened to be tuning in late one night in Philly, for example, you might hear radio host Joel Dorn ring in the new day with the sound of Carter's voice, saying: "It's midnight in Philadelphia: here's the girlfriend," followed by a cut from the Ray Charles duets or *The Modern Sound*.[2]

Having emerged from the "journeyman" phase of her career by the first years of the 1960s, Carter seemed poised for that elusive big break that would catapult her to national celebrity. Her recent successes fueled her self-confidence, and her reputation as a prima donna dates from around this time. As she put it: "That's when I started acting like a star."[3] This attitude was double-edged: while it stemmed from her hopeful outlook, it also gave her the hubris to believe she could achieve fame without compromising her ideals. Meanwhile, jazz continued to lose ground to music of a less intricate, more accessible design, as a new generation of listeners asserted its impact on the market. Unlike several of her colleagues, and in the face of pressure to adapt to the changing scene, Carter persisted in defining herself exclusively as a jazz singer. Spurning the electronic instruments that were gaining ascendance, in favor of acoustic ones, she took the chord changes of songs, usually standards, and created new themes to serve as the head—the way Jay Jay Johnson had created "Jay Bird" over rhythm changes, for example—rather than reiterate the songs' familiar melodies. Being a vocalist, however, she also had to contend with words. By modifying each restatement of musical material to conform to the evolving phonetic and semantic content of the lyrics, as she did in the second half of "The Good Life," for example, as well as in response to each band member's contribution, Carter kept her renditions changing, growing, and moving, virtually forcing the listener to stay involved in her creative process. This process generally continued into later choruses, as in "I Can't Help It," sustaining the music's growth to the end of the performance. As a result, listeners found few "handles"—the literal repetitions such as refrains, hooks, and the like—with which to grasp the music's form easily; the kind of handles that made the current pop music so easy to digest on first hearing. As we have seen, her complex approach had already antagonized some jazz critics, so it is not surprising that it denied other listeners what they were looking for as well, especially during this period of simplification in popular music. Predictably, her perseverance during this time led her to become identified as a jazz purist. Primarily concerned with turning a profit, major labels grew less and less interested in catering to the shrinking jazz audience.[4] Viewed strictly in commercial terms, Carter's refusal to sing anything but jazz was therefore bound to undermine her marketability, as she herself later acknowledged: "I'm not *supposed* to have a hit record. . . . I've always been a jazz singer. If you're a jazz singer from the beginning, it'll stay. You can't get away from that feeling. I've tried to compromise and couldn't sleep. I'll stay with what I'm doing and be happy on the stage rather than compromise."[5]

Carter's prima donna attitude also stemmed from the knowledge and experience she had gained since she left Detroit sixteen years before, which gave her strong opinions about how to proceed with her career. These opinions, coupled with her forceful personality, led her to feel entitled to more control over her destiny than many singers, and most women, then claimed. Still smarting from the Atco fiasco, she was more determined than ever to accept no one's input. Given the gender politics of the day, a woman who stood up for herself as Carter did was bound to experience adverse effects. With the industry's consolidation into a handful of dominant labels, or majors, and its increased power to determine an artist's success, her prospects began to stall. The big break she anticipated never materialized, and her dream of reaching the stature of Ella Fitzgerald or Sarah Vaughan slipped out of reach.

Because jazz expressed her experience as an African American, Carter's stance was partly a function of racial pride. She was mainly interested in addressing black listeners—the only ones, in her eyes, who had the authority to validate a jazz artist's work. Caving in to pressure from businessmen would have entailed reshaping her work to make it accessible to the largely white mainstream. Even as her audiences grew whiter during the course of the decade, Carter continued to identify jazz solely with black culture. During the preceding decade the audiences Carter had been delighting at such venues as the Apollo Theater had been embracing a wide range of styles that drew heavily upon the blues. As long as black performers were producing these styles for black audiences, and as long as these audiences continued to accept jazz, Carter did not see the current styles as a threat. In fact, several of the people she had formed connections to—Dinah Washington, Lionel Hampton, Don Robey, and Ray Charles, among others—had contributed to the development of these styles. For Carter, segregation made these different musics compatible. As the following for these styles expanded to include white listeners and jazz was edged out of the popular market, however, she became less broad-minded.

Carter was not the only one troubled by the marketing of black styles to white listeners. She was among a contingent within the African American community that took Ray Charles to task, for example, for commercializing the gospel style by bringing it out of the church and adding secular lyrics. In the liner notes to *Ray Charles at Newport,* for example, blues singer and former preacher William Lee "Big Bill" Conley Broonzy was quoted as saying that Charles was "mixin' the blues with spirituals. I know that's wrong. . . . He should be singing in a church."[6] Ironically, while Charles's work had long been rooted in these African American sources, in the course of moving from Atlantic records to ABC-Paramount, his sound underwent a shift toward a mainstream pop sound. But the cat had been let out of the bag, and British rock groups such as the Rolling Stones were now openly emulating Charles's earlier work and that of other blues-based black musicians. Carter said little about such acts as the Supremes and the Four Tops (incidentally from her hometown), who also helped establish the crossover potential for African American musical styles on the black-owned label Motown. But in 1976 she recalled nostalgically that, before 1959, "there wasn't the influx of the white world in our music like we have today, . . . an influx of white artists who have learned more about black music."[7]

The effect on jazz produced by the shift in mainstream audience tastes started to become apparent by the mid-1960s, when the prospects of musicians who worked from a bop-based sensibility began to deteriorate. To be sure, the groundswell had begun much earlier, but the tide seemed to turn suddenly in 1964 with the wave of rock musicians arriving from across the Atlantic. The Beatles' "I Want to Hold Your Hand" reached number one on the *Billboard* singles chart on 1 February and remained in that spot for seven weeks.[8] The group's appearances on the *Ed Sullivan Show* that month fueled the rising tide of Beatlemania, and by the time the film *A Hard Day's Night* was released in the United States in August it had already become clear that the music world would never be the same.[9] In the following decade, when Carter recalled the setbacks that struck around the time British rockers invaded, she wryly noted: "I'm in real trouble now, because I haven't gotten nowhere in the first place."[10]

With their fabulous success, British R&B-styled musicians, and the Beatles in particular, became easy scapegoats for the effect rock had on the record industry and, by extension, on the market for jazz. As a disgruntled Carter put it: "It wasn't until the 1960s when the Beatles came on the scene that the impact in the music business was money—instantly."[11] Carter felt that the Beatles' open acknowledgment of their debt to black music "gave permission to every white artist who wanted to do some black material or to approach the black world of music—it was the stamp of approval."[12] There were earlier instances of this kind of acknowledgment, when Frank Sinatra admitted in 1958 that Billie Holiday's singing had left a strong impression on him, for example.[13] Furthermore, as in the case of Sarah Vaughan, who credited certain white singers, including Dinah Shore and Doris Day, as strong inspirations, there were also instances of black artists acknowledging the influence of white performers.[14] But for Carter, the floodgates for musical cross-pollination suddenly opened wide in 1964, when "the barrier for white people to go out and buy black music lifted."[15] Associating the Beatles' arrival in America with the moment when the record industry effectively stopped making race records, Carter lamented the dissolution of the musical division between blacks and whites. By focusing blame for the situation on the British rockers, Carter could initially ignore the growing rejection of jazz by her own people.

Typically white musicians reaped more benefits from musical cross-fertilization than black musicians, so Carter had reason to decry the musical desegregation then taking place. For her, the emphasis on quick money invariably inhibited musicians' adventurousness and cheapened the quality of their musical output by leading them to borrow from others rather than produce their own original work. "Now it was okay for white people to simulate us, mimic us, do the black music, get over, and they could freely do it. . . . Everybody struck out with a sigh of relief; now I can [sing] like Muddy Waters. It became integration time, musically. [Nat] King Cole got into Las Vegas. Everything became everything, right. Think about it. Now money is the most important thing, not creativity."[16]

In retrospect it is clear that whatever desegregation the music business experienced during this time was not occurring in a social vacuum. On 2 July 1964 President Lyndon Baines Johnson signed the Civil Rights Act. The resultant migration of middle-class black people from cities such as Newark to outlying suburbs added to the effect white flight had already been having on black urban neighborhoods since the early 1950s.[17] Before the new legislation, these neighborhoods had depended upon the economic stratification of their residents to sustain the sense of community that held them together. According to C. Vann Woodward, the increased opportunity desegregation presented for black people posed the threat of cultural disappearance and intensified the pressure for black separatism that was being voiced by the militant wing of the civil rights movement.[18] Carter never adopted a public position on the civil rights movement or on the Nation of Islam; her own brand of militancy came out in the defiance with which she maintained her personal style. This stance clearly had musical implications, but it ultimately stemmed from her image of herself as a black artist. Speaking in 1979, Carter said: "When the '60s came, and money became the most important thing to an artist and to a record company, it [the commercial market] had a lot to do with what happened to artists. Most of our [black] artists decided they wanted to make some money. . . . So all of them conformed to make money. That cut down on the musicianship."[19] The price Carter's defiance exacted was steep because it entailed renouncing the aspirations for personal advancement her middle-class upbringing had instilled in her. Her stance reflected her dedication to jazz, not only as a musical tradition, but also as an outgrowth of African American culture.

Still, it took a while for the full impact of all these forces to be felt in the day-to-day business of making music. In 1964 Carter visited Europe briefly without much response.[20] Back at home, however, some people were beginning to take note of a new direction in the development of her concept. Amiri Baraka (also known as Leroi Jones) wrote positively of this direction:

> The word around now is listen to Betty Carter! She's gone way past those Ray Charles duets. I heard a recent tape at one citizen's house that was really something else, maybe more than that. She also turned out a benefit this summer at the Five Spot, singing with her own trio. Miss Carter seems to hear her voice now more personally, as a human extension of human feeling, rather than as say, some formal (revived) artifact that must wade wearily through word after word of essentially vapid "popular" songs. To say that she "uses her voice as an instrument," is to cheapen her intent. She uses her voice toward the limits of its physical (and emotional) expressiveness . . . past mere melody, as a constantly stated, recurring theme, to a way of collecting very hidden facets of emotion by giving very individual . . . values to her notes, rests, slurs, etc. I mean, she sounds very good.[21]

The stylistic elements Baraka was noticing, while present in Carter's previous commercial recordings, started becoming more pronounced at least as early as 1963—the private recording of a performance in Japan documents this. Reflective of the singer's deepened commitment to a bop-based concept of jazz, in spite of its diminishing commercial viability, these elements began to seep into her commercially produced recordings.

In the spring of 1964 Monte Kay arranged for Carter to make a record for the independent producer Alan Douglas. A session that took place that April at Sound Makers in New York City generated eight tracks that the United Artists label released as *Inside Betty Carter*.[22] The instrumentalists at this session consisted of pianist Harold Mabern and bassist Bob Cranshaw, as well as drummer Roy McCurdy, who had been on Rollins's Japanese tour.[23] In its resemblance to her recent live work, this record shows how Carter was rethinking her approach to commercial recordings. The substitution of a rhythm section for the lush orchestral contexts in which she had been recording, for example, represents an important step, giving her more flexibility to interact with her accompaniment and vice versa. In some respects her vocal delivery did not depart radically from the approach she had taken on *'Round Midnight*, especially with Oliver Nelson's sparer charts, which gave her more space than Ogerman's did. But finally Carter had a record she liked unequivocally. In 1976, citing a demand for *Inside Betty Carter*, she felt that United Artists should have reissued the record,[24] and three years later she stated that, out of the eleven records she had made to date, *Inside* was one of her two favorite albums.[25] In the late 1980s, she obtained the rights to reissue it on Capitol, and once having acquired these rights, Carter retroactively catalogued it as the first recording on her own label.

The fact that she did her own arranging for the record indicates the greater control she was now exercising over her recorded output. Certain songs on the record came to define her emerging sound from this time. Her idiosyncratic renditions of "My Favorite Things" and "Spring Can Hang You Up the Most"—with the former cast in 4/4, unlike Richard Rodgers's waltz time, shifting suddenly from a moderate to a breakneck tempo, and the latter set in a languorously slow tempo—made these songs signature tunes for Carter in the years that followed the record's release. The song "Something Big," with its oblique reference to the civil rights movement, could stand as a fanfare announcing Carter's latest assertion of her artistic voice.

According to Carter her own composition "Open the Door" grew from the effect financial pressures were having on her relationship with her husband: "I was trying to get him to understand . . . why I couldn't give up what I was doing to go for the money."[26] The song became a staple of her repertoire thereafter, and she would go on to record it more times than any other song (example 8).

At first it is hard to relate Carter's free-verse lyrics for "Open the Door" to her motive for writing the song, for they follow their own logic, making their point more by suggestion than by literal meaning. The song's persistent bossa nova rhythm and its haunting, sensual melody make it easy to hear the lyrics as a sexy come-on. But in such phrases as "I must get in your heart" and "No matter how you try to avoid me you can't get away so easily," hints of aggressiveness surface, suggesting that, although the narrator seems to be offering herself, she is in fact seeking her lover's surrender. Her sexuality becomes a means of obtaining control over the object of her desire and making him accept her as she is. In this respect this song's lyrics are an extension of a theme she introduced in "I Can't Help It."

The song's harmony also follows its own logic, with the striking insertion of a IV^7 at measure 21 between the ii^7 at measure 17 and the V at measure 23, and its unusual use of the ♭III in the bridge. The slow harmonic rhythm—especially the opening and closing harmonic vamps—may reflect the influence of modal jazz, to which she was exposed while working opposite Miles Davis, and the fragmented delivery of the text is reminiscent of the trumpeter's phrasing. Consistent with her approach to standards, her delivery's irregular phrase structure obscures the form in places by stretching the line across the song's formal articulations, most noticeably at the start of the bridge, which begins in measure 45 (at rehearsal figure B) midway through the line "No matter how you try to avoid me . . ." Indeed, only the recurrences of the lyrics' title phrase signal the song's major structural divisions, initiating each A section in measures 13, 29, and 61. Unusual too is the interruption of the last A section by an A-flat minor6 chord, which precipitates the ensuing tag: three statements of a descending chromatic progression at measures 73,

81, and 89. The melody's structural fluidity, coupled with the largely unrhymed lyrics, gave Carter room to respond to the words and the music as they unfolded.

On *Inside Betty Carter* Carter displays a fondness for pairing her voice with individual instruments—a technique she may have absorbed from Gigi Gryce and Richard Wess. Starting a song this way helped to contrast it with the preceding number, creating a sense of movement between each number on the record, or in the set. Carter also used this approach to create movement within each song, while also articulating the form, by adding instruments at such key structural moments as the bridge, the repeats of the A section, or the start of each new chorus. On *Inside* she sings the entire first chorus of the song "Look No Further" with only bass, saving the remaining instruments to help spur on the more intense second chorus. Beginning the ballad "Beware My Heart" with just voice and piano gives the tune a reflective intimacy. Her arrangement of "Some Other Time" juxtaposes piano-voice and bass-voice pairings effectively both for timbral contrasts and for mood changes. Carter kept instrumental colors fresh by pacing their entrances, as she did in the pyramid-like introduction to "Open the Door." Taking this principle to an extreme in "You're a Sweetheart," which was not commercially available until the album was later reissued on CD, she sings the verse a capella.

Carter began to explore the possibility of performing at black colleges as early as 1964. As her career prospects began to dim, it was logical for her to approach institutions of higher learning for support, as they have traditionally served as havens for art forms that lack commercial viability. But Carter also wanted to help rebuild the black audience for jazz and educate black students about their cultural heritage. In 1980 she described the resistance she initially encountered:

> When I tried to get a grant to get into these black schools, the person I asked about the grant was on the board of NEA, one of the branches, New York or the international branch. Anyway, he told me flatly, which discouraged me completely, that the school itself would have to be interested in me in order for me to write up a proposal to get a grant to go to this school. I know the school is not interested in me. I'm not going there for that reason. I'm trying to get into the school to expose myself to the kids. . . . So I'm thinking of a real period where it's very necessary for it [jazz] to be heard by the youth before the continuity is broken, you see.[27]

Perhaps Carter's role as a parent sensitized her to the important function music can serve in nurturing community. During the summer of 1964 she was pregnant with her second child, and on 1 February 1965 she gave birth to Kagle Redding.[28] By then she and James Redding had moved their family to a house at 139 Goodwin Avenue in Newark and he had taken a job as warehouse manager for Active Distributors. They were not there for long, however, for on 1 June Carter bought a house at 881 South Fifteenth Street, in the largely white Irvington community on the outskirts of Newark.[29] Clearly she was doing well enough to provide a home for her family similar to the one in which she had grown up. From an economic standpoint at least, she had vindicated her teenage disobedience by fulfilling her family of origin's middle-class aspirations.

Musically Betty Carter was also settling down, becoming a keeper of the flame. To speak of preserving the jazz tradition is to approach it retrospectively rather than from the radical stance of her youth. Jazz's position in the cultural hierarchy had shifted considerably from the time when Lillie Mae Jones had auditioned for Lionel Hampton. Urban neighborhoods across the country where jazz had flourished a decade earlier were now economically depressed, and the scene continued to erode as the 1960s wore on. As the situation worsened, Carter came to feel that sustaining the jazz tradition was a powerful way that African Americans could keep their distinctive cultural identity from being swallowed up by mainstream America.

Gigs were starting to get harder to come by, and Carter treated each one as a precious opportunity. She recalled that around New Year's Day 1965—when she was about eight months pregnant with Kagle—a snowstorm nearly kept her from making a gig at Philadelphia's Cadillac Club; but, rather than cancel, she drove through the blizzard and made the date. Later that year, about two months after her new son was born, she was in the company of John Coltrane, Archie Shepp, Albert Ayler, and others associated with free jazz on Sunday, 28 March for an afternoon concert entitled "New Black Music." This benefit for the Black Arts Repertory Theater School that took place at the Village Gate also included Charles Tolliver, Bobby Hutcherson, and Grachan Moncur III, and much of the music performed there was released by Impulse records.[30] Amiri Baraka's liner notes spelled out the event's agenda: "The expression and instinctive (natural) reflection that characterize black art and culture, listen to these players, transcends any emotional state (human realization) the white man knows."[31] In some respects this is a surprising bill for Betty Carter to have appeared on, for as much as she may have identified with the participants' expression of black pride, she did not support their use of music to promote a political agenda. Referring to free jazz musicians in general, perhaps with this event in mind, she would later tell radio host Art Roberts: "I think that politics has a lot to do with . . . the destruction of the music, of jazz in particular. And their music was political. It was hard; it wasn't soulful; it didn't have any warmth, any depth; it was out telling us what to do, and how to live, and badgering us; it was angry music."[32] Carter felt that many of the avant-garde players were imposters who used "the new thing," as it was then also termed, to dupe white listeners who didn't know good music from bad. Furthermore, she blamed the movement for driving black listeners away from jazz.[33] Thinking about the training of young musicians, she also felt that free jazz threatened the continuity of the jazz tradition. "I knew that a musician who jumped on the free music [bandwagon] would be lost as far as education in musicianship is concerned."[34] Having adopted the jazz world as her surrogate family when she left Lionel Hampton's band, she took personally any development she felt might jeopardize its existence, and her attacks on free jazz became more scathing as the jazz economy worsened.

With the closing of jazz clubs, Carter relied on her connections to the Apollo Theater and venues in Greenwich Village to get gigs. For the 1966 New Year's celebration at the Apollo, she worked "a package" with John Lee Hooker, T-Bone Walker, and Sonny Terry and Brownie McGhee.[35] Old friends in the black entertainment world also steered work her way. Her association with Sammy Davis Jr., for example, dated from her time with Lionel Hampton, who presented the entertainer when he was still teamed up with the Will Maston Trio. Davis was riding a crest of popularity from his triumphant performance in the musical *Golden Boy* in 1964 and the film *A Man Called Adam,* so this was an opportune time to be associated with him, and she appeared on the penultimate episode of his television show in 1965.[36] After coming to hear her sing at Wells in Harlem—famous for its chicken and waffles—Davis invited Carter to inaugurate a new space at the Living Room, of which he was part owner.[37]

This was in July 1966, and Carter was contracting her own dates. She was backed by pianist John Hicks, bassist Cecil McBee, and drummer Jack DeJohnette—players who also worked as a unit without her. Later that month she began an extended engagement at the Five Spot Cafe that lasted much of the summer, backed by a quartet consisting of tenor saxophone—first Joe Henderson, then George Coleman—plus a rhythm section with Hicks, drummer Freddie Waits, and, initially, Walter Booker on bass, with McBee later taking his place.[38] Even though the relative stability of her personnel for much of the summer came about more by chance than by design, she came to consider the rhythm section for these dates as "her trio." The declining prospects for work made these remarkable instrumentalists available to Carter for relatively minor compensation. It was unusual for Carter to have a horn on her dates—doing so entailed splitting the proceeds five ways instead of four—but because Henderson and Coleman were doing other gigs with Hicks, they came along with the package.[39]

Carter enjoyed a fruitful collaboration with John Hicks intermittently over the next dozen years or so. Born in Atlanta in 1941, raised in Los Angeles and later, in St. Louis, Hicks had moved to New York City in 1962 after attending Berklee College of Music. He played piano in Art Blakey's Jazz Messengers in the fall of 1964, and by 1965 he was working with trumpeter Charles Tolliver and saxophonist Gary Bartz, as well as McBee and DeJohnette. In fact, it was DeJohnette who recommended Hicks to Carter, after the pianist had heard her at the Five Spot on earlier occasions. For roughly two years, from September 1965 to July 1967, Hicks worked with her on and off, at such local sites as Harouts, Wells, the Five Spot, the Half Note, the Village Gate, the Apollo Theater, and Town Hall.[40] Frank Foster had a big band that rehearsed at the Five Spot—pre-"Loud Minority," as Hicks recalled—and performed there on Sunday afternoons, and Carter was backed by that group as well during this time.[41] According to Hicks the singer always drew a big crowd.

Ironically, as the work situation deteriorated, the response Carter's work received from jazz fans and writers improved. The following fall, critic Nat Hentoff wrote in *Down Beat:*

> I heard Miss Carter one night this last summer in New York and wondered how a musician of such stunning individuality, drive, subtlety, depth, and wit could be so underrepresented on records. And of her few albums, most bristle with the conflicting imperatives of Betty and various a&r men.
>
> Left free, and with musicians of her choice, she could record a series of albums that would help set a new criteria for what jazz singing can be in terms of where the music is taking us. So where are Bob Thiele or Alfred Lion or Nesuhi Ertegun?[42]

She was also interviewed by Bill McLarney for *Down Beat* that summer. Although Carter, like many jazz artists, resisted putting certain matters into words—she refused to define jazz, for example, saying only that "it's not technical. It's a feeling you receive from a performer"—she had, by this time, clearly formulated many of the ideas that would guide her throughout her career. She acknowledged the importance of technique, however, of having a strong foundation before doing anything creative or personal, or as she put it, of "knowing where you are."[43] Only when that foundation was established, she added, could you improvise "and interpret, think, and play with taste."

For her, the musicians were the final arbiters of quality, and she named as her favorite pianists Bobby Timmons, Harold Mabern, and John Hicks, indirectly identifying some of the sources of her sound image from this time. Choosing her players largely on a subjective basis, she emphasized that "if a group has a feeling for jazz like mine, we'll get a good interaction going."[44] This last point is especially significant because, unlike many singers, who view their sidemen largely as accompanists, Carter actively participated with her rhythm section in creating the music. The musical exchange with the rhythm section influenced her improvising, which depended upon the flow of musical ideas coming from the group. "It's often a question of whether or not the musicians feed me."[45] This interaction extended beyond individual performances as well, to include her exposure to new ideas. Carter resisted stylistic inertia. Having moved on to a stylistic outgrowth of bebop, she was intolerant of singers who "fall back into the bebop element when they scat."[46] She subjected her work to the exacting standards of improvising musicians, who have little patience for those who spout clichés, because she wanted her music to be interesting to the young musicians who inspired and encouraged her. The original approach she took in "Open the Door," for example, while hardly radical compared to avant-garde jazz, shows how much she had grown stylistically since "Jay Bird" and "I Can't Help It."

Carter's impatience about "the new thing" surfaced in this interview. For her the application of bop-derived principles to the raw materials provided by the existing repertoire of standards was enough grist to generate new, exciting work, so there was no need to synthesize elements from outside jazz. The stylistic boundaries the singer drew around the music she made, which placed not only current pop music but also free jazz, and later, fusion, outside of the jazz domain, partly account for Carmen McRae's naming Carter the sole representative of pure jazz vocalism. Striving to keep out what she felt were corrupting influences, Carter only endorsed musicians who continued to explore the musical vocabulary and procedures provided by bebop's spin-off styles. As with her straight-ahead colleagues, she placed a high premium on swing, so she disliked any unhinging of jazz from the groove. In this context the style's removal of the chorus structure, the recurrent cycle of chord changes that gave the form its shape, was not only a harmonic phenomenon but also a rhythmic one. She remarked, "If I don't want to hear something that swings, I play the classics [European classical music]."[47] Clearly, even though bop was not primarily a dance music, the dance impulse from which swing stems was crucial to the music's aesthetic. Carter's movements onstage expressed this impulse and helped convey it to her rhythm section.

Carter also stressed the importance of pacing sets, of giving them an aesthetic wholeness. After having gone for forty-five minutes without scatting, for example, she would close a set "way up," using scat to energize her finale.[48] Listeners who had come to hear Betty Bebop scat had to wait, their expectations building for the duration of the set. As she did with instrumental colors, she made each scat episode count by holding the technique in reserve rather than overuse it. Unfortunately, because Carter did not record between 1965 and 1969, there is no documentation of her adventurous scatting from this period.

This time marked a turning point in the lives and careers of many jazz musicians regardless of their stature. Several talented performers became session musicians while others took work outside the field of music. Even such legends as Duke Ellington had difficulty securing recording contracts. As Carter's gigging prospects slowed to a trickle in the latter half of the decade, it became difficult to sustain the middle-class lifestyle she had worked so hard to attain. Enjoying the autonomy that came from being the primary wage earner of her household, she also did not relish the prospect of depending upon her husband for financial support. With two small children to raise, however, she also had no romantic illusions about the virtues of being a starving artist. This circumstance makes her refusal to sing pop all the more remarkable. Deciding that making the music was more important to her than making a killing, Carter kept plugging away. She certainly did not take time off "to have a family," as was mistakenly reported. But with the cover of *Newsweek* asking "Is Jazz Dead," and the black urban communities that had been sustaining her work shaken by riots, it is not so surprising that the singer seemed to be slowly but steadily disappearing from view to all but the hippest of insiders. The difficulties Carter encountered in getting work during this time deepened her resentment of the racial inequities she felt had cheated her out of the success she deserved. Still embittered nearly two decades later, she would tell Leslie Gourse: "If I had been a white female, I would have been a big star earlier. If I were white, with my drive and concept, I'd have had a contract with Columbia."[49] Feeling like an outsider to a hostile industry, Carter began to lose sight of her earlier successes: "I stayed with Hampton for two and a half years, then I left him and went to New York to try my luck. From then it's been a bitter fight from one club to the next."[50]

A momentary boost was provided by an invitation to participate in the Antibes Jazz Festival at Juan-les-Pins, France. Benny Bailey, whom Carter had known from her time with Hampton, was working with the Boy Edgar big band from Holland, and he may have encouraged the leader to bring her over. The summer of 1968 was a tumultuous time in France as well as in the States, and student unrest left its mark on the festival. Nevertheless, impressed with the musicality and panache she displayed at this event, *Down Beat* reviewer Mike Hennessey found her one of the few performers deserving of praise: "Carter came on stage in trousers and a jaunty cap and sang with such verve and command that she almost got the band to swing."[51] But the crowd remained unmoved, and Ted Joans recalled that her sets were not well received.[52] She returned to Newark without much to show for this brief excursion.

The downward turn of fortune Carter faced late in the 1960s was especially disillusioning because the opportunities she received early in her career had nurtured her hopes of a steady rise to fame. She was approaching forty years old, with her youthfulness, a critical selling point for a female artist, slipping away, and scraping by from gig to gig had lost the excitement it had when she first came to New York looking for her big break. Her disappointments ultimately took their toll on her marriage. In the summer of 1968 Carter loaded Myles and Kagle into their 1964 Bonneville, leaving James Redding and Newark behind. Redding described how, one morning that summer, she said she needed to use the car and arranged to pick him up at work when he was done. That afternoon there was no sign of his lift. When he finally got a ride home, he found a note saying she had the kids. She had no driver's license and little driving experience, but she was undeterred. As Redding put it: "Once she got an idea in her head, you got on the wagon for the ride 'cause the trip was going to be made."[53]

The wayfarers' first stop was Detroit, where they stayed with Carter's sister and brother-in-law, C.B. and Ellis Rogers. At first her hosts were supportive of her efforts to line up gigs at local clubs, but these proved as futile there as in New York. After a few months C.B. and James Jones III lost patience with their sister and insisted that she take a job bagging groceries at a supermarket. With her back to the wall, the out-of-work singer reluctantly agreed, but on the day she was supposed to start work she did not show up. When she returned to her sister's home later that day she found her packed bags on the front step. This incident created a deep rift between Carter and her siblings: she resented their lack of unconditional support, while they felt she was being irresponsible. Being back in Detroit led her to revisit the antagonism she had experienced with Bertha. It was no doubt hard for her siblings to see her fall short of the Jones's ambitions of achieving the American dream.

With her two sons, Carter continued westward, performing one-nighters wherever she could get work, and ended up in Oakland where she stayed with her sister Louise. The prospects for work were no better on the West Coast, however, and after a few months she found herself out on the street again. She and the boys stayed with Redding's sister Helen for a short time, but Carter sent Myles home by plane that fall. She then moved on to San Francisco, where she and Kagle settled for the winter and spring.[54] There was little opportunity for work and when she did perform, the audience response was cool at best. Ten years later she told a California audience: "I worked right here in San Francisco, and you all looked at me like 'what is she doing?' "[55] Over two decades had passed since Carter had sung at the Golden Gate in San Francisco with Hampton's thriving musical organization. Her failure to draw an audience on the West Coast pointed up how little she had to show for all her efforts. Yet as the chasm between Carter's dreams and the reality she was living continued to widen, her resolve to stay true to her vision only deepened.

Elmira "Ain'tie" Dixon Jones surrounded by nine of her grandchildren, in Detroit, ca. 1940. ***Clockwise from top left:*** **Lillie Mae Jones (Betty Carter), Irene Jones Meadows-Blanding, Ain'tie holding Barbara Marion, Jewella Jones, infant Ronald Jones, Gilbert Jones, Elayne Jones Robinson** ***(in front),*** **James T. Jones III** ***(in suit),*** **Laverne Jones Ahmed. (Photograph courtesy of Kagle Redding.)**

At the cannon in front of Detroit's Northwestern High School, ca. 1946. *Standing,* Lillie Mae Jones; *far right,* Anna Duncan; third person unidentified. (Photograph courtesy of the WestSiders.)

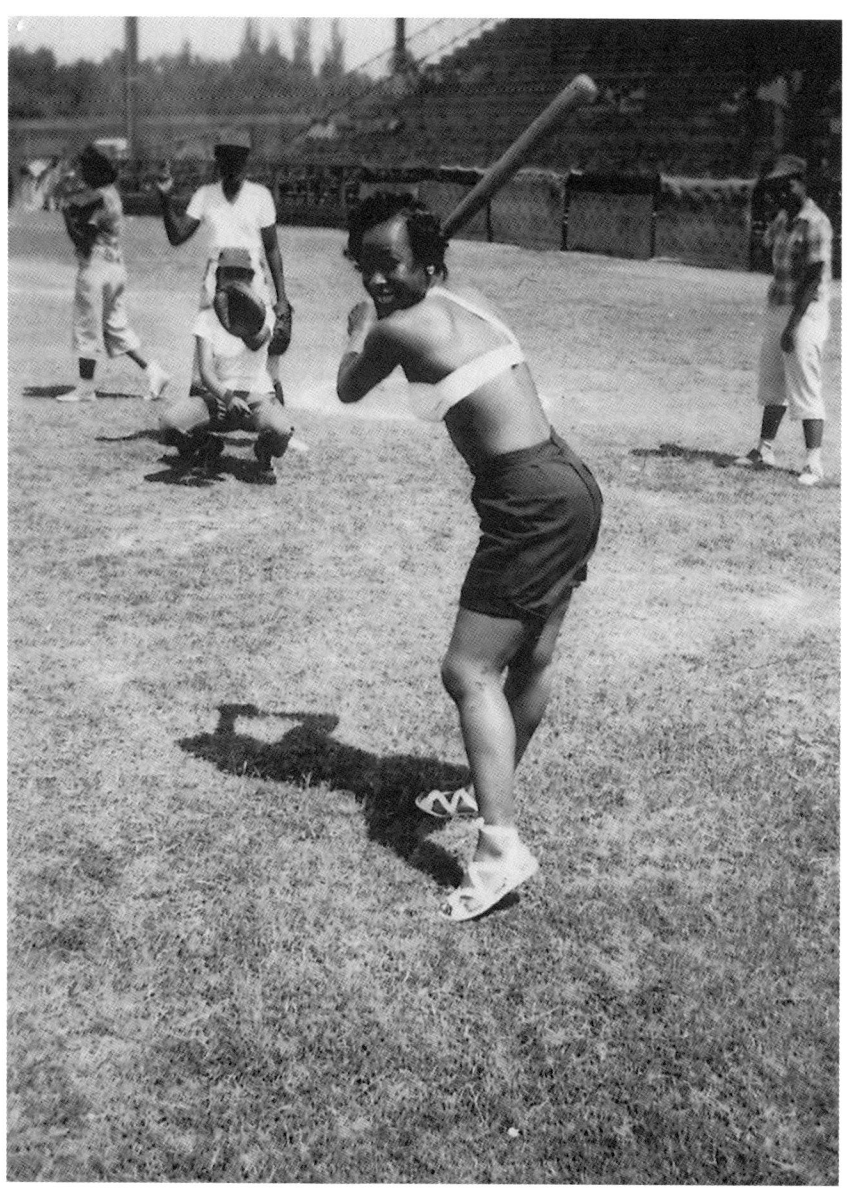

Showing off her superb form at the plate. (Photograph courtesy of Kagle Redding.)

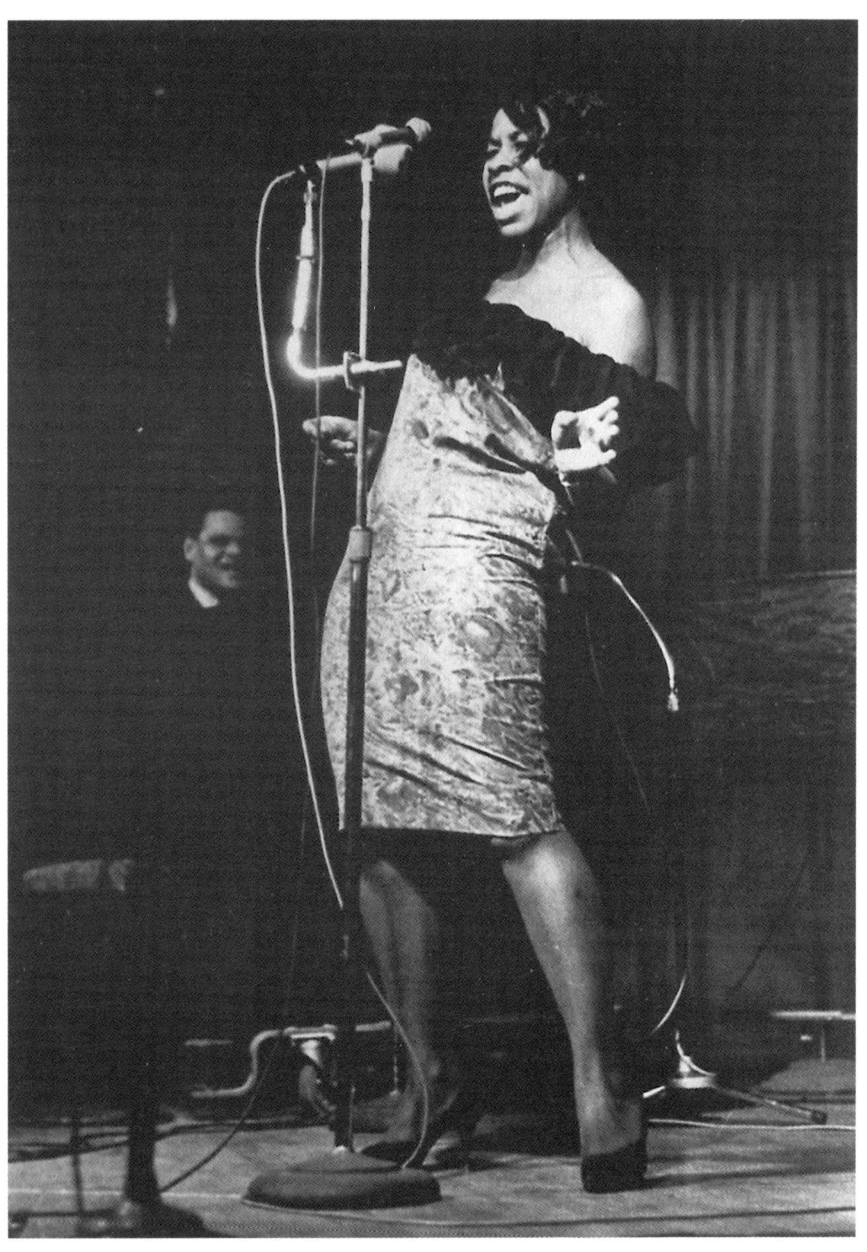

At the Village Gate in March 1968, with Walter Davis Jr. on piano. (Photograph courtesy of Charles Stewart.)

Promotional shot from the time when John Levy was booking Carter in the mid-1950s. (Photograph courtesy of Frank Driggs.)

Ray Charles and Betty Carter, ca. 1960. (Photograph courtesy of Kagle Redding.)

Sporting her transgender look in late 1976. (Photograph courtesy of Kagle Redding.)

At Le Bataclan, Paris, November 1979. (Photograph courtesy of Photo Horace.)

Performing at the bandshell in Prospect Park, Brooklyn, 1981. (Photograph courtesy of Hilda Daily.)

Striking a pose at the Prospect Park band shell, with Curtis Lundy on bass, Brooklyn, 1981. (Photograph courtesy of Hilda Daily.)

Performing for a broadcast in Hamburg, Germany, in 1983, with David Penn on bass. (Photograph courtesy of Thomas J. Krebs.)

Backstage at New York's Blue Note Cafe with Freddie Hubbard, 25 August 1992. (Photograph courtesy of Verve Records.)

At Carnegie Hall for Verve's Fiftieth Anniversary celebration, 6 April 1994. (Photograph courtesy of Steve J. Sherman.)

With Hillary Clinton at the White House for a dinner honoring the trustees of the Democratic National Committee, 19 April 1994. (Photograph courtesy of Kagle Redding.)

Dr. Betty Carter receiving her honorary Ph.D. from Williams College, 8 June 1997. (Courtesy of Dean David L. Smith, photo by Mark Kimball.)

"Everything she did was done in a natural fashion—it grew out of who she was; it wasn't put on" (David Amram). (Photograph courtesy of Kagle Redding.)

8

A New Direction

While Carter languished on the West Coast for what was undoubtedly the longest year of her life, the musical landscape continued to change. Over the course of the 1960s musicians experimenting with free and modal styles had increasingly challenged a fundamental tenet of jazz performance practice: that chord changes provide the basis for jazz improvisation. With the sovereignty of harmonic progression already under assault from these earlier developments, the path was cleared for musicians to integrate rock techniques and styles into a new approach that used electronic instruments and relied more on vamps or ostinatos than on harmonic motion. The resulting fusion of jazz and rock held out the possibility of having greater mass appeal, luring several players away from the straight-ahead sound. The most prominent of these players was Miles Davis.

After having steadily made moves toward integrating the sounds of rock into his approach during the end of the 1960s, Davis produced his landmark jazz-rock album *Bitches Brew* in August, 1969. Feeling that he had sold out, Carter openly expressed her disregard for this new direction in Davis's work in her interview with Arthur Taylor: "It wasn't until he did *Bitches Brew* and came up with the sound that they decided to put his picture on the trade magazine *Record World.* He'd made money for Columbia for years. How come they didn't respect him enough then to put his picture on the trade magazine?" adding, "He has disappointed me, because I want to hear something, not just sound."[1] Even though the new style drew upon funk, blues, and other African American styles, and in spite of Davis's own belief that it would rebuild jazz's black following, Carter openly proclaimed her disdain for musicians who abandoned the principles of bop, attributing fusion to white influences:

> So they do a play called *The Musical Tragedy of Billie Holiday* and Archie Shepp writes the music. To me . . . it was an insult to Billie Holiday, because he wrote rock music. . . . [T]hey were influenced by the white media. They [whites] put up the money and hoped it would be another *Jesus Christ Superstar* or *Hair*. . . . I heard the music and I know that Archie Shepp wasn't the man who should've written that music. Maybe the white people thought he could do it, but you can go uptown and ask ten people on the street who Archie Shepp is and they won't be able to tell you. Ninety percent of his audience is white.[2]

Given the depths to which Carter's career prospects had sunk, it is hardly surprising that she should frown upon the commercial success of musicians working in a style that, in her eyes, required less virtuosity than bop.

In the summer of 1969 Carter rejoined James Redding in Newark, apparently no better off than when she had left. But the trip West had changed her. It made her more determined than ever to perform jazz on her terms. A decade later she reported proudly, "A lot of people thought I quit. . . . Didn't have no job other than singing jazz, never had any kind of public assistance, and had no help from what you'd call a husband. I had a husband but it wasn't where I could relax because my husband was making enough money to support me."[3] Meanwhile, the situation for jazz musicians back east had not improved; if anything, it had deteriorated even further. But a handful of people who had formed Jazz Spotlite Productions, an organization designed to keep jazz musicians working, would provide her with occasional gigs over the next few years: "There was one guy here named Jim Harrison who was putting on a lot of concerts around New York City at that time, not a lot of big places, but he was doing the best he could. He lost his shirt putting on me and a whole lot of other guys during that whole period, but he was really trying. And it kind of helped us in our egos that somebody was trying at that time to keep us going."[4] Harrison had started producing concerts by forming a fan club for Jackie McLean in the early 1960s. The purpose of the club was to present McLean in a concert format because the saxophonist did not have a cabaret license and therefore could not work in clubs that served alcohol. Harrison and his collaborators presented McLean simply because they wanted to hear him; they did not expect to make a profit: "You have to be not afraid not to lose money because [drawing a crowd's] not a sure thing."[5] Since 1965, Harrison had been working for Jazzmobile, an organization dedicated to bringing jazz to black neighborhoods by literally taking it to the streets. With money he made doing promotion work for clubs, working with Jazzmobile and with bassist Larry Ridley at Rutgers University in New Brunswick, he put on concerts. "We tried to create outlets for these artists.

Did a lot of stuff with Hank Mobley and [Art] Blakey and Betty [Carter], Tina Brooks . . . Milt Jackson and Jimmy Heath."[6] With two or three other promoters who pooled their resources to present the music, Harrison helped keep the sounds of straight-ahead jazz alive.[7]

Initially Jazz Spotlite Productions presented jazz events mainly out of Club Ruby in Jamaica, New York, from 1965 to 1969. After that club closed, several venues in New York City eventually came to form a kind of circuit that included Cami Hall, the Mark Ballroom in Union Square, at West Sixteenth Street and Broadway, Town Hall, and later, Club Baron at Lenox Avenue and 132nd Street. In the early 1970s Harrison often presented Carter and Art Blakey on the same bill. The arrangement between Carter and Harrison was informal, not exclusive, and he recalled that other promoters also presented Carter during this period.[8] Nor did he book her when she went on the road. Nevertheless, the promotional literature Carter circulated then as part of a press kit included contact information for Harrison's organization. With no chance of making a dent in a recording industry gone cold on her brand of jazz, Carter managed to scrape by from gig to gig. Apart from her devoted followers, whose dedication sustained her through this dark period, many who had once admired her work thought she had quit singing, or even died.

Then, at the very end of the decade the singer struck upon the idea of producing her own records. This was hardly a novel idea. Some musicians including Lionel Hampton and Dizzy Gillespie had done so years before, and others such as Charles Mingus were still pursuing this option. Furthermore, the notion that she could take charge of her recording career, in addition to being consistent with her need for autonomy, was a logical outgrowth of her associations with Gladys Hampton and Gigi Gryce. The spark for Carter came from two people associated with Jazz Spotlite Productions—Orville O'Brien and Ben Taylor. O'Brien had done sound at Club Ruby, and, according to Harrison, with some success, he had already taped and sold an event that took place there, a concert of four or five trumpets and a rhythm section.[9] By this time Carter had given up any hope of finding a label that would not try to mold her into a hit singer. This business venture gave her more say in how her music was produced and promoted than she had previously known. Another important element in the scheme was the idea of recording her live rather than in a studio setting. Perhaps the key feature of the deal was that she "got a piece of the company,"[10] or would receive a portion of the profits from its sales. They called the label Bush Records. "We were ambitious blacks starting our own record company jazz-wise."[11]

This next step was made possible by the fact that Carter had begun to think of the musicians she contracted for club dates as her own trio. At first this shift was more a matter of attitude than any concrete change in the way she did business. She certainly was not paying her musicians any more than she had before her residency in California, nor was she providing them with steady work. But working consistently with John Hicks through much of 1966 had helped solidify her charts. From that experience she learned that having a stable rapport with her musicians—especially with her pianist—was necessary to develop her ideas.

Her pianist at this time was Norman Sarney Simmons. Born in Chicago on 6 October 1929, Simmons had made a reputation in the Chicago scene working first with saxophonist Clifford Jordan in 1946 and then as the house pianist of the Bee Hive until 1956, where he backed singles who were visiting the Windy City on their Midwest tours. After working at the C & C Lounge until 1959 backing singers Dakota Staton and, later, Ernestine Anderson, he came to New York City. During the 1960s he was Carmen McRae's pianist, and Carter first met him at such venues as the Half Note and the Village Gate when McRae performed there.[12] Simmons recalled an impromptu jam session that evolved from one of these dates:

> Several musicians of note mounted the stand to jam—Jimmy Cobb on drums, Willie Ruff on French horn, Vic Sproles on bass. I can't remember who else, but Betty was up there. There were several musicians in the audience also, including Miles Davis and Bobby Hackett. Betty sang some notes I wish I could find on the piano. She sounded as far into it as any horn I'd heard play and she was singing fantastic lines and intervals. Miles got turned on and borrowed Bobby Hackett's trumpet to get up there and join her. It was really a beautiful session.[13]

The pianist had recently ended his long association with McRae, who had moved to Los Angeles in 1967. As a collaborator, he appreciated Carter's self-reliance, her ability to deal with harmonic complexity, and her approach to arranging: "Most singers' formats rest heavily on the piano as an orchestral instrument; Betty's does not. Her format has no orchestral sound that is planned or expected. . . . The mind is therefore freer because you do not have to orchestrate for her high notes, breathing, [etc.]."[14] In addition to her new pianist she also had bassist Lyle Atkinson and drummer Al Harewood, who had been in Gigi Gryce's circle in the mid-1950s.[15] She later told Stuart Nicholson that she had been with these players for "about a year, eighteen months" by the time they recorded, so, in addition to having jelled as an ensemble, the rhythm section understood her musical expectations: "By then they *knew* what I wanted, OK!"[16] The group's cohesiveness, forged more in performance than rehearsal, allowed Carter to expand upon her charts and galvanized her to record.

Bush Records was officially launched toward the end of 1969 when O'Brien and Taylor taped shows at two different locations: Judson Hall and Club Ruby on Long Island.[17] In September they had also recorded a set at the latter venue, but the bulk of the material for their first record probably came from two sets that Carter performed at Judson Hall on 6 December. For reasons that will become clear, the tracks from this date were not released until nearly seven years later, when Roulette records issued them with the titles *Finally–Betty Carter* and *Betty Carter: Round Midnight.*

Working live energized Carter. Speaking of this concert, she later reported, "An audience makes me think, makes me reach for things I'd never try in the studio."[18] *Down Beat* reviewer Tam Fiofori reported that "she transformed the concert setting at Judson Hall into an intimate club-like environment, holding listeners spellbound," adding that "she had the audience so geared to listening and responding naturally that there was no need for a pep talk from the producer prior to the concert or other props one suspects are normally used at live recordings."[19] The original order of the songs was not retained when this material was released, but these sets are important for being the first commercially available document of Carter's live approach.

One of the central challenges of constructing a set is generating enough contrast to sustain listeners' attention over the course of an hour or so. Carter employed all the weapons in her arsenal, tunes and arrangements, as well as changes of tempo, meter, dynamic, key, and texture, to engage her audience in the aesthetic process. After the trio's warm-up numbers, for example, she would typically change the energy—if it had been up, she would sing a ballad; if not, she would break into an up-tempo tune. The opposition this created with what came before amplified the impact of her entrance. As the set progressed, her choice of tune could also be dictated by the crowd's energy and response: if the audience seemed excited, a ballad would bring her listeners into a more reflective frame of mind; if, on the other hand, the audience was subdued, a comic tune or sizzling up tempo number would lift the mood. According to Fiofori, after the instrumental numbers Carter appeared on the bandstand dressed in black pants, a black blouse, a gold scarf, and a peaked gold cap.[20]

She started her segment with "What's New," followed by a medley of nostalgic tunes: "Seems Like Old Times," "I Remember You," and "(You Forgot To) Remember." She had experimented with putting songs together to create longer narratives along a single theme before. Her medley of tunes associated with Billie Holiday, consisting of "God Bless the Child," "Don't Weep for the Lady," and "I'm Pulling Through,"[21] dated back to her shows opposite Miles Davis and Ray Charles. But doing so now became a strategy for varying the musical flow within her sets, enabling her to counteract the fragmenting effect individual songs can have. Recently she had linked "Body and Soul" with "Heart and Soul," which she had recorded for Atco. In such extended arrangements, she showed off her musicality by organizing the tunes so as to create a formal sense of growth, with a clear beginning, middle, and end. Arranging such tunes as "I Didn't Know What Time It Was," "All the Things You Are," and "I Could Write a Book," in the form of a medley, for example, enabled Carter to move through a sequence of tempos, as if performing a suite—with the two choruses of the latter tune corresponding to the slow movement and finale, respectively. Embedded in medleys, staples from her repertoire were juxtaposed with newer songs, creating fresh contexts that allowed them to take on new meanings.

Carter's growing proficiency as an arranger was on display in individual tunes as well. This growth is perhaps especially evident on tunes she had recorded before, such as "'Round Midnight." Here Carter imaginatively applies the idea of long meter, stretching each measure of Thelonious Monk's tune into four measures of 3/4 time, with each ternary beat of the original now expanding to fill out the new measure. As the band moves in an up-tempo feel, the vocal line floats over it in slow motion, creating a haunting disjunction. Modifying the tune's metric structure forced her to reconceive the line rhythmically, shifting the metric placement of Babs Gonzales's words. Rather than being an accidental by-product of her approach, this was an effect she sought in order to spur herself on creatively: "If you change to three-four time, you have to deal with the lyrics differently and the words flow differently."[22]

Her propensity for creating timbral contrast was increasing as well. A striking amount of unaccompanied singing occurs in these performances. In such passages Carter demonstrates that she could stay on pitch and hear complex harmonic relationships, but she also made use of the texture for dramatic effect. Her a capella delivery of the closing lines of "Body and Soul," for example, fragmented into short phrases separated by long pauses to intensify the lyrics' emotion, helped her sustain the song's musical growth as well as its dramatic line into the following tune of the medley. After Carter sings "it looks like the ending" at the final measures of the bridge [4:27], the trio drops out (a musical pun on ending?), and, unaccompanied, Carter sings, "unless I can have just one more chance to prove, dear. My life's a wreck, you're making; you know, I'm yours so please just take me, I'd gladly surrender, myself, my body, and [my heart and soul]." Without benefit of harmonic support she makes a transition from F-sharp major back to the tune's tonic of G major, then on to the B flat-major of "Heart and Soul." By musically depicting her nakedness—stripped of the musical fabric, so to speak—and offering herself so vulnerably, she turns what is normally delivered as an earnest cry of distress into a sexual gambit.

Betty Carter's bold use of the unaccompanied vocal line on these dates seems to herald the greater independence she exhibited after her return from California. It also is reminiscent of Miles Davis's use of cadenzas in his arrangements, such as at the end of his versions of "My Funny Valentine" from the 1950s, or his entrance in the version from Philharmonic Hall in 1964. Davis's oblique use of the melody in these performances and others like them may have drawn the singer toward her increasingly free approach to standards. Her exceedingly slow ballad tempos could also be traced to Davis, but more likely she was drawing upon the inspiration of her friend Jimmy Scott, who was hugely influential among singers from Carter's generation. From as far back as her time with Hampton, with whom Scott also sang, Carter was conscious of Scott's use of laying back, or back phrasing, to create swing, and from him she learned how to sustain a slow ballad's mood and growth for an entire chorus convincingly. In her interview with Leonard Lyons she referred to Scott as the best "delay action" singer.[23]

In addition to timbral contrast, Carter increasingly used changes in dynamics to reinforce the emotional journey of a song's lyrics to its climax as well as to sustain the music's growth from beginning to end. During this time she came to pay close attention to the power of dynamics to impart movement to an arrangement. Her sudden changes of energy, from deeply interior to explosively extroverted, also forced her band members to operate at peak alertness. The music's emotional volatility, in addition to keeping the players actively engaged in the music-making process, brought listeners to the edge of their seat as well. Later in her career the singer would forbid the engineer who ran the mixing board during her performances from following her dynamic level, demanding that he just set the microphone levels so she could control the dynamics vocally.[24]

The "grand finale" with which Carter closed the first set of her Judson Hall date, an eight-and-a-half-minute rendition of "The Surrey with the Fringe on Top," illustrates how effectively she could use dynamics to build and sustain movement over long stretches of time. She launches the arrangement simply enough by paraphrasing the melody over a walking bassline, saving piano and drums for surprising accents at measure 8, and again at measure 16, at the words "and their eyes will pop!" As much as they evoked chuckles from the crowd, these explosions are not entirely frivolous, for they give audible shape to the form by marking its structural points; but, onstage, she amplified the accents' comic effect with facial expressions. Using the same lyrics in the next chorus she moves further away from the tune, exploiting the richer harmonic support and dynamic intensity the full rhythm section is now providing. Carter then takes two scat choruses. The first of these recalls the opening, with the band returning to the head's instrumentation and Carter again paraphrasing the melody. In the following chorus the band plays time, helping her to escalate the energy of her improvisation, which then spills out into an extended coda, where the rhythm section generates a stream of variations on the turnaround while Carter shows off her rhythmic and melodic inventiveness.[25] Although she insisted that she did not intentionally adopt the sound quality of any instrument, here Carter responds to the timbre of her supporting instruments to create a dialogue with each player in turn. Her rhythmic ingenuity is most apparent when she riffs, layering short repeated melodic figures polyrhythmically against the time to create powerful surges of movement that crest and dissipate in waves of sound. As a horn player would, Carter directs the rhythm section with her line, stirring it to overflowing or reining it in via abrupt or gradual changes in dynamics and rhythmic feel.

She conducted the rhythm section as well through her characteristic way of moving onstage, which grew naturally from her physical response to the music.[26] In her movements about the stage Carter played to different segments of the house.[27] By directing passages of her singing to each player individually she also guided the audience to an awareness of his particular role in the proceedings. The turnaround codas of her set closers gave her an opportunity to announce the names of her band members, further drawing attention to each player's contribution. By merging her vocal sound into the intricate textures she created in her arrangements, Carter challenged listeners to hear her voice not as the centerpiece with an accompaniment but as an integrated component within a complex web of sound. In later recordings she would require that her voice not be given undue prominence in the final mix down. Likening her method to a cooking technique in which sugar and whipped egg whites are mixed together to make a smoothly textured meringue, Carter once described her approach to lyrics as "folding your line."[28] I suspect it was this approach, which exemplifies her convictions about the rootedness of the music in community, that won Carter the advocacy of instrumentalists. As much as she could act like a prima donna, as much as she was the band leader, arranger, contractor, and boss, when she was performing she was simply one of the musicians, working with them shoulder-to-shoulder to make the music happen.

Compared to her studio recordings from before, these performances reveal a higher degree of risk taking. Her earliest scat solos were constrained by the big-band arrangements she was fitting into, but even in her own arrangements on *Inside Betty Carter* there is a greater reliance on forethought.

Carter reinforced this point in 1978, saying of her improvising that "nobody's doing it the way I'm doing it, and I'm scatting now from the hip—it's never the same."[29]

The second set further illustrates Carter's growing command of arranging and improvising, including "I Only Have Eyes for You," "My Shining Hour," "Girl Talk," and ending with a version of "All through the Day," complete with scatted finale to culminate the set. Her greater sophistication made it possible for such tunes as "By the Bend of the River," and "I Could Write a Book," to remain in her book for over a dozen years without losing any of their luster. While Carter was constantly on the lookout for new songs, she herself admitted that it took her a long time to forge an interpretation. Her deliberation over new material contributed to the slow turnover of her book. Periodically she renewed her repertoire by overhauling her charts, and from one night to the next she kept them interesting by improvising on them in varying degrees. A recording of her material from this time, performed live at the Village Vanguard soon after the Judson date, reveals that, when she was singing lyrics, the broad outlines of what she sang were fixed ahead of time, providing a framework for interpretive touches that lent her renditions spontaneity.

A comparison of the version of "I Could Write a Book" (example 9) from the Roulette release of the Bush tapes with the one she had done in 1955 (example 2) reveals the extent to which she reworked her tunes. Performing the opening statement rubato, accompanied only by piano, Carter leads Norman Simmons through a range of tempos from 84 to 168 beats per minute (in the transcription the changes indicate only the form, not the rhythmic placement of the chords or the substitutions Simmons uses). As Carter sustains the final pitch of this statement, the rest of the band enters to introduce the next chorus's breakneck tempo, which moves between 264 and 276 beats per minute. She then proceeds to deliver the lyrics yet again. The new line she sings here shares certain structural features with the opening statement, but the dramatically new tempo, dynamics, and feeling obscure these similarities. With the band churning away, she wisely places the bulk of her line at the top of her chest voice to rival the players' strong dynamic. Ignoring repetitions within the original melody's ABAB′ scheme—the return of the original melody's A section at measure 49, for example—she casts formal articulations aside. Instead, a restless unpredictability propels the music's mad dash to the finish, where Carter wryly comments on the coda of her Epic recording of the same tune by converting the earlier arrangement's falling cycle of fifths figure into a descending chromatic sequence.

By this time Carter was unabashedly using standards as grist for her creative process. Aside from sharing lyrics and chord changes with Richard

Rodgers's composition, for example, this version of "I Could Write a Book" is unrecognizable as his song. To her ears, rhythmically and melodically recasting the original melodic line so it more closely conformed to the way she spoke not only personalized her rendition, it also rescued the lyrics from the rhythmic straightjacket imposed upon them by the line's motivic structure. Her revisions frequently masked the lyrics' rhyme scheme, for example, averting the "jingle" at phrase endings that can often trivialize a song's message. The resulting interpretations were so far afield of the original melody that they reflected her personal aesthetic only, and the songwriter's not at all. She reasoned that the composer may have to organize the music a particular way, "just to make the package good, make the thirty-two bars come out right" even though the music he comes up with may not fit the words all that well, adding, "Everything else, 90 percent of the song is OK, but there may be one phrase that he just may have to write a certain way that if you don't read that lyric carefully, you will lose the meaning of it."[30] Judging from Carter's approach to teaching singers at the end of her career, she probably began to form an interpretation by removing the lyrics from their musical setting and speaking them, perhaps over the changes, so that her delivery was guided by her own reading of the song's text.[31] Such an approach enabled her to spin a new line out of the words' inherent musical qualities. This line evolved into a somewhat fixed melody of her own devising, a bebop head in effect, built upon the song's changes. Carter kept her renditions of this newly composed—but not written-out—theme fresh by inventing nuances on the spur of the moment that obscured the connection between one performance and another. The effect, however, was of improvising an entirely new line while singing the lyrics.

By bringing out the music inherent in the words, words that a lyricist had often added onto the composer's melody after it had been written, Carter was able both to focus her interpretation on the verbal meaning of the lyrics—indeed, convey most effectively her understanding of them—while also creating a rendition that was viable as music. She advised other singers not to sacrifice meaning when forging their interpretations: "If you can improve on the composers lyrics, make them more understandable. Now my musicianship allows me to improvise, . . . change the composer's melody . . . [but] I never lost the meaning of the lyric. . . . I've heard people attempt to change a song around and lost the lyric too."[32]

During the Bush date the record production went according to plan. Then, after having engineered the tapes, Ben Taylor and Orville O'Brien consulted with Carter and put together a tape of the songs she wanted released, and they catalogued their first master as Bush 907. Carter now had a recorded document of her latest work, which acceptably represented her art despite its crude sound quality. Her partners were in charge of the postproduction phase: having the masters pressed into LPs, the LPs wrapped in record jackets, and the product distributed to retail outlets, et cetera.

But something was not right. Carter sensed trouble when O'Brien started talking about buying an airplane with money derived from the project. Lillian Conrad, who worked at Peerless Plastics, the pressing plant, was the first to realize that O'Brien intended to release the tapes on his own. At Conrad's suggestion, James Redding and Carter drove together to the factory at 333 North Drive in North Plainfield, New Jersey, loaded up all five thousand of the record jackets O'Brien was expecting to have mailed to him, and brought them home.[33] They thwarted O'Brien's scheme for the time being. But he still had the masters, and he could still sell them.[34] Carter was generally discreet about discussing the Bush debacle directly, but much later she acknowledged that the people she had gotten involved with were no better than gangsters and that she was in over her head for "a few minutes."[35]

Betty Carter was now resolved to form a record label that was hers alone. Because the planned release of the Judson Hall material had been mentioned in the concert review, the singer felt she had no choice but to produce herself in order to avoid professional embarrassment. As she later put it: "We had created such a demand by saying it was going to be released on Bush."[36] She named her company Bet-Car Records, perhaps with echoes of Gladys Hampton's label, Glad-Hamp, ringing in her ear. She even found a way to include her sons in this project. Preceded by an "MK," the catalog number she used for each recording was a reference to their names, Myles and Kagle, as was the name of her publishing company, MyKag. Later, when speaking of Bet-Car she often traced the company's beginnings back to the tapes of her Judson Hall concert, even though they were never released on her label.

To pursue the venture entirely on her own would have been impossible. Fortunately, Carter had a few guardian angels waiting in the wings. Without the encouragement of Lillian Conrad, for example, she might not have sustained the momentum toward her goal.[37] The older woman allowed her set up office space at Peerless Plastics and use the location as a mailing address for her label.[38] With Conrad on hand to help with postproduction, Carter proceeded with her plan.[39]

She booked the Village Vanguard on 24 May 1970 from 3:00 to 8:00 P.M., and, using identical personnel and many of the tunes she had performed for her Bush dates, she recorded this date for her newly formed company. Because her forty-first birthday had fallen about a week before, Carter had the event catered by Stegwood Caterers from the Bronx and billed it as a birthday celebration,[40] although she later suggested that it was her father's birthday that she had had in mind.[41] Judging from the recording, those in attendance formed a small but spirited audience. Undeterred by the low turnout, Carter sounds even more self-assured than she did at Judson Hall. Taken together, the Bush and Bet-Car recordings give us the nearest instances we have to alternate takes in the Carter discography. Carter admitted that her first foray into record production, which she called, simply, *Betty Carter,* suffered technically because of sound "bleeding over everything." Despite the poor mixing job, however, she took pride in the record because "the feeling was there."[42] Carter did not initially recoup the four thousand dollars it cost to make the record, but she did ultimately see some returns from its sales. By 1985 she had done about two and a half pressings of it at five thousand records per pressing.[43]

While she initially formed Bet-Car Records out of necessity, Carter ultimately came to embrace this course of action wholeheartedly: "I'm going it myself, and I'm very proud. . . . Well, it's not very difficult once you get through the initial package. The pressing, labels, jackets—then it's up to the technicians the label people, the jacket people."[44] By 1972, Carter had taken in stride her new role as entrepreneur: "I can hire my own engineer and go into the studio and do it. It will take me maybe six months, where it may take a record company two weeks. . . . I can do what I want to do, sing the way I want to sing, and nobody tells me what to do. I don't have to worry about the executives in the booth. I tell them what to do when it comes to recording."[45] In December of that year, speaking to Arthur Taylor, she emphasized the control she now had over the business end as well: "I recorded myself, and it actually did quite well. In other words, I know exactly how many records I sold and I got the money, so it was to my advantage. It's out there, and people are buying it. It's not overwhelming, but its mine."[46]

In her new role Carter had to learn about aspects of the music business with which musicians rarely come in contact, such as marketing and distribution.[47] Without a distributor, Carter initially had no formal avenue for getting the record out to the public. She refused to sell records at her club dates because she wanted to create a market demand for her records, so she opted instead to act as her own sales representative to record shops: "I used to just tear out the record store listings in the Yellow Pages everywhere I went, then contact the shops to take records. . . . There were a few mom-and-pop record shops in every city that took five or ten copies on consignment. . . . Lillian Conrad used to press Folkways albums, so she had some ins with distributors."[48] The New Music Distribution Service of the Jazz Composer's Orchestra Association also sent out her records on consignment. At first the sales were nominal, but the novice executive's highly disciplined marketing strategy ultimately paid off: by the time Bet-Car was ten years old, demand for her records was high enough to warrant the services of a larger independent distributor. It was then that Carter arranged with Rounder Records in Somerville, Massachusetts, another outfit associated primarily with the folk music market, to distribute her records.[49]

During this time opportunities for gigging had not improved much, and Betty Carter was therefore not receiving much press coverage. When she did, however, the critical response to her singing was positive. John Wilson's review of Carter's appearance at Cami Hall (formerly Judson Hall) at the end of March 1971—which was apparently recorded but never issued commercially—reveals that her concept had begun to grow on him:

> For a time Betty Carter has obscured her vocal talents under a cumbersome set of mannerisms that were sometimes laid on so thick that whatever she might be singing disappeared completely. But she is beginning to use these vocal gambits to advantage. . . . She has a supple voice that ranges from sonorous low notes to a well-controlled falsetto, a voice with subtle shadings and nuances and an appealing texture. It has been her tendency to exaggerate these elements that has resulted in her mannered style. But when she uses them with sensitivity, she lets her true qualities come out. . . . She still overwhelms some of her songs with vocal tricks, but the gimmickry is becoming less obvious and, in some of her more playful scat numbers, she uses it judiciously to good effect.[50]

During 1971 Carter's marriage to James Redding, which had been tenuous for some time, frayed to the breaking point, and she left him. Nevertheless, although the two had not been formally wed, by this time they had certainly established a common-law marriage and Carter identified herself as married in a press release from the early 1970s. Nor did the two take any action to formally end the marriage. By 1972 Daniel Mixon had become her regular pianist, and this working relationship soon evolved into a romantic one.

Born in New York in 1949, Mixon had made a name for himself in Atlantic City during the mid-1960s, originally playing organ behind rock and R&B acts such as Patty LaBelle and the Bluebells. More recently, from 1967 to 1970 he had accompanied singer Joe Lee Wilson and he had been working with Kenny Dorham not long before the trumpeter died in December 1972. According to Mixon, Jim Harrison had sought him out at Slugs in order to put him in touch with Carter, and she arranged an audition for him at a studio in Manhattan. During his first years as her pianist he also led his own trio and worked with Stanley Cowell's Piano Choir, but shortly he would drop the latter association in order to lead her rhythm section exclusively. Carter had grown close to Mixon in this period, and soon she, Mixon, and her sons moved into a brownstone in the pianist's old neighborhood, the Fort Greene section of Brooklyn, at 117 Saint Felix Street.[51]

Many African Americans had moved to Brooklyn during the 1960s and 1970s, spilling beyond the predominantly black neighborhoods of Bedford-Stuyvesant and Crown Heights into nearby sections.[52] By 1979 the Fort Greene community would consist largely of low-income families.[53] The projects to the west of Fort Greene Park were rife with drug traffic. The public schools in the area were essentially segregated.[54] A sizable proportion of the relatively small number of residents in Fort Greene—it would be about 73,600 by 1974—formed a close-knit neighborhood, however,[55] and as the jazz community continued to become more and more embattled and fractured, the neighborhood's cohesiveness gave Carter a sense of place. It certainly helped that other musicians soon followed her lead, with saxophonist Gary Bartz, drummer Clifford Barbaro, and bassist Stafford James all making their homes nearby.[56] Carter's new surroundings inspired her to participate locally, appearing with Art Blakey in a benefit concert at the East, a thriving black cultural center in Bedford Stuyvesant founded in 1969 by Muslim activist Jitu Weusi (formerly Les Campbell).[57]

Being able to rehearse with her pianist to her heart's content enhanced Carter's musical growth, and she began to compose more prolifically than at any other time in her career. Aside from Mixon, however, her trio personnel was unstable.[58] From 1972 to 1975 she went through a string of bassists, including Wayne Dockery, Wilbur Little, Stafford James, George "Duke" Cleamons, Milton Suggs, and Buster Williams—who had worked with her a decade earlier and who lasted longer than most. The drum chair was somewhat more stable during this period, being occupied at turns by Clifford Barbaro, Greg Bandy, and Alfred "Chip" Lyles. In August 1972 Carter took her trio to Alice Tully Hall to perform in a double bill with Max Roach's percussion ensemble M'Boom, but this was an exceptionally high-profile gig amid her much less glamorous standard fare. If she was working at all, she would more likely be found singing in some dive—Slugs, for example, which was notorious for being the site where Lee Morgan had been shot dead by his mistress eight months earlier. Mixon recalled working with fair regularity at the Needle's Eye on Little West Twelfth Street, a storefront with the bandstand in the window where the musicians had to climb under the bar to get onstage. They worked there every other month for about a year, mostly on weekends.[59] In general, however, the work was tight, with weeks elapsing between gigs. When on the road they often saved money by staying with friends.

Having a newly minted record enabled Carter to promote her work by sending samples to college radio stations, and as a result, such institutions started to become important venues for her. In February 1972 she took her trio to Goddard College in Vermont,[60] and later that year she performed at Antioch College and—at Larry Ridley's invitation—at Livingston College of Rutgers University. These dates were significant to Carter because she had wanted to bring her work to colleges as early as the mid-1960s. Since those early efforts she had formulated an educational agenda. Around this time she spoke candidly about the status of jazz as a black cultural legacy and about the authority of African American musicians within this legacy: "The black is authentic jazz. Sure, some white musicians have made their mark in jazz. They play well, interpret well. Sure some blacks listen to some whites. There are white singers I like. But the leaders, the originators have all been black."[61] For Carter it was the responsibility of black musicians and the black community to sustain their heritage. She felt strongly that the control exercised by the media prevented jazz from reaching its people. "What worries me is that black people are not hearing Charlie Parker and Lester Young. . . . Just turn on your radio and see what you get. It ain't jazz. The kids up in Harlem are not getting the straight, pure, swinging sounds. Their music. Their history. Their culture."[62] Going beyond grumbling, Carter offered pragmatic solutions to the problem, solutions she felt were within her people's control: "If every black disc jockey in the country would play one jazz track every hour he's on the air, just think how much jazz would be heard nationally! . . . Just a few minutes of each hour is all it amounts to. No one would suffer, no one would lose any *money.*"[63] She also wanted to expand upon Jazz Month, an event that took place in New York each April in which concerts, lectures, record sales, and radio programs were used to promote jazz. She felt that, if each of twelve major cities adopted a different month of the year as its Jazz Month, not only would it provide musicians with more work, it would also effectively spread jazz across the country.[64]

Early in 1972 she began to make plans to produce a children's record called *Who Said Jazz Is Dead?*—her direct response to a *Newsweek* cover story that had implied as much at the end of the 1960s. This question preoccupied her, according to Mixon.[65] Using a *Down Beat* interview to address her black listeners, Carter proclaimed: "Jazz is your culture. Don't believe them when they go around saying jazz is dead. You can't kill culture that easily. Not black culture. 'Cause if jazz is dead, so are you."[66] She hoped to fight the erosion of black people's heritage by taking her children's record into the schools. By the end of the year Carter had formed a clear idea of where she was going with this project and had even begun to negotiate a distribution deal with Scholastic Records:[67]

> It's not going to be eenie, meenie, miney, mo. It's going to be my introduction to music so far as jazz is concerned, for children. We're going to do lively things, advisable things and nice things but they're all going to do with the jazz atmosphere. . . . My album, I hope, will put a new dimension on what they've been learning in school, in terms of "Jack and Jill went up the hill." If I do "Jack and Jill went up the hill," it will be done a different way than it was ever done before. . . . It's going through the educational system first and I hope I can put it on the racks in the record shops.[68]

As she observed the influence pop music had on children, including her own, she became more and more interested in reaching people when they were young: "I read somewhere that music has to have a folk feeling to get across to kids, but I don't believe it. . . . If kids hear jazz young enough, they'll understand what it's supposed to feel like. Why should they wait until they're in high school or college before they're exposed to it?"[69]

During this time her repertoire included material from the children's album, including such titles as "Congolese Children" (which included lyrics in both English and Swahili), "Listen to Thy Parents," and "Life Is Growing Up, Daughter."[70] Later she spoke of the positive tone of the material: "It would be fun lyrics for kids, but it would be swung for adults. Well you know that's the way you're gonna get the kids. You gotta tell it like it is. You can't swing any way, but the one way. So that's very important that the kids hear that."[71] Carter did not use a didactic approach, but instead, offered words of encouragement to aspiring young artists: "One of the tunes on the children's album I'm putting together says: 'Don't be afraid of a mistake! A mistake is all that it is.'"[72] For Carter, another purpose of the project was to stimulate young peoples' creativity, a goal that transcended racial boundaries. "The youth of today is lacking in individualism, and I don't mean just black youths; I mean white youth, too. . . . In other words, I want to be able to tell the difference between one tenor player and another tenor player."[73] Her highest ideals, independence and individualism, were ones Carter impressed not only on her own children, but on her trio members as well. If she sensed ambivalence in one of her players, she would grow impatient, urging him to think for himself. Carter sustained her belief in *Who Said Jazz Is Dead?* until 1976, but she did not complete it, nor did she mention it after that time.

Carter had other plans for promoting African American culture, such as forming a foundation to present scholarships in Ella Fitzgerald's name. In December 1972 she was optimistic about this project:

> I have put all the wheels in motion that will make it successful, and I hope I won't have too much of a problem. I want to do two shows a day

> in Harlem for a week, with individual singers at each show. For instance, Lena Horne, Sarah Vaughan, Carmen McRae, Aretha Franklin, Barbra Streisand, Morgana King, Vikki Carr, Nancy Wilson, Totie Fields and Moms Mabley—all women, in other words. We black people have never paid tribute to Ella Fitzgerald, and I don't think we should wait until it's too late.[74]

As late as the following April she still had plans to do a tribute concert with Aretha Franklin. According to Mixon she made phone calls and wrote letters, but as with the children's record, this idea did not make it off the drawing board.

In February 1973 Carter gave an important concert in Boston. Her friend Ora Ross Harris, who would become her booking agent much later on, and singer Mattie Mangrum arranged for her to appear in Brown Recital Hall at the New England Conservatory.[75] After the trio played their opening numbers Carter emerged from the crowd singing Emil Boyd and Hal Smith's "I Love Music." The set included songs from the projected children's album. Surprisingly, she also performed the Jackson Five hit "Never Can Say Goodbye" in an arrangement that ranged through a variety of styles and grooves from Latin to rock to straight four.[76] The following afternoon Carter gave a master class at the conservatory.[77] This event and a concert in June at Town Hall in New York City organized by Jazz Spotlite Productions gave Carter a much needed boost in an otherwise uneventful year, as did a reissue of *Inside Betty Carter*.[78] Incorrectly describing the record as Carter's most recent commercial endeavor—due to slow distribution, her first record on her own label would take a while to make an impression—and erroneously dating it from 1963, an otherwise strong review of *Inside Betty Carter* in *Coda* may have added to the notion among those unfamiliar with her recent work that she had dropped out of the jazz scene.

Toward the end of 1973 Carter began to produce her second record for Bet-Car records, which she had planned to release by July 1974.[79] Disruptions in the personnel of her trio would lead to delays in its release, and the record ultimately took shape during several sessions over the next few years. When she began the record her trio included, in addition to Mixon, Buster Williams on bass and Chip Lyles on drums, and she cut four tracks with this group. Later she replaced Lyles with Louis Hayes for three other tracks. During a period of conflict with Mixon she replaced him with pianist Onaje Allen Gumbs for the remaining three tracks.

Carter's longtime friend Joel Dorn arranged for studio time at Regent Sound, where she had made *Inside Betty Carter* a decade before. Dorn ran his production company, the Masked Announcer, out of this studio and he owed her a favor.[80] Due to personality conflicts with Carter, the studio owner, Bob

Lifton, would have nothing to do with her, and he assigned sound engineer Joe Ferla to record her sessions. Ferla was twenty-four years old and had recorded much rock and R&B, but had no prior experience with jazz. Capitalizing upon the fact that she was not paying for studio time, Carter and Ferla spent hours developing recording and mixing techniques by trial and error to confront the jazz idiom's, and the singer's, idiosyncratic demands. After the songs were recorded, Carter worked closely with Ferla to convey how she wanted her concept to come across. While monitoring Ferla's every fader adjustment, she was also educating herself about the art of sculpting sound with recording technology. She learned how sounds may be tailed off, or tucked into the texture, and how to exploit stereo technology to create movement by directing the signal from an unmixed track to one speaker or another—that is, adjusting the panning position—as well as how to fix musical errors that marred an otherwise excellent take through tape editing and other means.[81] Overdubbing scatted "fills" for her own vocals on the first and last cuts of the album, "You're a Sweetheart" and "Sounds," and singing harmony with herself on "Sunday, Monday, or Always," Carter took advantage of the different possibilities the medium offered her to realize her sound image on tape.[82] According to Ferla, the final version of "Sounds" is the amalgam of different takes spliced together, suggesting that its episodic form grew in part from the recording process. Ferla would become her recording engineer for the rest of her career, recording and mixing all but two of her remaining LPs.

Significantly, of the album's ten tracks, six are Carter originals, including an up-tempo remake of "I Can't Help It," "What Is It?" "We Tried," "Happy," "Tight," and the tour de force "Sounds," more than seven minutes long and featuring extensive scatting. The lyrics to several of the songs have a confessional character, and it is easy to read meanings into them that relate to her personal life. If this is the case, she was opening up new avenues of expression and new levels of intimacy with her listener. The record was released in 1976 with the title *The Betty Carter Album,* but Carter affectionately referred to her first two Bet-Car issues as volumes 1 and 2.

Carter's new version of her anthem "I Can't Help It" has a cocky reassurance that is conveyed primarily by her choice of tempo, but her phrasing also signals the song's new mood (example 10). In retrospect, the ballad version from 1957 (example 5) sounds almost apologetic when held up to this fresh reading of the lyrics. Simply in the way the singer suspends the word "I" for a moment at the outset announces that the central topic under discussion will be Betty Carter. In the bold bends and swoops and the passages that start out of tune and gradually resolve, such as in measures 22–24 and measures 30–31, the singer forcefully asserts of her own unique way of singing. Her use of blues gestures in measures 66–68 is striking, as is the change to waltz time at the end.

The familiar verse "Children Live What They Learn" set to music by Dorothy Law Nolt was likely a vestige of her children's album. Built upon a figure that is reminiscent of the bass line to "All Blues," the song closes with a funky groove, a surprising twist given Carter's attitude about fusion. She encouraged Ferla to bring his experience with popular music to the song, and he muffled the sound of the bass drum head so the drummer could play with a rock feel without covering the sound of the bass.[83] This song, as well as her interpretation of "Girl Talk"—and her performance of "Never Can Say Goodbye," which was never commercially recorded—demonstrates that, as much as Carter had strong feelings about free jazz and fusion, she was not enslaved to her opinions. Carter's two sons appear on the back cover of the album, adding to the impression that it represents an especially personal level of expression. She felt positively about this record, and by 1985 it had been in three pressings.[84] But that was a decade later. In the meantime, she focused on surviving from one week to the next.

9

Breakthrough

In the spring of 1975 the work began to improve. As Carter put it, since April she had been "picking her jobs."[1] By this time Jack Whittemore had begun booking her on a regular basis. In addition to Miles Davis, Whittemore handled several other important jazz acts and was able to give Carter the access to jazz venues that for so long she had been denied. In contrast to many in his line of work, he had a reputation for being honest and treating his acts with respect. Carter had wanted him to book her since the late-1950s, when she had met him through Davis, but he did not generally take on female vocalists. The agent was certainly positioned to have a big impact on her career, but the fact that he added her to his roster was also indicative of the impression she was now making in her own right. Furthermore, in the scene at large there were stirrings of a revived interest in jazz from mainstream audiences and, as a result, from club owners and record executives. Having survived the long drought—indeed, having used it to grow artistically—Carter now stood to benefit from the music's new audience, which included more young people.

That April, Carter had a well-attended appearance at the Keystone Korner on her way back from a successful tour of Japan. "We'd been shipping quite a few of my records by mail order to that area [San Francisco], so I figured it was worth taking a chance. I had made good money in Japan, but Todd Barkan at Keystone couldn't afford me and my musicians, so I just paid for my regular pianist, John Hicks, and his trio to come from New York. Well, we played to six days of standing room only audiences."[2] She had been in touch with her former pianist since he had returned to New York from a teaching job at Southern Illinois University and had hired him for various tasks, such as to write out charts for her.[3] Although she had toured Japan not with her trio but an with all-star combo, it is curious that she turned to Hicks instead of Daniel Mixon, who was living with her and was, in fact, still her regular pianist.

In his enthusiasm for her work, club owner Todd Barkan urged Bob Krasnow, who was interested in acquiring jazz talent for the Warner Brothers label, to listen to *Inside Betty Carter.* Krasnow noticed on the back of the record jacket that she had made the record at Regent Sound, and he proposed that Joel Dorn introduce him to Carter.[4] After Dorn informed Carter that Warner Brothers was interested, Krasnow came to New York and met with her at Regent Sound. She left the meeting believing she was on the verge of an agreement with a major label, one that would give her wider distribution and greater visibility than she could get with her small, independent label.[5] Carter felt she had made it clear that, while she was interested in recording for Warner Brothers, she had no intention of working with a producer.

Then, at the end of July, Carter did something out of the ordinary. Taking a break from her trio work, she accepted a starring role in a play-with-music called *Don't Call Me Man.* The play was written by tenor saxophonist Howard Moore, who also acted in the play along with Claude Bossette.[6] In an old converted milk factory in Bedford-Stuyvesant—renamed the Billie Holiday Theater—Carter made her acting debut, playing the role of a singer "hung up on a no-account piano player"[7] who was using her to "get his songs over."[8] Apart from Carter's involvement in the production, which included her singing four of her own songs and lyrics, little about the play was memorable.[9] Given the dramatic sense she brought to her vocal interpretations, the project seems a logical extension of her talents. There was little remuneration involved, but at this point she felt she had nothing to lose by exploring a different forum for her work and a new avenue for exposure: "This is this year's new thing . . . every year the Kid does at least one new thing to keep her going. Money is a small thing, this is good for my artistic spirit."[10] The play ran for two weeks in Brooklyn, and then, after a week's break, moved to the Five Spot in Greenwich Village during the last week of August, where it was not as well attended.[11] Carter's "cult" audience, friends and fellow musicians, including sidemen from Rahsaan Roland Kirk's and Frank Foster's bands, as well as disc jockeys from WRVR and WWRL, came to see her.

A major article appeared in the *Village Voice* proclaiming with a touch of irony, "Betty Carter Is Alive in Bed-Stuy," a fact of which all but her devoted followers had seemed to lose track. Rather than feel embarrassed about her obscurity, however, Carter took pride in her capacity to transcend her difficulties and define success on her own terms: "I had something bigger than being a star. I had this talent that could keep growing. That was something no-one could ever take away from me, no matter what happened. Knowing that made me free."[12] The media coverage the singer garnered from her experiment on the boards gave the general public a new awareness of her talents. Unexpectedly, her role in a shoestring production of a minor theatrical work gained her greater recognition than she had known in the fourteen years since her time with Ray Charles.[13]

During the week between her acting appearances, Carter had an engagement at the Jazz Workshop at 733 Boylston Street in Boston. Carter had had well-attended appearances in the Boston-Cambridge area during the preceding two years, starting with her performance at the New England Conservatory and then later at the University of Massachusetts. Furthermore, she had been keeping track of her record sales, and according to her calculations, 60 percent of the correspondence about her records was then coming from Massachusetts.[14] She was making enough to stay in the Lenox Hotel, but she paid her musicians five hundred dollars each out of her eighteen-hundred-dollar salary, as she had done at the Keystone Korner in April.[15] The ambitious singer had had her sights set on appearing at the Jazz Workshop for some time,[16] but it was not until Todd Barkan told Fred Taylor how well she had done at the Keystone, a room of about the same size as the Workshop, that the Boston club owner offered her a bona fide booking.[17] Accompanied by Daniel Mixon, bassist Milton Suggs, and drummer "Chip" Lyles, she performed to a full house every night.

During the run Carter fired Mixon and Suggs. She was known to dismiss players in a callously offhand manner, but this personnel change was especially turbulent because her relationship with Mixon was both professional and personal. By serving as the fixed center of her trio for the preceding four years, Mixon had provided some stability amid the succession of bassists and drummers. More than any other player she worked with during this period, it was his concept that gave definition to the trio and to her arrangements. Mixon has claimed that they were married;[18] but, although the two had lived together since 1972, Carter did not describe him as her husband. There is no doubt that Mixon played a crucial role in her artistic development, however, and she was probably referring to him when she told Leslie Gourse that a younger musician helped her to feel good about her work during a difficult time in her life. "I was in love with a musician once. One time. After the marriage. . . . I'm not going to tell you who. But it was a new, young experience. Of course he was younger than me. You can't get a new experience with old head. He influenced my music. He was very instrumental in the new spirit I have now."[19]

Carter called John Hicks in the middle of the week to ask him to come to Boston the next day, telling him that she and Mixon had had a falling out. When Hicks couldn't come right away, she got Reggie Moore to come up, but Hicks ended up replacing him later on in the run and joining the trio on a regular basis later that year. He also played for her performances of *Don't Call Me Man* when the show moved to the Five Spot.[20] Apparently the disruptions did not adversely affect her performing. Before a packed house at the Jazz Workshop each night she sang material that came largely from her Bet-Car LPs, and these shows soon generated record sales.

These results fueled Carter's ambition. She was hopeful that Taylor would book her in Paul's Mall, located in an adjacent room on the same premises as the Workshop, which catered to a pop-rock clientele and had a larger room that seated about three hundred. Carter now had reason to believe she could fill such a space. Following her Greenwich Village run of *Don't Call Me Man* she had an important four-day stint at the Bottom Line in New York coming up. Obviously thrilled with her sudden turn of fortune, she was also a bit baffled. She did not have a hit record on the charts; in fact, people could barely find her records in the bins at record shops. Optimistic about the prospect of securing a record contract, she leaked word of the Warner Brothers deal to Bill McLarney while in Boston.[21]

In light of all the attention she was receiving, Carter had come to feel that she was now in a strong bargaining position with Warner Brothers. When she returned from Boston, she called Joel Dorn to apply pressure indirectly on Bob Krasnow to make her a lucrative offer. As she told Leonard Lyons, she confronted Dorn saying: "Look, I'm going to the Bottom Line; and if you all keep from fooling around and I go into the Bottom Line and *pack* it, I won't need Warner Brothers. I have Bet-Car as a label. If things keep going the way they're going, Bet-Car'll be the hip label." Dorn arranged for Krasnow to come to New York City to hear her at the Bottom Line. According to Carter, when she and Dorn spoke a few days later, the conversation went something like this:

> "Well, I think that we have a deal."
> I said, "We've got a *deal?*"
> He said, "You know what the deal was?"
> I said, "What is the deal?"
> He said, "Forty-five to fifty thousand dollars."
> I guess I was supposed to say, "Whee! Wow! Ooh!" But the word "we," the word "*we,*" stuck me cold."[22]

Carter surmised that Dorn had been working behind the scenes to insinuate his production company into her contract, and she was dumbfounded at the realization that he would assume she wanted him on board. As she recounted it, she told him: "'Joel, after all these years, I want to sign up with you, and a lawyer? And you want me to have a manager too, don't you? [Next] I gotta have a roadie—I need all that?'"[23] As she spoke to him, she could see her percentage slipping away into the hands of all the other people who would get involved. She told Lyons: "What did the production company have to do with the success of Betty Carter? Why, *now,* after all these years, do I need to give money to a production company that comes in on the tail end of things?"[24] Then there was the matter of artistic control. Dorn himself has stated that, since her Atco recording, she did not trust anyone else to produce her.[25] She suggested that another reason she did not sign with The Masked Announcer was because she did business by word of mouth: "Joel knows me well enough to know that I wouldn't sign with my *mother* at this stage of the game. What for? I had a booking agent, I didn't [even] sign with him. *I keep my word.* Everybody know, I keep my word. I've lived that way."[26]

In spite of the opportunity presented to her, Carter held her ground. After all she had been through, she was wary of being exploited. As she put it: "They wouldn't come to me if they didn't think that I could make them some *money.*"[27] The politics of race also figured in her decision, which was as much a matter of black autonomy as of personal integrity. In the process, however, she denied herself access to the channels that were enabling other artists to reach a mainstream audience. When she performed at the Bottom Line to sellout crowds, accompanied by John Hicks, Stafford James, and Chip Lyles, Krasnow was not in the audience.[28] The record deal ultimately fell through, and Carter held Dorn responsible. Dorn had several clients who recorded for Atlantic records, including Rahsaan Roland Kirk, Yusef Lateef, and David "Fathead" Newman. Krasnow wanted to sign those artists, as well as Carter, to Warner Brothers. During this period, Kirk and Newman did in fact leave Atlantic records to sign with Warner Brothers.[29] Carter was convinced that, in order to pressure Krasnow to sign his production company into her contract, Dorn had threatened to withhold his clients.[30] She felt that, even though Krasnow wanted the prestige of having recorded her, he had no choice but to back down. Dorn confirmed that he wanted to produce Carter for Warner Brothers and that he had hoped to facilitate her signing with the label so she could get greater distribution, as he had done for Kirk and Newman. He felt he could do her justice, that he had some ideas that would help her "get over." As he put it, he wished she could have "played ball" and been more open to input, but he also acknowledged that her way of doing things was what got her where she finally ended up.[31] He denied that he blocked Carter's Warner Brothers deal, however, and Todd Barkan reinforced this view.

Carter's perspective on this incident helps to explain the position she ultimately took toward other record labels: "A major label must understand and respect the fact that I am what I am and who I am. I've never gone to them to try to be something different. I've never pursued them to try to get some of that money that they *have,* so if they come to me and say to me, 'We want you to record for our company,' then they must know in the beginning what I'm all about. . . . They must understand that and not try to involve me with *producers.*"[32] The loss of the contract was a disappointment, but Carter proceeded as if nothing had happened. She took advantage of this period of transition in her personnel to modify her arrangements so they took into account the talents of her new accompanists.[33] Since she had moved to Brooklyn, she had developed an effective system for drawing upon the unique talents of her sidemen while also exerting enough influence over the rehearsal process to make the outcome bear her mark. This process entailed having the players run through the book upstairs, where the piano was located, while she appeared to be busy with other concerns downstairs. Having listened intently and made mental notes, she would then go up and offer suggestions and observations, guiding and coaxing them, all the while having a pretty good idea of where she was headed. While any single element of an arrangement might therefore reflect the contribution of a particular player, the form the chart ultimately took grew from her concept. John Hicks recalled, "There was always something different that she wanted to do with a tune."[34] Even though she may have done it several years before, "now it was time to upgrade it." He always had to bring blank manuscript paper: "She'll be talking it [the arrangement] down, they'd play something, '*No*' she didn't want that. Sometimes she could do that in one bar. Four beats, it was: '*No.*'"[35] But even though he might write out what happened in a given rehearsal, it was still just a guide, and in performance she always wanted the players to expand upon the basic idea of the chart.[36] A change in personnel therefore would require a period of resetting the arrangement for the new group that resulted. After a breaking-in period, a new player would make a place for himself and the group would gel.

In the fall of 1975 Betty Carter appeared at the Village Vanguard for the first time since she had booked the club to record herself for Bet-Car Records. Vanguard owner Max Gordon had given her a job about a dozen years before but recalled that, for her last show of that run, there was nobody in the club: "There she was, singing to a lot of empty chairs and tables. I could never get that picture out of my mind."[37] Although Carter repeatedly approached him, it was only after hearing her at Well's that he decided to book her again. A number of fellow musicians attended her Vanguard date, including Cecil Taylor, Roy Brooks, Leon Thomas, and Rashied Ali.[38] Musicians formed a core element of Carter's audience, indicating how strongly the jazz community endorsed her work. Likewise, when Carter was not on the bandstand on a given night, she could most likely be found in a club catching one of her colleagues at work, or scouting for potential sidemen. Carter was deeply enmeshed in the scene, hanging out and making her presence felt. Her musical prowess, her self-sufficiency, her willingness to "pay dues" as a practicing jazz musician, and her ability to interact as "just one of the guys," enabled her to get over in a man's world.

Carter's stance was not a matter of feminist politics per se. She did not see assertiveness as a freedom women needed to fight for so much as a birthright that any individual, male of female, needed to seize. In this respect she identified less with women than men, whose conventional role grants them the social license to assert their will directly. Photos of the singer, often dressed in pants, hair tucked under her cap, suggest that she toyed with a traditionally masculine persona onstage at this time. Her exploration of the customary boundaries between genders often made men, especially those from her generation, uncomfortable. She was aware of this, stating in an interview for *Jazz Forum* in 1978, "Most of the female singers could swing. We could play the horns but we just didn't dig into it like men and you had to dig into it like men in order to compete with men. So that meant you were a lesbian, right? I had somebody say that about me, say that I handle my business like a man when he discovered that I had my own record company—because I'm doing that independent thing. Males are afraid of that."[39] But among young people, her probing of gender boundaries was also a factor in her new popularity, especially in San Francisco. It added a layer of complexity to her interpretation of certain songs. Describing her wistful reading of "I Love Music," which featured prominently in her book from this time onward, she told Leonard Lyons: "It's a song about how much this young lady loves music, but yet she loves a man or a woman too," adding, in the narrator's voice: "'You know, when I'm with you I love music, I dream of beauty and everything,'" but still "she thinks of him . . . or her."[40]

At the end of September, Carter returned to San Francisco for a triumphant weeklong run at the Keystone Korner. "Chip" Lyles received billing as the trio's head,[41] but the players looked for leadership to Hicks, who was the veteran. She was so pleased with the turnout that she boasted she had outsold Miles Davis's run there around this same time.[42] These concerts at the Keystone were taped, but according to Dorn, the tapes were returned to Carter around 1990. During her stay in San Francisco she also made an early appearance in the role of teacher, giving a seminar on jazz singing.

One would think that by this time Carter had fully recovered from Orville O'Brien's disappearance and the loss of her Judson Hall tapes. Yet even as late as 1975 the Bush nightmare had not yet come to an end. During the intervening years O'Brien still had the tapes, and he kept trying to offer them to record label owners. Carter was vigilant in her efforts to stop him: "Fortunately for me I'm catching him every time he could place his deal,"[43] but ultimately he succeeded in eluding her. According to Carter, it was only after Morris Levy, owner of Roulette Records, had paid O'Brien a mere five hundred dollars for the tapes that she found out about the deal between O'Brien and Levy. Carter had known Levy from the time when Monte Kay was her manager, and she had performed at Birdland, which Levy and Kay had opened in December 1949 to compete with Bop City.[44] In a chapter entitled "Lullaby of Gangland," Frederic Dannen has described Levy as little more than an avaricious, power-hungry hoodlum with ties to the Mob who required the protection of a bodyguard. In 1988 he was convicted on two counts of conspiracy to commit extortion, but he died before serving time.[45]

Levy had formed Roulette in 1956 as a rock-and-roll label, but he had also recorded Count Basie and Joe Williams.[46] By the time he had acquired the Bush tapes he co-owned a lucrative operation called Promo Records that specialized in reselling cutouts, or discontinued records, and allegedly counterfeiting them as well. Purchasing unsold records, Promo would proceed to unload copies of them wholesale onto discount retailers.[47] Record companies typically designed artist contracts so that they were released from their royalty obligations if an artist's record went into the cutout bin, so there was a built-in incentive for companies to relegate a product that wasn't a hit to this status and regain production costs on records they had overproduced.[48]

In 1976 Roulette issued the Bush tapes as *Finally Betty Carter* and *Round Midnight*, the latter consisting of the performances Carter had rejected when putting together Bush 907. In his hurry to get the records out, Levy neglected to find out that Atco had already released a recording of Carter's with the same title. Carter was understandably displeased with the release of performances that she had not personally endorsed.[49] A bootleg version of the tapes also came out on the Joy label.[50] According to Carter, Levy approached her about making a record for Roulette and then told her about the Bush tapes. Apparently after he had put the tapes out he discovered that, in addition to being the singer on them, she also owned part of Bush Records.[51] In an effort to secure some compensation for the tapes, Carter worked out an agreement with Levy, signing with his label early in 1976. Speaking to Herb Nolan for *Down Beat* that year, Carter said that she had arranged a recording contract with Levy because she preferred working for a smaller label, adding that she did not like the impersonal way large corporations dealt with their artists.[52] In addition to stipulating that she produce one recording of her own work for Roulette, her contract also made provision for her to record other artists for the label's newly created Birdland series. She had hopes of using her position at Roulette to encourage young talent, beginning with John Hicks.[53] A hard-won bond seemed to exist between the singer and the label owner that enabled her to trust him in spite of, perhaps because of, their disagreements: "Morris Levy and I have a kind of handshake agreement, he respects what I'm about. . . . I'm personal with the man I'm with, if he says 'no' we fight and holler—he respects me enough to know that I will holler—and I know he'll holler. I've listened to him holler. But this is what I want, I'd much rather have it out in the open, on top, than underneath."[54] Carter's experiences with Bush and Warner Brothers undoubtedly had a lasting affect on her trust of people in the music business.

Carter's career continued to warm up during this period as she began to receive more and more exposure. Early in 1976 she appeared at the Bottom Line again and on 13 March as a substitute guest on NBC's *Saturday Night Live,* when Anthony Perkins hosted the show: "This chick had seen me work at the Bottom Line, and she got me recommended for the gig."[55] Having only found out about it on the preceding Monday, she recalled being "petrified."[56] By this time Walter Booker, who had played with both Carter and Hicks ten years earlier, had replaced Stafford James on bass, and Clifford Barbaro had taken Chip Lyles's place on drums. Carter appeared on two different segments of the show in a dazzling white tuxedo, singing new additions to her book, "Swing Brother, Swing," and "I Was Telling Him about You," that she would include on her forthcoming recording. Appearing on television meant a lot to her because she saw the medium as having enormous potential, not only for promoting her own work, but for generating interest in jazz as a whole.

Her latest successes did not necessarily improve her outlook on the jazz scene, however, despite general agreement that a bebop revival was taking place. She told Chris White that April: "I hear people tell me jazz is on the up. I'm still waiting. . . . I gotta wait a little longer."[57] With typical media hyperbole, a *Newsweek* cover from the following year would announce: *Jazz Comes Back!*[58] Even so, her suspicions lingered: "There's too much money for anything really creative to happen in jazz. . . . When jazz becomes popular, it's like all music today: produced, controlled, computerized."[59] Carter was skeptical, partly because of the suddenness of her own ascent, which seemed almost random to her: "I can't put my finger on why it has changed. . . . I haven't changed. I've just developed."[60] The airplay she received during this period did a lot to contribute to the public's awareness of her and helps to account for her success: "College radio stations began playing my stuff . . . and I was getting across to young listeners. College radio and word-of-mouth and appearances on college campuses were what did it."[61] The college stations certainly gave Carter a way to evade the system of independent promotion that barred her access to commercial radio stations.

The Roulette project proceeded as planned when Carter took her trio, her current repertoire, and her sound engineer, Joe Ferla, into Sound Ideas Studio for four recording sessions on 9 and 10 March and 21 and 22 June

1976. According to Clifford Barbaro, Eddie Moore took over for him on "Wagon Wheels," "Making Dreams Come True," and one other song, possibly "With No Words."[62] The trio provides superb support, with Booker and Barbaro adding to the music's constant feeling of renewal by imaginatively digressing from straight timekeeping in key passages. The recording mix emphasizes Hicks's able comping and his remarkably clairvoyant connection with Carter.

The dates resulted in nine tracks that Roulette issued as *Now It's My Turn.* In addition to choices of repertoire inspired by Billie Holiday ("Swing, Brother, Swing"), Charlie Parker ("Just Friends/Star Eyes"), and Sonny Rollins ("Wagon Wheels"), Carter also recorded three originals: "New Blues (You Purr)," a ballad that does not follow the standard blues form or feeling, "No More Words," and "Open the Door." Her setting of the latter song, which she had recorded over ten years before on *Inside Betty Carter* (example 8), exploits long meter to good effect. With the harmonic rhythm now proceeding twice as slow as the earlier version, Carter had more time to "fold her line" into a significantly faster groove, making this performance (example 11) more subtle, yet more urgent, than that one.

The tantalizing way Carter breaks up her sentences with pauses and sustained pitches, easing each phrase out little by little, provides the listener with aural punctuation that clarifies her meaning even as it delays closure: "Open the door, [pause] dear. I must—get in—your heart; you're making—it so hard [pause] to be true." She had used this technique in her earlier version, but the long meter's slowing of the harmonic rhythm allows her to probe each chord change more deeply. A more substantial difference is the way Carter suspends the time at measures 137, 153, and 169, to color the tag's chromatically descending chord progression, only resuming the bossa groove at the arrival of the tonic chord at measures 149, 165, and 181—with the last of these becoming the closing vamp-to-fade. In her handwritten chord chart, Carter wrote the terms "rubato" and "tempo bossa" to indicate these shifts in the time feel (pp. 139–40).

Now It's My Turn includes Carter's reading of Cole Porter's archly satirical "Most Gentlemen Don't Like Love," set in up-tempo waltz time, a tune that remained a staple of her repertoire for much of her career. As with the song "Ego"—Randy Weston's "Berkshire Blues" with Carter's own lyrics—Porter's tune used scathing wit to confront men obliquely about their treatment of women, as well as to rally women to their own cause. The song gave Carter a playful way to vent her frustration with men. She was coy about her addition of this song to her book. But, as with other social critics, her intent was not entirely whimsical: "I had to test it out on some fellow musicians and ask them if they got offended by the lyrics—I'm thinking of the audience.

Betty Carter's handwritten chord chart of the song "Open the Door."

PLAY
RUBATO
TEMPO BOSSA
RUBATO
TEMPO BOSSA
RUBATO
TEMPO BOSSA
VAMP OUT

They all laughed, so I figured I'm in shape, I can do them . . . such cute lyrics."[63] In live performances she disavowed any credit for the lyrics, but her superior acting skills made it hard to doubt that they captured her personal sentiments. Compared to her live renditions, which depended for effect on Carter's playing off the audience's reactions, the recording falls a bit flat. At the end of her performances of this tune she would often heighten its irony by quipping: "But we just don't get it; do we girls? We still have to say: [singing] everything I have is yours," thereby leavening her comic assault on men by teasing women about their complicity in their own exploitation. Always sensitive to the mood of her audience, she rarely continued with the whole ballad, bowing out of it by saying: "No, we won't do that; that's too heavy."

The amount of scatting on *Now It's My Turn,* with one tune sung entirely "With No Words," suggests that Carter was improvising more than ever. Partly because of slicker audio production, the performances sound more polished than on any record she had made to date. Although a variant of the album's title occurs in her rendition of Porter's song ("Now ladies, it's your turn"), Carter did not choose the title, and she felt self-conscious about its presumption of entitlement.[64] Nevertheless, until 1980, she felt that it was the best album she had done.[65] Toward the end of 1976, Roulette released the record to favorable reviews in *Billboard* magazine and London's *Melody Maker.* Her second recording for Bet-Car, *The Betty Carter Album,* was also coming out at around this time. Impulse Records saw that she was marketable enough to warrant a reissue of *Out There* and *The Modern Sound,* which was now offered together in one LP entitled *What a Little Moonlight Can Do.* Gary Giddins's glowing appraisal of these rereleases gave Carter a mention in the *Village Voice.*[66] Coupled with Morris Levy's releases of *Finally* and *Round Midnight,* the drought in Betty Carter recordings ended with a flood of material presenting her listeners with a welcome, if disorienting, profusion of choices. Most of this material represented her work from the preceding seven years, which in itself had witnessed significant growth. However, coupled with the Impulse reissue, it included music that reached back nearly two decades, when her approach had been markedly different. Enthusiastic reviews in *Cadence* of these releases, and in *Coda* of her recent performances, certainly didn't hurt.[67]

Betty Carter's romance with Roulette records did not last long. Relations with Levy soured when he decided not to give her credit as composer and publisher for her own compositions on *Now It's My Turn,* thereby denying her royalties. When the record came out, there were also a couple of cuts that she did not want released, including "Star Eyes." She was so angry about this that, at a gig after the record was released, she actually told people *not* to buy the record,[68] and she never listed the record in her publicity materials. By

October 1976 Carter had decided to sue Levy over ownership of the rights to release *Round Midnight,* a situation that obviously brought to a halt any of her other planned activities for Roulette. As late as the end of 1979 she refused to discuss the matter publicly.[69] A fact sheet in her press kit from several years later reported that *Finally* and *Round Midnight* were sold to Roulette in 1981, which suggests that a favorable resolution of the matter had not been reached until nearly a dozen years after she and O'Brien had made the tapes.[70] The remarkable vigilance she showed in pursuing a just resolution to the Bush affair speaks volumes about her tenacity.

With each new gig Carter commanded greater visibility. Her participation in the Berkeley Jazz Festival in the fall of 1976 led to an interview in *Rolling Stone* magazine. A tour of Europe that included stops in Berlin and Paris in November was followed by a weeklong engagement at the Vanguard that was favorably reviewed in the *New York Times.*[71] At this time Hicks and Barbaro formed the core of the rhythm section. Carter admitted to being especially tough on bass players, and there was a steady succession of them over the next few years, including Stafford James, Chip Jackson, Dennis Irwin, Calvin Hill, Juni Booth, Ray Drummond, Walter Booker, Dave Holland, Clint Houston, Jerome Hunter, and Ratzo Harris. In spite of her misgivings about white jazz musicians Carter had enormous respect for Dave Holland, and Barbaro felt that, among the bassists she worked with at this time, it was Holland who had the most impact on her singing: "Dave was very open with his playing. Instead of just playing a straight bassline, Dave sort of opened the music up a little bit. We felt more loose. During that period Dave was playing with Sam Rivers. So he brought that open feeling. And then Betty started singing open."[72] But Holland never became a regular, only filling in occasionally.

Carter was working more than she had in years, in venues that had a higher profile than the small rooms to which she had grown accustomed. The time she had spent in obscurity certainly deepened her appreciation for the success she was finally beginning to enjoy. But she did not lose her perspective on her struggles, on how they fit into her career and into her lifelong development as an artist: "Paying of dues *is* shaping. And it's living. You pay dues *to* live. But it is really shaping your self, your body. You're maturing. 20 years ago, 10 years ago, I wouldn't have been ready for what's happening to me now; I like what's happening to me now better than I would have liked it 10 years ago."[73] In an interview with journalist Don Nelson she expanded upon this idea, saying, "Though I had rapport with audiences years ago, I didn't have what I wanted. I really didn't have range or depth then. No, there's something you have to feel inside that tells you you're ready—and I am now."[74] Nevertheless, she expressed some reservations about the pace and magnitude of her recent accomplishments. She told Joel Dreyfuss of *Rolling Stone* that she was afraid: "It's almost like becoming commercial. You're overwhelmed. What if you don't have time to think, to be creative?"[75] After all of the potholes she had hit on the road to her current success, Carter could not help suspecting that the musical establishment would only grant her access to the mainstream audience if she compromised her artistic standards.

The year 1977 proved the best one Betty Carter had had so far. In addition to working more and drawing larger crowds, suddenly she was enjoying an unparalleled degree of attention from the media and critics. She spent a good amount of time on the road with her trio, taking in a tour of Europe that summer, and she claimed that by year's end she had earned one hundred thousand dollars.[76] Carter even presented a master class at Harvard University with her onetime mentor Dizzy Gillespie in April.[77] Since the late-1950s she had had ambitions to appear in the prestigious Newport Jazz Festival, but she had never received an invitation. As her power to draw crowds increased, being asked to sing there became a matter of pride: "George Wein [Newport Festival promoter] doesn't respect me. I'll make him respect me."[78] By June she had accomplished her goal, making a triumphant midnight appearance at Carnegie Hall, one of the venues used for the festival. According to John Wilson, Carter's performance overshadowed the main event of the evening, a reunion of the singer's fellow Detroiters, the Jones brothers, Hank, Elvin, and Thad.[79]

In the spring of 1978, Joseph Papp and the New York Shakespeare Festival included Carter in a jazz series at the Public Theater Cabaret, a small, intimate space upstairs from the main stage, where Elizabeth Swados's *Runaways* was playing. Independent producer Robert Kantor arranged a videotaping of the last of Carter's four sold-out shows at the instigation of PBS's cultural programming department, which hoped to broadcast it on National Educational Television.[80] Funded with thirty thousand dollars seed money from the Mellon Foundation, the pilot project was intended as a catalyst for airing jazz on television. Ultimately Channel 13 did not pick it up, and the master has been lost, but the idea did spark some interest from the National Endowment for the Arts, and this interest ultimately led to the Jazz in America series.[81] Sound engineer Danny Michael preserved an audio tape that captures most of this performance, nearly two hours of material. The tape reveals how dramatically Carter's presentation had grown, as well as how much freer her approach had become since her live recording dates eight years earlier. Renditions of such staples as "'Round Midnight," "I Didn't Know What Time It Was," "Open the Door," and "Sounds" show Carter exploring the idea of improvising while singing words, further blurring the line between singing scat and delivering lyrics. The trio's playing is fluid and dynamic, with Hicks providing such rich counterpoint to Carter's line that he often crosses over from comping to soloing. Holland—whom Carter described as "on loan from Sam Rivers"—added another level of rhythmic intricacy to the counterpoint, and Barbaro bobbed and wove in and out of the musical fabric with the agility of a Sugar Ray Robinson. The balance of the recording would have pleased Carter as it highlights the four musicians' interaction, which stayed on a very high plane throughout the performance.[82]

At Carter's return appearance in the twenty-fifth Newport Festival, at Avery Fisher Hall on 25 June, she stole the show. The performance earned her enthusiastic write-ups in the *New York Times* as well as national publications *Newsweek* and *Time.* Noting her unusual repertoire and her reliance upon scat, *Times* critic Robert Palmer remarked upon her recent emergence from relative obscurity into the front rank of jazz vocalists, as though the process had taken place overnight.[83] Tony Schwartz of *Newsweek* went a bit deeper, pointing out that "she is unknown to many jazz enthusiasts. Her name does not even appear in many books about jazz and none of her eleven recordings are widely available." Observing that "the very qualities that so distinguish her singing—aggressiveness, relentless experimentation, a fierce refusal to compromise—have long limited her appeal," Schwartz contributed to the growing Carter mystique.[84]

After years of lukewarm receptions in Europe, Carter was also beginning to generate a following there, as audiences and critics alike favorably received her records. With Ratzo Harris now on bass she toured Europe in the summer of 1978, on a trip organized by George Wein's Festival Productions, which included a stop at the Montreux Festival.[85] Not long after returning to the United States, Carter ended her long association with drummer Clifford Barbaro, bringing Kenny Washington into the group to replace him. That fall other European engagements followed, mainly in Poland but also Norway.[86] While on that tour she was interviewed at length for *Jazz Forum* and, after coming back to New York, by Linda Prince for *Down Beat,* which ran the interview as its cover article in May the following year. The press was taking great interest in the views of this outspoken woman, and characteristically, she did not hesitate to speak her mind.

By the beginning of November Cameron Brown had taken over for Ratzo Harris, whom Carter had fired in Poland. Stalwart John Hicks smoothed the transition, helping the new players learn the book. While the preparation was immediately directed toward a run at Blues Alley in Washington, D.C., and a one-day trip out to the Galveston Jazz Festival, the focus was on a high-profile concert to take place in two weeks: a performance at the Schubert Theater during Thanksgiving weekend—billed as the first time a jazz artist had ever performed on Broadway. The gig grew out of Carter's dates at the Public Theater earlier that year, and it held such special significance for her that she insisted the trio members rent tuxedos for the occasion.[87] At 9 P.M. on Sunday night, 26 November, Joseph Papp introduced Betty Carter as "the greatest jazz singer in the world," and she proceeded to prove him right. She ended her performance with "Sounds (Movin' On)," which had evolved into a twenty-minute tour de force that traversed a wide range of meters and tempos.[88]

There was not much time to catch a breath as the pace of events continued to pick up. Trips to Amherst; Dayton, Ohio; Lincoln, Nebraska—to play at a prison—and Evanston, Illinois, kept Carter and the band busy through early December.[89] The week leading up to Christmas Eve found her at the Vanguard, a gig that had become something of a winter ritual.[90] January 1979 brought a trip to Michigan, and while she was in her hometown, Carter visited with relatives.[91] Her success helped heal the wounds her pride had suffered the decade before and made it possible for her to face her family with dignity. By the end of February, Carter had incorporated bassist Curtis Lundy in the group and had begun a tour out west and through Canada.[92] At Sarah Vaughan's invitation she appeared at Carnegie Hall in March, participating in a concert that also included singer Eddie Jefferson. In June Carter returned to Carnegie Hall, this time to organize an evening of her own for the Newport Jazz Festival. Carter assembled an all-star quintet, and pianist Dorothy Donegan also appeared in a segment of the concert. Performing instrumental numbers only, these musicians set the stage for Carter.[93] Around this time an advertisement for the classified section of the *Boston Phoenix* featured a photo of the singer, indicating that she had achieved enough recognition to make a commercial endorsement. For Carter, her new success justified all those years of struggling in the underground: "It makes you feel like the rest was worthwhile. You don't have to kiss nobody's behind, sell yourself, be somebody you don't want to be. And you can still win."[94] She could even afford to joke about her success, saying, "Don't say that there is a resurgence of interest in my singing. After all, there was never really any 'surgence.'"[95]

On 6–8 December 1979 Carter took her trio, now seasoned by nearly a year of touring together, and her sound technician Joe Ferla, to the Great American Music Hall in San Francisco. There she produced the third record for her own label before a spirited and clearly devoted audience. She had just come from performing at several midwestern colleges, and she was energized by the positive responses she had gotten at them.[96] Carter had strong feelings of gratitude toward her audiences, especially those in the San Francisco area, where she felt her career turnaround had begun.[97] She had worked at many of the major venues there, the Keystone Korner, the Greek Theater, the University of California at Berkeley.[98] Tom Bradshaw, the owner of the Great American Music Hall, had recently wooed her from the Keystone, which she had outgrown by this time. Carter had taped various live dates since her first Bet-Car recording, but she had not released a live recording for almost a decade and she wanted the presence of an audience to have an impact on her performance. The singer felt she was developing rapidly—surpassing even her most recent efforts—and this led her to hesitate about releasing the tracks she had put down previously. "They are not the same tunes they were five months ago. That's the reason I have to do it live, and do it then and there and put it out, and don't hesitate. I got to go straight ahead; I can't wait."[99]

Matthew Yaple, then a graduate student at Temple University, videotaped Carter's performance at the Great American Music Hall as well as various talks and interviews she gave around the same time.[100] Interlacing this footage into a documentary entitled *Jazz Is Betty Carter: Is She the Last Jazz Singer?* Yaple succeeded in communicating the passion Carter brought to her performances and her public lectures. The video, as well as the unedited footage from the shooting, contains rare alternate takes of several performances that made it onto the album, revealing that her renditions of tunes often deviated widely from one set to another, even in passages where she was not scatting.

The recording, which Carter called *The Audience with Betty Carter* in recognition of her fans' dedication, reflects a clear summation of everything Carter stood for musically. With her rhythm section consolidated into a cohesive unit, the record represents her best work from this period. Part of the credit for the record's finish belongs to Joe Ferla, who worked in a sound truck to bring Carter's aesthetic vision to life. The record includes several originals, including "Tight," now with a slower, cooler delivery than the version on *The Betty Carter Album;* "I Think I Got It Now," a ballad; "Fake," a relaxed jazz waltz; "So . . . ," a confessional recitation about infidelity cast in a Latin feel with unusual interruptions of the tempo; and a twenty-five-minute version of "Sounds (Movin' On)," which had continued to evolve since her Public Theater performance almost two years earlier.[101] She also sang her theme song, "Open the Door," which she was symbolically reclaiming from Morris Levy's clutches by including in this recording. Her inclusion of this last song, as well as "Spring Can Really Hang You Up the Most" and "My Favorite Things" inevitably harked back to *Inside Betty Carter.* Her old standby, "I Could Write a Book," recorded in 1955, 1969, and 1970, also reappears in a new guise. While these tunes had attained the status of signature numbers, they had hardly remained static in form.

Carter's several versions of "Open the Door" reveal the characteristic ways she used pitch as an expressive device. This feature of her style is immediately evident in her treatment of her vocal compass, for she used the registers of her voice as an important means of creating variety within numbers as well as over the course of an entire set. Her choice of key was designed to place certain tunes in a specific tessitura, partly to create a particular mood. Within a song, she might avoid using a certain register until a specific moment, reserving it for its full expressive effect. While Carter often made transitions to a different vocal register by arpeggiating a chord, she also created striking contrasts by leaping an octave or more. Generally she did not use leaps to break up sustained pitches in the melody with parenthetic inner voice movement, in the manner of Louis Armstrong, or to create compound melody as Bobby McFerrin later would. Within the context of a largely diatonic vocabulary, Carter used pentatonic scale segments, flatted scale degrees in blues-based licks, and chromatically altered chord tones to create varieties of melodic movement, as well as harmonic tension and release. Listen to how her use of her high register in the 1979 rendition of "Open the Door" (example 12) contributes to this version's powerful sense of movement and growth.

Since her earliest reading of this song Carter had increasingly come to use contour rhythm to create contrast and growth in her melodic lines. Her lines had always been characterized by a frequent rising and falling, a series of asymmetrical undulations, which—coupled with her rhythmic flexibility—gave them a restless quality. Listening for peaks and lows, and how she prepares for them, reveals the ways that her pacing of melodic events contributes in the broadest terms to the sense of movement she generated over the course of an entire arrangement. Carter steadily increased her command over this aspect of her music throughout her career, but she especially did so during the late 1970s.

The first recorded version of "Open the Door" (example 8) already shows an awareness of the potential for melodic movement to help sustain the dramatic tension of an arrangement. Here she situates the first sixteen bars (mm. 13–28) within her low octave, and then moves into her midrange for the next sixteen (mm. 29–44), emphasizing the high B-flat below her break. Her leap up a diminished fourth to the song's highest pitch, a D-flat, initiates the bridge and draws attention to the surprising harmonic move to the ♭III harmony. Over the next eight bars (mm. 45–52) Carter descends a tenth to a low B-flat, and the following eight bars (mm. 54–60) echo this broad descent, bringing her line to a low G-flat at the end of the bridge. This effectively sets up the return of three distinct elements at measure 61: the tonic harmony, the A section, which is now varied to accommodate new lyrics, and her low octave. In order to reinforce the sense of imminent closure generated by the coda's chromatically descending root progression (m. 73ff.), Carter places much of her remaining vocal line toward the lower half of her midrange.

For her next recording of this song (example 11) Carter's use of space between phrases, now timed more irregularly, and her rhythmic interaction with the groove—which is now enhanced by Clifford Barbaro's flexibility—gives the bossa nova feel a less rigid, more playful quality. While its broad outlines resemble her earlier rendition, Carter's greater assurance in the use of different registers and dynamic levels is apparent. She uses her low register more effectively as a foil for what immediately follows, as in measure 47, where it makes way for the varied A section, or at measures 73–76 and measures 90–96, where it sets up the highest pitches of the performance. The climaxes at measures 81–89 and at measures 97–105, with their intensified dynamics and Walter Booker's animated strumming beneath them, give the bridge greater definition than it had in its 1964 guise, especially in light of the relaxed responses that follow them.

Reversing this procedure, Carter uses her high register at the high E-flat in measures 169–72 to set up the startling plunge of a ninth to the word "love" in measures 173–75. In delivering the word "love" in this way, Carter seems to recoil shyly from the expansive statement "I've got," as though she suddenly realized that she didn't want to play all of her cards at once. The sudden change in register and dynamic has the flirtatious quality of someone coyly diverting her gaze after having announced amorous feelings. Carter's melodic setting here adds to the complexity of the reading of her own lyrics. This reversal also helps to signal the tune's imminent close. While her parting glances on the phrase "I've got love," at measures 181–84 and measures 190–93, recall this dramatic passage, they now entail shorter descents, which—combined with the repetitions of text—help to release the tension of the earlier melodic profile on these same words.

Recorded only three years later, Carter's arrangement of "Open the Door" on *The Audience* bears the mark of her further refinement and control, as well as that of the new musicians in the group. Although it has a lower tessitura and a slightly more restrained quality overall, its faster tempo and subtler dynamic nuances intimate a deeper emotional undercurrent that ebbs beneath the surface. A scatted introduction over a vamp on the tonic harmony sets the tone for the whole song by descending to a low E-flat. From this point to the end of the bridge, Carter reserves the bottom of her range for the title phrase, which now descends the III hexachord of the E-flat major scale to a low G-natural (mm. 32–35 and mm. 68–72). As in earlier versions, her return to this range at the end of the bridge in measure 126 sets up the return to the title phrase at measures 132–35, which in turn initiates a varied restatement of the A section. Carter's withholding of her high pitches provides further evidence of her registral control, for she has gradually increased the tension through the first A section by saving notes above her lowest octave for measure 40. By then successively peaking on G-natural in measure 45 and A-flat in measure 60 she paces a climb that will culminate in the second A section, at the B-flat in measure 74. Hovering around this B-flat, she sustains this culmination for eight measures, until measure 81, before pulling back for the bridge, as in the 1976 version. In measure 96, at the words "how you (try to avoid me)," she produces an expressive leap of an octave to emphasize the line's apex when she sings the words "how you" to bring her to the high E-flat.

In an extended coda, beginning at measure 197, Carter restores the tonic vamp of the introduction and returns to her low register, which now has the effect of rounding out the shape of the entire arrangement. In order to accomplish this she has isolated the occurrence of high E-flats to their climactic appearance in the bridge and eliminated their recurrence elsewhere. The net effect is a more satisfying, more integrated structure than those of her earlier versions, which allows her to phrase the line more freely, pace the growth of the form more effectively, and air out the phrases without sacrificing continuity and linear tension. She had always displayed a sensitivity to the ways that pitch can create movement, demonstrated as early as her solo on "Jay Bird," but as her career progressed, she increasingly realized the expressive power that placing a whole phrase or a portion of a phrase at the extremes of her vocal range can have.

Carter's ability to build a solo notwithstanding, her treatment of pitch rarely produces connections between successive phrases that add up to a large-scale pitch structure, or strong motivic links that span the entire performance. In fact, in some ways, her melodic lines almost discourage the long-term association of melodic events. Her frequent changes of melodic direction, her use of irregular phrase lengths and breaks in the line, and her additive phraseology, or building of new phrases out of material from the preceding phrase ending, govern the flow of events. In her scatting especially, sections of Carter's lines coalesce around the immediate repetition of melodic ideas, or riffs, which she subsequently abandons for fresh material. By doing so she tends to promote listening on the local level, guiding the ear to notice the relationship between each phrase and what came immediately before it. All of these methods enabled her to generate a sense of alertness and surprise in her listeners, as well as in her trio. Brought into the present by her compelling melodic, dynamic, and rhythmic twists and turns, by the intriguing rhythmic and harmonic interplay between her line and the rhythm section, and by her entirely fresh delivery of lyrics, her audiences hung on her every syllable.[102]

Carter's reputation for introducing tempo changes into a chart was renowned.[103] In her up-tempo arrangements, Carter used tempo contrast effectively to convey a sense of perpetual motion, especially in such long charts as "Sounds (Movin' On)." Sometimes changes of tempo also helped Carter enact the story of a song and convey her evolving response to events in the lyrics. In her shrewd reworking of "The Trolley Song," for example, the change from the anxious tempo of the verse into the slower, heavy-swinging groove of the refrain expresses a shift in the narrator's experience of the trolley ride. This temporal displacement mirrors the narrator's movement from an objective sensation of the trolley's speed to the subjective involvement with her feelings for the new passenger, a shift that alters the narrator's awareness of the sounds and movements of the trolley. The sound effects in the lyrics give Carter an opportunity to explore the line between scat and onomatopoeia, to great comic effect. This in turn is made possible by the slower tempo, which gives her time to back phrase expressively. The faster tempo's return at the end rounds out the chart by conjuring an image of the narrator riding off into the sunset with her new love. It seems likely that the Detroiter's reminiscences of riding the trolley to Paradise Valley grounded her fanciful rendition in her own lived experience. Carter's novel arrangement and her hip delivery challenged Judy Garland's claim to this vignette of a woman overcoming her shyness, by replacing the latter's earnest reading of the lyric with an ironic, sexually assertive one.

Carter's latest arrangement of "I Could Write a Book" (example 13) inverts standard procedure by beginning with the singer scatting for two choruses, playfully concealing the song from all but the most savvy audience member. This approach prepares us for her idiosyncratic statement of the lyrics, which does not even bear a passing resemblance to Richard Rodgers's melody. The spaces she leaves in her line give it an understated, laid-back quality and allow Hicks to intertwine a beautiful melodic commentary with the vocal line. The transition she makes from her extended scat introduction into the song's lyrics gives us a clear illustration of the smooth integration of the two modes of singing that she had achieved by this time. Carter also capitalizes on her dark low register here, which gives pianissimo passages a chalumeau quality, especially in ballads. Her appreciation of Wini Brown's deep chest tones had clearly not gone to waste. The low tessitura of her 1979 renditions of "I Could Write a Book" and "Open the Door" give us a good illustrations of the expressive mastery she acquired over this range, which expanded downward as she matured.

The two-record set released by Bet-Car from the performances demonstrates the self-confidence Betty Carter had achieved by this time: "I'm hearing more and thinking more than I've ever thought in my life at this point, musically. I'm having fun."[104] As a tribute to her San Francisco following, Carter gave each person who attended the date a rose. She also took their names and addresses and mailed each of them a free copy of the recording.

Naturally, her improved financial situation also helped her feel confident: "It's not a million dollars, but I'm putting some money in the bank. I'm not starving. My kids are going to a private school at this time. I'm paying for my kids' education too."[105] By this time Myles was attending C. W. Post College in Long Island, and Kagle was enrolled at the Friends Academy. On 8 August 1978 Carter took out a mortgage for fifty-five thousand dollars and bought the three-story brownstone she had been renting.[106] Even though she did not conceive of herself as being from a particular local scene, she was committed to her neighborhood in the Fort Greene section of Brooklyn. As much as she was grateful to her West Coast following, she had no intention of relocating, for it was the New York scene that had gotten her through her tough times. "New York kept me alive. It kept me thinking, my continuity going, because that's what the East will do for you, keep you on your toes. . . . It keeps you working hard. You don't get a chance to lay back, like you can do in California. So when California gets me, they get me on top of things."[107] With her friend Ora Harris living in California, Carter had a West Coast base of operations that would continue to expand her outreach there into the next decade. In the time since her ill-fated trip to California, she had turned her career around. This fact alone justified all the struggles she had been through along the way. At last she was fulfilling her dreams from over thirty years before, when an idealistic Lillie Mae Jones had left home to become a performer.

10

Reaching for More

As pleased as Carter was with *The Audience*, as significant as it was for her career, its triumph was clouded over. Echoing the events during another important gig she had done at the Jazz Workshop in Boston less than five years earlier—significantly, when her prospects had first started to turn around—Carter gave John Hicks his walking papers during the run at the Great American Music Hall. This was especially hard for her because she was so fond of her long-time collaborator. Hicks had been drinking lately and the bandleader was outraged that he would risk jeopardizing the evening's success. On the recording it is hard to hear evidence of his altered state of consciousness. No error eluded Carter's hawklike attention, however, and because so much hung in the balance on this particular occasion—not only her record but Yaples's filming as well—Hicks's transgression proved the final straw.

In many ways firing Hicks brought to a head many tensions that had remained buried beneath the surface for some time, not only between the pianist and his boss. As Carter came to assert herself more forcefully as a band leader, it became harder for the musicians to tolerate her leadership style. Art Blakey and other male band leaders employed tactics similar to the ones she used to retain control over the men in her trio, such as creating division among the ranks by triangulating, criticizing a player to others behind his back knowing full well that he would eventually hear it.[1] Being a woman, however, Carter felt especially under pressure to assert her authority in order to maintain control.

In this regard Carter found younger musicians easier to work with than men from her generation, who did not take kindly to her directness, her criticism, her volatility, or her rage. The battle lines between the sexes were no less firmly drawn with younger players, but her greater experience increased the likelihood that they would accept her authority. As she wryly put it then: "I know more than they do, even though they don't think I do."[2] Square into the face of her players' chauvinism she projected a certainty that, at this point in her career, she could give them a better training than anyone else: "Most young musicians would *much* rather have a horn . . . a male horn player that he's backing up. That's a matter of fact. I think that I offer, at this point musically, more music than any horn player in the business for a young musician."[3]

In spite of her talent and her experience she knew she had to overcome a double hurdle—as a singer and as a woman—to win the respect of her players. As she told reporter Curtis Wenzel: "Most musicians have trouble handling the fact that here's a singer who knows what she's talking about. But after they're with me a while they find it's very necessary and it's a good thing [for her to be in control]," adding, "I *do* believe that the dues for a woman musician are tougher than for a male. However, you know that from the beginning. So get ready! Brace yourself and do what you're going to do."[4] Her brusque manner did not make it any easier for her players to take orders from her. Carter provoked resentment in other ways as well—setting an impossibly high standard and then criticizing players—often publicly—when they fell short. She would also delve into players' personal lives during periods of truce and use this ammunition later to lash out at them.[5] When subtle psychological manipulations did not work, she was not averse to using direct verbal assaults on her players' manhood to get her way.[6] At a sound check at Fat Tuesday's described by Stanley Crouch, the band leader taunted her players in order to get results: "Don't lay down on me, now, put some strength in it. Let's hear some of that man stuff, put some shoulders in that music. Don't worry about drowning me out. That's my problem."[7] She was also known to belittle players who had received a formal musical education—not an uncommon tactic, even among her male counterparts from that generation. She appeared to feel that any means of gaining the upper hand was fair, even if it risked destroying the relationship.

Bass players seemed most ill suited to her leadership style, as she herself acknowledged: "Every time I turned around, it was a new bass player. I guess I was just very hard on bass players. They didn't want to work that hard."[8] She would later clarify to Willard Jenkins that this also had to do with her extreme reliance upon the double bass: "My voice is more in tune with the bass fiddle [than the other instruments]. I just feel that my bass player has to be someone who wants to learn his instrument, wants to *know* his instrument, and can keep time. If the bassist goes out of time it messes everybody up. The bassist is holding everything together in a sense, although a lot of bass players don't want that responsibility—they lean on the drummer."[9]

While the force of her artistic convictions justified her strong need for control, her embattled role as a woman in charge of men led her to exaggerate this tendency. Often before a show, typically during the sound checks that routinely evolved into rehearsals, she would provoke arguments that inflamed her musicians' rage. This elicited impassioned performances from them, performances that surpassed what they were capable of without her. By putting them off balance emotionally, Carter forced her players to produce music that was truly created on the spot, rather than based upon the precomposed ideas that are an instrumentalist's stock in trade. As bassist Ira Coleman eloquently put it, she "thrived on conflict."[10] But the toll it took on her relationships was steep. While pianist Khalid Moss likened her approach to that of former Green Bay Packers coach Vince Lombardi, who would "get you so mad that you would go out and play hard just to get back at him,"[11] several musicians, Moss included, echoed the sentiment that her approach often did more harm than good.[12]

One side effect of this dynamic was that her trio members occasionally engaged in masked attempts to undermine Carter's leadership. The hardships of touring invite a certain amount of frivolity, essential to maintaining one's sanity. Kenny Washington recalled the trio performing such pranks as rebooking airline reservations she had arranged for a tour, so they could arrive on a later flight.[13] But some of the player's shenanigans hinted at a not-so-subtle subversion of the Carter "matriarchy." Washington also recalled how the players would take out their aggression on the singer during fast numbers such as "The Trolley Song" by pushing the tempo, forcing Carter to deliver the lyrics at breakneck speed.[14] Given the timing, Hicks's drinking and his showing up late for gigs, may have been such an oblique assault on his band leader. On the surface it would seem foolish, given jazz's rigorous technical demands, for a player to risk hampering his motor coordination by using alcohol or other mind-altering substances. Yet it is hardly uncommon among musicians to settle jittery nerves and release inhibitions via chemical means. In the past, when drug use was more prevalent among musicians, Carter tolerated it as long as it didn't interfere with their work. Otherwise her personnel options would have been severely limited. She could hardly object on moral grounds given her own use of marijuana to arrive at a suitably relaxed state. What's more, when it came to drinking off the bandstand, she could apparently keep up with the best of them.

On the night of Yaples's filming, when Carter had orchestrated a complex network of elements so they would coalesce, she felt Hicks had gone too far. During the sound check she blew up at him, and from that point on things only went downhill. Afterward, she was discreet about the split, explaining it as an inevitable result of having been together for so long. They remained lifelong friends, and she continued to promote his musical efforts: a year after she fired him, she would take Crouch to hear him play in a duo with Ron Carter at the Knickerbocker Saloon on University Place.[15] Hicks would work with Betty Carter on several subsequent occasions, but never again as a regular trio member.

For Carter this was a time of steady gigging, and she had no trouble getting players. Band members who moved on were soon replaced by others who eagerly wanted the opportunity to work. With her impeccable ear for talent, Carter never failed to find gifted young players who were technically ready to break into the professional arena, but who also needed the polish that only comes from time spent in front of an audience. Early in 1980, Carter hired a youthful Mulgrew Miller to take Hicks's place. Greg Bandy, who had worked with her briefly in early 1973, signed on to replace Washington, who left in the wake of Hicks's firing.[16] Curtis Lundy stayed on as the mainstay of her next trio, but at times other bass players, including David Eubanks, filled in for him. By March, Carter had recovered from the dissolution of her group and was taking her new trio out on the road, bringing it to her hometown, among other places.[17]

Jack Whittemore had a rule about booking his artists that Carter would ultimately make her own: do not overexpose yourself in any one locale. As a result, Carter was on the move a lot of the time. The staple of her schedule was weeklong runs at such venues as Blues Alley in Washington, Jazz Showcase and Rick's Cafe Americain in Chicago, the Great American Music Hall in San Francisco, and of course various clubs in New York City such as Fat Tuesday's and the Bottom Line. She appeared at festivals, doing the Montreux/Detroit Jazz Festival in July. There were also isolated evenings scattered among the extended engagements. In August, for example, Carter did a gig in Philadelphia opposite a small group led by Count Basie. For Carter, sharing the bill with such a legendary figure was emblematic of the new stature she was attaining: "I never thought I would get to that point, doing a gig with Count Basie."[18] Then there were the occasional college dates, such as the one Carter did in March at Rutgers University.[19] New York City, however, remained her center of operations.

A performance at Howard University in 1980 was the scene of another filming, this time by Michelle Parkerson. Carter had been to Howard the year before, to perform a set at Crampton Auditorium during a two-week-long festival, fulfilling a long-harbored wish she had to bring her art to a black college. She may have found some irony in the festival's theme: "Survival of the Black Artist." She shared the program with Lionel Hampton's band, their first performance together in many years. Their quarrelsome history did not keep her from joining in the spirit of the evening, jamming with the vibraphonist at the end of his set, which closed the evening.[20] The two would continue to maintain ties after this. In September 1981 she was invited by President Reagan to attend a tribute to Hampton at the White House and a performance at the Kennedy Center that was later aired on PBS.[21] Carter glowed in the recognition: "After all these years Lionel has come around to understanding what I'm all about . . . and I'm happy that he's finally calling me Betty Carter."[22] Appropriately enough, Carter sang an extended version of "Seems Like Old Times." The event may have brought back memories of Hampton's performance at the White House thirty years earlier for Harry Truman's inauguration.

Hampton was also on hand to reminisce with Carter on film when Parkerson was shooting her documentary in 1980. The filmmaker had begun her movie about Carter, entitled . . . *But Then, She's Betty Carter* in 1976, but due to various setbacks the project's completion had been delayed. In the film's opening segment Carter can be heard insisting that Parkerson get new footage because she felt that her singing had changed so much since they had begun shooting. Working with new musicians always sparked her growth, and by this time her new trio members were bringing a fresh energy to her book. While much of the music they did had been recorded on *Now It's My Turn* and *The Audience,* her improvisatory approach led to differences in this performance. In the first musical selection on the film, "I Could Write a Book," for example, while the arrangement is the same as the one she had recorded less than year before, her rendition digresses significantly from that version, even while she is singing the lyrics. Interspersed amid highlights of Carter's performance at Howard University are interview segments that touch upon Carter's artistic and personal values. There is also footage of her son Myles's graduation from high school. By the fall of 1980, with the help of essential grant money, Parkerson was finally able to complete the project.[23] At the film's premiere, a crowd of over three hundred filled the District Building for the event as Mayor Marion Barry proclaimed 23 October 1980 Betty Carter Day in Washington, D.C.[24] The film would be aired the following year on PBS for Black History Month and was telecast at other times over the following years. It was also screened at several other venues, including various film festivals, giving mainstream viewers a chance to discover Carter's work.[25]

Sensitive to television's potential for capturing the visual aspect of her work, Carter continued to pursue opportunities to have her work filmed and broadcast. In November 1981 she was filmed again, this time performing for a studio audience. Record producer Michael Cuscuna produced the show, entitled *Call Me Betty Carter,* for CBS Cable. In addition to an interview with Alex Katy, the film featured saxophonist Sonny Stitt in what would turn out to be one of his last performances, as well as saxophonist Ricky Ford, and drummer Michael Carvin.[26] John Hicks returned to play for this gig, and pianist Khalid Moss, who was then in her trio, recalled serving as a consultant, showing Hicks how the charts had changed since he had left the band. As Moss put it, Carter paid him seven hundred dollars "not to play piano."[27] CBS Cable folded shortly after the film was made, and it did not air much.

During the period when Carter had been preparing to bring out *The Audience* on Bet-Car, Columbia Records was also pursuing the reissue of *Meet Betty Carter and Ray Bryant*, along with the sessions that had never been released when she recorded with Gigi Gryce in 1956. This collection would be issued with the title *Social Call*. Unlike previous reissues, the singer was pleased about this release. Not only had someone from the label called her to let her know it was coming it out, but unlike past reissues, Columbia Records also paid her some royalties.[28] In October, glowing reviews began to come in for material she had recorded twenty-five years before.[29]

By November 1980, Khalid Moss had taken over for a pianist named Kasah Ali, who had worked with Carter for about a month after Mulgrew Miller left the band.[30] Indicative of Carter's growing fame, Pomegranate Artbooks included her picture in its 1981 Jazz Calendar. New Year's Day brought Carter and her trio to the Bottom Line.[31] JoAnne Jimenez, a close friend of Carter's, recalled that members of the singer's family, including her brother James and one of her sisters, flew out to New York to hear Carter perform during this run. Her success made it possible for her to look her family in the eye knowing that bagging the supermarket job they had lined up for her in 1968 was the right decision. This visit indicated a gradual thawing of relations between them.[32]

Enthusiastic reviews for *The Audience* began to appear early in 1981,[33] and the record was nominated by the National Academy of Recording Arts and Science (NARAS) for a Grammy later that spring. The award for best female jazz performance went to Ella Fitzgerald, but there was a consolation prize. That June the National Association of Independent Record Distributors gave the Bet-Car founder an "Indie" award for producing *The Audience*.[34] In addition to the renown she was getting as a musician, Carter was gaining recognition as a record producer. The success of this record vindicated all the efforts that had gone into forming her label and keeping it afloat.

Then in July, Carter embarked upon a new path, appearing as a special guest soloist at a free concert in Brooklyn's Prospect Park with forty strings from the Brooklyn Philharmonia conducted by composer David Amram. Amram had played French horn in various jazz contexts early in his career, and several of his compositions explored ways of introducing the jazz idiom into a classical setting. He had known about Carter's work as far back as 1955, when he had come to New York from Washington, D.C., and heard Charles

Mingus and members of his band speak admiringly of her.[35] According to Amram, the idea to work together grew out of his visit backstage after one of Carter's performances at the Great American Music Hall in 1977. Once she discovered that he was in San Francisco to attend a conference having to do with expanding National Public Radio programming to include more world music and jazz, Carter offered to sign on to the undertaking. In the course of making a case for this cause, the two got to know each other and had several discussions about the relationship between classical music and jazz, and when they parted, Amram gave her a recording of his 1972 composition for woodwind, brass, and jazz quintets.[36]

Carter had an earnest love of European classical music. Other than jazz, it was the only kind of music she had allowed her sons to listen to on Sundays, at least until their teen years, indicating the religious zeal she had for both kinds of music. Daniel Mixon recalled that she had turned him on to the music of Dvorak;[37] her son Myles spoke of her passion for Sibelius;[38] and JoAnne Jimenez described how she and Carter enjoyed going to concerts together.[39] The wide dynamic range and sudden dynamic contrasts Carter used are features of European classical music as well as jazz, and her expansion of the song format into extended compositions, as in "Surrey with the Fringe on Top," "All through the Day," "Wagon Wheels," and her current chart for "What a Little Moonlight Can Do," or her own "Sounds (Movin' On)," may have had roots in her exposure to this music. Her distaste for musical quotations, which can take the listener out of the performance at hand, echoes of classical composers' efforts to mold self-contained—so-called absolute—musical entities.[40] Carter even took cello lessons at the Brooklyn Music School, which was situated directly opposite her brownstone, literally in her own front yard. It is not surprising, then, that she—like her hero Charlie Parker—seized upon the chance to perform with strings. Having an alto saxophone soloist in the person of Paquito D'Rivera—who had just arrived in the United States from Cuba—on the program, brought Bird with Strings to mind even more.[41]

The first half of the program included compositions by Alberto Ginastera, Gershwin, Ellington, and Amram that explored the boundaries between jazz and symphonic music. It ended with three string arrangements that featured Carter and her trio, which now included Lewis Nash on drums. The charts, which she had never performed live, came from her ABC-Paramount recording sessions.[42] For the second half of the program Carter returned to the stage with just her trio. In an interview with Leonard Feather later that summer, Carter estimated that there had been about four thousand people in the crowd, which was made up of "black, white, young, old," noting that "they were absolutely quiet and respectful."[43] After having spent much of her early career battling to get her message across to noisy mobs in dimly lit grottos, the attentiveness with which the open-air audience received her work left a deep impression on her.

Carter was so pleased with the results that she wanted to expand upon the concept. One of the owners of the Bottom Line had heard the outdoor concert, and soon after the concert he, Carter, and Amram began to explore the possibility of doing the program at his club.[44] Carter had been harboring a wish to work with a larger group at least as far back as 1980: "If this record [*The Audience with Betty Carter*] does anything like maybe I hope it does, with the new number of fans I've gained over the years, maybe then I will be able to hire fifteen, sixteen, or seventeen pieces."[45] Now she had the means to finance such a venture. Amram was too busy to do the additional charts, so she contracted the arranger Herman Dennison.[46] For the Bottom Line dates, Amram assembled a fifteen-piece string group plus harp consisting mostly of Brooklyn Philharmonia players. Although he felt that Dennison's charts were well done, the conductor ultimately had to modify the arrangements during rehearsals so they fit more closely what Carter was actually doing, because the arranger was not able to attend rehearsals.[47]

These modifications are revealing. In some of the string sections certain passages were simply omitted or moved up an octave so the sound of the low- to midrange instruments would not cancel out Carter's low register and deep tone color.[48] By giving the harmonies a more open voicing, these changes also made the texture transparent enough to allow Carter's voice to emerge out of the mass of sound. In other cases Amram made the charts more responsive to Carter so she could improvise without being locked into a rigid sequence of events. In "With No Words," which she had recorded in 1976 on Roulette, Dennison's charts did not give Carter enough room to improvise, partly because of the tune's structure. Built on the same chord root throughout, the tune is a study of the shifting moods that can result simply from modifying a chord's quality. Its modal approach, akin to the one Miles Davis explored in such tunes as "Milestones" and "So What," required the improviser to alter the scale degrees of the C scale in response to chord changes. Much of the time the tune remains on a C minor6 chord (Dorian mode), but moves through C major7 and C7 (C major scale to C mixolydian) for the bridge, with brief passes through C6, C diminished, and C augmented. The minimalism of the concept fascinated Carter: "You still have that 'modal' sound going through it, like that C that is going straight through it. Actually the chord is changing you know, and it takes just one note to change a chord."[49] To the musicians Carter referred to the tune as "The Mode"; but perhaps she felt that name was too abstract for the general listener.[50] Because of the lack of words, it seems at first as though she's simply blowing on the changes from the start, but a comparison with other performances reveals that there is indeed a head, even if it is not indicated on the chart.

In response to the idiosyncratic concept of "With No Words," Amram devised an elaborate system of conducting signals to cue the string players. They would in turn vary their timbres using different bowing techniques, as well as various types of pizzicato, to create timbral interest while playing essentially a tonic drone. The shifting fabric of sound paralleled the tune's kaleidoscopic harmonic mutations. In addition, for each performance, the ending was created on the spur of the moment. Being a composer in his own right, Amram was able to use extended and aleatoric techniques employed by the classical avant-garde, in order to coax the classically trained string players of the Brooklyn Philharmonia to match Carter's mercurial leaps of imagination. In performance Amram adopted such an improvisational approach that he felt he was conducting in the same way he would play in a jazz group.[51] The rapport between conductor and soloist was so intuitive, he recalled, they hardly ever had to speak to each other. "The string players would flip out at the different endings that we would arrive at as we worked our way to the end of the chart, each night producing a different way to get there," the conductor marveled. "They would follow me and I'd follow her and she'd follow me, and eventually we'd talk about it and agree that we were both following the music, we would kind of instinctively know what to do. . . . It was almost like ESP. That's what it was like when I played with Mingus and with Monk."[52]

Amram's jazz experience also prepared him to deal with Carter's extreme back phrasing, or "delayed action singing," in her ballads. He recalled the first time they rehearsed "Cocktails for Two," which unfolded at an incredibly slow tempo. At a certain point during the reading, she surprised him by making an entrance "at a different place" than the one notated in the chart. Based upon his experience conducting opera, he slowed down to adjust to her. As he described it, after a couple of measures went by, she stopped and said: "No, David, forget about the music [the score], don't follow me. Just lay it out. I'll do everything else."[53] Relying upon the tight ensemble of the rhythm section, the conductor in turn told the trio members: "Just pretend that I'm not even here." From then on, in order to time his conducting to the groove, he watched Curtis Lundy's fingers on the bass, and the high hat on Lewis Nash's drums, much as in a concerto he might have timed a crucial orchestral entrance by watching an instrumental soloist's hands. Then, in order to coordinate the acoustics of the different instruments, so as to bring the sounds of the disparate subgroups together, he conducted a slight bit ahead of the trio. Otherwise, lacking the percussive attack of rhythm section instruments, the strings would have seemed behind—especially when playing pianissimo, where it can take a moment to get the string to "speak," or vibrate. Keeping the musicians all together was a challenge because, when Carter started to do her "rubato" singing, as he put it, some of the string players thought they were in the wrong place.[54] Nash himself admitted the "huge trust factor" that comping for Carter's extreme back phrasing entailed. The musicians had to be confident that the singer knew where she was in the chord changes and would catch up when she wanted to. She was so daring that he usually did not know when and how she would catch up.[55]

For Amram and Carter, the concerts with strings were an opportunity to promote the mission they shared, to elevate jazz to its proper place in the culture, as an art music—an American classical music. They did the programs several more times over the following years, modifying the repertoire to the demands of each new situation. Carter even did the arrangements once with the Kronos Quartet at the Great American Music Hall.[56] To Amram, echoing Dave Brubeck's view of jazz from thirty years before, they were presenting "a magnificent high art as opposed to the tawdry commercial stuff that was being presented to young people."[57] Wanting jazz musicians to earn the respect that classical musicians receive,[58] Carter followed the conventions of the concert world and insisted that the musicians wear black tie for the performances at the Bottom Line, which took place on 26–28 March 1982. Leslie Gourse noted that when Carter returned for the program's second half, when the strings took the stage, she had changed from a "black crepe jump suit and bejeweled belt" to a "high necked, lacy sky-blue gown."[59] Afterward, Carter told the writer that she had ambitions of doing the program at Carnegie Hall.[60] The concert itself, however, was not a stiffly formal affair.

As a record label owner, Carter did not want to miss this opportunity to document the event. She arranged for Joe Ferla to be there with a sound truck so he could engineer and mix a recording of the performance. For the release Carter used the best takes from two sets, nine tracks in all. The record, entitled *Whatever Happened to Love,* was the fourth Carter had brought out on her own label and the third she had produced live. As with her other live recordings, this one documents the remarkable power Carter could exert over the listener. At the end of Gordon Jenkins's "Goodbye,"[61] for example, the audience remained rapt in silence for almost thirty seconds, held in Carter's thrall by her last unaccompanied note, before showering her with applause. Citing the lyrics of "Cocktails for Two" in the liner notes, Carter referred to her audience as the "principal ingredient." As pianist Benny Green would later report: "She told me that people, regardless of the amount of exposure they've had to so-called jazz music, can still sense where your heart is. If you're playing out of love, if you're just making the gig, if you're trying to impress them, if you're trying to reach them, the level of respect you have for them, the level of respect for the music . . . People can sense all that within the first few notes."[62]

Produced less than a year after *The Audience*'s release, *Whatever Happened to Love* may have grown from the pragmatic wish to issue a new record on her label quickly so she could capitalize on the wave of interest her recent work had been generating. Carter generally resisted listening to her prior recordings, feeling that she had already moved on from earlier ways of doing a song. Around this time she told Kitty Grime: "When I record a tune, I know I'm never going to sing that tune like that again. That's *over.*"[63] But in light of her current success she had begun to look back over her career. She had told Matthew Yaple: "I'm dealing with yesterday more than ever before, because to be at this point where anybody would be interested in my yesterdays is quite an achievement."[64] Including eight songs that she had recorded before, *Whatever Happened to Love* reflects this tendency. In their new settings the songs have a wistful, retrospective quality, especially those accompanied by strings. Some of the record's material came from the earliest years of her career, including an imaginative reworking of Gigi Gryce's "Social Call," which Columbia had only just issued. "What a Little Moonlight Can Do" dated back to *The Modern Sound of Betty Carter.* The tune had served as the title song for that album's reissue by MCA records, coupled with *Out There,* in 1976. By rejuvenating the title songs from these releases, the singer was referring back to her earlier effort while also promoting it. "Cocktails for Two," "Goodbye," and "Every Time We Say Goodbye" built upon her work with Ray Charles, and she used the string charts Marty Paich had done as the basis for her current arrangements.[65] In addition to "With No Words," the record included the two other originals that she had recorded on *Now Its My Turn* but for which Morris Levy had not given her composer or publisher credit, "New Blues (You Purr)," also with string arrangements, and "Abre La Puerta." The last of these was none other than her theme song, "Open the Door," now fully abstracted from the words and sung entirely in scat. This deconstruction of her own work was not without precedent, for she had recently performed "Fake" with scat syllables instead of lyrics at the Montreux/Detroit Jazz Festival in July 1980. According to Carter, the decision to scat here was made "on the spot."[66] Carter was aware of the abstract quality of scatting, and she rarely overindulged her taste for it at the expense of her audience. The presence of two entirely scatted tunes on this album is therefore an anomaly. On a few of the songs, "New Blues (You Purr)," for example, saxophonist Jerry Dodgion took the role Paquito D'Rivera had played in Brooklyn, but he is not given credit on the liner notes and his sound is lost in the live mix. Other tunes from the dates at the Bottom Line did not make it onto the record.[67]

Carter's reconception of "What a Little Moonlight Can Do" from *Whatever Happened to Love* illustrates how far she could take her creative process, transforming the song from her original explosion of high-energy vocal pyrotechnics lasting just over two minutes (example 6) into a probing exploration of various moods lasting more than ten. The song as it was originally conceived is in long meter, a rhythmic approach she was fond of. Perhaps this feature gave her the impetus to take the rhythmic transformation of her materials one step further, setting the whole first chorus in 5/4 time. Having used this tricky meter in "Sounds (Movin' On)," she had already demonstrated that she could improvise fluently in it. Here she displays further rhythmic virtuosity by singing the tune's lyrics to a melody recast to fit a different time signature, as she had once done with "'Round Midnight." In the conspicuous way she counted off the tempo it is clear that she wanted to put this feature of the chart on display (example 14).

At first glance Carter's approach seems to add a needless level of complexity to a fairly simple tune, perhaps even obscuring its happy-go-lucky message. Instead of sounding fussy, however, the effect is to release the beat from common time's four-square predictability and float it effortlessly on the rhythm section's asymmetrical groove, which has a three-plus-two feel similar to Paul Desmond's "Take Five." Moss's suave touch, Lundy's easy rhythmic precision, and Nash's subtle propulsion of the music through time all contribute to the meter's laid-back intensity. Within this luxurious atmosphere, Carter's back phrasing and rhythmic hesitations stretch out languorously, creating a clever evocation of the moon's power to render an unsuspecting soul vulnerable to love's charms.

Rather than disrupt the meaning of the lyrics, Carter's fragmentation of the text into shorter sense units allows the listener to take in the words while also delighting in the interplay she creates with the rhythm section. In measure 5 [0:13–0:15], for instance, she takes advantage of the fluidity of the words "what a little," all short vowel sounds and voiced consonants placed near the front of the mouth (/wədəlidl/), to get quickly to "moonlight," stressing the word's first vowel, /uw/, with a longer rhythmic value. The motion this initial activity generates continues to diffuse through the next long vowel "do," /duw/, which receives a slight accent as it comes from the G-natural below, until it arrives on the word "you," /yuw/, which she lengthens for emphasis. Here Carter shows how she can put the words' inherent rhythmic energy to good use, shaping the music's motion with it while also enunciating the lyrics.

To balance the persistence of the /uw/ vowel sound here, she collapses the song's urgent repetition of that sound, "oo, oo, oo," into a single /uw/ [0:04–0:10]. While she also had dispensed with the opening repetition in 1960, by setting her 1982 version in a slower tempo, she gave the /uw/ a plaintive character that sets an entirely different tone from her earlier heart-pounding version. Carter's matter-of-fact delivery in 1982 suggests a cool distance from the moon's lunacy, giving the words an understated irony and hinting at the narrator's wisdom in matters of love. She is no longer acting out the love-struck victim of the moon, playing instead a sage counselor who recalls how it once felt to lose her reason to the exigencies of romance. In this opening statement, at least, she has moved from inside the experience to outside, adopting a mature, removed perspective on the havoc love can wreak.

At the next statement of the title phrase at measures 12–15 [0:32–0:41], Carter follows the same principle she used earlier in the song, but now increases the accentuation on "moon," "do," and "you," by pulling apart the phrases that hold these words, and lengthening each of them, as well as adding grace notes to the latter two. Listen to how, in these last instances, Carter places the word-accent off the beat, to increase the richness of interaction with the groove's layers of rhythmic activity. Incidentally, the melodic idea used at measure 12 [0:32–0:34] will take on importance later in the chart, but we do not know that at this point in the performance. When the title phrase comes back again at measures 36–39 [1:36–1:45], Carter draws it out even more, setting "what a little" to a ternary skipping rhythm against the 5/4, extending "moon" and "do" more than a half note in length, and elaborating further on the latter word with a quick ornament that echoes her first statement of these words. In this third statement she delays the phrase for so long that she must omit the closing words, "to you." The effect of this elision is to suppress the sense of closure these words would have brought, holding the listener in suspense until the next phrase. Even the way she unveils the lyrics serves to generate swing, for by denying the listener's expectations here, she propels the music forward.

Carter reinforces the music's continuity and keeps the momentum from flagging in other ways as well. While the arrangement follows the broad outlines of the tune's original changes, her rhythmic approach to the form required an elaboration of its original changes. The harmonic structure has therefore been expanded in places with the insertion of chord substitutions that generate greater tonal motion. The increased harmonic pace that results keeps the slower tempo and the long meter from weighing down the momentum. Instead of remaining on the tonic harmony during the opening four measures for example, the chords here guide the harmony from the tonic, B-flat major, through an E-flat7 (IV^7), D minor7–G7 (ii^7/ii–V^7/ii) [00:0–0:13], to the C minor in measure 5. This sequence will become a recurrent feature of the chart, returning at measures 21–24 [0:55–1:05], and again at measures 33–36 [1:26–1:37], as well as later in the arrangement. By approaching the area of the C minor via its ii^7–V^7, and then remaining in it for the next eight measures, Carter tonicizes it. In this context, even the dominant of the home key in measure 8 is treated momentarily as a IV^7 of C minor. This treatment gives the tune a tantalizing harmonic instability as it lingers in a secondary area, creating suspense as we await the return of a tonic at which Carter has so far barely hinted.

Later in the chart Carter amplifies this avoidance of the home key and the emphasis on the supertonic. When the opening statement ends in a deceptive cadence to an A-flat altered dominant at measure 61 [2:41], it undermines the finality that the return to the tonic would normally produce at this point in the form. An "out" section follows in which Carter intones the song's title against free time and sharply dissonant harmony, suspended over an A-flat pedal [2:41–2:58]: under the moon's influence even the turnaround has gone awry. From this passage emerges a hard-swinging 4/4 groove that shatters the song's dreamy mood with the delicacy of an early-morning wake-up call [2:58]. Replacing the opening "oo, oo, oo" with a scat idea built out of melodic material from measure 12 (mm. 65–68), the singer now uses a harmonic progression that slides down from an A-flat7 to a G7 ($\flat VII^7$–VI^7 of B-flat, or $\flat VI^7/ii$–V^7/ii) [2:58–3:03] to introduce a second reading of the lyrics. These substitutions replace the initial tonic harmony, preventing a resolution that would have depleted the music's tonal energy, and lead to the supertonic in measure 69 [3:03]. The same approach is used at the form's midpoint, measures 97–100 [3:37–3:42] averting a similar resolution. At the end of this statement a standard turnaround leads to a full-chorus scat solo, which she had prefigured in her earlier scatted fragments at measures 65–68 and at measures 97–100. In making the use of scat itself into an outgrowth of the song's opening vocal gesture, Carter keeps it from seeming inserted merely for technical display. In this chart, at least, the presence of nonsense lyrics becomes a giddy speaking-in-tongues induced by the harmony of the spheres.

Atypically for Carter the chart includes full-chorus instrumental solos, measures 193–256, first by Curtis Lundy and then by Khalid Moss. These no doubt helped her to pace her own performance as well as sustain the listener's interest in the vocal sonority. During these solos the singer murmurs short fills that outline the harmonies, comping for the soloist as a horn player might. Carter next pits herself against Lewis Nash's rapid-fire drum solo, measures 257–320, singing a near-literal statement of the original tune in double time [8:08–8:46]. The band then joins her for half a chorus in this new tempo, measures 321–52, and she reiterates the lyric for the B section of the form, entering where the harmony turns to the subdominant, at measure 337. Echoing the earlier deceptive cadence, the music dramatically shifts back to the first 4/4 tempo at measure 353, while Carter reasserts the measure 12 figure [9:04–9:09]. She proceeds to scat again for the remainder of the chorus, which would have ended at measure 384, but which dovetails into a coda that begins at measure 377 [9:34]. This coda makes use of of the tune's characteristic harmonic gesture, from measures 1–4, with Carter scatting a threefold variation of a new idea that occurs successively at measures 377, measure 385 [9:44], and measure 393 [9:54], ending with a startling two-octave leap into her head voice. As an arranger, Carter designed this chart as a showpiece for her many strengths and those of her musicians. In performance she used it as a show opener, after the trio had warmed up the house, to immediately grab the listener's attention and establish her authority onstage.

A comparison of the version of "What a Little Moonlight Can Do" she released with those in private recordings reveals how much Carter modified the arrangement in performance. In those performances Carter back phrased more, suggesting that for the recording she had done a relatively "straight" version of her reconstituted line. This was partly a function of their faster tempos: the version she did in East Berlin three years later was nearly twice as fast.[68] At that performance she back-phrased so much during the opening chorus—as much as four whole measures at times—that by its end she had run out of time, causing the last lines of the lyrics to spill over into the free section. By delaying the lyrics so much that she had to improvise to stay inside the changes she took the back-phrasing technique well beyond the pale.

Coming as it does on the heels of *The Audience with Betty Carter,* which fans often referred to as Carter's classic recording, *Whatever Happened to Love* has suffered in comparison. *The Audience* is certainly a remarkable record, so remarkable that it served as a template for her trios during the early 1980s. Khalid Moss recalled that listening to John Hicks on that album was a formative experience, even as the younger pianist worked to establish his own voice.[69] Although Moss provides exemplary support for Carter on *Whatever Happened to Love,* at this point in his career, his playing could not compare to that of Hicks. Nevertheless, to judge the record on the basis of Carter's sidemen, as is sometimes done with singers—as though a singer's work is ornamental—is to suggest that what she contributed to the record does not bear scrutiny on its own merits. To be sure, *The Audience* effectively conveys the telepathic level of communication the singer and her ensemble had achieved in 1979. Furthermore, she herself was nostalgic about *The Audience,* feeling it marked a turning point in her career, when she "started taking risks."[70] Nevertheless, *Whatever Happened to Love* shows that in her work as composer, arranger, band leader, and performer, Betty Carter had continued to grow and had honed all of her tools to produce very complex layers of expression, in many cases surpassing her work on *The Audience.* The later record should not be discounted because the group dynamic was occasionally less than magical or because of limitations the strings occasionally placed on Carter's spontaneity. As with *The Audience,* it would be nominated for a Grammy, but it fell short of winning. Later the singer clarified that the title did not refer to romantic love, but "love for people. People caring for one another. Yeah, I worry about that 'cuz people just are not nice anymore. They do something, they want to get paid."[71]

This was a rich time for Carter in more ways than one. She was getting more press than ever before and was charging more for her appearances. In September 1982, a finely detailed word-portrait of her by Whitney Balliett appeared in the *New Yorker,* further increasing her exposure to the mainstream audience.[72] The piece was warmly complimentary, and its timing was especially opportune. Carter was on the verge of announcing the release of *Whatever Happened to Love,* which she did at a press party thrown by Liljay Productions at Studio 54 in November. She wisely capitalized on the occasion by also publicizing a forthcoming appearance at the Brooklyn Academy of Music with David Amram and the Brooklyn Philharmonic, Jerry Dodgion, and her trio.

Carter was also receiving a wave of recognition in the African American community, with greater attention from the black press than she had ever received.[73] Having spent years berating the African American community for abandoning its own cultural heritage, she must have welcomed these signs of its renewed support for the music. But Carter did more than berate. As her fame grew, she gave performances directed squarely at expanding black listenership for jazz. In September 1979 she had brought her trio to Harlem World to perform opposite Art Blakey's Jazz Messengers for the Uptown Jazz Junta, a group dedicated to bringing the music back uptown.[74] In May 1982, upon returning from a stint in Marseille, France, she had performed at a benefit for the Young Musicians of New York City Jazz Ensemble at the High School of Music and Art in Harlem.[75] She would continue to seek out similar opportunities to bring the music to her people and stimulate their interest in it. In this vein, Carter had begun to include the South in her touring itinerary, with an appearance in Atlanta the preceding April, which led to a road trip through the South the following spring and ambitions for further ventures into what she called jazz's "virgin territory."[76] Unlike her earlier attempts to attract a black crowd, these efforts were welcomed. She was one of five honorees at "A Salute to Black Women" held at Howard University in October 1982, where she had received a College of Fine Arts Award in 1980.[77] In addition, she continued to build an audience overseas, with trips to Europe becoming an obligatory feature of her touring schedule.

Out of necessity Betty Carter had become a sophisticated promoter of her own work, and she was now learning more about the mechanics of generating ink, such as the above press party. She needed to take the initiative now partly because of a transition she was going through in the handling of her bookings. Due to a prolonged illness that started in 1981 Jack Whittemore was often unavailable when she most needed his attention, and she began seeking others to support her activities. Around this time JoAnne Jimenez began to take over certain tasks, organizing Carter's office and making travel arrangements. After seeing Carter perform on *Saturday Night Live* in 1976, Jimenez decided she "had to meet this woman."[78] She recalled arranging for the singer to perform in Boulder, Colorado, and interviewing her for her college radio station. Shortly after, Jimenez came to New York. She had been doing bookings with a European agent before she started helping Carter out and had had dealings with Whittemore, so she already had some knowledge of the terrain; but she considered her work for the singer her first real experience in the business. Eventually she moved into an apartment in Carter's neighborhood. Since 1979 the singer had begun to acquire an entourage, including a fashion consultant and an office secretary, partly because she was juggling so many aspects of the music business.[79] She even began employing the owner of the Great American Music Hall, Tom Bradshaw, as her personal manager, a startling about-face for the autonomous singer suggesting that she felt the time was ripe to reach for celebrity.[80] The seasoned businesswoman knew how to exploit her increased marketability, and, according to Jimenez, she let Bradshaw negotiate with Whittemore for higher fees and other concessions.[81] By the time Whittemore died in 1983, Carter had moved on to the Willard Alexander Agency, which booked other singers and several big bands. She would later add publicists and press agents in major cities such as Detroit and Los Angeles, who worked on short-term assignment to promote her local appearances. All of these accessories coalesced into a production company, which she called Liljay after Lillie Mae Jones. Liljay Productions had begun to take shape as early as December 1979 with the help of JoAnne Jimenez, and, once formed, it served as an umbrella for her recording label, her performing activities, and other related concerns.[82]

During this transition in her booking and management personnel, the rhythm section had been relatively stable. From the spring of 1981, when Carter had fired Greg Bandy and hired Lewis Nash to take over on drums,[83] until around October 1982, when David Penn replaced Curtis Lundy on bass, the working unit had had as much time to gel as any of her preceding groups. Ever the vigilant talent scout, Carter had heard Penn play the preceding spring when he had been a member of the Young Musicians of New York City Jazz Ensemble. Lundy had been with her for nearly four years and had provided an anchor amid the changes that followed John Hicks's departure. During the current round of changes it was Lewis Nash's turn to provide such continuity. On the southern tour in the spring of 1983, Carter let Khalid Moss go. The band leader had been planning to replace him for some time, and by the time she gave him notice, she had already made arrangements for Benny

Green to take his place. By May, a new face looked up from the piano bench as the ensemble made its way across the Midwest, playing dates in Detroit, Milwaukee, and Minneapolis.[84]

Carter had been hiring talented young players for some time, but she had not actively used this feature of her act as a selling point until now. At the age of fifty-four she was reaching out to the young adult audience, the large cohort born during the 1950s that was now a critical market in the selling of American entertainment. To this end, when she introduced her players at performances, she made a great show of telling their ages—which were generally in the low to middle twenties, in some cases even the late teens. Betty Carter's reputation as a finishing school for promising young musicians, a one-woman university, would grow into an important feature of her act. In many ways she took on a maternal image for her musicians, dispensing moral wisdom along with musical tips, and her players viewed her as a mother hen at times.

In light of the events in her own family during the summer of 1983, this perception of the singer carries a certain irony. With Kagle, seventeen, finishing his schooling at the Friends Academy and about to attend the School of Visual Arts in Manhattan, and Myles, twenty-one, studying communications at C. W. Post College, Carter's children were now quite grown. Given the demands her performing schedule had often made during the preceding eight years, however, the transition to an "empty nest" would not be all that notable. Remarkably, she had juggled the demands of having a career and a family and had included her sons in her work in a variety of ways, using a photograph of them with her for the back cover of *The Betty Carter Album*, for example, and naming her publishing company MyKag. She obviously loved her children, but despite her best intentions she had been away a lot of the time during their upbringing, and as her touring schedule got busier, she was often on the road for birthdays and other special occasions. By word and by example she had taught her sons to be independent, much in the way she had learned from her mother. She was proud of them and undoubtedly relieved as well, that "the kids didn't go wrong," telling Leslie Gourse, "My friends and their father helped me raise them."[85] Her younger son appreciated that she had worked hard to make their lives as "normal" as possible, and as entertainer's children generally do, he took for granted the aspects of their life that were not.[86]

Carter admitted that her career had left little time to cultivate deep personal connections with anyone: "People remind me of things I did years ago. And I don't remember at all, if it wasn't to do with music. I'm so busy concentrating on the music, I forget people or things I should have remembered."[87] In many ways her dedication to her muse made her unavailable for intimacy, and she was loathe to let anyone, especially men, into the private place in which she held herself apart.

> I suppose a lot of men are attracted to you because of what you do. You're special, you know. And they would like to be with somebody special. But can they handle that? Once they get into that special world, can they deal with that? A lot of us singers have a particular attitude about things, and men can't handle it. They can't handle the aggressiveness. I know they can't handle *my* aggressiveness. Because I know I'm aggressive.[88]

Betty Carter's relationship with a few select women may have been the greatest source of stability in her personal life. Over her lifetime, one of her closest friendships was with Ora Harris, whom Carter credited with planting the seeds of her success. Carter's alliance with JoAnne Jimenez had evolved from a personal to a professional one. Beyond her inner circle, the singer was outwardly gracious to acquaintances but generally unapproachable on an intimate level, and few others ever drew close enough to win her trust. She was a staunch supporter and loyal friend, but once she felt betrayed by someone, she did not hesitate to cut him or her off entirely. As with other highly capable people, she made a great show of her autonomy. But in many ways she was emotionally needful and required the complete devotion of the people around her.

Not one to stand still, Carter's recent successes fueled grander ambitions. It was with great expectations, then, that Liljay Productions prepared to present a concert with strings at Symphony Hall in Boston on 22 October 1983. Carter had performed there the preceding March on a bill with the Modern Jazz Quartet for the Boston Globe Jazz Festival and had appreciated the hall's acoustics.[89] Home of the Boston Symphony, the space cried out for the string arrangements, and she embarked upon having David Amram assemble a group for the event which was billed "On an Autumn Evening." Unlike the preceding string dates, in which Amram had programmed the jazz into a concert of European classical music, the evening was to be all Carter.

Now a concert promoter as well, Betty Carter had much at stake in the venture, financially and emotionally, and she brought all of her media savvy to bear on the marketing of this concert. In addition to a press party at the Performance Center of the Berklee College of Music, numerous radio and television stations blanketed the region with advance promotion three days before the concert.[90] On the show *Say Brother,* WGBH devoted a half hour segment to her, targeted specifically at Boston's black audience and aired three times that fall. It was also broadcast at times during the following January, and Carter had hopes that it would be syndicated through PBS. At Berklee she spoke to a packed hall, accepting a plaque from Lee Berk in honor of her distinguished career, and she even autographed albums at the well-known Beantown record shop Strawberries.[91]

Given her past relationship with the city of Boston, Carter was convinced that she would fill the house. As she told radio host Art Roberts: "I was in The Workshop before it closed, I was in Lou Lou Whites when it closed and then Tinket's when it closed. . . . Now I do Jonathan Swifts, so that's the only one that's still hanging around. I've been to Sandy's, so this area has been very good to me. And *all* the colleges, I've done them all, practically all of them and there's more to do, so it's been a great relationship really with this area."[92] Her distributor, Rounder Records, was also located nearby, and Carter's confidence came partly from her past record sales in the Boston area.

An audience of about a thousand devoted followers assembled for the affair, and the evening received glowing reviews in the *Boston Globe* and in *Down Beat.* In a smaller hall such a response would have been a gratifying reward for all the effort spent promoting the concert. By selling only about a third of the house, however, the event was a failure financially. Having used personal resources to produce the event, Carter had good reason to be disheartened by the dismal box office receipts, and the recognition that she had misjudged her popularity wounded her deeply. Blaming Jimenez—who had been in charge of publicity—Carter fired her and then proceeded to sever their relationship. Jimenez turned her attention to the booking agency that she had started the preceding summer and named The Bridge at Carter's urging.[93] In the aftermath of yet another painful falling out with an intimate, Carter threw herself into her performing schedule, heading to Colby College in Maine that November to do her concert with strings accompanied by the college's own ensembles. As in the past, life would go on.

11

Celebrity

By the early-1980s the winds of fashion had shifted again, and it became stylish to be a jazz singer. People who had had little to do with the music were now clamoring to lay claim to the designation. There had been isolated signs of this direction earlier. Pop rock singer Phoebe Snow had included Gershwin's "There's a Boat That's Leaving Soon for New York" on her album *Second Childhood,* released in January 1976. At the end of that decade, Joni Mitchell made her record *Mingus* in collaboration with the bass player just before he died in 1979. Even then Carter had criticized the practice, telling Herb Nolan: "Now they want to put a jazz label on a singer and yet recording companies don't want to record jazz singers. . . . So here all of a sudden they want to *make* a jazz singer? What is it? What are they thinking?"[1]

In 1984, Linda Ronstadt reached for jazz legitimacy with her record *Lush Life,* backed by Nelson Riddle's arrangements. While describing her conversion in a *Down Beat* interview the following year, the reformed rocker spoke highly of Carter's earliest available recorded work: "Betty Carter completely slays me. That record with "Just Tell Him I Said Hello" [*sic*] on it just knocks me out. I love the way she sang the melody. That record was a big influence on me."[2] Later in the decade other young singers would begin to receive recognition on the basis of a jazz-inflected approach, including Phyllis Hyman, Susannah McCorkle, and Maria Muldaur, reinforcing the notion that jazz singing was back "in."[3] By then, media pundits were beginning to wonder who would follow in the footsteps of the older generation of singers who had roots in jazz soil.

Prophetically, Carter had already expressed dismay over the tradition's prospects long before, when she told Arthur Taylor in 1972: "After me there are no more jazz singers. What I mean is there's nobody scaring me to death.

No young woman is giving me any trouble when it comes to singing jazz. I'm not even worried about it and that's a shame. It's sad that there's nobody stepping on my heels so I can look back and say, I better get myself together because this little girl is singing her thing off."[4] Her current view had not improved. Now, over a decade after she had made these remarks, and well after the continuity of the jazz vocal tradition had been shaken, recent efforts to graft a new generation of singers onto the family tree seemed futile. She could not conceive of these singers' forays into jazz territory as anything but the treading of imposters on sacred turf. Perhaps the attempts of younger singers to connect their expression with the music's original sources were destined to sound forced to her. After all, they lacked access to the kinds of experiences she had enjoyed in the 1950s as she had worked her way up through the ranks.

In conjunction with this recent trend, Carter's name had now become big enough for other singers to drop, so as to implicate themselves obliquely with jazz's newly revived luster. As early as 1981, Puma Jones, the defining voice of the Jamaican reggae group Black Uhuru, had cited the jazz singer as her favorite vocalist.[5] Bernice Reagon, founder of the Washington-based gospel group Sweet Honey in the Rock, said she had learned much from Carter's singing.[6] Critics, too, compared other vocalists, such as Chaka Kahn, to Carter. For many, the veteran had become the standard by which a jazz singer's credibility was now measured.[7] Impatiently dismissing all the hype, Carmen McRae quipped to Richard Harrington: "I don't hear anybody young doing what I do, or what Sass [Sarah Vaughan] does, or what Fitz [Ella Fitzgerald] does, or even what Betty Carter does."[8] To Carter, this meant taking risks: "Very few singers challenge themselves like I do—stick their neck out and do the things I do."[9]

Of the singers from the older generation who were still active, Carter stands out for having consistently updated her concept. As much as this growth had taken its impetus from a drive to set herself apart from other musicians, especially from other singers, it followed a course determined by her character and her artistic convictions rather than by a wish simply to appear novel. With regard to the musical materials she used, she worked largely within the established boundaries laid by the musicians of her generation. The common practice of bop, both the musical vocabulary and the set of skills and procedures shared by the musicians, provided the backdrop against which her uniqueness as an artist stood in relief. In the process of developing her own sound she had taken the principles of bebop and postbop—styles more often associated with instrumental music—to their logical conclusion. Of necessity this forced her to burst through the bounds placed upon the singer's role. She innovated, therefore, not only at the level of sound but also at the level of community, of social organization. This aspect of a musician's life can easily elude critics' assessment because it is not internal to the music itself, but provides the context within which the music making takes place.

Simply by going about the business of asserting her own distinctive artistic vision, and allowing the expression of that vision to evolve, Carter was demonstrating that bop-based jazz had not become a quaint historical style whose day had passed, an artifact to be relegated to museum-like settings, but was indeed very much alive. In giving bop currency, Carter's imaginative approach helped spur interest in jazz vocalism among young singers. By surviving the music's near death and by helping to prompt its resurrection, working in the trenches when the going had gotten toughest and generating work for up-and-coming jazz players, Betty Carter had also proved that an enterprising young person could earn a living making this music. But anyone driven to do so would have to do it her own way, as Carter had done.

Only a handful of singers—most notably Al Jarreau and Cassandra Wilson—absorbed any of the lessons Carter was teaching by example.[10] The former singer's recording *Al Jarreau: 1965,* only released in 1982, already revealed style elements that may be attributed to Carter, as well as to Jon Hendricks, Sarah Vaughan, and Carmen McRae, among others. In his work from the mid-1970s, captured in his European tour and released as *Look to the Rainbow,* Jarreau offers clear evidence he had studied Carter's work, especially the music she was performing during this same time period. Hearing the extended scat solo he takes on Paul Desmond's "Take Five," modulating up a half step with each chorus, brings Carter to mind. But by 1983, Jarreau's sound had shifted and Carter was noting, "He's not a jazz singer. He's pop. Manufactured."[11]

Cassandra Wilson first heard the older singer in person at the Jazz and Heritage Festival in New Orleans sometime in the early-1980s. She was so overpowered that she described the experience as an "alien abduction."[12] Later, after a performance of Carter's in Chicago, Wilson approached her for lessons, only to be turned away brusquely.[13] In her earliest recorded work, Wilson drew too heavily on the kinds of jazz dismissed by the more conservative singer to display any obvious resemblance to her. Toward the end of the decade, however, when she recorded standards backed by a rhythm section that included Mulgrew Miller on *Blue Skies,* she showed signs of the master singer's influence. Tellingly, it is in the record's textures that one is most aware of Carter's impact, the unaccompanied scat introduction to "My One and Only Love," for instance, as well as passages accompanied by just bass or drums. When Wilson plunges into her bottom register we can hear echoes of Carter's vocal sonority. In many other respects, however, the presence of instrumental solos on every track, a tendency to phrase with the beat, a closer adherence to the tunes when singing lyrics, Wilson does not follow Carter's lead.

In performance Wilson's far-off manner lacks the gregarious warmth that Carter exuded, making her appear less interested in communicating with her audience. The younger singer's restraint may come from having missed the big-band experience, which required singers from Carter's generation to demonstrate showmanship as well as musicianship, but it also may derive from a tendency among some jazz musicians to view the role of entertainer as something beneath their dignity. In contrast, Betty Carter had a commanding presence on stage. Her charm and her ability to put people at ease could create a remarkable rapport with the audience, and as David Amram has pointed out, her presence elicited a palpable energy from the house.[14] Having learned her craft by doing, at a time when presenting four or five shows a day gave a performer ample opportunity to gain experience onstage, and having grown up in a thriving jazz scene where role models abounded, Carter goaded novices to pass quickly from mimicry to personal expression as soon as they developed enough skill. Coupled with her sometimes callous emphasis on self-reliance, the intuitive way she had gone about creating her own style made her insensitive to the needs of young singers looking to her for guidance. In order to awaken their individual voices, Carter was known to discourage young artists' tendency to emulate the giants from her generation. If this failed, she urged them to seek out musicians who used a medium of expression other than theirs—with vocalists exploring instrumentalists' work and vice versa.

She herself listened voraciously, however, and she spoke knowledgeably about many different musicians' distinctive qualities, including those of singers. Her comments about Phoebe Snow's jazz experiment in the mid-1970s, for example, reveal the depth to which she had analyzed the younger singer's work. Speaking of Pat Williams's arrangement for Snow of "There's a Boat That's Leaving Soon for New York," Carter noted, "He didn't hear her—what her sound was all about—what her bottoms are and her tops are about, what her vibrato is all about; she's got the kind of vibrato you can't get in the way of, it needs freedom, it needs the air."[15] Beyond merely listening, Carter was able to articulate what she expected in a singer's work. Later in the same interview, for example, she asked: "What I want to know is, can these young girls like Flora [Purim], Phoebe [Snow], or Ursula [Dudziak] take a song and *do* a song? I really don't know that; I don't know if they can take a melody and portray the lyric like it should be portrayed—in other words, make me believe it."[16] In her interview with Ben Sidran she stressed the importance of the dramatic element in her own work: "You're an actor actually. You've got to make that audience *understand* that lyric. I mean, you can't just say the words and expect the audience to feel it. You've got to really believe them at the moment, and believe in what you're singing about."[17] She denounced vocalists who succeeded by copying others, comparing them to Anita O'Day. As she put it: "Most jazz singers today . . . haven't got Anita O'Day out of their system."[18]

While there is little support for the notion that any influence flowed from either Carter to O'Day or vice versa, it is intriguing to consider the parallels between their careers. Born ten years before Carter, O'Day was making strides in the music business at a time when Betty Bebop was struggling to gain a foothold. While Carter was getting her start with Hampton, O'Day was gaining renown working with such organizations as Buddy Rich's band, which had access to the mainstream media and routinely played at the higher-priced venues. In 1958, while Carter's performance of "Frenesi" languished on the shelves at Epic records, Verve issued a recording of O'Day singing the same song backed by Russ Garcia and his orchestra, in a reading that is decidedly tamer. Yet unlike Carter's early recordings, O'Day's Verve issues from this period won her acclaim. Carter felt a strong affinity for "Frenesi," featuring it on her shows with Ray Charles in 1961 and recording it again, this time for ABC-Paramount, in November 1962. As her efforts to a produce a hit with the song were frustrated—ABC-Paramount never released that track—O'Day's good fortune seemed boundless. An important appearance at the Newport festival in 1958 secured the white singer's fame during the years that immediately followed, while her black rival would wait until 1977 for her first appearance at the same festival. Gradually over the ensuing decades, however, the tables turned. In 1972, perhaps inspired by her competitor's example, O'Day formed her own label, and as late as 1984 it was generating new releases. O'Day produced a concert at Carnegie Hall in 1985 to celebrate a fifty-year career in the music business. By this time Carter's earlier release of "Frenesi" had seen the light of day on *Social Call* and she was moving on to ever fresh ways of doing the material on that record.

For a number of reasons, then, Betty Carter did not engender many direct imitators. Other singers might have had comparable or even superior vocal technique, "pipes" as she would say, but few could match her intensity of vision and her distinctive execution of it. As with Billie Holiday, she took all of her traits, virtues and flaws, and molded them into a statement that was profoundly hers. Her unique musical experience and life experience informed everything she sang, and she expected other musicians to share what was uniquely theirs, rather than don the jazz idiom as though it were the latest fashion. Carter's independence has, in turn, affected the critical estimation of her contribution. Artists are often judged in terms of the degree to which they inspire other individuals to follow along similar lines, as Charlie

Parker, Dizzy Gillespie, and Miles Davis had done. Because she pushed jazz artists to think for themselves, the ways she inspired other musicians have not come out overtly in their musical style, leaving the traces of her impact buried beneath the surface. The lonely stance Carter took has added to a perception that she was an eccentric mannerist whose work was "out" simply for the sake of being "out" and has thus complicated critical appraisal of her accomplishments.

In the mid-1980s, however, such attitudes were in the minority among jazz writers. Carter was enjoying a sustained run of critical support, and she was thrilled to be making a living singing jazz. Only a few years earlier, Linda Prince had dubbed her *Down Beat* profile of Carter "Bebopper Breathes Fire." Now, having made it on her terms, she could tell Barbara Barrow-Murray the message that she hoped would survive her work: "You can do anything you want if you work hard . . . nothing that's gonna send you to your grave with a smile on your face comes easy. . . . It's about doing what you love. Find out what it is and improve on it."[19] When it came to her work on the bandstand, the fire-breathing bebopper generally kept a clear boundary between art and politics, even at her lowest moments. As much as she may have railed against the social realities of race and the economic realities of the music business, as much as she battled to assert herself as a woman in a man's world and as a singer in an instrumentalist's world, she rarely brought her feelings about these injustices into her bond with the audience. Songs that make a political statement are therefore exceedingly rare in her repertoire. In her performances Carter avoided creating too heavy a mood, being careful to follow a song about love lost, such as "Goodbye," with an up tempo number to dispel the earlier song's gloom. For her, music was meant to be held apart from day-to-day concerns—not so much an escape as a chance to experience spiritual renewal by way of immersion in the emotional realms sound can evoke. "We come to forget about the politics and the day and to try and learn something else, to relieve our minds. We wanna smile, we wanna be happy, we wanna touch, we wanna feel, we wanna make love. So politics has got nothing to do with that."[20]

In 1984 Wynton Marsalis was emerging as a force in the music business, making a splash in the jazz and the European classical worlds by being the first musician to win a Grammy in both categories in a single year. In light of the fact that he and Carter shared similar views about free jazz and fusion, it is not surprising that the two would develop a rapport. She approved of what he had accomplished for so-called straight-ahead jazz, feeling that it ultimately had positive ramifications for the musicians. "Wynton is opening doors. We need somebody to open doors, whatever it takes, so this is what's happening there."[21] This alliance would prove beneficial to Carter in her search for potential sidemen, and when Marsalis became artistic director of Jazz at Lincoln Center, she enjoyed further benefits of having an "in" with him.[22]

Judging from the volume of press she was generating at this time, there was a relative slackening in her performing activities in the mid-1980s. The absence of a follow-up release in the wake of *Whatever Happened to Love* may have caused the gigging to tail off slightly, and she was starting to think about putting out another record soon, but disruptions in her personnel kept her from building up enough material in the studio to do this immediately. In July 1984 Lewis Nash had given notice, and by September she had replaced him with Winard Harper on drums. Later that year Tarik Shah took over for David Penn on bass. At the end of the year Carter's activities were confined to the northeast, with gigs in Boston, New York City, and Philadelphia.

In the summer of 1985, she took the trio on a European tour. At a performance in East Berlin that June someone in the audience made a digital-quality bootleg recording and released it on Repertoire Records under the title *Jazz Bühne Berlin.* In addition to the trio's warm-up number, Herbie Hancock's "One Finger Snap," it included "What a Little Moonlight Can Do," "The Man I Love," "With No Words," "Caribbean Sun," "Every Thing I Have Is Yours," "My Favorite Things," "Every Time We Say Good-Bye," and "Sounds." Carter threatened to go to court over this infringement of the copyright law and quickly had it withdrawn. Burned from her experience with Bush records, and later with Roulette, she now knew how to respond effectively to bootleggers who tried to profit from her efforts. More important, she now had the financial means to make use of her lawyer, Gail Boyd, to stand up for her legal rights. After her experiences with Orville O'Brien and Morris Levy, she was determined not to be made use of again.

By the start of 1986 Carter's trio—which now consisted of Benny Green on piano and Winard Harper on drums, in addition to the new bassist Michael Bowie—had stabilized and would remain together until the first months of 1987. Once the group had become a cohesive ensemble, she recorded six songs. Three of them, "Look What I Got," "Just Like the Movies," and "Mr. Gentleman"—a sequel to "Tight" whose title came from an after-hours club in Detroit[23]—were Carter's original compositions, with the first of these making use of a melodic idea from a scatted passage in her 1979 version of "Sounds (Movin' On)" to which she added lyrics. The remaining three, "The Man I Love," "All I Got," which she had recorded for Peacock in 1958, and "Imagination," were standards. Carter broke with her usual practice of using only a trio and hired tenor saxophonist Don Braden to play on two of these tracks, "The Man I Love" and "Just Like the Movies." Finally making good on a wish she had expressed a decade earlier to produce young jazz artists for Roulette, Carter also recorded a few instrumental numbers with the Harper Brothers' Quintet, which included Braden, as well as her drummer's brother, Philip Harper, on trumpet. Braden recalled that all the tunes he played on were done at Clinton Recording in New York around mid-August 1986.[24] The other tracks were put down at Media Sound during the same period. Much of the material ultimately made its way onto the album *Look What I Got,* but at this point it fell short of what she felt she needed in order to issue it.

The decision not to record live is a curious one, given the success of *Whatever Happened to Love* and *The Audience.* Furthermore, remarks she made in 1985 in an interview with Graham Lock reveal that her attitude about studio recording had not changed: "I've always had problems with being in a studio, in a cubicle, where all the musicians are far removed from me and there's not that closeness, that camaraderie you get when you're all together. I like being close to people—an audience makes me *think,* makes me reach for things I'd never even try in a studio."[25] But while the work seemed to pick up throughout 1986, the need to increase her visibility made the release of a new album more pressing, leading her to cast aside whatever concerns she still had about studio recording. Furthermore, she had learned how to promote interaction in the studio by arranging the players so they all could see her visual cues and by giving verbal signals that Ferla would later edit out in the final mix. Still, it would be over a year before she generated enough material to release. In the fall, after she had returned from appearing with her trio at the Prague Jazz Festival, Carter and conductor Andre Previn of the Los Angeles Philharmonic cochaired the Committee of Sponsors for American Music Week, which consisted of over one hundred celebrities.

Then Carter made another of her occasional breaks with standard practice and teamed up with Carmen McRae to perform a series of concerts as a duo, backed by a rhythm section. Seven years Carter's elder, McRae had come up in the mid-1940s singing with the big bands of Benny Carter, Count Basie, and Mercer Ellington. A familiar face at festivals in the United States and abroad, McRae had settled in the Los Angeles area in 1967, and, around the time Carter was starting to hit her stride in San Francisco in 1976, McRae made a live recording for Blue Note records at the Great American Music Hall. The idea of these two high-powered ladies occupying the same stage together conjures up images of dueling divas; but the fact that they had a long, collegial relationship, and a mutual connection to Tom Bradshaw, makes the association logical. The collaboration grew spontaneously from an evening when Carmen McRae was performing at the Blue Note Cafe in New York City. Carter had come to hear McRae and ended up sitting in, as she had done at the Half Note roughly twenty years before when Norman Simmons was with McRae. This serendipitous pairing led the senior vocalist to invite her younger colleague to team up with her to present a program in San Francisco, Atlanta, and possibly other locations as well. In preparation for the partnership, Carter spent three days at McRae's Beverly Hills home, where they chose the songs, tempos, keys, and order of solos.[26] The songs they chose drew from both singers' repertoires with "What's New," "But Beautiful," and "Where or When" (included in a medley with "Glad to Be Unhappy") being familiar Carter titles. While much of the material only had the singers tossing phrases back and forth in dialogue, "Stolen Moments" featured the two singing in close harmony. The collaboration enticed Carter to sing tunes that she normally sidestepped, such as "Sometimes I'm Happy," which she would subsequently add to her repertoire, "Isn't It Romantic," and "Am I Blue?" The singers archly turned this last song's lyric on its head with the conclusion that, despite their man's disappearance (more likely, because of it), they were far from blue. The program also featured two Duke Ellington tunes, "Sophisticated Lady" and "It Don't Mean a Thing (If It Ain't Got That Swing)," which was the closing number. In general, Carter deferred to McRae, who had acquired a reputation for being surly.[27] The duo was to be accompanied by McRae's pianist and bass player, Eric Gunnison and Jim Hughart, respectively. No blushing violet herself, however, Carter made her presence felt in several ways. The rhythm section included her drummer, Winard Harper, whose skills were highlighted in the finale, and several of the arrangements bore Carter's imprint.

In late January and early February 1987, the two singers gave the first of these concerts, a run of six shows at the Great American Music Hall. Not surprisingly, the concerts sold out. Tom Bradshaw had made arrangements to record the event, and Carter was especially pleased with the results. She wanted Bradshaw either to let her release the recording on Bet-Car or to shop it around to major labels. JoAnne Jimenez, who was booking Carmen McRae at the time, recalled that McRae knew Bradshaw was planning to use the tape to start his own label—the two had already come to this agreement independent of Carter. McRae did not want the recording to come out on Bet-Car because the label's distribution was limited, although it is doubtful that Bradshaw had any better access to retailers than Carter did. Despite the fact that Bradshaw was Carter's manager, in this situation he seems to have forged a stronger alliance with McRae. While Carter had signed an agreement to record the concert, it did not include a clause releasing the tapes to Bradshaw. Nevertheless, he proceeded to launch Great American Music Hall Records, collecting eight of the numbers the singers had done together and releasing them as an album in August of 1987.[28]

Once again Betty Carter felt betrayed over a record release and was predictably enraged. During the time leading up to the record's release she had been in touch with Richard Seidel, at Polygram Record's jazz subsidiary, Verve. Seidel had admired her work since he had seen her perform in Boston when her career started to warm up. Verve was now in the business of acquiring such singers as Marlena Shaw, Nina Simone, and Shirley Horn, and it would later add Abbey Lincoln to its roster, so this was an opportune time for Carter to test the waters with the label. She claims to have asked him if he was interested in the tape of her duets with McRae, but he surprised her by asking if she had any other recent material. In response she sent him the tracks she had recorded the preceding year, which she had been accumulating for future release on Bet-Car. Carter would ultimately take legal action to keep Bradshaw's recording off the shelves, suing him and his company, Great American Music Hall, Inc., in January 1991 for breach of contract.

In March 1987, the two singers appeared in Manhattan during the same week, but not at the same venue, with Carter at Fat Tuesday's and McRae at Michael's Pub. In April, at a concert originally intended to be done in tandem at Atlanta's Symphony Hall, McRae did not appear due to a "contract dispute."[29] The Ahmad Jamal trio filled in as an opening act, and Carter carried on as though nothing had happened. This was a turbulent time for her in other ways as well. Within a few months, when she headed out on a short tour of the West Coast via Cleveland, she now had an eighteen-year-old Stephen Scott at the keyboard instead of Benny Green. When her duets with McRae hit the shelves, she was back in New York for a concert at Alice Tully Hall entitled "Ladies First: A Tribute to the Great Women of Jazz."[30]

Through the spring, Carter had been actively negotiating a contract with Verve, and at the time of this concert she announced the forthcoming release of a new record on an unnamed label.[31] By November, Gail Boyd had ironed out the details of the deal and Carter was proclaiming the news that, early the following year, Verve would be bringing out the tracks she had sent to Seidel with the title *Look What I Got.* No one was more astonished at this turn of events than Carter herself. Less than two years earlier she had stated unequivocally: "Nobody's jumping over themselves to ask me to record for them; Columbia's not after me, Warner Brothers aren't after me. And they won't be unless they find a producer to produce me, and that's almost impossible 'cause everybody's *younger* than I am. So how they gonna tell *me* what to do?"[32]

The key to the deal was that Carter would retain complete artistic control over her releases, a fairly unusual arrangement, especially for a singer. In addition to stipulating that Verve/Polygram would distribute three new Bet-Car releases, the contract also made provision for the reissue of her four previous Bet-Car albums in CD and cassette format as well as vinyl. While this was just the kind of offer Carter had hoped for, one can hear a trace of wistfulness in her comments to the press, as though allowing a large corporation to absorb her work constituted a loss instead of a gain. Proudly defending the honor of Bet-Car, and of having made her own records, Carter revealed that the four releases she had produced for her own label had each already sold between twenty-five thousand and thirty thousand copies.[33] In the same announcements, Carter also revealed that "an album with Carmen McRae was in the works."[34] As of February 1988 the duet record's release on Verve was still held up due to some "legal wrangling," as Carter put it,[35] but Bradshaw ultimately settled the pending suit in July 1991. By June 1988, however, Verve was already announcing the record's release. The next year Bradshaw and McRae would collaborate on *Carmen Sings Monk,* with Jimenez's help.

Ironically, the dispute over the duet tapes led to something Carter had been unable to manufacture on her own: a contract with a major label on her terms. The Verve deal represented a turning point in her career as a recording artist. In the immediate future it produced an explosion of publicity for Betty Carter, with a cover story about her in the *Daily News Magazine,*[36] and a long segment about her woven into a substantial piece in the Sunday magazine section of the *New York Times.*[37] These came out at the top of 1988, in conjunction with Carter's appearance at Fat Tuesday's at the end of January.

As much as 1987 had been an eventful year for Carter professionally, it had also brought significant events in her personal life. When it began, her younger sister Vivian Brooks had been diagnosed with pancreatic cancer. According to Benny Green, the singer took a month off to be with her sister in March.[38] That November, while Betty Carter was performing in the United Kingdom as part of a European road trip that traversed nine countries,[39] her sister succumbed to liver failure. Brooks bequeathed her residence at 15713 Sussex Street in Detroit to her older sister, enabling Carter to have a satellite office for Bet-Car in her hometown. The label now served as her production company, since Liljay had lapsed at the end of 1983. By this time she had also purchased a house in San Francisco, at 307 Lake Street, which served as the West Coast office for Bet-Car.[40] Although she now had a major label behind her, Bet-Car still served a crucial function in handling various aspects of her activities. While she had relinquished the house in Irvington, New Jersey, to James Redding, Carter had owned her house in Brooklyn outright since the end of the 1970s. Investing her earnings in real estate across the country, she revealed yet another way that she had taken Gladys Hampton's example to heart.

The collapse of her relationship with Bradshaw led Carter to resolve upon doing her own publicity in-house. Certainly her association with a major label provided an important supplement to her own efforts. But because Carter refused to put her fate entirely in anyone else's hands, the marketing and promotion of her work remained a central concern of Bet-Car Productions. By this time, Ora Harris, who maintained Bet-Car Productions' Los Angeles office, had already taken on a more active role in coordinating aspects of Carter's business. Now her assignments expanded to include such activities as securing the *Inside Betty Carter* material for release on Bet-Car. Increasingly the singer called upon Harris to take on more work for her, publicizing gigs, making travel and lodging arrangements, contacting new band members and booking dates. Gail Boyd, who had received her start in entertainment law with Carter, would strike out on her own during the next few years, and Harris became a point of stability in the ever-shifting landscape of Betty Carter's personal and professional relationships.

On Winard Harper's recommendation, Carter had acquired bassist Ira Coleman in Michael Bowie's stead before embarking on her European tour the preceding fall. Born in 1956 and raised in France and Germany, Coleman brought a bit more life experience to the group than Carter's usual hires. His command of French and German proved a useful accessory to his musical abilities. According to Coleman, the tour was meticulously organized by the promoter Tomas Stöwsand, who subcontracted European tours for many American acts, including Jack DeJohnette.[41] With train travel between gigs worked out to the letter, it was an arduous seven weeks with the days off spent traveling instead of sightseeing. Coleman recalled that pianist Stephen Scott, on his first road trip, had brought dumbbells along to stay in shape, not anticipating the exercise he would get simply from carrying his luggage.

Scott was not the first musician Carter ever introduced to the rigors of being on the road, nor would he be the last. Serving a similar function to the one that Art Blakey's Jazz Messengers served in the jazz scene, Carter's trios had begun to gain a reputation as a finishing school for young talent. Her emphasis on a band leader's responsibility to enlist youthful players in the service of the jazz tradition echoes Lionel Hampton's endorsement of young talent. With the celebrity she had gained from her Verve deal, Carter was now in a strong position to give the players in her band a leg up at a time when it was difficult for an artist who was not already established to get a record deal on his or her own: "I'm really trying to stretch out and get ready to record other musicians that I think need to be nourished instead of being controlled by the vultures out there who have literally destroyed a lot of young lives."[42] In line with this wish, Carter had included in the tape submitted to Richard Seidel the two instrumental cuts that featured the Harper Brothers' Quintet, and she planned to include these on *Look What I Got.* By building more instrumental solos into her arrangements. Carter was also letting her musicians stretch out more in her performances.

Shortly before the record was scheduled for release, however, the Harper brothers and Seidel cut a separate record deal without telling Carter about it. When Carter found out about it, the ensuing blowup between Harper and her led to the drummer's immediate firing. As a result of the Harper brothers' going behind her back, she decided to replace their two instrumental tracks with ones using her current trio. On 2 March 1988, Carter took Scott and Coleman into Clinton Sound with Lewis Nash, who was brought in on special assignment, and recorded "That Sunday, That Summer," "The Good Life," and a tune called "The Sparkles" that did not make it onto the record. Then on 20 April, after a short tour of the South, Carter took her new drummer, Troy Davis, into the studio to record "Make It Last," which she had recorded for Peacock thirty years before. All of these last-minute changes led to delays in the record's release, which finally occurred in June.[43] The record betrays no signs of the troubled journey it had taken from inception to release; indeed, largely by virtue of Carter's consistency in sound and concept, the record hangs together quite well. Of necessity she had discovered that she could record without giving her rhythm section several months together to gel, and this revelation opened up the possibility of recording more frequently.

Carter's conception of "The Good Life" (example 15) spins a complex web of time relationships and timbral interactions. She had given her musicians Claus Ogerman's piano chart for Sacha Distel's "The Good Life" when the song was added to the book not long after Benny Green joined the band in the spring of 1983, and it had remained in the book since. This new rendition of "The Good Life" begins with a plaintive, yet restrained, unaccompanied tenor saxophone introduction by Don Braden. Dovetailing into the rhythm section's entrance in an up-tempo Latin feel, the saxophone then drops out. Not until shortly after the vocal enters in measure 3 [0:59], at the first harmonic move away from the tonic, does it become clear that the rhythm section has been playing the form in long meter and that Carter has delayed her entrance. This chart illustrates the extreme degree of back phrasing the singer had come to use by this point in her career. Hanging back as much as two or three measures into the form at times, rather than catch up at the end of phrases as other "delay action" singers do, Carter remains consistently delayed throughout the head. By the time she reaches the tune's midpoint, measure 33 [1:43] she is singing the preceding section's closing lines: "don't try to fake romance." In this context it is surprising how much of the original line she is able to retain, as she maneuvers through the changes while singing the rhythmically displaced lyrics. Her recasting of the form into long meter facilitates this by giving her more time to hear and respond to the changes, while also working against a faster tempo in the rhythm section. In effect she could now sing a ballad as an up-tempo number without having to rush the lyrics and squeeze her melodic excursions into rapidly shifting chord changes.

Carter back-phrases so much that, when she gets to what would normally be the end of the form at measure 61 [2:28], she still has the lyrics' final lines yet to sing. To give herself additional time into which to spill over and complete the lyric, Carter extends the (doubled) form by eight measures, measures 65–72 [2:34–2:46], using the harmonic idea that Claus Ogerman had invented for the tag. After this tag the tempo doubles, at measure 73 [2:46], exponentially augmenting the already rhythmically attenuated form by taking it to another level of long meter. In effect, each beat of the original ballad now lasts for an entire measure of time. Stephen Scott enters at this point and plays a climactic solo for the first forty-four measures of the second chorus, from measure 77 to measure 120 [2:46–3:23]. Braden solos for the next fourteen bars, measures 121–34 [3:23–3:34], increasing the music's intensification. When Carter enters a little before the second half of the chorus, at measure 135 [3:34], Braden continues to play an obligato behind her. With the entire ensemble now sounding all together, the dynamics peak and the emotion overflows.

Carter's phrasing here is instructive. While her line is unfolding at essentially the same rate as before, she nuances it differently in response to the heightened rhythmic activity now swirling about her, such as at the words "to be free," at measures 144–45 [3:41]. As the listener absorbs the impact created by this superimposing of different levels of rhythmic activity, the tension created by Scott's and Braden's solos gradually dissipates. The extended coda that follows this chorus beginning at measure 217 [4:36], is built upon ten repetitions of Ogerman's idea, and because it grows out of the tag that had extended the form, it takes on a quality of endless unfolding. By sustaining a diminuendo over successive repetitions of this tag and by repeating the final words of the song, Carter and the group prolong the feeling of release that started at her reentry. Clocking in at 160 measures, the coda constitutes over one-third of the arrangement, but it serves the essential function of resolving the tension created by the rhythmic disturbance introduced at the end of the head.

Private recordings from the Greek Theater in San Francisco (1984)[44] and at Tufts University (1986)[45] reveal how Carter's concept for the chart grew. Those versions bear a closer relation to the original ballad, for example, because she did not use long meter in her opening statement and started in a slower tempo. As with the version on *Look What I Got,* the piano solo in those versions also doubles the time. When she reenters for the second half of the form, she is now singing against this new feel. Back phrasing against the long meter here was probably what led Carter to hit upon the idea of starting the song in this feel. The version done at the Greek lacks the extended coda, relying on a short unaccompanied cadenza to dissipate the rhythmic energy and bring the chart to a close. At Tufts in 1986 she did essentially the same arrangement as before, but in a faster tempo and a more defined bossa groove.

Carter's rendition of "The Man I Love" on *Look What I Got* illustrates how the singer had expanded her ability to use recording technology as a compositional tool. Working closely with her sound engineer Joe Ferla as he mixed down the multitrack session reel to a stereo master, the singer would often lay in fresh vocal tracks if she was unhappy with what she had done when the musicians had been there. Because this technique saved her from having to produce numerous alternate takes, it reduced the amount of costly studio time needed to produce a master take. Unhappy with Benny Green's playing on the latter part of the tape she had made of "The Man I Love" when she recorded it in 1986, Carter extended this tape-editing technique in an imaginative way. In order to salvage an otherwise acceptable take, she inserted other tracks, first over and then in place of Green's piano track. Initially she asked Don Braden to play over Green's solo, ostensibly to flesh out the texture, so Braden overdubbed a sax line about midway through the solo. This explains why Braden comes in over the piano solo, even though he had already soloed. In spite of the fact that it sounded strange to have sax and piano soloing at once, perhaps Carter had it in mind to build the texture up at that point, to distract the listener from what she felt was an unsatisfactory piano solo. When this did not work, she had Stephen Scott dub in a piano track there that was less soloistic, more in a comping style.[46] Ferla felt that dubbing in fresh tracks was not as extreme as splicing together segments from different takes, which would have been difficult since her performances varied so much from one take to another. The singer liberally dubbed in tracks at this stage in her career, however, to the point that, during the mix phase, the sound engineer often had to set up a microphone and send the unmixed rhythm section tracks to a set of headphones because Carter had rethought her vocal line. Ferla marveled at her ability to repair a sagging groove by "rewriting" the vocal line so it interacted differently with what the players had recorded while she had sung the original vocal track. But he also found these last-minute changes intruded upon his mixing, which requires an entirely different sensibility on the part of the sound engineer. Much more experienced in recording jazz now, he had for some time been forming strong ideas about what he wanted to bring to the mix. However, until her last recording the singer retained strong control over the mixing process.[47]

When *Look What I Got* was released, Carter was on a Midwest road trip that took in a date with Amram and strings at Chicago's Grant Park, and the Hampton/Chevron Jazz Festival in Moscow, Idaho. At the end of June 1988 she was honored at the Schomberg Center for Research in Black Culture, in Harlem, along with Ella Fitzgerald, Melba Liston, and Abbey Lincoln, in a photo exhibition entitled "Black Visions '88: Lady Legends in Jazz." By July, when she sang at the Bottom Line, pianist Darrell Grant had joined Coleman and Davis. For this date she also brought along saxophonist Wes Anderson, who took Don Braden's former role. Meanwhile *Look What I Got* began to receive favorable reviews in newspapers across the country.[48]

In addition to the releases of her own record and the duets with McRae, the long-wished-for reissue of her duets with Ray Charles came out on Dunhill Compact Classics (DCC) around this time. One night in October the following year, Carter would open for Charles at Constitution Hall in Washington, D.C. They also shared the bill at two amphitheaters in Massachusetts, including Tanglewood, and four evenings at the Paul Masson Winery in California, but those who came expecting to savor the blending of these two voices had to take their delight in single servings.[49] With three records coming out nearly at once, the jazz market was again flooded with Betty Carter's material, as it had been in 1976. Polygram's promotional machinery was putting her into the mainstream loop and stirring interest in her work to an extent she had never before known. By October 1988, *Look What I Got* had been at the top of the jazz charts for four weeks. That same month Hal Willner, *Saturday Night Live*'s music director, released *Stay Awake: Various Interpretations of Music from Vintage Disney Films,* which included one cut contributed by Carter: "I'm Wishing" from *Snow White and the Seven Dwarfs.* Using a group assembled for the session, Carter recorded an arrangement that is busy with contrapuntal activity as the musicians each solo behind her at various points.

In November, Carter went to Kaufman studios in Astoria to tape her appearance on the highest-rated television program of the time, *The Bill Cosby Show,* in an episode scheduled to air on Thanksgiving. A jazz enthusiast, Cosby had included jazz artists on his show in the past, including Dizzy Gillespie and Joe Williams.[50] Carter had been invited by Cosby to appear on the show after they had both performed in the spring at a tribute to Lionel Hampton at Manhattan's Town Hall. In an episode entitled "How Do You Get to Carnegie Hall," the singer played a vocal coach named Amanda Woods, whom Vanessa Huxtable, Cosby's TV daughter, approaches for voice lessons. At the end of the episode, Woods sang the title song of Betty Carter's new release, "Look What I Got," with the album's cover art conveniently displayed in a poster behind her. Ira Coleman recalled that Carter kept the band members late to do several takes in the hopes that a video would be made of the song.[51] Cosby did ultimately sponsor the production of a video in which he and his costar Phylicia Rashad appeared with Carter. Unfortunately, Verve did little to follow up.[52] Carter soon began to push the label to produce and distribute jazz videos in order to expose the work of jazz musicians on such television stations as MTV and VH1.

During this time Cosby would also produce a thirty-second commercial for Coca-Cola entitled "Betty and Bill" that featured the new Verve artist. Set in a nightclub, the spot shows Carter singing "Sounds (Movin' On)" with lyrics from Coke's "Can't Beat the Feeling" ad campaign. Meanwhile, dancers perform choreography by George Faison, who had won a Tony award for his work on *The Wiz,* while Cosby—through the benefit of video technology—backs her on piano, bass, and drums all at once. Spun out of Cosby's own concept, the commercial debuted at 8:00 P.M. on 15 August 1989 on the ABC Television Network, to a prime-time audience.[53] Betty Carter's face appeared on network television in other contexts as well, including David Sanborn's syndicated NBC show produced by Hal Willner, *Night Music*—where she traded fours with saxophonist Branford Marsalis—and on *Good Morning America.* Her voice could also be heard on commercials for Listerine and Budweiser.[54] Carter's photo was featured in *Rolling Stone* alongside photos of pop stars Tracy Chapman and Terence Trent D'Arby. She was finally making the leap from cult figure to celebrity.

All of this media attention stimulated sales of her recent issues and reissues, and in the beginning of 1989, both *Look What I Got* and *The Carmen McRae–Betty Carter Duets* were nominated for Grammy Awards. Carter's touring schedule was in high gear. Her gigging was getting more press than it ever had, and wherever she appeared, she drew sold-out houses. Having just replaced her bassist Ira Coleman with Tarus Mateen from Georgia, she spent much of February bringing her act to Chicago, Cambridge, Massachusetts, and St. Paul, Minnesota. That month, *Look What I Got* was honored with a Grammy Award for the best female performance in jazz. The record had stayed at the top of Billboard's sales chart for six weeks and was still on Billboard's Top Ten List, along with Dunhill's reissue of her duets with Ray Charles. It would remain there for thirty-nine weeks. In fact, Carter enjoyed the unusual distinction of having two records appear simultaneously in Billboard's top fifteen. She was receiving a new kind of prestige now, as indicated by such frivolous news items as *USA Today*'s report the following August that San Diego Padres pitcher Eric Show named Carter second on his list of top female jazz vocalists.

There is perhaps some irony in Carter's receiving a Grammy for *Look What I Got,* since it is hardly any better than *The Audience* or *Whatever Happened to Love.* Convinced that the record's success had less to do with its intrinsic merits than with the fact that she now had a powerful record company promoting her work, Carter noted that the records that had preceded it "didn't have a chance."[55] Where Bet-Car had to fight simply to get records into retail outlets, Polygram had the means virtually to manufacture a Grammy by pushing the record in a wide array of media outlets. Carter observed, "It took me longer to cross over with the white audience the way Sarah and Ella and Carmen did. I think the fact that my records finally are on a major label and *available* has something to so with it. Now that a large record company is involved it gives me some clout."[56]

Perhaps this is why she seemed so nonchalant about the Grammy itself. She did not attend the award ceremony in Los Angeles, ostensibly because the presentation of awards to jazz artists does not take place on television—an indication to her that jazz was being put on the "back burner"[57]—but also because Verve did not pay her travel expenses there.[58] In fact, receiving the Grammy only seems to have reinforced her belief that jazz wasn't as big as it should be, because record labels were not doing enough to promote it. Referring to her shows at the Regattabar earlier that year, she told Willard Jenkins that she had been "drawing crowds anyway," independent of the latest harvest of Betty Carter recordings, adding: "I can tell you that only about twenty percent of those people knew I had a record out."[59]

To many these seemed to be heady days for jazz artists, but Betty Carter was never content with the status quo, and the veteran singer saw things differently. Having already witnessed how easily the jazz community could be broken by an indifferent music industry and public, Carter's confidence in the jazz renaissance that had been sparked in part by the reissue of classic jazz recordings in CD format was measured at best.[60] Her feeling had less to do with how much promise was shown by young players, many of whom she had brought into the professional arena, than it did with her belief that the fate of jazz was in the hands of greedy executives—a belief she had been harboring for some twenty-five years or more. She felt that the moment had arrived for record labels to aggressively promote the recent work of living musicians and to spur the sales of newly released recordings, not just issue boxed sets of classic jazz. "It's only a good time for jazz *if* the major people in the record business think it is. . . . If they marketed it differently than they have over the years, and if they stopped assuming that jazz is only going to sell a certain number of records, then maybe it would be a good time for jazz."[61]

For Carter, the issue was not only about sales. It ultimately spoke to the matter of creating an economy that would support the next generation's involvement in jazz. She argued that, in a business in which artists need to have recordings out in order to secure club dates, if record companies do not get behind young players and stick with them long enough for them to establish a voice, there is no way for the players to get work and continue their artistic development. Without an environment that rewards the enormous amount of time and energy that must go into forging a personal style, the music has little hope of sustaining a high level of quality. In conjunction with this rebirth of interest in jazz, the conservative contingent secured much of the available sponsorship. This was when Wynton Marsalis began his retrenchment into historical jazz styles in an effort to purge jazz of the "impurities" he felt players of jazz-rock, fusion, and free jazz had introduced.

By the end of 1989, Carter had also won best female singer in both the critic's and the reader's polls of *Down Beat.* As early as the beginning of 1989, Polygram began urging her to produce another record right away.[62] Carter had initially resisted, feeling that the glut in recordings would "over-expose" her. But by the time she had replaced pianist Darrell Grant with Marc Cary, and drummer Troy Davis with Gregory Hutchinson, around the start of the new decade, she was having thoughts about producing another release with possibly a ten-piece band. Tarus Mateen was in the process of vacating the bass chair, and Hutchinson's friend Dwayne Burno would ultimately take over, although Carter had initially lined up Christian McBride to take Mateen's place.[63]

Over the preceding years the rate of turnover in Betty Carter's personnel had begun to increase, with some players lasting little more than a year. By this time such instability did not seem to pose the kind of obstacle to recording that it had in the past. For one thing, she was not putting together as many elaborate charts because her new players were expected to know her arrangements from her recordings. In addition she had evolved a mission of exposing as many musicians to her approach as possible. When French writer Pascal Kober asked her why she had so many upheavals she responded: "Jazz is always in motion, it's always moving. And also I have to teach these young musicians I'm with today who I am, what music I was playing before, and what kind of music I want to play now."[64] Around this time her press material began referring to her as "The Duchess of Jazz," a sobriquet that never really took.

By early May 1990, Polygram was announcing that Betty Carter would make a live recording later that month at the site where she had made *Whatever Happened to Love,* which Verve would reissue two months later. The resulting recording, *Droppin' Things,* which ultimately included some tracks that were put down in the studio, featured guest artists Freddie Hubbard and Geri Allen in addition to saxophonist Craig Handy and Carter's new trio. According to the log at Clinton Recording, Carter took her trio and Craig Handy into the studio on 23 May and recorded five titles: Lerner and Lane's "Why Him," which Carter had recently added to her book, enhancing the performance with her eloquent facial expressions and sense of timing, to much comic effect; and four originals, "Open the Door," taken out of its bossa nova groove and done largely as an instrumental, "Thirty Years," "Dull Day in Chicago," a tune without lyrics, and "Droppin' Things."

"Droppin' Things" is none other than Carter's scat tune "Jumps," now with clever lyrics about how disruptive falling in love can be, to match the tune's "jumpy" character. Similarly, Carter claimed that "Thirty Years" had been composed long before, when she spoke of the tune's genesis: "I did '30 Years' about 12 years ago, when there was a rash of gentlemen I knew who were leaving their wives after 20 and 30 years. . . . The title was different then. It was 'Someone Else Will (Soon) Grow Old, Too.'"[65] The song is an astute enactment of a wife's desperate, yet dignified, attempt to hold onto her husband, who is leaving her for a younger woman. When performing live, Carter would inevitably break the somber mood of the song by modifying its closing line, "Thirty years is a long time," to ever shorter time spans, until the punch line, "Two days is a long time." As with the title song of *Look What I Got,* Carter was reaching into her trunk now to meet the demand for new material that the increased pace of these recordings placed upon her. Yet the music on this recording hardly sounds stale; in fact, it displays several innovations. Discussing "Dull Day" in her press kit for the record, Carter described how the tune's novel procedure evolved: "It was raining cats and dogs [at an outdoor festival in the Windy City]. We had a few diehards in the audience, sitting in the mud, and my trio just went out there and they hit. I walked out onto the stage, and they started the theme that's the beginning of "Dull Day." And I listened to a tape and I said, it's swinging like crazy. So I just added a bridge to it."[66] The press release adds that she designed the tune so that "whenever a musician wants to play the bridge, he plays it. Anywhere. That means the other musicians have to keep their ears open." Craig Handy confirmed that the bridge was done on cue.[67]

The above description reveals other ways in which Carter made use of recording technology in her compositional process, as she had done in making "Look What I Got." She would later tell Pascal Kober of *Jazz Hot* that sometimes she composed "on the piano, but very often singing while driving. There is no place quieter and more intimate to sing than the car. When I think of something, lyrics, idea, melody, or subject, I record it on a small Dictaphone that I always carry with me."[68]

Craig Handy recalled that, in addition to scheduling several rehearsals, Carter used the recording session as a dry run for the forthcoming Bottom Line dates, which took place in the following days. She also taped some tracks in the studio, although it is unclear how she ultimately used them.[69] Freddie Hubbard came to the session in an ill humor, according to Handy. When Carter saw the effect this was having on the mood of the session, she told the others to take a break and took the veteran trumpeter aside. When the younger players returned from the break he was "just as polite as could be—congenial, funny."[70] Bassist Christian McBride was apparently also present at one of these sessions, in anticipation of his joining her trio, but Carter never used him. Dwayne Burno ended up playing bass on a version of "When It's Sleepy Time Down South" for vocal, trumpet, and bass that did not make it onto the record because Carter was displeased with Hubbard's performance.[71] The repertoire was rounded out with "What's the Use of Wonderin'" and "I Love Music," the latter of which Carter had been performing since the 1970s, but had never recorded. On 7 June, at Mastersound Studios, Carter also recorded a medley of "Star Dust/Memories of You" with Geri Allen in a rendition that unearths levels of emotion connected to love's loss that few performers achieve. Polygram released *Droppin' Things* that September to a warm critical reception.

The record's title song is perhaps the most rhythmically intricate of Betty Carter's inventions. On the recording, the singer initially counts the tune off in four; but after the players come in she changes her mind saying "sorry, sorry," and restarts the tune in a rapid jazz waltz feel. This false start—which anticipates the composition's characteristic metric volatility—could easily have been edited out, so its inclusion suggests that she wanted to draw the listener's attention to the tune's rhythmic complexity, much as she had done with her 1982 version of "What a Little Moonlight Can Do." After the introduction, built on a drone figure on C-natural [0:10–0:31] played by Mateen over which Cary plays in C Lydian, Carter comes in with the lyric of the first A section.

> He came into my life so suddenly;
> I tried to tell this man that I'm not free;
> He gave me such a sexy look, I shook nervously and then,
> There I go, breathing hard, stumblin' and
> Droppin' things.

The scansion of the lyrics follow the tune's phrase structure, making this structure audible. But the lyrics also exploit this structure, which in turn reinforces their syntactic structure, as well as their meaning, by providing aural punctuation. Carter designed the first thirty-six beats of the form [0:31–0:39] to flow in straight quarter notes without a strong sense of meter. This approach allows the speech rhythm of the lyrics to lead the time, as if she were not so much singing as urgently intoning the words. While one could measure this passage in nine bars of common time, this would not account for its overall breakdown into phrase lengths of fourteen, fourteen, and eight beats successively, or for each of the first two phrase's breakdown into subgroupings of eight plus six beats.

In such an idiosyncratic rhythmic context it is the contour rhythm created by repetitions of the melodic line that makes the rhythmic structure hang together. The melodic idea to which the opening line of text is set [0:31–0:34] is restated in the second line of text [0:34–0:38], with a varied ending. The third time we hear this idea, it leads into the form's first clear sense of meter, as a 3/4 feel emerges at the words "look—I—shook—nervously and then" [0:39–0:42], which stress each downbeat. At the word "then," where we hear the first departure from C major, the time goes into 4/4 for the song's hook [0:42–0:49]: "there I go, breathing hard, stumblin' and droppin' things." When she reaches these last two words, the bass reasserts the introductory drone figure for two measures of 3/4, preparing us to plunge ahead into the restatement of the A section, now, of course, with different lyrics. Only about twenty seconds of music have passed our ears during this first A section, but because the quarter note races along at a tempo of about 264–276, we have already encountered several restless metric shifts.

The next A section runs in similar fashion [0:51–1:09], ending with the hook as before [1:02], which now leads into the bridge. Compared to the A section, the bridge is relatively straightforward, but not by much. In 4/4 time throughout, it consists of eight measures of E-flat minor7 [1:09–1:17], twelve measures of A-flat minor7 [1:17–1:28], and four measures of D-flat minor with a major seventh [1:28–1:31]. At this last harmonic change, the time is momentarily suspended in a "rubato" effect similar to the one Carter had used in later versions of "Open the Door," reflecting the tonal uncertainty of this moment. In response to this quality, Carter set the passage to lyrics that instigate the narrator's change of heart. In conjunction with her friend's remark, "If you really don't want him, he'll go away," the music's tentative character hints at the woman's realization that she might be "free" to respond to his interest after all. Here the music supplies a meaning the words alone cannot provide. The D-flat minor harmony will soon function as an altered ♭II, preparing for the return to C major, but in this brief, suspended moment, the listener does not yet know this.

Without benefit of the opening drone figure, the listener is now sent hurling into the return of the A section at the words "Determination is his middle name" [1:31–1:51]. The narrator is back in the throes of lovesickness, describing how she soon "gave in to keep from going insane." By the end of this section, however, it is the pursuer who is losing his balance: "and now the tables turned and he—now—knows—how it feels to fall. There he goes, breathing hard, stumblin' and droppin' things." In about ninety seconds

Carter has bared the emotional essence of courtship, the rolling and tumbling that makes this phase of a relationship so enticing and unsettling all at once.

Carter claimed that she had added the song to the book because her musicians were intrigued when she was "fooling with it" on the piano at a rehearsal. They also wanted to try "another of Carter's ideas on it, playing in what she called a 'wave,' a continually shifting tempo."[72] One obvious occurrence of this wave happens during the opening statement of the melody when the bass and drums dramatically increase the density of rhythmic events occurring behind the second A section's opening segment [0:51–1:02] without affecting the passage's harmonic rhythm. When this happens, it sounds like all hell breaking loose, but Carter and Cary steadily maintain the original tempo, creating an incredible sense of rhythmic disjunction that captures the emotional turbulence Carter is singing about. This passage is all the more remarkable because it occurs during the part of the form that lacked a strong metric impulse to begin with, so the parts do not mesh neatly. Here Carter is exploiting the tune's harmonic freedom—its modal aspect—to create an original rhythmic effect that few musicians of her generation would have attempted, let alone conceived of.

In reworking "Jumps" into "Droppin' Things," Carter eliminated the original version's contrasting section, replacing it with horn solos built upon the bridge. She inserts the opening melodic idea from the A section between each bridge-chorus, using it much the way a big-band lead-in works, to set up each successive solo. When Hubbard first enters—on fluegelhorn, not trumpet—he starts eight measures into the bridge, at the A-flat minor7 harmony, but the second time through the changes, he has the full twenty-four measures to work with. When Carter introduces Handy's solo, she sings the words, "Determination is his middle name," setting up her return at the end of his solo, when she repeats these words and then proceeds to sing the final A section. This leads to an extended scat coda in C Lydian, with a C major9(#11) quality, that turns into a group jam when Hubbard and Handy join in to fill out the texture. To pull the strands together and effect a close, Carter scats the tune's principal motive, rising dramatically at the end to a high D-natural (the ninth of the chord), in her head voice. Judging from the recording, this is how she ended the set.

Around the turn of the decade, the jazz community was dealt a series of devastating blows with the deaths of several artists, many from Carter's generation. In the fall of 1989 saxophonist Sahib Shihab and drummer Freddie Waits had died. On 3 April 1990, Sarah Vaughan died, an especially profound loss for Carter. Saxophonist Dexter Gordon died that April as well, and drummer Eddie Moore, who had played with Carter on *Now It's My Turn,* died that May, a few days before she made *Droppin' Things.* Pianist Walter

Davis Jr., who had played on one of Carter's Atco sessions for *'Round Midnight,* among other occasions died in June. In July, singer Joe Turner died. That October, while Carter was on tour in Japan, Art Blakey would die, and in less than a year Miles Davis would also be dead. These greats were more than just colleagues to Betty Carter. They were family members. In addition to leaving her deeply saddened, the events gave greater urgency to her mission of passing jazz on to future generations. In response to several of these passings, she added tunes to her book in memory of the artists, including a medley of songs associated with Vaughan that featured "Everything I Have Is Yours," "The Nearness of You," "Mean to Me," and "Tenderly."[73] At some gigs she even had the band play the Jazz Messengers' theme song, Benny Golson's "Blues March," while she proclaimed the names of important figures who had recently died.[74] No matter how well documented the artist's work is, in jazz—a medium that relies so heavily upon oral transmission and improvisation—every death chips away at the music culture. The loss of these singers and instrumentalists, and many others who made important contributions during the period when much of the musical vocabulary had taken shape, would spell the demise of jazz to many.

As deeply as Carter mourned the loss of these rare individuals, however, she did not fall prey to defeatism. Instead, she pinned her hopes for the durability of the art of jazz improvisation on the young people she was inducting into the society of musicians. Having witnessed the collapse of the jazz economy in the 1960s and survived it, she felt that those who were still among the living needed to redouble their efforts to reach more young people and share the excitement of making this music. Beyond her tributes to Sarah Vaughan, Art Blakey, and others, this commitment to perpetuating the music was the highest form of homage she could pay the dead. So with the sound of Golson's blues-turned-funeral-march ringing in her ears, she soldiered on.

12

Recognition

The somber news of her fallen comrades notwithstanding, the new decade held much promise for Betty Carter, and she embarked upon it with optimistic vigor. At sixty-one years old, she was going strong, maintaining an active touring schedule and basking in her hard-won celebrity. If she had given any thought to slowing down, she gave no indication of it. She would later report to David Amram that the reason she did not retire was because she had to keep "her kids"—meaning her band—working. The fact is, she was thoroughly enjoying herself. In addition, Carter was temperamentally ill-equipped to allow herself the luxury of feeling she had arrived. Furthermore, having waited so long for this kind of recognition, she was not about to hang up her hat. She quipped that only when she had to sing from a stool would she quit.

At the start of 1991, around the time Carter was participating in tributes to Dr. Martin Luther King Jr. at the Brooklyn Academy of Music and to Langston Hughes at the Schomberg Center, *Droppin' Things* began to receive a strong critical response. That February, it was nominated for a Grammy Award for best female jazz performance of the year. McRae's *Carmen Sings Monk* was also nominated, but both singers were passed up in favor of Ella Fitzgerald. McRae felt especially cheated, and in a fit of pique, lashed out at her former collaborator in a *Down Beat* interview with James Taylor Jones IV, probably unaware that she was speaking to Carter's own nephew: "Give me a break. They even gave one [Grammy] to Betty Carter, and I know I sing better than her. Shit."[1] In the interview, McRae refused to elaborate upon the events that had soured their relationship. But Carter's name is conspicuously absent from the irate singer's list of great improvisers, and in light of her past encomium of the one "pure jazz singer" the omission speaks volumes.

As with other Carter releases, *Droppin' Things* spurred the reissue of long-forgotten material. Blue Note records—now the jazz subsidiary of EMI records—had acquired Roulette's catalog and reissued *Finally,* with *Round Midnight* soon to follow. This release, too, received a strong critical response. Record producer Michael Cuscuna digitally remixed the original four-track masters for both records at the Beatles' Abbey Road Studios in London. Carter's receiving producer and arranger credit for the material was a step toward setting to right the unsanctioned release of her music over two decades earlier.

Having crossed over to a mainstream audience, Carter's name and music was now cropping up in the most unlikely of places. A verse from Gangstarr's rap "Jazz Thing" from the sound track to Spike Lee's 1990 film *mo' better blues* praised Carter's contribution to jazz, and she herself appeared on the tune's music video. Ironically, the song used rap, a pop idiom, to promote an awareness of jazz history among the younger generation of listeners.[2] Carter had known about rap since the late 1970s, when her then teenage son Kagle had been peripherally involved with some of the style's earliest innovators. While she admired the young black record producers' entrepreneurial initiative, on an aesthetic basis she was disparaging of the new sound. Betty Carter would grow to become an icon to some members of the hip-hop community, receiving mention in songs by Black Star and Saul Williams.[3] Eager to capitalize upon her visibility to the mainstream audience, Carter also accepted a job from the advertising agency 4/4 Productions, to do a voice-over on a Dr. Pepper commercial during this period.[4] Later in the year she would be featured in an ad campaign for a clothing line.

The spring of 1991 was a volatile time for Carter's trio. In April, she fired pianist Marc Cary on a gig in his hometown of Washington, D.C., and the following month Peter Martin joined the band as Carter and her group set out on a monthlong road trip through the South.[5] The tour consisted of a series of performances and workshops at several southern colleges. While on this trip, a long-standing disagreement with her bassist, Dwayne Burno, about how she wanted the bass to be amplified—along with other differences of opinion—flared up, and this relationship also deteriorated. That July, during an extended European road trip, Carter gave him notice, and he walked out midtour.[6] Surprisingly, on such short notice, she was able to get bassist Ariel Roland from Tel Aviv to fill in for Burno. She resumed the tour, apparently none the worse for the disruption, but she never spoke to Burno again. By the end of the summer, Cyrus Chestnut had taken over on piano.

Carter had met Chestnut at Berklee in 1983, when she had given a workshop in conjunction with her Symphony Hall concert. While he was in her trio, she liked to recount to her audiences how, during that workshop, she had asked the students if anyone wanted to play. When the assembled students all chanted "Cyrus, Cyrus," the bashful pianist reluctantly came up. She called "Body and Soul" in her usual key of G major, not the standard key of D-flat major. The pianist was mortified, because he had not had much experience transposing. While a videotape of the event shows that he covered for his lack of preparation admirably, he had not made the best impression. Since that time he had grown into a physical performer who tackled the instrument, wrenching orchestral effects from its entire range. Chestnut was older than her usual initiate when he joined the band, and she welcomed his fervor.

During this period, Carter started doing something different in her stage act. Instead of speaking the entertaining banter she inserted between songs in preparation for the number to follow, she would occasionally sing it, creating an almost continuous flow of music in the fashion of a recitative-aria sequence. While the rhythm section cycled through a modified turnaround progression (iii–vi–ii–V), changing tempo and key on cue, Carter addressed her audience in improvised song. She first began to experiment with this procedure during her opening monologue, as a novel way of holding the listeners' attention and keeping up the mood through song. In the course of these jazz intonations, she might describe how she had acquired each of her musicians, or how a particular song came into her book, or some comic insight about the song's message. The way Carter musicalized her own everyday speaking—improvising the words as well as the melodic line—reinforces the impression that it was partly through the infusion of her speech rhythms into others' lyrics that she energized her reworking of songs' rhythmic and melodic material.

Carter was notoriously tough on her players, but she also watched out for them. When speaking/singing about her current or former musicians to the audience or to the press, she occasionally covered for them. For instance, instead of describing how Burno had walked out on her, she would describe in song how Roland had joined the band because her former bassist broke his leg while she was in Europe. When Benny Green left the entire piano book in a taxicab in New York, Carter told audiences that she herself had misplaced it. Aware of how unforgiving the public could be, she could be protective of her "charges," shielding them from negative scrutiny. In a later interview, she would attribute Chestnut's confusion at their first meeting to his mishearing her state the tune's key as D major. In his recollection, however, he had known exactly what the demanding singer had wanted. "Like Zorro would put a *Z* in someone's back when he would finish . . . [a swordfight], she says the words to me '*in G!*' And that 'G' went through me like a knife. I was never really up on transposition at the time—I knew 'Body and Soul' in one key. And that was one of the first of many lessons that Betty taught me. If you're going to be a *good* accompanist, you *have* to be able to adjust."[7] In the fall, drummer Clarence Penn took over for Gregory Hutchinson. The new unit consisting of Chestnut, Roland, and Penn would be together for less than a year, until the end of the following summer.

In January, 1992 the National Endowment of the Arts honored Betty Carter with the American Jazz Masters Fellowship Award at the Nineteenth Annual Conference of the International Association of Jazz Educators (IAJE) in Miami. Carter's fellow recipients were trumpeter Harry "Sweets" Edison and pianist Dorothy Donegan. The fellowship, launched a decade before—with Carter's mentor Dizzy Gillespie as one of the initial recipients—reflected the NEA's commitment to acknowledging living jazz legends. Carter accepted the award graciously: "I've had a rewarding career, believe it or not. . . . For somebody to give me an award for doing what I do (laughs) is really a surprise."[8] The ceremony closed with a performance of "Major Butts" by the Count Basie Orchestra led by Frank Foster, with Carter and Edison both soloing to Donegan's comping.[9]

At first the NEA had presented these awards independently of the International Jazz Educator's Association, but in 1991 the IAJE began to present them as a way of raising the NEA award program's profile. As significant as the NEA's recognition was for Carter, of more lasting consequence was the connection it created for her with the IAJE, a connection that would deepen into an extremely productive relationship. This was an unexpected outcome given Carter's stance on formal jazz education, and it suggests that Carter was tempering her perspective on the subject. Recent changes in the IAJE may have contributed to this shift in her stance: the organization had been drawing more black educators and students lately through the efforts of its leadership, particularly the efforts of president Bunky Green and vice president Ellis Marsalis.[10]

Perhaps because she eyed the formal schooling of musicians with some skepticism, Carter had at first been slow to express an interest in teaching. To her, nothing could replace on-the-job training as a means of realizing the stored energy of talent. It was largely how all of the jazz masters from her generation had become performers, and she expressed doubts about whether schools could convey the essential quality of jazz: its feeling. "You get education by doing. In jazz you have to *do* it. You can't get education sitting in a room or going to school. You can get your technique, your theory. But it's on-the-job working for people that you really learn about the business."[11] Speaking later that year about her new drummer, Clarence Penn, she elaborated upon her position on formal jazz training: "Clarence is very well schooled: he knows a lot; has a lot of degrees." Ominously she added that, when a student has an education, "you have to crack it, show the person that the education was for naught and that now it's really time to start the education."[12]

As time went on, Carter was destined to hire more and more schooled players because most of the current crop were coming out of colleges such as Berklee. Of necessity these institutions were becoming a key piece of the jazz network because of the dearth of venues, especially the low-profile ones in which Carter had cut her teeth. Long gone was the time when a large number of clubs, informal jam sessions, and other situations supported a wide range of playing abilities and provided opportunities for musical and professional development. The few club owners who persevered could not afford to take a chance on a performer who did not have a demonstrated capacity to draw an audience.

An increasing number of music schools were beginning to add jazz studies to their curricula, signaling a growing acceptance of jazz by academics. While some took this as a vindication of the music's worth, others felt it was a mixed blessing, partly because a large proportion of those hired to teach jazz were white. At the heart of jazz lies a fundamental resistance to the formal structures schools typically impose on learning. This comes partly from an ambivalence the musicians have about rules. Jazz consists of a highly structured musical language from which one could derive a set of rules—in order for a musician to play "outside" there must be an "inside" to work against.[13] But playing by the rules does not produce jazz. In fact, it is partly in the idiosyncratic breaking of the rules that a musician displays originality and taste. As Cyrus Chestnut put it in an interview with Gene Santoro: "Like any language, music has a logic. My whole aim is to understand that, and then toss in something that's illogical but still sounds like it makes sense. People don't react to music theory, after all; they react to what they hear."[14] The relationship jazz creates between asserting a normalized structure—discrete scale degrees or the meter, say—and then intentionally cutting across this structure in ways that challenge it—say by "smearing" the pitch or delaying the time—gives it a distinctive aesthetic that features intentionally unmeasured plasticity. In a traditional academic setting such an approach can have subversive overtones.

Remarks Carter made during this time suggest that she was beginning to think more concretely about the skills involved in becoming a jazz artist and wrestling with the question of how to spur artistry in young musicians. Commenting on musicians "who have been inspired to become jazz musicians but don't have the concept—the feeling—for the music," she asked: "Why did Miles, or Ella Fitzgerald, or Billie Holiday have the concepts of music that they've had? And why is it that other singers who aspire to be like Ella or Billie just don't succeed?"[15] She was painfully aware from her own experience that one does not forge a personal concept overnight: "Those who have the patience and can hang in there to grow and develop, and find out who they are—to *really* find their style and their identity—they will be the survivors."[16] Holding the jazz community responsible the transmission of its cultural values, Carter expressed her disappointment in it: "The jazz community has let a lot of young musicians down by not providing the work for them. . . . We have a bunch of young players out there who are really serious and want to play jazz. I hope I had a lot to do with it; I think that Wynton Marsalis had a lot to do with it"[17] Later that year she amplified her views on the survival of the music, telling critic Peter Watrous that it "depends upon people playing it and living the life," adding that "the young guys playing it . . . will be taking the music somewhere else [in twenty years]."[18]

Despite her reservations about music education, Carter recognized the need for a "farm system" for jazz players, and she was beginning to grant that jazz educators might now have some role in this system, especially given the scarcity of gigging opportunities for young players. As she put it: "There should be more people like Art Blakey to provide work for young players and encourage them to get into the business."[19] Since Blakey's death the similarity between him and Carter in this regard had become more apparent, especially because the singer's celebrity now raised the profile of anyone who worked with her. Carter had been employing young musicians for the preceding twenty-five years, but now she framed this approach in specifically educational terms.

Seeking to build jazz's audience and hence its share of the music industry's market, Carter's interest in young players partly served to hook young listeners as well: "I could probably go out there and get some old guys my age to work with me, but then I don't develop any young listeners, either."[20] Setting herself apart from many of her own generation of musicians, Carter castigated those who did not support novices. "There are a lot of musicians my age that can't deal with hiring younger players because they think it's too much work rehearsing, practicing, and teaching them. . . . [They] don't have the patience . . . don't have the time. . . . In some cases it's a jealousy factor, which I think is pretty sad."[21] Carter acknowledged that "it's tough to take their mistakes and understand them. When you're 18 or 19 you have a lot to learn. Which is fine. Everybody started somewhere."[22] There were some older musicians such as Barry Harris who had always worked to bring young musicians into the jazz fold, but few had as much visibility as Carter. Others from Carter's generation, such as Ron Carter, understandably expressed resentment of record labels' current marketing of young players who had not paid much in the way of dues, while established masters were languishing without contracts and club dates. There were few enough gigs to go around as it was—for older players to be bypassed in favor of these "wunderkinds" added insult to injury. But Carter had no problem with the so-called young lions craze, referring derisively to the attitude of "some bass players I know who seem to be bitter because the young people are moving ahead."[23] In fact, Carter felt that the positive changes in the industry were largely due to the presence of young talent. "The sheer pressure of so many young musicians, and all the good things they're doing, has moved people who might not have ordinarily been moved."[24] She also challenged people from her milieu to take the long view with regard to the music: "If the music is to continue, if it is a culture of value, it would seem to me [older players and fans] would have no problems with young people coming along, wanting to play. It's a culture that must be sustained."[25] In identifying with young people she was drawing upon a vivid recollection of her own youthful enthusiasm for Dizzy and Bird when they were still quite young, but there were other benefits to her strategy as well. The presence of young players in her groups proved an effective marketing tool, and Carter increasingly made a point of telling their ages in her shows, interviews, and press releases. Furthermore, by only having to lay out entry-level salaries she was able to keep her overhead down and profits up—"economizing" as Gladys Hampton had done. She herself admitted that the benefits of her recruitment strategy went both ways, claiming that her players' youthful energy kept her young.

On Saturday, 28 March 1992, Jazz at Lincoln Center presented Carter in a program at Alice Tully Hall entitled "Betty Carter Big Band with Strings: The Music Never Stops." Symbolically, this was an important event for the singer, for she was returning to the big-band format after thirty years. As one might expect, however, Carter added a unique twist: the singer would perform a program of continuous music for some ninety minutes straight. Carter described this as a dream project. In addition to her current trio—Chestnut, Roland, and Penn—the concert included two guest trios featuring several of Carter's former colleagues: Geri Allen, Cecil McBee, and Jack DeJohnette; and John Hicks, Lyle Atkinson, and Kenny Washington. The latter group served as rhythm section for a seventeen-piece big band supplemented with four cellos and two basses. The singer's former drummer Gregory Hutchinson also played drums on a few numbers. Carter used the twenty-thousand-dollar honorarium from her American Jazz Masters Fellowship to help finance the concerts.[26] A matinee the next afternoon at City College in Harlem made the concert accessible to those who could not afford Lincoln Center's admission prices.

Carter's design of the event expanded upon her conception of an entire set or concert as an aesthetic whole. Singing the improvised patter she had been using lately to smooth transitions between songs, she treated the evening almost as if it were an extended medley. Several tunes were grouped according to lyric themes, such as good-bye songs. Interspersed among tunes from her current book, performed with the various rhythm sections she had assembled, were big-band arrangements from earlier in her career that reached as far back as Gigi Gryce's settings of "Social Call" and "Frenesi." As with *Whatever Happened to Love,* the reuse of charts from the entire span of her career had a retrospective quality and served to highlight how the singer's approach had changed over time. Carter counted off the numbers and conducted the large group with her physical movements, as she normally did with her trios. The singer made effective use of the trios' flexibility to create transitions between many of the numbers, but from an economic standpoint the concert was inefficient. As critic George Kanzler observed in his review, most of the musicians played only in a handful of numbers, sitting idle on the stage for long stretches of the performance while Carter flitted from group to group.[27] The full houses for both concerts responded enthusiastically to her every turn of expression, however, and in size and response the audience vindicated the disappointment of the similarly ambitious Boston Symphony Hall project nine years earlier. Carter stressed that her central goal was spontaneity: "That's what makes it interesting for me. I don't memorize what I do. I know what the band does and when I come in."[28] By having the entire evening unfold in a nearly seamless flow—interrupted only by applause—she further demonstrated her capacity to reframe her work in new contexts.

Betty Carter's association with Lincoln Center extended into 1993, when she headlined "Prelude to a Kiss: Jazz for Valentines," a program presented on 14 February at Alice Tully Hall. Other performers on the bill included Harold Ashby, Roy Hargrove, Bobby Watson, and Jimmy Heath, all backed by the evening's "house trio," which was made up of Carter alumni Mulgrew Miller, Curtis Lundy, and Lewis Nash. On Carter's final number Wynton Marsalis joined her as an unannounced guest. In June of that year she also spoke at the Stanley H. Kaplan Penthouse for a Lincoln Center Off Stage "Conversation" with WBGO disc jockey James Brown, in anticipation of her appearance a week later as the opening act for the JVC Jazz Festival. Karen Carillo described her "dressed in a long, cascading black dress draped by gold colored pearls, gold earrings and [wearing] a woven taupe hat."[29]

During the months following "The Music Never Stops" Carter replaced Ariel Roland on bass with Chris Thomas, who had been recommended by Clarence Penn,[30] and by August she was on the road with her reconstituted group: Chestnut, Thomas, and Penn. This tour of North America was scheduled to coincide with the release of her forthcoming CD. Speaking to Peter Watrous of the new addition to her rhythm section, she gives us an idea of what she was looking for in a bass player: "I can live off swing and Chris has that, and such enthusiasm. He's got a strong, big, fat sound on bass," adding playfully, "and I like the way he looks on the instrument."[31] Later that year,

Carter listed "all the things that are eventually going to make a good performer, a good artist" in an interview with Willard Jenkins:

> Their enthusiasm and what they know. How hard are they gonna work for the job. Do they practice at home; when they leave rehearsal do they practice at home again? Do they want to memorize the music, do they want to learn the music? Are they good listeners? Do they have a good time; their creative abilities. . . . All those things; even though they may be young you can almost smell it if it's good, especially when you've been around as long as I have.[32]

By this time the advance press for her CD *It's Not about the Melody* was coming out in anticipation of Verve's 8 September release date. The label's spin machinery was in overdrive, and in sheer volume the media response to Carter's latest effort was impressive, with reviews and notices appearing in a gamut of music and entertainment publications. It had been two years since she had last recorded, and Verve was making this release into a media event. The singer evidently felt no special urgency about recording while under contract with Verve, for she expressed little interest in surpassing the pace she had established throughout her career, an average of one record every two and a half years. Referring to the label's executives, she told Chip Deffaa of *New York Post,* "Boy, they get uptight! But you should really come up with something different on each album. And that takes time."[33] Nevertheless, the pressure Verve put on her to generate a product ultimately proved a positive force.

The record's title neatly summed up her aesthetic.[34] In Verve's press release for the recording she patiently defended her concept: "There is no way I can approach a song now and not change it. It's part of me. I think that's why it's accepted. It's not forced. People understand that it's really happening at that moment." She offered that one reason why more people now accepted her approach was because young fans experienced the canon of classic American popular songs differently than older listeners did. "It takes some getting used to for a listener who is my age. I understand that. The young kids who have not been over-exposed to a melody accept it for what it is. It's only when they get interested in that melody's source, will they reflect and understand what I did with the piece of music."[35]

Taped at Clinton and Eastside Sound studios in New York during the first months of 1992, *It's Not about the Melody* was pieced together from material cut at several sessions with different groupings of musicians, in the same manner as *Look What I Got,* but multitrack digital technology now made it even easier to go back and redo passages of her vocal line that she felt didn't work. *It's Not about the Melody* represents a departure from Carter's established practice in several ways. More than ever before, she drew upon the services of several former band members, such as John Hicks, who was concurrently working with her on "The Music Never Stops." Aside from current trio members the staff consisted mostly of seasoned Carter alumni. She did this partly because she wanted the variety each individual's approach gave to the music.[36] Due to the volatility of her personnel, however, during the period following *Droppin' Things,* she also had lacked the time to allow the trio she had then—who had only combined forces the preceding October—to coalesce and settle into the material during months of live performance, as she had done in the past. She needed the core members to be musicians she could count on, musicians who understood her approach and its special demands. Craig Handy and John Hicks provided the nucleus for two cuts, with Walter Booker playing bass on one of these, "The Love We Had Yesterday." The three had been working together at Bradley's at the time, so this lent the group a certain cohesiveness. Carter brought Hicks in specifically to do his composition "Naima's Love Song" and reasoned that "there's no sense doing just one song together in the studio, so I might as well use [that] band on two songs."[37] Mulgrew Miller and Lewis Nash played together on three tracks, and her regular trio played on six more, with Nash filling in for Clarence Penn on two of them. "I didn't like what Clarence was doing on some of the songs so I hired Lewis Nash. And again, you might as well use them if you've got them there."[38] Two players new to Carter completed the roster: drummer Jeff "Tain" Watts and bassist Christian McBride, the former working with Hicks's contingent, the latter with Miller's. Carter may have hired Watts to spur him to develop in new directions but offered, nonchalantly, that she brought him in because he was "just hanging around Bradley's one night doing nothing and I asked him if he wanted to do my date."[39] Handy suggested that Watts's wide dynamic range may have influenced Carter's choice: "Jeff can really, really play quiet and swing hard and then he can just bring the house down, not just loud, there's quality too."[40] The band leader gave these experienced players considerably more space to stretch out and solo than she had given musicians on previous records, and they seized the opportunity with zeal. As one would expect, they also comped at a very high level, bringing an inventiveness to textures and an intricacy to the rhythmic interaction that can only come from years in the business. Carter was highly sensitive to the sweep of brushes on the snare head and often frowned on their use, but Nash's imaginative playing on "Stay as Sweet as You Are" and "You Go to My Head" convinced her that they could work when used tastefully.

Unlike several of Carter's other records, *It's Not about the Melody* contains very little of her previously recorded repertoire, with most of the tunes new to her book since *Droppin' Things.* Originally intended for the earlier record, a new arrangement of "When It's Sleepy Time Down South" made it onto this one. Her rendition of "You Go to My Head," in which she took her approach to back phrasing to extreme lengths, had been well honed in performances over the preceding year or so. Both that tune and her original "Make Him Believe" had been presented at "The Music Never Stops," the latter with a string arrangement minus drums, conducted by Geri Allen. The singer had added "You're Mine, You" to her repertoire as a tribute to the memory of Sarah Vaughan shortly after her death.

Carter's third record with Verve, *It's Not about the Melody,* received an enthusiastic critical response, and in December Carter was named Female Jazz Singer of the Year for the fourth year in a row in *Down Beat*'s annual Critics Poll, as well as taking first place in the Fifty-seventh Annual Reader's Poll for the third time, ahead of Abbey Lincoln, Shirley Horn, and Cassandra Wilson. The record and its singer also garnered the American Jazz Awards for Album of the Year and Vocalist of the Year respectively. By June 1994, sales for the recording totaled $34,348.[41]

In May 1992, Betty Carter's long association with the Brooklyn Academy of Music began to take on a greater significance. At that time she performed there on the same bill as the Count Basie Orchestra for the One Hundred Years of Jazz and Blues Festival. The festival was sponsored by 651, named for the address of the Majestic Theater at 651 Fulton Street. Carter's participation in the festival led to the development of a program designed to bring a select group of budding jazz talents together for a residency and performance at BAM that would give them professional experience and media exposure. She had originally proposed the idea of this project, which the forward-thinking singer named Jazz Ahead, to BAM executives when she had performed there in 1982 with David Amram and strings, but in light of her increased stature, the notion now took on greater weight, and the venue's current executives followed up on it.[42]

The organization 651—also known as the Kings Majestic Corporation—was developed four years earlier as a not-for-profit organization specifically designed for arts outreach into the Fort Greene and neighboring communities, and had a specific mission to expand the black audience for jazz and blues.[43] In retrospect the partnership of artistic director, Leonard Goines, coproducer Mikki Shepard, and Betty Carter seems inevitable given 651's mission. For Carter the association with 651 reflected her deepening commitment to her local community: "I love living in a neighborhood where there is so much talent, where young jazz musicians live and you can see young musicians coming to take classical lessons or visit BAM. I can see the future of this area from my front window. I hope I have contributed to it in some way."[44]

Carter's alliance with 651 also reflected her recognition of the growing importance of cultural institutions to jazz's future and her optimism about the music's prospects: "I think Lincoln Center and Carnegie Hall having done what they've done helps other people try things. . . . For now I'm excited because I'm looking ahead to what's in front of me. I want to go forward."[45]

Carter had already begun to explore the idea of showcasing up-and-coming musicians as far back as 1986, when she wanted to feature the Harper Brothers' Quintet on *Look What I Got.* The blow-out with Winard Harper had led her to draw back from the idea, but now she was back at it, aggressively. By the end of 1992 arrangements with 651 were in place for her first Jazz Ahead program.[46] In a bold statement of the program's central purpose: to sustain the continuity of the jazz tradition, Carter linked the program to the future by naming it Jazz Ahead '94, even though it was to take place in the spring of 1993—much as automobile manufacturers make a given year's new car models available during the preceding year. In January 1993 she was at the next IAJE conference in Houston, listening to student groups and consulting with trumpeter Roy Hargrove. In the following years such active participation in IAJE conferences would become an annual ritual for Carter. She also held auditions in Boston, probably in February while there for a gig at the Regattabar, with the help of saxophonist and teacher Billy Pierce. Gregory Hutchinson made some recommendations, and as word about the program spread, Carter also received tapes from musicians from across the country.

The singer had always prided herself on her ability to notice incipient talent, and the cast of sixteen musicians she assembled for Jazz Ahead '94, plus her trio, proved that she had not lost her touch. Some of the players, such as drummer Adonis Rose and trumpeter Marcus Printup, had already received some exposure in New York. Gregory Hutchinson, who was working with Roy Hargrove at the time, was also on hand, as well as drummer Brian Blade, who had been touring with Joshua Redman and pianist Jacky Terrasson. These more experienced players served as ringers to ensure that the evening would produce a high caliber of music. In addition to Rose, half of the other musicians represented Berklee, including tenor saxophonists Melvin Butler and Teodross Avery, who had been one of the five recipients of the Clifford Brown and Stan Getz Fellowship Award at the 1992 IAJE conference on tenor, bassists Mark Zubek, Matthew Garrison, and Reuben Rogers, and pianist Anthony Wonsey. Tenor player Chris Byars had reached the semifinals of the Thelonious Monk Competition in 1991. The players ranged in age from eighteen to twenty-nine, with Cyrus Chestnut being the oldest, and most of them being in their early twenties. Rehearsals had the quality of a workshop, with Carter diligently instructing players on the fine points of jazz performance, "showing a drummer how to accent and shade the rhythm;

voicing the saxophone harmonies; calling up specific chords from the pianist; coaxing a trumpeter to answer her vocal statements in an antiphonal exercise."[47] Betty Carter was stepping into the role of jazz educator, and not surprisingly she was adept at it.

On 17 and 18 April 1993, Carter presented "Betty Carter: Jazz Ahead '94," and Mayor David Dinkins declared the first of these dates Jazz Ahead Day. She performed a few numbers that evening with her own trio and with occasional backup from her showcased artists, including a seamless duet with Marcus Printup on "The Nearness of You" set against a hushed rhythm section backdrop. Most of the performance, however, was devoted to the next generation. All the musicians, divided into four groups with two groups playing in each half, were seated onstage behind two sets of drums and two grand pianos. The unique format was significant, sharing some features with the jam sessions in which Lillie Mae Jones had forged her skills as a teenager, as well as with the showcases Betty Bebop had participated in at theaters like the Apollo when she herself was coming up through the ranks. Carter orchestrated a sense of collective support among these musicians comparable to the one that had pervaded the jazz world when she was younger, and the musicians responded to this environment heartily, cheering each other's efforts. The message was clear: jazz is not just about the sounds—jazz is a way of being, a way of connecting.

Extending the benefits of Jazz Ahead, Carter had trumpeter Peven Everett and Melvin Butler join her and her trio when she kicked off the JVC Jazz Festival—a role formerly reserved for such stars as Sarah Vaughan and Ella Fitzgerald—at Carnegie Hall in June. Carter was billed with Gerry Mulligan, and Bill Cosby emceed the program. The title, *Sounds of Life,* came from her lyrics to "Sounds (Movin' On)." Later in the evening the *Tonight Show* band, led by Branford Marsalis, backed her on a number.[48] That October, Carter replaced Clarence Penn with Jazz Ahead alumnus Will Terrill III, and Everett continued to participate in some of her gigs, but this aggregation would only last a fortnight.

In the fall of 1993 the singer produced saxophonist Javon Jackson's debut recording with Blue Note, *When the Time Is Right.*[49] Having been told by label executives to get an established musician to produce the record, Jackson sought out Betty Carter.[50] Hinting at the respect he had for her, Jackson later spoke about the singer's impact on his playing: "She has a knack for laying behind the beat, taking her time in really delivering the melody. That's something I began to incorporate into my playing, in terms of pacing myself . . . so that people really get the gist of what you're trying to deliver."[51] This project was something of a dream come true for Carter, and she was pleasantly surprised when the saxophonist called her. Jackson chose all of the personnel for the date himself. For the first session on 7 September he used bassist Chris Thomas and drummer Clarence Penn, who were with Carter at the time, as well as singer Dianne Reeves for one number. Much of the personnel changed for the second session on 13 October with Peter Washington and Carl Allen now on bass and drums respectively, and Kenny Garrett playing on two numbers. Jacky Terrasson played piano on all the cuts.

Carter's former Liljay Productions coordinator and estranged friend, JoAnne Jimenez, was booking Jackson at the time, and there was some awkwardness between the women at the first meeting, but the project ultimately led them to bridge the distance that had grown between them. Carter's approach to her role as producer was initially somewhat laissez-faire. As a band leader the singer typically allowed her own musicians to get a feel for each other and generate a group dynamic before she added her own ideas. At the session she may have been intentionally hanging back so she could discern the musicians' nascent voices before exerting any influence. Jackson recalled a particular example of how, on Lerner and Lowe's "If Ever I Should Leave You" from *Camelot,* Carter ultimately made her presence felt:

> The first version that we did is a version where we just played the melody. I played the melody, took a solo. . . . It was kind of straightforward, and we took it back out. So when we finished the take, we thought, you know, first take—wasn't bad. So Betty came into the studio from the booth and she said "*bor-ing*" [in a singsong tone]. . . . So she said, "Let's try it again, and Javon you play an intro. Don't play anything that has to do with the melody, and when you're finished playing your intro, just start the song."[52]

The CD commences with this cut, so Jackson's unaccompanied solo sets the tone for all that follows, sending the signal that this will not be an ordinary recording. The use of an unaccompanied horn to open the tune recalls Carter's use of Don Braden on "The Good Life" from *Look What I Got.* Listening to this cut, one can notice some other features it shares with Carter's own charts. In her own arrangements, for example, she wanted the statement of the melody to display as much creativity as a solo, and, as we have seen, she often accomplished this by saving each instrument's entrance until it would have the maximum impact, meting out the fresh sounds little by little. Jackson's rendering of "If Ever I Could Leave You" displays a similar awareness of the effect each player's entrance can create. Having player's entrances cut unpredictability against the form kept the music moving forward. In its use of double time, the arrangement of "If Ever I Could Leave You" also recalls Carter's playfulness with meter. According to Jackson, however, Carter did not directly involve herself in the arrangement, which grew largely out of his concept for the tune and out of choices that each of the musicians made spontaneously. Nevertheless, her comment to him that the first take sounded "too typical" and her suggestion that everybody try some different things to make the chart unique guided the musicians in a fresh direction. Aside from suggesting the ballad "Something to Remember You By," Carter did not influence the choice of tunes.

Even as Betty Carter was involved in *When the Time Is Right* and taking her trio on a short road trip to the Midwest, final preparations were being made for yet another unprecedented project, one that would bring her together with a group of her own peers for a tour to sites in France, England, and Spain. Bassist Dave Holland had planted the seeds for this undertaking earlier that year, after his gig at Fat Tuesday's with Hank Jones. Rushing to catch his former boss as she left the performance, Holland paid his respects to the singer. As they spoke of a mutual wish to work together again, the notion seemed more than an idle pleasantry. At the time Holland had been performing on solo bass in Europe and had just released his second solo bass recording, *Ones All.* Initially Holland had been thinking of just vocals and bass, but they ultimately settled on a trio format.[53] Carter had wanted to perform again with Geri Allen, and this project seemed a suitable vehicle for them to get together. Holland suggested drummer Jack DeJohnette, with whom he had a long and varied history, having both worked together with Miles Davis in 1969 and John Abercrombie in 1975, as well as with Herbie Hancock and Pat Metheny in 1990. Allen and DeJohnette had worked together before, participating in one of the trios backing Carter in "The Music Never Stops." Understandably, Carter enjoyed the break this all-star cast gave her from teaching: "You know that they're seasoned, they have plenty of experience, and you don't have to tell them what to do, or how to do it. They know about shading, they know about textures, they know about things that young musicians get as they grow older."[54] It was also a relief not to be introducing standard repertoire to her rhythm section; in fact, Allen recommended at least one of the tunes, "I'm All Smiles,"[55] and possibly "Lullaby of the Leaves" as well. Carter intended to return from the trip with a live recording of their work together, and during preparations for the tour arrangements were made for the British Broadcasting Corporation's Audio International to record the group's performance on 30 October at Royal Festival Hall in London.[56] Verve/PolyGram later released the document of this remarkable event under the title *Feed the Fire.* Although the BBC taped the entire concert, which included 105 minutes of music, Carter released only ten of the fourteen tunes performed, presenting some in a different order from that of the concert.

The concert was a study in contrasts. As was Carter's custom, after the trio opened the first half, the singer entered to perform Geri Allen's original, "Feed the Fire." On the next tune, "Love Notes"—composed by Jazz Ahead alumnus Mark Zubek—DeJohnette played much of the ballad pianissimo on sponge-headed mallets, and throughout much of the song his presence was felt more than heard. The resulting warmth of sonority reinforced Carter's lyrics, which conveyed her love for music's power to soothe, and punned on the word *notes* as both written messages and musical sounds. The group proceeded directly into a playful up-tempo arrangement of "Sometimes I'm Happy," a tune Carter had done in her concerts with Carmen McRae in 1987. This version featured Carter singing the A sections of the tune against a repeated ascending figure played by Allen and Holland with DeJohnette reinforcing the rhythmic pattern. During the head and later in Carter's solo, the trio's reiteration of this climbing figure built tension that exploded into the B sections, when the group went into straight time. After Carter's original tune "Fake," the group finished the first half of the concert with a highly energetic rendition of Michael Leonard's "I'm All Smiles."

Carter's complete reconception of "Lover Man," which opened the concert's second half, banishes any thought of Billie Holiday's rendition, or any other singer's for that matter. The recording deserves close listening because it illustrates how Carter used formal procedures to hint at nonverbal meanings. As complex as the following description is, in probing the song's emotional content it merely touches upon all that Carter was able to get across. Even so, its complexity belies the immediacy of her rendition's emotional force.

"Lover Man" conveys a dark, dark yearning coupled with a deep sense of foreboding through the obsessive recurrence of a rhythmic figure that I will refer to as *X*. Fashioned upon a modified clave pattern—akin to the ostinato from Herbie Hancock's "Maiden Voyage," the figure extends across two measures in a feel that moves twice as slow as the song's tempo of ninety-six beats per minute. In its staccato phrasing, Geri Allen's muted hammering on the figure's F-sharp minor9 (13) chord hints at the tempo without stating it. Broken only briefly by a move to the IV^{7,} on the last quarter-note of its second measure, the chord's repetitions have the futility of a faintly pounded fist.

Initially heard as an introduction (0:00–0:30), figure X persists throughout the first half of the A section (0:30–1:10) with gentle shifts in the harmonic coloration. In fact, because figure X is first heard as a vamp, its repetitions obscure the formal beginning of the A section. This ambiguity cuts the stabilizing effect of the figure's throbbing reiteration by surrounding it with an air of uncertainty: time has come to a standstill just when the narrator is yearning to know what to expect. The harmonic move at the end of X contributes ambiguity, because it is the only legato moment in the figure. By shifting rhythmic weight to the anacrusis, it sounds as though it might be falling on the downbeat—an effect that Allen amplifies by accentuation. The figure's syncopated structure—which suggests a two-against-three polyrhythm—coupled with the rhythm section's withholding of straight time also creates an unsettling ambiguity about the groove, because figure X has no rhythmic anchor against which to swing. The many ways in which this figure undermines stability keep its nagging recurrence from wearing on the ear, while at the same time suggesting a world-weary numbness. All of this in turn gives Carter's vocal line a strangely suspended character as she enters on the words "I don't know why . . . but I'm feeling so sad," with the weight of despair hanging over them. The sense of dislocation provoked by the rhythm lends the words a new, disturbing quality.

The music suddenly changes character at the moment in the form that corresponds to the fifth measure of the original song (1:10). Carter's extreme back phrasing leads the last words of the next line of text—"I long to try something . . . I never had"—to spill over into this new music. In shifting to the relative major, the A section's second half (1:10–1:42), which is built upon a contrasting figure that I will call *Y*, lightens the song's mood. DeJohnette clarifies the metric situation here by introducing the high-hat click on 2 and 4, which leads the Y idea to feel faster than the X idea. Against a progression of I^7 moving to IV^7—the characteristic harmonic turn of the blues—in A major, Carter continues: "Never had no kissing; never had no loving."

Bringing up the reins, so to speak, the rhythm section closes the A section by playing the next two harmonies as repeated block chords in octave displacements while also marking the half note to prepare for the return of the slower feel.[57] At this point Carter's voice sinks to the darkest part of her vocal range on the words "Lover man." Partly because the X idea preempts the Y figure by returning before each A section's formal reiteration (at 1:42–1:52 and later at 3:06–3:17), its somberness dominates the arrangement. When the harmony resolves to the song's tonic of F-sharp minor—which functions locally as a deceptive cadence as it comes out of the A major section—Carter calls out "where can you be?" on a rising line, giving the song's hook a questioning urgency.

Only after a second hearing does it become apparent that the arrangement had started in double long meter, which makes each A section last thirty-two measures instead of the usual eight, with each subsection, X plus Y, consisting of sixteen measures apiece. Put another way, Carter's vocal line and its supporting harmony move at a pace four times as slow as the time feel produced by the rhythm section—as she had in the second chorus of "The Good Life" (example 15)—allowing Carter to sing the lyrics with the emotional intensity of a ballad while the band creates the effect of a faster tempo.

The lyrics of the second A section's first half (1:52–2:34) amplify the sense of desolation: "The night is cold—and I'm so—all alone." Typically, Carter's musical phrases fragment the verbal phrases, giving the words a new meaning and punctuation. She sings: "I'd give my soul—just to call you," before adding, almost as an afterthought, "my own." The mood shift in the second half of the A section (2:34–3:06) lends the lyrics an ironic bemusement: "Got a moon above me but no one to love me." But by the final words, "love me," the sustained chords that signal the cadence have arrived to usher in the X idea, over which Carter sings "Lover man." The plea "where can you be?" dovetails into the bridge this time, denying the cadence its power to bring about an ending.

In the bridge (3:17–4:00) the trio plays straight time now, but twice as slow, which would bring the groove into simple long meter except for the fact that the changes now double in frequency, thus bringing the harmonic rhythm and the meter into a standard metric relationship. This supports the speedier exposition of the narrative, which evokes a fantasy world in which all doubts have been washed away: "I've heard it said that the thrill of romance is like a heavenly dream. I go to bed with a prayer that you'll make love to me." Setting these words against straight time and the normal meter here—which sounds even more solid because of what has come before—carries an implication that the narrator's escape into a state of reverie has more substance for her than facing the painful truth of her emptiness.

With muted drama, this rhythmic state of affairs prevails when the A harmonic phrase returns (4:00–4:49), promoting a sense of continuity where one would expect a contrast thus undermining the large-scale relationship that this moment in the form bears to the earlier A phrases. Withholding the X idea here obscures the arrival of the tonic at the form's most important structural moment. By suppressing the sense of impending closure that the recapitulation of the A phrase in the AABA form usually brings, Carter generates a sense of movement through the end of the so-called melody statement into the solo chorus. Doing this also bestows a hopeful quality upon the closing lines of the lyric: "Someday we'll meet and you'll dry all my tears and whisper sweet little things in my ears." When she reaches the lyrics' hook, however, the X idea brings back the haunting anguish from which we had momentarily been spared.

The X idea now functions as an ostinato for DeJohnette's solo, and he exploits its rifflike structure by folding rhythmic ideas into its creases. Soloing through the A section's repeat, DeJohnette builds a feeling of unbroken growth across the formal articulation, intensifying the agitation with increased volume and rhythmic activity. Using sponge-headed mallets, as he had with "Love Notes," he now creates the sinister effect rolling thunder has when it presages a summer storm. After Allen solos on just the bridge, providing another passing respite from the song's gloom, she collapses back into X as Carter's voice returns for the song's final A section (7:10–9:05). In addition to a reprise of the opening measures' brooding quality, the original harmonic-metric relationship of double long meter now returns with a concomitant halving of the harmonic rhythm. All of these factors, coupled with a return to the tonic (now clearly signaled by the X figure's reappearance), brings to mind the song's beginning and rounds out the arrangement, thus inducing the sense of closure denied earlier at this point in the form.[58] The words that sounded so hopeful when she had sung them before now ring false as the X figure drives home the hopelessness of the situation.

Carter's performance of "Lover Man" reveals much about her concept. For her, reshaping the melody was an integral step in creating an arrangement that utilized all the resources of the ensemble, empowering her to bring feelings to the surface that the original tune only hints at. Rather than being inserted for virtuosic display, the instrumental solos sustain the song's overall emotional thrust, even when Allen briefly parts the clouds to remind us that, somewhere else, the sun may be shining. By exploiting words' capacity to link music's nonverbal meanings to specific images from life, Carter weaves the abstract excursions of absolute music into the narrative art of the storyteller, allowing the listener to hear her singing on several levels at once. While communicating with emotional clarity and precision, she also left each individual listener room to formulate his or her own response. In the process, she is no longer merely interpreting a song, but using it as raw material for the creation of a unique composition that succeeds on its own merits.

Consistent with Carter's approach to programming and arranging, which for her were intimately linked, the remainder of the evening featured an exploration of different ways of combining the forces assembled. After "Lullaby of the Leaves,"[59] three duets with Allen, Holland, and DeJohnette each in turn followed on "If I Should Lose You" (an expansion of the approach Carter and Allen had used in "The Music Never Stops"), "All or Nothing at All," and "What Is This Tune?" respectively. This last tune, consisting entirely of more than seven minutes of improvised dialogue between voice and drums—in which each musician fed the other rhythmic and melodic shapes, and both modified their timbre in response—did not have a title until the CD was to be released. As the two brought the busy conversation to a reflective conclusion, Holland entered on a bowed tremolo, smoothly leading into an unaccompanied arco solo that served as the introduction to Billy Strayhorn's "Day Dream." The concert closed with a truncated rendition of Carter's "B's Blues." The incorrigible singer sounds as if she could have kept singing all night—she was known to extend sets to over two hours in length—but perhaps the concert presenters were urging her to conclude the evening, as often happened in such cases.

Geri Allen reported to Michael Bourne the following year that for her the tour was a master class in audience rapport: "Every time we would play I was amazed at Betty's command, at her ability to communicate *directly* to each person in the audience, no matter how big or small the venue. Every place was Betty's *house*. . . . It was like that every night. She was able to *connect*."[60] The recording shows the heights of invention to which Carter could rise in the presence of equals. Indeed, it is hard to imagine any other singer who could go head-to-head with these musicians and display the creative abandon Carter did. By collaborating with peers she put to rest any notion that she could only work with promising greenhorns who depended upon her to realize the full force of their talents.

With *Feed the Fire,* Carter had succeeding in making her next recording for Verve just over a year after the label had issued *It's Not about the Melody.* The four reels did not arrive in the States until April 1994, however, and contract negotiations between Bet-Car, PolyGram Records, and the BBC delayed the recording's release. By June the two parties had agreed upon terms whereby the BBC would license the master tapes of the event to PolyGram. In return PolyGram would pay the BBC an advance of fifteen thousand dollars and a royalty of 5 percent on the published dealer price over a ten-year period. PolyGram retained exclusive rights to remix the multitrack masters. The terms of the contract were contingent upon Carter's royalty agreement, for which PolyGram was responsible.[61] Listed as executive producer of the recording, Carter received full recognition for her artistic control of the product.

The group Carter had assembled for the European tour worked together only once again, around a year later, when it reunited for the United States premiere of the repertoire at the San Francisco Jazz Festival, on the same bill as Abbey Lincoln.[62] Verve had issued *Feed the Fire* that September 1994, and the event helped draw attention to its release. With the modest ambition of generating twenty-five thousand dollars from CD sales and five thousand from cassette sales, the label did not market the recording as aggressively as it had her preceding records, confirming Carter's contention that record companies did not actively promote jazz.[63] The recording was a huge artistic success, however, proving that at sixty-four years of age Betty Carter was still very much on top of her game.

Due to the rapid turnover of the singer's trio personnel during these years, an army of young talents marched through the halls of "Betty Carter University." In a performance at Seattle's Jazz Alley around this time she quipped: "These guys are sticking with me about two weeks now and then they're off and running."[64] At the end of 1993, Carter was back on the road, touring the West Coast with an entirely new trio consisting of pianist Jacky Terrasson,[65] whom JoAnne Jimenez was now managing, Larry Grenadier on bass, and Jazz Ahead alumnus Alvester Garnett on drums. This aggregation did not last long: Terrasson stayed on until the following summer; Grenadier and Garnett until February. The good news was, if a budding musician had the chops and the drive it took to make Carter's cut, there was always a realistic hope that a window of opportunity might suddenly open up for him.[66] The bad news was, it might just as suddenly slam shut.

13

Movin' On

The idea of exploiting the medium of music video to promote jazz would continue to preoccupy Betty Carter over the next few years. Having given much thought to her own physical presentation, she knew the power of visual imagery to communicate and reinforce music's impact. Furthermore, she kept herself apprised of various trends in television. She was very aware of the success of music video channels MTV and VH1 and the roles each had played in revitalizing a sagging recording industry.[1] Claiming it was an idea she had had for over a dozen years—no doubt referring to the video of her Public Theater performance that was never telecast—Carter spoke in several interviews of how conceptual jazz videos could be used to develop existing and new audiences, and most important for her, to reclaim black listeners who had moved on to other styles.

As passionately as she argued for this idea, Carter was certainly not the first to conceive of it. Shortly after she had left Lionel Hampton's band, for example, her former boss had publicly expressed similar sentiments during television's first years: "The band business has got to get hip to television, or television will get hip to the idea of creating its own bands."[2] He had already appeared on *The Perry Como Show, Cavalcade of Bands,* and *The Frank Sinatra Show.* Hampton was convinced that the big-band era would not have ended if band leaders had exploited television. The band leader was onto something, for later on, one of the few remaining places one could hear the sound of a big band was on television, where such late-night programs as Johnny Carson's *Tonight Show* typically had orchestras.

The storyteller and actress in Carter felt strongly that a narrative approach, and not simply a documentary one, would enliven the presentation of jazz performers: "That's what the technology is all about. That's what all the pop artists are doing. There are a lot of songs that tell stories that could come alive on film."[3] She was aware, however, of the formidable obstacles she was facing within the industry. In 1993 she told Sheila Rule of the *New York Times* that record company executives claimed that, in respect to jazz, such an idea required too much money to make it worthwhile.[4] Undaunted, Carter had a long-term goal in mind and she was not about to let up. Speaking to WKCR radio host Evan Spring, she elaborated on this point, playing with the multiple meanings of the word *vision:* "I can't for the life of me understand why the powers that be don't get on the ball and deal with jazz as a visual part of the music. It can be visual. You *can* come up with some creative ideas for it. But nobody's done so, and it's crazy because there's no vision, they're not looking ahead."[5] Ever pragmatic about the business side of her job, Carter related jazz's need for a television presence directly to her concerns about the music's promotion and distribution: "We've lost a percentage point; we're down to four percent of the market, even though we're getting more records out there. We need that one percent back, and to do something about getting on to eight, nine, or ten percent."[6]

As vocal as she was about her cause, Carter was not one to leave off merely at voicing her opinion, and several of her projects from this period were devoted to achieving her goal. At the end of January, 1994, she participated in a "musical variety hour" entitled "A World of Different Music" aired on WCVB-TV in Boston, performing "Love Notes."[7] Around this same time Carter was in Toronto for the filming of her cameo appearance in *Lost in the Stars,* a tribute to Kurt Weill, coproduced by Rhombus Media—the company responsible for *Thirty-Two Short Films about Glenn Gould,* which had just come out the preceding year—and by ZDF German Television. Given the mission of Rhombus, it is clear why Carter found the project appealing. In its fifteen-year existence, the company had acquired a reputation for becoming "classical music's answer to rock video" by making classical music "sexy, human, and accessible," according to Brian Johnson of *McLeans.*[8] In a segment set in a dimly lit factory, a hollow brick shell of a structure with tall ceilings, the singer was presented in an eerie, surreal fashion. Standing virtually motionless, she intones Weill's "Lonely House,"[9] including the song's rarely-performed verse, accompanied by a trio put together for the session that included Geri Allen on piano. Carter's stillness is all the more striking for being entirely out of character for her. This effort was also atypical in that Carter allowed Hal Willner to take credit for producing the recording, although it is doubtful that he had much say about the final outcome. The material she performed would be released on CD by Sony in 1997 as an anthology entitled *September Songs,* in a project similar to the Disney recording Carter had done for Willner in 1988.

The release of *Feed the Fire* was still in preparation, and the record would not be issued until the fall, but some of Carter's past efforts were being released in various contexts. In January 1994, Verve reissued her first Bet-Car record, now titled *Betty Carter: At the Village Vanguard.* That February, *Jazz at Lincoln Center Presents: The Fire of the Fundamentals* was released, a compilation of ten live performances from Jazz at Lincoln Center's first two seasons that included some of Carter's material from "The Music Never Stops."[10]

Changes in her trio personnel continued into the new year. By mid-February George Frudas had taken Alvester Garnett's place on the drum stool—but he was there for "only a minute"—and by the time Carter was singing in London at Ronnie Scott's that March, Will Terrill III had come back into the fold. Apart from a brief return visit from Alvester Garnett, Terrill would hold the chair for the following two years. Around this time twenty-seven-year-old Eric S. Revis of Fresno, California, took over for Larry Grenadier on bass.[11] This group would form a working unit behind Carter for the next few months. In the meantime her pianist Jacky Terrasson created a stir by winning the Thelonious Monk piano competition and then signing with Blue Note Records.

On 6 April 1994 Carter was on hand, along with some thirty other musicians including Herbie Hancock, Joe Henderson, Hank Jones, and J. J. Johnson, for a celebration at Carnegie Hall of Verve Records' fiftieth anniversary. The event also served as a benefit for Carnegie Hall's jazz program with tickets ranging from twenty-five to one thousand dollars. In tribute to Ella Fitzgerald, who had helped Verve founder Norman Granz launch the label with a series of "songbooks"—recordings devoted to such composers as George Gershwin and Cole Porter—Carter sang one of her mentor's signature tunes, "How High the Moon." Fitzgerald had been inactive professionally since 1992, and later in 1994 Carter would add to her book an homage to the older singer in the form of a hip rendition of "A-Tisket, A-Tasket."[12] While this bore only a faint resemblance to her much earlier idea to present an Ella Fitzgerald tribute concert to benefit a jazz foundation, this performance was a welcome chance for Betty Carter to honor one of her idols. She also participated in the jam on "Now's the Time" that closed the program. The event was videotaped and aired the following month. Soon after, the label released selections from the event on CD as *Carnegie Hall Salutes the Jazz Masters: Verve 50th Anniversary.*[13]

Carter had also been gearing up for her Jazz Ahead '95 program during the first months of 1994. She had attended the IAJE conference in Boston that January, as she had done the preceding year, to scout for talent. For Jazz Ahead '95 Carter assembled seventeen musicians ranging in age from twelve to thirty, with Peven Everett, Mark Zubek, Andre Hayward, and Melvin Butler returning to provide continuity from the preceding year's program. Responding to criticism that she had not included any women and/or vocalists, she made a point of doing both this year, inviting a young vocal harmony trio from Milwaukee named the Reed Sisters: Brittany, age twelve; Tanya, age thirteen; and, Brandi, age sixteen. After a week of intensive rehearsing that included the development of several original compositions created by the participants, and only days after her Carnegie Hall appearance, she led her young charges in the "second annual showcase of a new generation of jazz musicians" at BAM's Majestic Theater on 9 April.[14] A matinee performance the following day made the program accessible to a young audience.

Betty Carter's work with the Jazz Ahead musicians led her to develop ideas about how to provide a learning environment for students. Sharing her views on teaching with Michael Bourne the following year, she revealed her understanding of the learning process:

> It's not about teaching. It's about doing and being allowed to do. I can't teach them. All I can say to them is that you've got to work in order to get better. What I've been able to offer them are *jobs*. . . . In the meantime I put in a dose of skill. I can tell them about what I've gone through and why this works and why this doesn't work. I can tell them about programming, what tunes should follow other tunes, how it should follow, why it should follow. . . . I want these young musicians to put their skills to use, to broaden what they have, to become more interested in the music than just playing it. I encourage them to write as much as they possibly can.[15]

Unlike those music teachers who tend to expect all of their students to develop a uniform technique, Carter was interested in the unique qualities her students could bring to their work with her. She took pains to know their idiosyncrasies as she worked with them: "They need the freedom to find out who they are and develop themselves, so I can see how loose they can become. If I'm going to give them any kind of advice, I've got to know something about them, their capabilities, their attitudes, how they really feel."[16]

Carter had spent the preceding year considering ways to increase the Jazz Ahead program's visibility and impact. This time around, the planning benefited from the experience of many savvy professionals in the entertainment industry. Corporate sponsorship made it possible to expand the program by providing room and board for the participants. A reception to benefit the Jazz Ahead program followed the concert, with gala tickets sold at one hundred dollars apiece. For the occasion, 651 formed a gala committee consisting of individuals in all aspects of the entertainment industry, including filmmaker Spike Lee, Carnegie Hall Jazz Orchestra director Jon Faddis, George and Joyce Wein of Festival Productions, writer Willard Jenkins, choreographer George Faison, Geri Allen, and John Schreiber.[17] Actor Billy Dee Williams, famous for his appearances in the film loosely based on Billie Holiday's *Lady Sings the Blues* and the *Star Wars* movies, chaired the gala committee and hosted the reception. His association with Betty Carter would continue throughout the year, and he would later emcee for her appearance at the San Francisco Jazz Festival and cohost the Thelonious Monk International Jazz Competition at Washington's Kennedy Center with Carter in the fall.

In line with her effort to raise the profile of Jazz Ahead, Carter expanded upon the participants' performance activities during the following year. As soon as the next week, she took the program to the Apollo Theater. In order to make the music affordable, tickets prices ranged from ten to twenty-four dollars. Bringing these young stars to a place so full of fond memories gave this performance special meaning for her, and she took pride in having arranged the date: "People hadn't seen this music in the Apollo for so long, especially the way I presented it."[18] From 17 to 22 May 1994, Carter featured the Reed Sisters and Peven Everett in performances with her trio in the Jazz Showcase at Chicago's Blackstone Hotel, and that August she brought several musicians from the program to Atlanta for the Black Arts Festival. Through her activities that year, Carter secured the program's foothold in the jazz world. The following year, thirteen musicians from Jazz Ahead '95 returned to provide continuity. In successive programs, Carter would continue to take a special interest in the Reed Sisters, the only vocalists she effectively took under her wing. For Jazz Ahead '97, in 1996, they sang a new version of Carter's first song "I Can't Help It" in 5/4 time.[19]

Betty Carter also integrated Jazz Ahead players in her regular performance schedule. Some of the members of Carter's working units—expanded now to include horns—were drawn from her Jazz Ahead finds. At the beginning of September, Xavier Davis jumped in to replace Terrasson, who had left ten days earlier.[20] As with many other initiates to Carter's traveling show, Davis was granted a preliminary one-nighter to settle in—an out-of-town preview—before embarking on a West Coast road trip. In December, Carter brought Everett and tenor saxophonist John D. Allen along for a three-day stint at Yoshi's in Seattle that included a New Year's Eve broadcast, as well as to other jobs early in 1995. In the years that followed, Carter would use her gigs more and more as a vehicle for putting the spotlight on her discoveries. In addition, she was busy opening up new markets for jazz, performing, for example, in Brisbane and Sydney, Australia, in May 1995. She would return to Australia the following year, in the fall, and then take her group on an extended tour of Brazil. During this period, Kagle Redding traveled with his energetic sixty-six-year-old mother, as her road manager.

Several Jazz Ahead players were finding work outside the training ground Carter had devised for them. Peven Everett toured with Branford Marsalis's new band, Buckshot LeFonque, in the summer of 1995,[21] and by then, nineteen-year-old drummer Karriem Riggins had joined Roy Hargrove's band. Twenty-one-year-old tenor player Mark Shim performed with the Lincoln Center Jazz Orchestra, and later he and Sherman Irby would both go on to sign with Blue Note records. GRP records would "introduce" Teodross Avery two years after Carter had discovered him.

The mid-1990s was a fertile time for jazz, and in June 1995, the *New York Times Magazine* dedicated twelve pages to a special section, "The New Jazz Age." A key sign of the renaissance, proclaimed by one of the section's coauthors, Stephen J. Dubner, was the emergence of stellar young players. While much of the momentum was attributed to Wynton Marsalis and the four-year-old Jazz at Lincoln Center program, Dubner gave Carter the final word. In a closing piece about the singer's recent Jazz Ahead '96, the writer went so far as to suggest that her program could easily be the source for the "next Miles Davis."[22] Ever protective of her charges, Carter was opposed to this way of thinking. She often encouraged young musicians in their creative efforts by saying that "they didn't stop giving out talent with Duke Ellington and John Coltrane." In her eyes, those who make a name for themselves playing or singing this music should be allowed to do so free of comparison to the giants of an earlier day.

As well as presenting her young finds from Jazz Ahead in live performance, Carter also made a point of recording them. In two sessions at the end of January 1996, she went into the Power Station in New York City with an ensemble that consisted of several Jazz Ahead players, including her current pianist Xavier Davis, bassist Matt Hughes, who had joined her regular trio in September 1995, saxophonist Mark Shim, who had participated in several live gigs starting around the same time, and trombonist Andre Hayward. Carter was between drummers at this point, with Byron Landham soon to join her group, so Gregory Hutchinson played drums for the sessions. Hughes would not last long in the bass chair, and steadfast Curtis Lundy also participated in the recording, playing bass on four of the CD's seven tunes. After making the recording, Lundy would stay on, stabilizing the group as Carter introduced new pianist Travis Shook that summer. With Landham, this rhythm section would remain fairly constant for the remainder of 1996, although bassist Vashon Johnson would step in briefly during the summer for Carter's European tour. Lundy would also serve as another pair of ears for Carter, recommending players whose talents may have eluded her attention. Released in late October with the title *I'm Yours, You're Mine,* the recording includes a new version of Weill's "Lonely House," as well as his "September Song," and several new additions to Carter's book: "East of the Sun," "Close Your Eyes," Jule Styne's "This Time," as well as an Antonio Carlos Jobim tune with English lyrics, entitled "Useless Landscape"—a rare example of Carter espousing a political cause in her work.

The recording's title song, credited to both Carter and Lundy, provides another example of how Carter ransacked her past efforts in search of raw material for new tunes. In this case, she built the new song on a coda she had devised for the version of "What's New" that she was doing around the time of "The Music Never Stops." The lyrics of "I'm Yours, You're Mine" consist entirely of scat vocables until the end, where she introduces the final lyrics from "What's New": "We haven't met since then—Gee but it's nice to see you again." The moderately slow tempo (MM = 66) and mezzo piano dynamic give the tune a wistful tenderness—the kind of mood Carter evoked from her players with the exhortation "make love." Constructed on a two-measure ostinato, and, in its contrasting material, on alternating chords, the tune lacks the intricacy one associates with Carter. Atypically, her solo line is entirely diatonic and strongly consonant with the harmony. The simplicity of the harmonic materials and the texture enables her to focus on creating melodic and rhythmic interest in her solo while using internal repetitions to give the line its own growth. In fact, it is a comment on her power as a soloist that she produced so compelling a line with such basic materials. The repetitive structure of this song suggests that she may have conceived of the tune as a vehicle for reaching out to a larger audience; certainly it is a far cry from the aggressive jazz Carter was weaned on as a teenager. In some ways it is consistent with a path that she had embarked upon over two decades earlier, when she had started to move away from the aesthetic she had learned from the beboppers and toward the cool sensibility Miles Davis exhibited in his work from the 1950s.

Perhaps convinced that the song was more marketable than her standard fare, Verve presented it in a music video format. Grapevine Pictures was enlisted to shoot the video and, according to Verve's accounting records, the total cost of the production was $17,863. The video's director was paid a measly $1,429, and the whole product has the look of a low-budget effort. Imposing a somewhat convoluted narrative upon the song, the video portrays Carter as a fortune-teller whose counsel is sought by two star-crossed lovers. The story is told through gesture and dance, and it operates largely on a symbolic plane, featuring a dancer who represents death. When Verve distributed the video to various national and local channels that summer the response from video programmers was lukewarm at best, ranging anywhere from

"You've gotta be kidding" (Illyotic Flava, Newton, Mass.), "Maybe next lifetime" (Dare-TV, NYC), and "Get that shit outa here" (Network One/Music on Demand, LA), to a description of how West Coast outlets were "generating some heat" with a few multiregional outlets showing the clip in rotation.[23] Most national outlets, such as the Box, rejected the video outright. Carter recorded two more tracks for Verve in April, for the *Verve Christmas Album: Jazz for Joy*, produced by Don Sickler, but after a spat with Verve's president, Chuck Mitchell, she would soon part ways with the label.

The close of 1996 was a turbulent time for Betty Carter. Toward the end of that year, a disagreement with the executives of 651 led Carter to withdraw her Jazz Ahead program from the Brooklyn Academy, and the following year there was no Jazz Ahead. The event's organizers wanted to present her program in the fall, along with its other jazz events. She felt strongly that it should take place in the spring, partly in order to exploit the timing of college students' spring break, and partly because of her own touring schedule. According to Kennedy Center's vice president for education, Derek Gordon, Dr. Billy Taylor had informed him that Carter needed a home for her program, and Gordon flew up to New York to propose the Kennedy Center.[24] By the spring of 1997, when she performed at the Kennedy Center, planning for the next Jazz Ahead was under way.

The shift of Jazz Ahead to the nation's capital fit in neatly with other ways Carter had recently become connected to that city. By early 1994, Washington, D.C., had become the site for several significant events in Carter's career. On 19 April of that year she had performed a forty-minute set at the White House for a dinner honoring the trustees of the Democratic National Committee. After the performance, Ann Stock, the president's social secretary, wrote Carter on behalf of the president: "The White House is still rocking from your awesome performance last evening!"[25] That June, Carter would return to perform with her trio again at a Rose Garden gala in a program that also included Lou Rawls and Carter's fellow Detroiter Aretha Franklin.[26] Then on 21 November 1994, she was at the Kennedy Center with Herbie Hancock for the Thelonious Monk International Jazz Competition. Through such events the center gave jazz a national forum, making it a likely place to broaden Jazz Ahead's outreach and influence. By April 1998, the foundation would be laid for Carter to present "Betty Carter's Jazz Ahead" in Washington.

The end of 1996 brought yet another round of personnel changes in Carter's rhythm section. Shortly after she returned from Brazil, she replaced drummer Byron Landham with Ralph Peterson. With Jacky Terrasson filling in on piano for a trip to Yoshi's in Oakland, Carter also dismissed Travis Shook at this time. By January 1997, when the singer brought her trio to

Switzerland at the invitation of the International Foundation for Creativity and Leadership, she now had Bruce Flowers on piano.

This gig was no ordinary club date. Betty Carter was one of a group of seven professionals at the top of their diverse fields, who were chosen to make presentations to the Seventh International Zermatt Symposium on Creativity in Economics, Art and Science about how they each addressed risk in their work. The group included Nobel Prize–winning physicist/neurobiologist Donald Glaser, who had won recognition in 1960 for the invention of the bubble chamber; physicist Edward Teller, who had helped develop the hydrogen bomb with the Manhattan Project in 1942; former MTV producer Josh Greenberg; Milanese photographer Oliviero Toscani, who was then creative director for Benetton; and writer-filmmaker team Diane Summers and Eric Valli, who had come from Kathmandu where they were conducting anthropological research.[27]

Carter kicked off the symposium, not with a performance, but with a lecture-demonstration on risk taking delivered in song. When she opened the floor for questions, she insisted that the participants sing their questions, so they could have a firsthand experience of the risks of jazz singing. Much more than any explanation, the format conveyed the concrete sensation of making jazz, albeit on a rudimentary level. It embodied Carter's "learning by doing" philosophy, and it was not new for her. Carter had conducted a master class along similar lines at the IAJE conference in Miami in 1993. Backed by continuous comping from her trio, cueing them to make changes in tempo and harmony when she felt the need for contrast, she sang her comments about music making to the audience and required audience members to sing their questions to her. While she had been quite tough with that crowd, which had included aspiring vocalists—exhorting them to "listen to the changes!"—Carter took a more encouraging approach with her pupils in Zermatt.[28]

That fall, Carter would expand upon her jazz pedagogy in a series of classes she taught for the Harman: How to Listen music education outreach program brought into public schools across the country by sound system manufacturer Harman International Industries. Spearheaded by Dr. Sydney Harman and Wynton Marsalis, the program grew out of a "mutual concern for the country's waning commitment [to] and interest in music education."[29] The premise was to bring established jazz artists to young people not simply to teach them about music but "to reveal the wonders of music."[30] Between 29 October and 5 November Carter visited four elementary and junior high schools in Chicago, Detroit, Dallas, and Houston. This was not an entirely new age group for her: she had given a workshop for children the preceding September while in she was in Oakland to perform at Yoshi's.[31]

Carter's friend John Schreiber, who had been her road manager for her

European tour of 1978, served as the middleman between Carter and Harman, bringing her in for the program's second year. Schreiber recalled that at first he had to "romance her about the program." Betty Carter wanted to meet Sydney Harman and his wife Lynn: "They had to prove their bona fides to her, that they were serious about this."[32] Once she made the decision to participate in the program, however, Carter brought a rare degree of enthusiasm and creativity to it. An employee of Schreiber's, Gail Goldstein, who accompanied Carter to the classes, contrasted her approach with that of other teachers: "She loved this program. It's funny, people say, 'Okay, I'll do a music education program,' and . . . then they get there and they're like, 'Okay, what am I going to do?' [whereas] she just did what was really natural for her. She talked to the kids about improvisation and listening and would sing to them . . . sing but talk to them."[33]

Each of the classes started with her trio playing, and then she would sing to the children. She would introduce each member of the trio, which in addition to Bruce Flowers now included Neil Caine on bass and Eric Harland on drums, and have the children listen to the different instruments one at a time, as she explained how musicians produce sound on them.[34] After drawing them deeper into the music, singing, "Listen close to the movement. Do you hear the music?" she told the children to think of questions that they might have for her.[35] Singing the whole time, she then had them line up in front of a microphone. Once there, Goldstein recalled, they were required to sing their questions.[36] Slowly, as the line moved along, more children, and even some teachers, got up and sang their questions as well. Carter didn't always accept what they sang but goaded the young artists-in-training to stretch. *Down Beat* writer David Zaworski, who was present for the first class in Chicago, described how she cajoled the children "to re-sing a question with a different melody or to mimic the way she repeated their questions."[37] Goldstein recalled that it really brought the kids out of themselves, particularly the younger ones, as they asked such questions as "What's your favorite color?" "What's your favorite song?" but also, "Why do you sing jazz?" and "How did you meet your band?" and "What famous people have you met?" Goldstein added, "They were all singing, and she sang back to them. . . . Her approach was great. . . . It was so much about who she was and how she thought about music, very intuitive. . . . It was over way too quickly."[38]

During this time, Carter was reaping a harvest of recognition the likes of which she had not dreamed possible. In June 1997, she had attended the graduation ceremony at Williams College in Massachusetts and received an honorary doctorate of music. Carter had sung at Williams twice before, at the invitation of the school's dean of faculty, David Lionel Smith, and she would give another concert and a workshop there in the fall.[39] The fact that several press releases issued by Bet-Car around this time refer to the singer as Dr. Carter indicates how much this degree meant to her. She would also receive an honorary doctorate from the New School for Social Research in June 1998. On 29 September 1997, Carter was in Washington, D.C., to receive the National Medal of Arts. President Clinton and the First Lady presented the award to a group of eleven recipients that included sculptor Louise Bourgeois, conductor James Levine, percussionist Tito Puente, actors Jason Robards and Angela Lansbury, choreographer Edward Villella, and the MacDowell Colony.[40] The normally brazen singer was clearly awed to be so honored. But there was no time to linger over these honors. Ever on the alert to expand the international market for jazz, Carter performed in Bombay that October and in Shanghai and Beijing for the Beijing Jazz Festival that November. The latter performances were taped by Black Entertainment Television's *BET on Jazz.*

Carter's ritual trip to Europe during the summer months of 1998 was marked by a number of outdoor performances in ancient forums and coliseums. She was the only jazz artist that year to perform in the festival at Spoleto, Italy. Back in the States, at a gig in Philadelphia that August, the band members noticed, according to Bruce Flowers, that Carter was extremely down, a state the singer rarely seemed to experience, let alone reveal to others. Despite their expression of concern, however, she refused to discuss what was bothering her and at show time she gave a sparkling performance. When JoAnne Jimenez called Carter later in the month to invite her to participate in an evening dedicated to singer Lena Horne, which the agent was planning for the fall at the Blue Note, the booking agent's old friend put her off initially, saying she wasn't feeling well. This took Jimenez aback because Carter was notoriously stoic when it came to illness. Jimenez recalled, for example, that Carter never let on to her trio members when she was ill, braving many a night on the bandstand with a hoarse throat rather than take to her bed.[41] Ira Coleman recalled that, while she may have been sympathetic about certain troubles, if the band leader found out that one of her players was ill, she would push the player even harder than usual.[42] In the years she had known her, Jimenez could recall only one instance when Carter had been sick enough to go to a doctor, albeit reluctantly.[43]

In an effort to get a commitment from Carter, Jimenez expressed a worry that Lena Horne's advanced age made the planned tribute somewhat urgent. Carter responded to this remark ominously, saying that she had to think about herself and then, reluctantly, disclosed that she was waiting for a diagnosis from a biopsy. When Jimenez called her back the following day, 17 August, Carter confessed that the doctor had discovered she had pancreatic cancer and had estimated that she had six months left to live.

Pancreatic cancer is known as a silent disease because in most cases it is not discovered until it has already advanced beyond a curable stage. Its onset often occurs several months before symptoms appear, and when they do, they are often so vague as to be ignored or misinterpreted.[44] Given Carter's stoicism, it seems likely that she waited until her symptoms were almost unbearable before seeking medical attention at the beginning of August. By then any treatment she received would be palliative at best.

According to Jimenez, Carter initially resisted telling anyone else, but ultimately she shared the grim news with James Redding, if only so she would not have to break the news to her sons herself. Redding recalled that he had been in touch with his former wife during the preceding months and that they had discussed plans to get together at his home in North Carolina for Thanksgiving.[45] That August, he received a call from her at his job in which she told him that she needed him. Such a summons was unheard of from Carter, and he responded immediately. When he got to New York, she was already in Sloan Kettering Hospital. Having witnessed the force of Carter's indomitable will, both Jimenez and Redding were certain she would somehow beat the odds. But she did not respond well to chemotherapy and decided to stop it. She summoned Redding with Myles and Kagle to her hospital room and said she wanted to go home. James knew her well enough not to argue with her, believing that she was getting ready to die. Her attending physician last saw her on 20 August.

When her sons brought her home, Carter was wheelchair-bound. The sidewalk of St. Felix Street had been torn up during that summer due to construction, and the workers had put up an elevated walkway that ran along the facades of the row of brownstones. Kagle recalled that the ramp made it easier to get her into the house. Carter had lost her appetite by this time, a common side effect of the disease. Redding told her that they were not going to let her starve herself to death, but he believes that "that's pretty much what she did. She shut down."[46] She refused to take her medications, ostensibly because she did not want to prolong the illness.

Initially the family had kept Carter's great friend and agent Ora Harris in the dark, clinging to the hope that Carter would miraculously recover and go on a tour booked for Brazil at the end of September. But soon after the singer came home, Carter asked that arrangements be made for Harris to come to Brooklyn. Harris immediately took an active role in the patient's care, and she also informed the musicians that Carter was fatally ill.[47] Word of Carter's illness spread quickly, if discretely, among her closest friends and her extended family. A handful of people in the music business knew about the situation as well, but she refused to see visitors. When singer Teri Thornton performed on 25 September at the Thelonious Monk International Jazz Vocals Competition—which she went on to win—she dedicated her soul-stirring performance to "her sister," Betty Carter. Early the following morning, with Ora Harris by her side, Carter succumbed to her illness.[48]

Because of the swift progress of her illness and the protective cloud of privacy that hung over her last days, and because she was known as a vivacious individual, the world received the news of Carter's death in stunned disbelief. The character and extent of the reporting suggest the stature Betty Carter had achieved. While her death was generally not considered front-page news, major newspapers across the United States and Europe ran full-page obituaries, many with a photo, and the public outpouring from Carter's fellow musicians was unparalleled. Several press items quoted extensively from musicians who fondly recalled her, recounting some telling detail from their time with her. For a band leader who had a reputation for being such a taskmaster, the open display of love for Carter was striking.

On 3 October a memorial service attended by over a thousand mourners was held for the singer at the chapel of Riverside Church near Harlem. Presided over by Reverend James A. Forbes, who spoke eloquently of Carter's impact on his life, the service included spoken tributes—from radio hosts Pat Prescott and Monifa Carson, Dr. David Lionel Smith, and Myles Redding—and musical tributes by the Reed Sisters and Abbey Lincoln, who sang Lionel Hampton's "Midnight Sun." A jam session followed the formal ceremony, which enabled friends old and new to step up and express their grief and celebrate Carter's life in a manner she would have appreciated. Among the musicians who took part were friends from her own generation, Max Roach, Jon Hendricks, Benny Golson, Jimmy Heath, Barry Harris; former band members, Buster Williams, Jack DeJohnette, Mulgrew Miller, John Hicks, Craig Handy, Lyle Atkinson, Daniel Mixon, Lewis Nash, Don Braden, Benny Green, Cyrus Chestnut, Jacky Terrasson; her last trio, Bruce Flowers, Neal Caine, and Eric Harland; as well as several Jazz Ahead alumni, Peven Everett, Andre Hayward, Mark Shim, and bassist Jennifer Vincent. This send-off seemed nowhere near ending when Reverend Forbes brought the service to a close. As Carter's family recessed down the center aisle, her rendition of "I'm Yours, Your Mine" issued from the sound system while a male dancer dressed in black followed the cortege out of the chapel.

On 12 June 1999, BAM presented a program entitled "Tribute to Betty Carter: The Music Never Stops" at the Majestic Theater. Planned in consultation with Ora Harris, Myles Redding, and Carter's friend Willard Jenkins and funded with support from the Verve Music Group, the concert affirmed the long relationship the Brooklyn Academy of Music had enjoyed with its community-minded neighbor. Many artists celebrated the singer's memory in performances that resonated with the profound impact she had had upon them. Geri Allen and Jack DeJohnette served as musical directors, Don Braden, Marc Cary, Dave Holland, and Curtis Lundy appeared as special guests, and Abbey Lincoln made a cameo appearance, singing "Down Here, Below" and reprising her reading of "Midnight Sun," with her pianist, Marc Cary. Several former Jazz Ahead players appeared, including the vocalists Brandi, Tanya, and Brittany Reed, violinists Miri Ben-Ari and Anand Bennett, saxophonist Casey Benjamin, trumpeter James Gibbs, trombonist Andre Hayward, pianist Brandon McCune, bassists Carlos Henderson and Vashon Johnson, and drummers Karriem Riggins and Nathan Smith. Hosted by Pat Prescott, the event included a performance of George Faison's choreography to "Sounds (Movin' On)" and the Reed Sisters' reworking of "I Can't Help It" in 5/4 and closed with a performance of "Feed the Fire" by Allen, Holland, and DeJohnette, which led into a jam on "B's Blues." The following year, BAM presented a second program entitled "The Music Never Stops," suggesting that the institution has intentions of sustaining its connection to Carter's vision.

Later that summer, Don Braden would lead groups in performances inspired in varying degrees by Carter's influence, at the Charlie Parker Jazz Festival in Tompkins Square Park and at the Museum of Modern Art's Jazz at MOMA series. Braden's CD *The Fire Within,* released on RCA Victor that summer, included Dwayne Burno and Darrell Grant, reinforcing his observation that he is attuned to the Carter alumni phenomenon and tends to surround himself with people who worked with her. This was not simply a matter of nostalgia. Ira Coleman has noted that he can tell right away when he is playing with someone who has worked with Carter: "It's like you speak the same language."[49] There were other forms of remembrance that year. Pianist Eric Reed, who had never been in Carter's trio but had once sat in with her, included a love letter to the late singer on his album *Manhattan Melodies.* The December issue of *Down Beat*[50] and the January 1999 issue of *Jazziz*[51] had cover stories about her, and the Twenty-sixth Annual IAJE Conference was dedicated to her memory. Indicative of her successful if tentative crossover into popular culture was her inclusion in *Entertainment Weekly*'s 1999 yearbook.[52] That August, in conjunction with *Down Beat*'s Forty-seventh Annual Critic's Poll, Carter was inducted into the magazine's Hall of Fame.

Carter's passing brought much speculation about the future of her Jazz Ahead initiative. The idea of proceeding in her absence made her loss that much more painful to contemplate. To imagine the program sailing without its captain at the helm seemed almost unthinkable. Before she died, however, the Kennedy Center had made a commitment to Carter, and on 13 April 1999, after securing permission from the singer's estate, a benefit concert was given at the Kennedy Center's Terrace Theater to raise money to help keep

Jazz Ahead alive. The list of jazz stars who participated included vocalists Jon Hendricks, Kurt Elling, Carmen Lundy, Nnenna Freelon, and Teri Thornton and pianists John Hicks, Jacky Terrasson, Cyrus Chestnut, and Dr. Billy Taylor, as well as Curtis Lundy.[53] If Carter had once wondered "whatever happened to love," she would have been especially warmed by this remarkable display of generosity. The following night, the preceding year's Jazz Ahead selectees—who had spent the week under the tutelage of five of Carter's alumni–were showcased in a Jazz Ahead format. While tickets for the benefit had been priced at seventy-five dollars, those for the showcase were only ten dollars. After the event, Derek Gordon charged the mentors to envision how they would recruit and audition young jazz musicians for the following year.[54] An advisory board was formed to serve as the ears of the Kennedy Center's Education Department, seeking out Jazz Ahead recruits and then adjudicating to select participants.

In April 2000, the Kennedy Center presented the second Betty Carter's Jazz Ahead project to follow her death. Vocalist Carmen Lundy, trumpeter Terence Blanchard, tenor saxophonist Nathan Davis, pianist George Cables, bassist John Patitucci, and drummer Winard Harper served as the mentors for twenty-four young musicians selected from a national applicant pool. As with previous Jazz Ahead programs, this one stressed the development and performance of original compositions. The residency began on 21 April and culminated in two free evening performances at the Millennium Stage on 27 and 28 April 2000, and an afternoon performance for schoolchildren on the second day. In addition, the evening performances were broadcast live over the Internet.[55] A press release about the program, available on the center's website, makes it clear that applicants must be composers as well as performers, and explains that the center covers the cost of housing, meals, and travel to and from Washington, D.C.[56] According to Gordon, the program costs the Kennedy Center between seventy-five thousand and one hundred thousand dollars to run, with much of the funding coming from the United States Department of Education and the Kennedy Center Corporate Fund.[57] The commitment the Kennedy Center has shown to the survival of Jazz Ahead is a tribute to the durability of Carter's vision.

Given that Carter was acknowledged to be the last of a breed of singers, it is not remarkable that her death would bring a new wave of hand-wringing about the loss of jazz singing as an art form. In spite of a surge of interest created by such luminaries as Harry Connick Jr. and Diana Krall, Columbia record's jazz vice president, Jeff Levenson, expressed a pessimism shared by many when he stated flatly, "The pure art of jazz singing is not in great shape. The soundscape is devoid of key personalities who have the power, chops, and charisma to capture people's interest."[58] In addition to the scarcity of these traits, there is another indicator of the precarious state of the jazz vocal craft. Many singers are able to get over simply by parroting a jazz vocabulary that was formed largely in the first half of the twentieth century, without involving themselves deeply in the improvisational processes through which a singer ultimately reveals his or her uniqueness. There are vocalists of a more improvisational bent, such as Kurt Elling and Marguerite Juenemann, to name a few, but they work in relative obscurity with little hope of a mainstream breakthrough in the near future. Even well-established talents such as Mark Murphy, Dee Dee Bridgewater, and Andy Bey lack a large enough following, at least in the States, to lend them the kind of visibility Carter had attained. All of this points up how remarkable Carter's celebrity was, given the challenging character of her music.

Several impediments continue to threaten the jazz vocal tradition's survival, some of them owing to the role of big business in the music industry. To a degree, these apply to instrumental performance as well, although there seems to be a larger pool of promising young players than there is of budding singers. As Carter often pointed out, learning the intricate art of jazz phrasing and improvisation takes a substantial investment of time and energy: unlike pop singers, whose success depends on their producers as much as, or more than it does on their own innate talents, jazz vocalists are not made overnight. For all musicians to development into artists, an environment must exist in which they can support themselves with their art. This cannot happen without the active participation of a knowledgeable audience that can delight in the initial glimmerings of an artist's raw talent, revealed in fledgling efforts. Moreover, given the media's hunger for hyperbole, jazz's subtlety makes it difficult to promote effectively in an industry where quick profit and adherence to the bottom line determine aesthetic choices. Furthermore, because singers have a greater likelihood of crossing over to mainstream celebrity than instrumentalists, they tend to encounter especially strong conflicting pulls in what they do and how they are defined. This may be why singers face a strong temptation to dilute their jazz content in order to straddle the pop and jazz worlds. Any singer who achieves the fame of a Connick or a Krall therefore risks losing the "pure jazz" designation.

Betty Carter resolved this conflict in her own career. In the last decade of her life, she found a way to embrace jazz purity and pop celebrity, partly because she had come of age before the rock era began and had remained true to her roots after jazz's heyday. By internalizing the fundamentals of a largely instrumental genre and transforming its vocabulary and syntax into a truly personal vehicle for her distinctive message, she was able to serve as a spokesperson for jazz. Through song and movement she was also able to make the intricacies of jazz approachable to all listeners. As well known as Betty

Carter's name became toward the end of her life, however, it did not truly became a household name. She never lost the aura of the hip insider, everybody's best-kept secret. Hers was a talent that emerged from the convergence of a distinctive personality and a particular historical moment, both of which will never come again. Let us therefore not speak of "the next Betty Carter." Let us instead hope that her life and work will inspire young singers to learn the jazz process and forge a personal style as deeply rooted in the music's aesthetic as hers was, for the presence of strong leadership in the vocal arena is crucial to jazz's survival in the marketplace. Singers remind listeners that music's power to move us derives from its source in a cry of joy or distress.

Defying categorization, Betty Carter encompassed many qualities and unified them into a singular expressive medium. She was a singer who became known as a musician. She was a consummate performer who explored the subtle transitional areas between improvising, arranging, and composing, between dancing and conducting, between leading a band and teaching, and between acting and storytelling, in order to bring to life her vivid musical conception. She was an artist as well as an entertainer, who communicated with her listeners without speaking down to them. On the bandstand she was a purist who compromised none of her exceedingly high ideals, yet off the bandstand she was an ambitious businesswoman who understood how to use power to achieve her ends. She was an African American woman who exuded a deep pride in her race and its heritage, yet she treasured the European classical tradition and drew upon it for inspiration. The one term that applied to her without qualification, *jazz singer,* is so rich, so complex, so personal, as to confound all efforts to define it.

Because this book has come soon after Betty Carter's death, it cannot comprehend all the ways this woman has contributed to the jazz world and to the American cultural scene. A realistic assessment of her impact will only come at a remove of some years' time. Certainly her recorded legacy, and her legacies as a band leader and jazz educator, will stand as a testament to the clarity of her artistic and social visions. But there are numerous intangible ways that she left her mark, ways that her absence has created a vacuum that can never be filled. As we learn the lessons that her life and work offer us, and help sustain her vision of what is possible, the significance of her impact will become clearer. Promoting a widespread acknowledgment of music's integral place in life will help fulfill Carter's dream, a dream whose trajectory extended beyond her lifetime. The battles she fought, to preserve the dignity of people who work for the love of what they do, regardless of how little their society rewards such efforts, must still be waged. Perhaps as people come to understand how crucial to their spiritual well-being is the simple ritual act of sharing a musical experience with one another, our society will come to appreciate more fully the depth of Carter's contribution. Those who attended her live performances carry within them a profound impression of this unique person and are renewed by the remembrance of her indomitable spirit. Those who attend live jazz performances in the future, who support the music, who learn this complex art, who reach for the levels of artistry that Carter exemplified, will be celebrating her life and music in the most tangible way possible and opening the door for others to share in music's life-affirming message.

Appendix: Reading the Phonetic Notation

Betty Carter's formative experiences as a scat singer led her to treat speech sounds both as words that carry meaning and as vocal raw material, to be manipulated for their sonic value. The mastery of the singer's phonetic tool kit that Carter forged early in her career enabled her to put the unique timbral capabilities of the human vocal mechanism to musical ends. Speaking to Leonard Lyons, she described some of the ways she exercised control over her vocal apparatus: "If you hold a note long enough and you move your lips around and close up your mouth, you eventually cut the sound off. . . . most people, when it's going to be a wild sound, their mouth stays completely open. If you want to ease it out and tail it in you have to do something [different] in order to do that."[1] Carter paid attention to other singers' vocal technique as well, closely observing what they do to modify the sound of their voice.

In order to reflect this essential aspect of her work, I have transcribed Carter's singing phonetically. The transcriptions expose connections between the words she sang and the musical choices she made, connections that standard English spelling cannot reveal. Standard spelling enables us to read for meaning, but it does not capture the sonic aspects of a language as effectively as phonetic notation does. A phone, the shortest unit of speech, may have several standard spellings that distract us from the way it contributes to patterns in sound and vocal production. In contrast, phonetic notation reveals the consistency of spoken language by providing one symbol for each phone.

Standard spelling also creates the false impression that words, the smallest sense units in language, constitute isolated speech gestures. In reality, fluent speakers produce a fairly continuous stream of phones interrupted by occasional breaks in the airflow, breaks that do not necessarily occur at word endings. In the phrase "I tend to be skeptical" (ay/tend/tuw/biy/skeptikəl/) notice that the only real stop occurs during the last word, after /skep/. Phonetic notation enables us to examine vocal expression and technique in great detail by showing how the speech organs' sequence of positions and movements produce speech sounds. I encourage the reader to "perform" each sound described below, to feel the physical changes necessary for their production. For English phones I have adopted the Trager-Smith notation and modified it for my purposes.[2]

Consonants

The phonetic notation of consonants resembles their standard spelling in more cases than the phonetic notation of vowels does. For example, there is a one-to-one correspondence between the standard English spelling and the Trager-Smith phonemes for /p/, /t/, /b/, /d/, /s/, /v/, /m/, /n/, /l/, /r/.

CHART 1. Consonants

	bilabial	labiodental	dental	alveolar	palatal	velar
1.	/p/ **pop** /pap/			/t/ **tight** /tayt/		/k/ **kick** /kik/
2.	/b/ **Bob** /bab/			/d/ **did** /did/		/g/ **gag** /gæg/
3.					/č/ **church** /čurč/	
4.					/j/ **judge** /jəj/	
5.		/f/ **fife** /fayf/	/θ/ **thin** /θin/	/s/ **sass** /sæs/	/š/ **shush** /šəš/	
6.		/v/ **valve** /valv/	/ð/ **this** /ðis/	/z/ **zebra** /ziybrə/	/ž/ measure /mežər/	
7.	/m/ **mum** /məm/			/n/ **nun** /nən/		/ŋ/ **sing** /siŋ/
8.				/l/ **lull** /ləl/	/r/ **rear** /rihr/	

Chart 1 shows the consonants arranged according to their vocal production. Consonants on the left of the chart are produced toward the front of the mouth (at the lips and teeth), while those on the right of the chart are produced toward the back of the mouth (at the hard and soft palate). Chart 1 also indicates the degree of air release or stoppage required to produce each consonant, as well as whether or not the vocal chords are engaged. Phonemes in rows 1, 3, and 5 are aspirated, requiring a puff of air, while those in rows 2, 4, and 6 are unaspirated. Reading down from row 1 to row 6, one therefore encounters alternating pairs of the same sound type, aspirated and unaspirated. The fricatives shown in rows 5 and 6 require the airflow to be constricted in various ways; the nasals and laterals shown in rows 7 and 8 respectively result from diverting the air in other ways. The alternating rows also indicate the absence or presence of definite pitch, with unvoiced consonants shown in rows 1, 3, and 5 and voiced consonants in all others.

With Trager-Smith phonemes only one symbol represents a sound that may have several standard English spellings. The phoneme /k/ is used for the hard "k" sound wherever it occurs, as in *kite* (/kayt/), *cat* (/kæt/), and *quit* (/kwit/). The phoneme /g/ is used only for the hard "g" sound, as in *gag* (/gæg/), while the phoneme /j/ covers both "j" and soft "g," as in *judge* (/jəj/). We use the phoneme /z/ for the initial sounds in both *xylem* (/zayləm/) and *zebra* (/ziybrə/), as well as for the final sound in *goals* (/gowlz/).

Likewise, the phoneme /f/ applies equally to the initial consonants in *fife* (/fayf/) and *phase* (/feyz/) as well as the final consonant in *rough* (/rəf/). In the latter two instances, one could mistake the standard English use of two letters for this sound to imply the presence of a consonantal cluster. For the same reason, in the Trager-Smith system the single phonemes /č/ and /š/ stand, respectively, for the initial and final sounds in the words *church* and *shush* (/čurč/ and /šəš/). Similarly, to illustrate the difference in sound between the initial consonants in the words *thin* and *this* (unvoiced and voiced, respectively) I have used the following symbols: /θ/ (/θin/) and /ð/ (/ðis/). The final sound in the word *sing* appears as /ŋ/ (/siŋ/). For the "z" in *azure* (/eyžər/) and the "s" in *measure* (/mežər/) Trager-Smith uses the symbol /ž/.

Short Vowels

The Trager-Smith phonemes give us a graphic way to represent the difference between short and long vowel sounds.

CHART 2. Short Vowel Sounds

/i/	**i** in p**i**t	/pit/	/ə/	c**u**t	/cət/	/u/	p**u**t	/put/
/e/	p**e**t	/pet	/eh/	p**ai**l	/pehl/	/oh/	c**augh**t	/koht/
/æ/	p**a**t	/pæt/				/a/	p**o**t	/pat/

The arrangement of short vowels in Chart 2 indicates the tongue position required to produce them. Moving from left to right, the tongue moves from front to back, accompanied by some rounding of the lips. Moving from top to bottom the tongue moves from a high to low position.

Several of the phonemes for short vowels are the same as their standard English spelling. For example, the letters *i, e,* and *u* are all used to spell their corresponding short vowel sounds: /i/, /e/, /u/, as in *pit, pet,* and *put* respectively. Standard English provides no other symbol to spell the first two short sounds, but the latter sound may be spelled several ways, as in *would* and *look* (/wud/ and /luk/). The phoneme /a/ is reserved only for the short "o" sound that occurs in the word *par* for example (/par/) as well as in *odd* and *John* (/ad/ and /jan/). The phoneme /o/ occurs in its pure form in some English dialects (*coat* and *home* in New England, for example). But it occurs more frequently in a modified form, indicated in the phonetic notation by the additional symbol /h/ (as in *caught* /koht/).

In standard spelling, the letter *a* serves so many phonetic masters that we need at least four phonemes to account for the many ways it is used. For the "a" in *pat* we use the phoneme /æ/ (/pæt/); for the "a" in *pale,* as well as the "ai" in *pail,* the "ei" in *veil* and the "au" in *laugh* we use the phoneme /eh/ (/pehl/, /pehl/, /vehl/, and /lehf/). For the "a" in *all* as well as the "o" in *song,* the "oa" in *oar,* the "aw" in *law,* and the "au" in *caught* we use the phoneme /oh/ (/ohl/, /sohŋ/, /ohr/, /loh/, and /koht/). The /h/ in these last two phonemes (/eh/ and /oh/) modifies the simple vowels that precede them, but not enough to create a long vowel. For both the "a" and "o" in *above,* the "u" in *up,* and the "ou" in *rough* we use the inverted "e" /ə/ (/əbəv/, /əp/, and /rəf/). Unlike its counterpart in the International Phonetic Alphabet (IPA), the schwa, this symbol may stand for a stressed syllable in the Trager-Smith system.

Semivowels, Long Vowels, and Diphthongs

CHART 3. Semivowels

/y/	**y**ell	/yel/	/h/	**h**ull	/həl/	/w/	**w**ill	/wil/

Often called glides, the semivowel phonemes listed in Chart 3 act as semiconsonants when they occur before vowels, for example, the initial sounds of the words *yell, hull,* and *will* (/yel/, /həl/, and /wil/).

On the other hand, when a /y/ or /w/ glide occurs after a short vowel, the combination produces either a long vowel or a diphthong. Glides therefore offer a graphic indication of increased vowel length. A glide lengthens the preceding vowel by altering its vocal production: to produce the /y/ glide after a short vowel the tongue moves forward and higher and the lips spread (compare "pit" /pit/ to "peat" /piyt/); to produce the /w/ glide after a short vowel, the tongue moves back and higher, and the lips round (compare "full" /ful/ to "fool" /fuwl/). For the /h/ glide the tongue moves toward a central position with little significant spreading or rounding of the lips, producing minimal lengthening of the preceding vowel. To experience the vocal changes that produce each vowel sound, try saying the phrase *two tall trees* (/tuw/tohl/triyz/). From an acoustical standpoint, the different lip and tongue positions of the semivowels serve to darken (/w/) or brighten (/y/) the vocal color by either muting or enhancing the upper partials of the overtone series.

CHART 4. Long Vowel Sounds and Diphthongs

/iy/	b**e**at	/biyt/	/yuw/	disp**u**te*	/dispyuwt/	/uw/	b**oo**t	/buwt/
/ey/	b**a**it	/beyt/	/oy/	bo**y***	/boy/	/ow/	b**o**at	/bowt/
/ay/	b**i**te	/bayt/				/æw/	b**ou**t	/bæwt/

Chart 4 shows the long vowels that occur in the English language. Those on the left show the effect of the /y/ phoneme when it occurs after the short vowels /i/, /e/, and /a/. Those on the right show the effect of the /w/ phoneme when it occurs after the short vowels /u/, /o/, and /æ/. Notice the spreading of the lips necessary for each of the former and the rounding of the lips necessary for each of the latter. The phonemes in the center, marked with asterisks, are considered diphthongs (/yuw/ and /oy/).

Musical Examples

Jay Bird

fast swing ♩= 224-232
Ab
Bb-7
Eb7
Ab
Bb-7
Eb7
Ab
B°7
Bb-7
Eb7
Ab
Ab
Bb-7
Eb7
Ab
F7
Bb-7
Eb7
Ab
Ab/C
Db
Eb7
Ab
G-11
C7

F7
F-11
Bb7
Eb7
Ab
Bb-7
Eb7
Ab
Bb-7
Eb7
Ab
Ab/C
Db
Eb
Ab
Carter: scat solo
mf
Ab
uw ə duw də uw . diy uw diŋ guw di
Bb-7
Eb7
Ab
ŋ guw yuw di duw di uw di di dliy ə dow də diy duw duw

36
B♭-7 A♭ A♭/C
. du du du diy ə du duw də buw dat uw
38
D♭ E♭7 A♭
3 3
*NB
yuw dn duw dn dwiy dow də biy dn dwiy ow biy dn dwiy a a, əm
41
A♭ B♭-7 E♭7 A♭ F7
ba diy diy uw, uw iy ə wiy a uw . biy ow, m diy duw biy
44
B♭-7 E♭7 A♭ A♭/C
3
biy ow də di dl yə da dn duw dn duw bap
46
D♭ E♭7 A♭
3
a yuw diy di dl iy duw diy dwey dap um diy
49
C7 F7
3
diy diy da duw duw diy da . də dl i diy ə n d diy ə n d

52
3
B♭7
di dli ya um də biy bə bə buw diy diy biy duw
E♭7
55
A♭
3
3
biy a duw duw duw diy . ə da yə duw dow duw . dow duw biy ow duw

B♭-7
E♭7
A♭
B♭-7
58
3
3
duw dn dwiy i ə duw iy a duw . dn duw duw . dn bliy i, uw diy

A♭
A♭/C
D♭
E♭
A♭
61
3
di dli yə duw diy uw ba bə dil ya duw da duw da də n d n d n d n d

A♭
64
3
mf
di dli ya n d bliy a da da da

*NB bars 39+40
3
3
3
3
biy dn dwiy ow . biy dn dwiy a a, əm

I Could Write a Book

1955

D7(♭9) G△ E- A- D7
- t ænd ðə si mpu - lsiy - kri tə ðə
— and the sim— ple — sec— — ret of the
G△ E- A- D7 G△ C♯-7(♭5) F♯7
pla - t i - zjə s tuw te lðəm - m ðæ
plot — is — just to tell them — — that
B-7 E7 A- A-/G D7/F♯ D7 D△/C
even
swing
tay lə - vyuw - ə - la - - - t ænd
I love — you — a — lot — — — and
G△/B E♭7/B♭ A-7 D7 D-7/G G7/B
ðə wur - ldi skə və - - rz hwen may - bu ke
the world — dis— co— vers — — when my — book ends
C△7 A-7(♭5) G/D E-/B A-7 D7
- - ndz hæw tuw mey ktuw l ə və
— — how to make two lo— — vers
G△ G△ E-
piano solo
- rz ə vfre - - ndz
— of friends — —

Thou Swell

(scat solo)

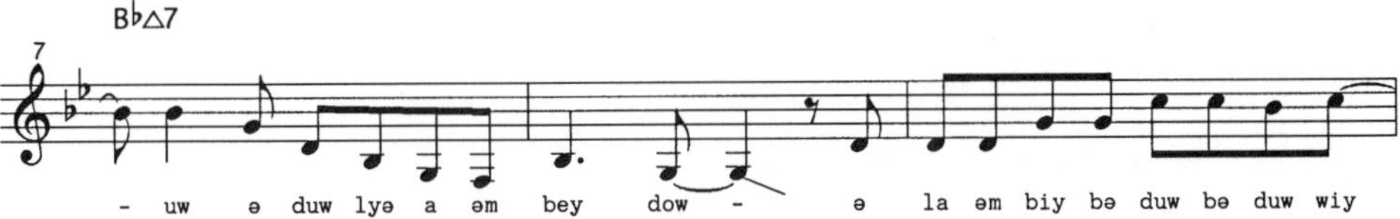

You're Driving Me Crazy

(scat solo)

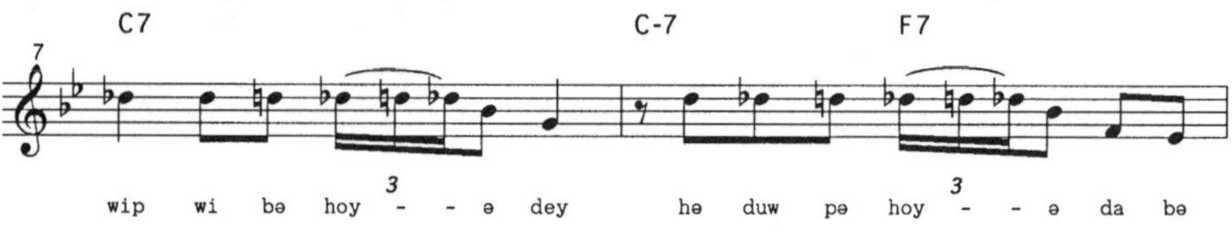

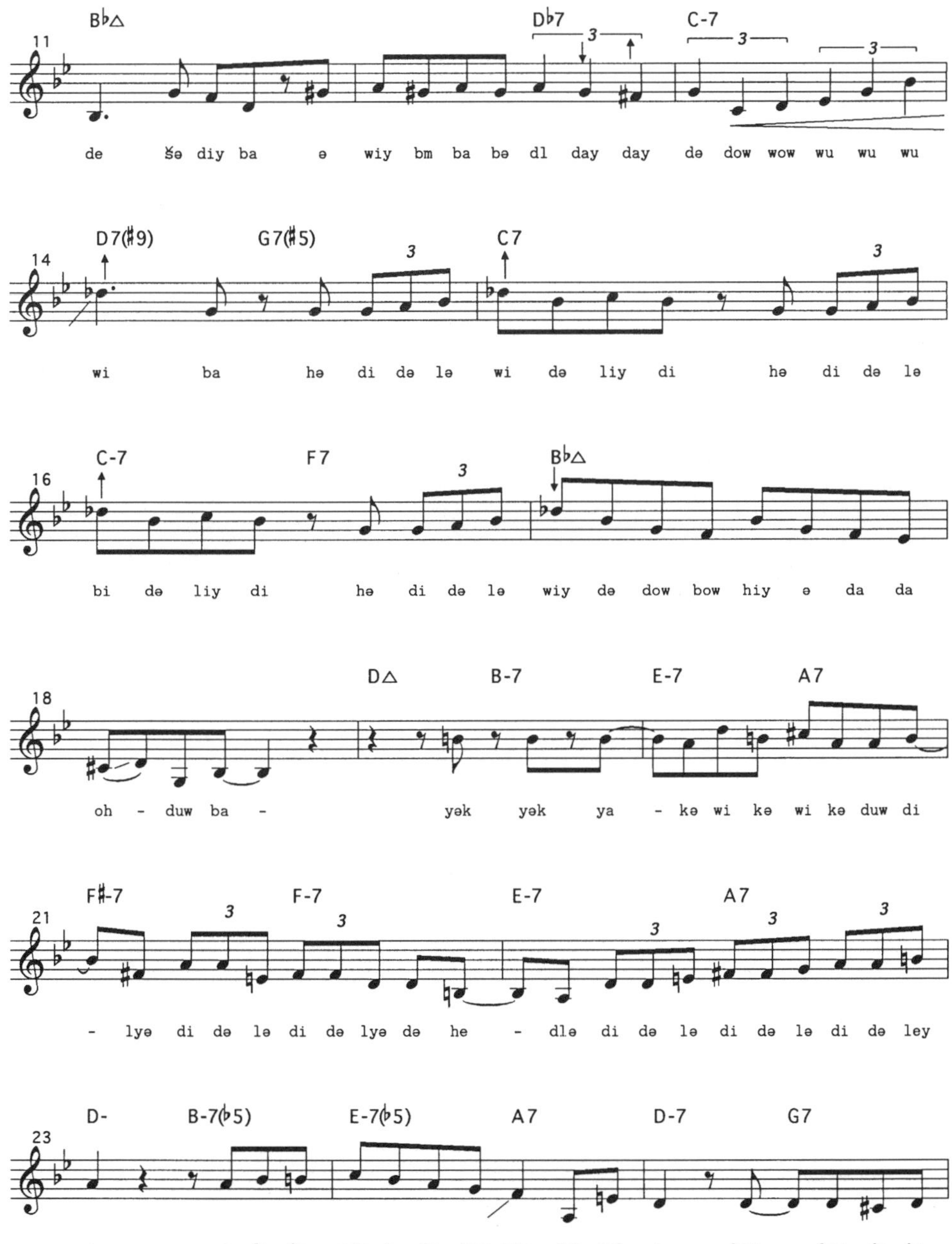
B♭△ D♭7 C-7
de šə diy ba ə wiy bm ba bə dl day day də dow wow wu wu wu
D7(♯9) G7(♯5) C7
wi ba hə di də lə wi də liy di hə di də lə
C-7 F7 B♭△
bi də liy di hə di də lə wiy də dow bow hiy ə da da
D△ B-7 E-7 A7
oh - duw ba - yək yək ya - kə wi kə wi kə duw di
F♯-7 F-7 E-7 A7
- lyə di də lə di də lyə də he - dlə di də lə di də lə di də ley
D- B-7(♭5) E-7(♭5) A7 D-7 G7
a ə la bə wiy bə duw buw wiy doh yeh a hey - lyə də ba

C-7
F7
B♭△
C-7
B♭/D
D♭°7
26
3
f
da duw - iy buw wiy ba a - də lə bi də li ba ba

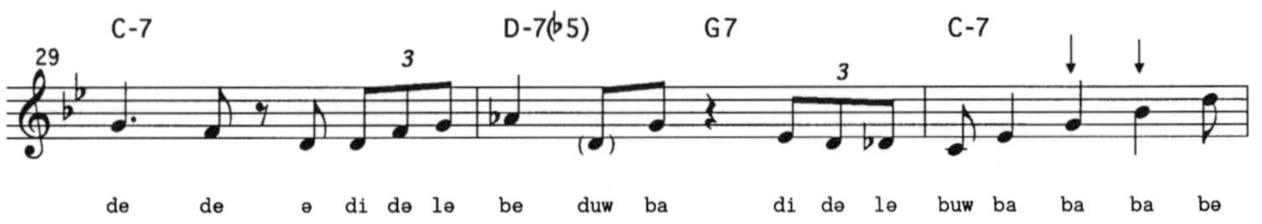
C-7
D-7(♭5)
G7
C-7
29
3
3
de de ə di də lə be duw ba di də lə buw ba ba ba bə

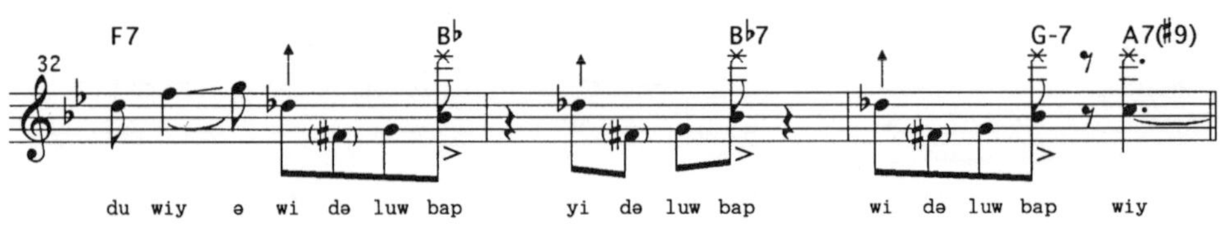
F7
B♭
B♭7
G-7
A7(♯9)
32
du wiy ə wi də luw bap yi də luw bap wi də luw bap wiy

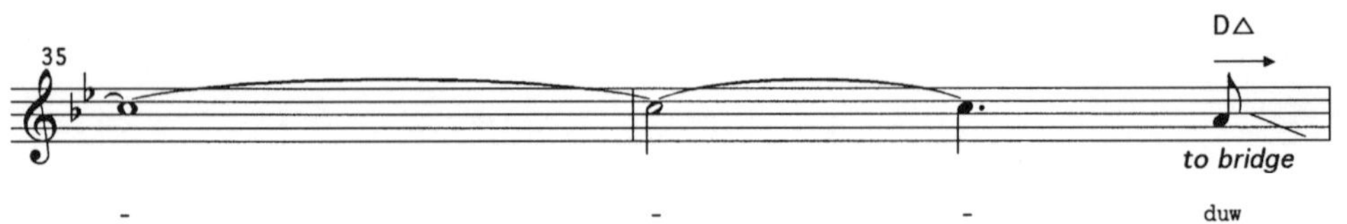
D△
35
to bridge
- - - duw

I Can't Help It

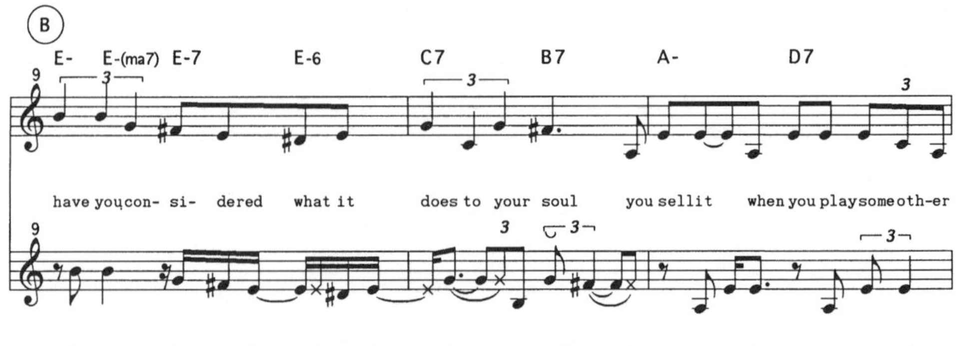
B
E- E-(ma7) E-7 E-6 C7 B7 A- D7
have youcon- si- dered what it does to your soul you sellit when you playsome oth-er
hæ- vyuw kən- si-dər- - d wə-di- t də - z tuwyohrsow- l yuwse-lit wen yuw pley

G7(13) A7♭9 C D7 G7♭9 C△7 A-7
role be your- self dear in what you chooseto be.ɪ'llnot
səm ə - - ðer z row- - l biy - yoh- self dih - in wə- t yuw- - čuwz tuwbiy

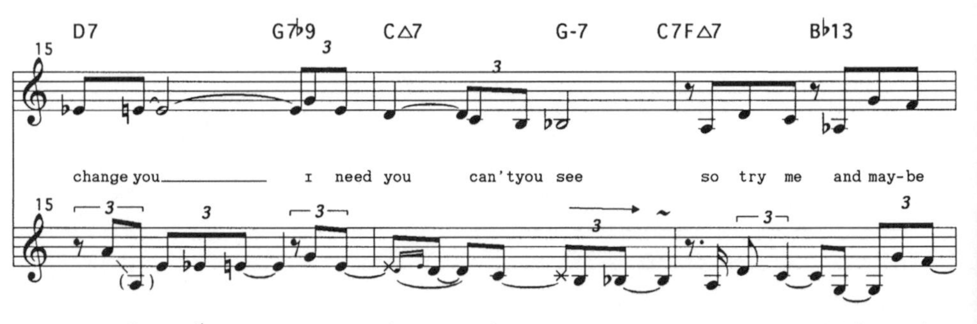
D7 G7♭9 C△7 G-7 C7F△7 B♭13
change you ɪ need you can'tyou see so try me and may-be
ay-l nat čeyn-ǰyuw- ay niy- dyuw - - kæn- t yuw siy - sowtraymiy - ænd - meybiy

C△7 B♭7 A7 D7 G7 C△7 E-11 E♭°7
you'll loveme cause I can't helpit that's the way that I am.
even
swing
- ye- -l- e v miy- - kezay - kænt hel - pi - t ðæ tsðe wey - ðæ tay- æm- -
D7 G7♭9 C△7 A-7 D7 G7♭9
help it that's the way that am. I can't help it I don't
tenor sax fill
reverb on
tenor sax fill
- ðæ- ts ðe wey - ðæ- t ay æm - - - ay down-
C△7 G-7 C7 F△7 F♯°7 C△7 A-7
know how to sham. I try to do the things I feel in side and be
reverb off
t now hæw tuw šæm - - ay - tray tuw duw ðe θiŋ- z ay fiy lin say- -

D7 G7♭9 C△ B E- E-(ma7) E-7 E-6
27
lieve me it's a real de- light. have you con- si- dered what it
27
d æn biy liy vmiy ðæts sə riyl diy lay - --t hæ- v yuw - kən si dər- d wət
C7 B7 A- D7 G7(13) A7♭9
30
does to your soul you sell it when you play some oth- er role be your-
30
it də- z tuw yohr sow - yuw seli- t wen yuw pley - sə mə ðərz row- - l biyyohr
C D7 G7♭9 C△7 A-7 D7 G7♭9
33
self dear in what you choose to be. ɪ'll not change you ɪ need
33
even
sel- f di - - - in wətyuw- - čuwztuwbiy ay- l na t čeyn-ǰ yuw - ay niy

C△7 G-7 C7 F△7 B♭13 C△7 B♭7 A7
36
you can't you see so try me and may be you'll love me cause ɪ can't
36
swing
even freely
d yuw- - kæn- t yuw siy - sow tray miy - æn- mey biy - yəl ləv miy kə zay kænt
D7 G7 C△7 D-7 E-7 F7(♯11)
39
help it that's the way that ɪ am.
39
hel pi- --t ðæts ðə - wey - ðæ tay æm-

What a Little Moonlight Can Do

up tempo swing ♩= 288

8

B♭

mf

uw uw
oo, oo,

10

uw - wət ə li- dəl muw- nlayt kæn
oo what a lit-tle moon - light can

F7

13

duw - - - -
do

F9

17

3 3

uw - - - - wət ə li- dəl muw- nlayt kæn
oo... what a lit-tle moon - light can

B♭ B♭7

21

duw tuw - - yuw -
do to you

E♭ E♭-6

25

yoh- rin lə- v yə ha- tsə flə- - - də- ri-
your in love your heart's a flutt - er - ing

B♭ G7
29
nohl - - dey - - lohŋ yuw ow- nliy - stə də - biy
all day long you on - ly stutt - er be -
C7
33
koz- zyoh/ə tə---ŋ jə- swil na ə- tə ðə
cause your tongue just will not utt - er the
C-7/F F°7 F7(♯5)
37
wur---d ay lə- vyuw - - - -
words I love you
B♭
41
- - - wət ə li- dəl muw- - - nlay- t kæn
(you) what a lit-tle moon - light can
F7
45
duw - - - - - - - - -
do
F7 (A-7(♭5)) D7
49
wey- də way- ---l ti- - lə li- dəl muwn- biym kəmz
wait a while till a lit-tle moon beam comes

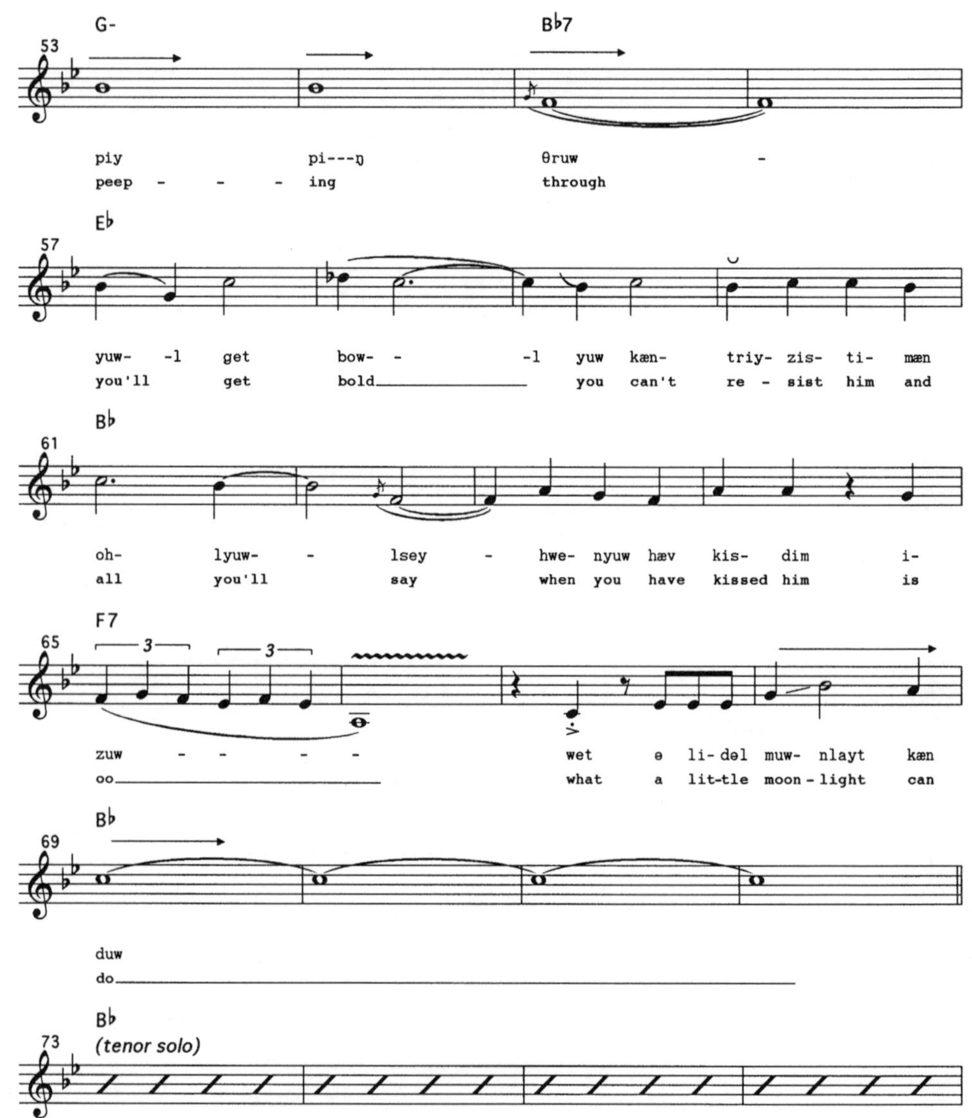
G-
B♭7
53
piy pi---ŋ θruw -
peep - - - ing through
E♭
57
yuw- -l get bow- - -l yuw kæn- triy- zis- ti- mæn
you'll get bold you can't re - sist him and
B♭
61
oh- lyuw- - lsey - hwe- nyuw hæv kis- dim i-
all you'll say when you have kissed him is
F7
65
3
3
zuw - - - - wet ə li- dəl muw- nlayt kæn
oo what a lit-tle moon-light can
B♭
69
duw
do
B♭
73
(tenor solo)

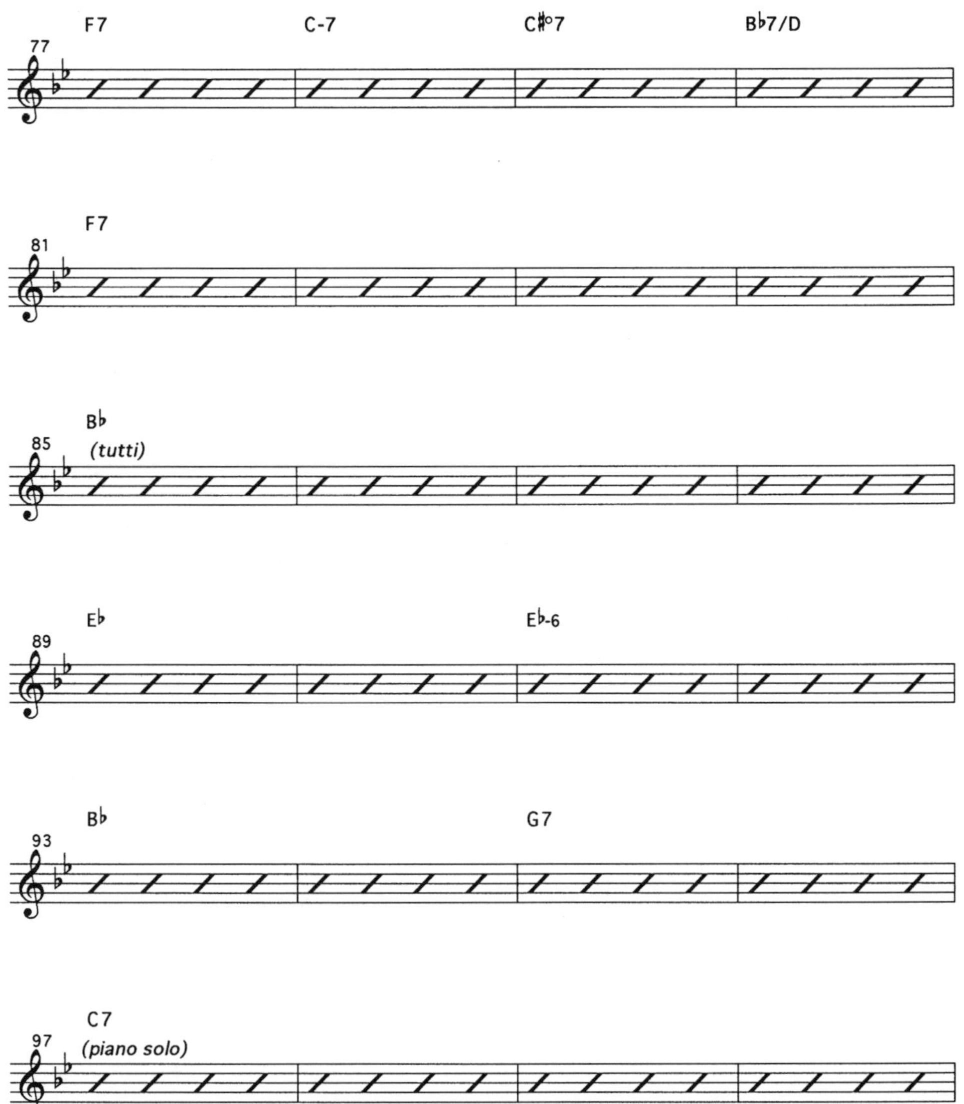
F7
C-7
C♯°7
B♭7/D
77
F7
81
B♭
85
(tutti)
E♭
E♭-6
89
B♭
G7
93
C7
97
(piano solo)

F7
101 (tutti)
uw
oo
B♭
105
3
- - - - - - - wet ə li- dəl muw- - - nlay - - t kæn
oo what a lit-tle moon - light can
F7
109
duw - - - - - - - - - -
do
F7
113
(A-7(♭5)) D7
wey də way- - - - l ti- - lə li- dəl muwn- biym kəmz
wait a while til a lit-tle moon beam comes
G-
117
B♭7
piy pi- - - ŋ θruw - -
peep - - - ing through
E♭
121
E♭-6
yuw- -l get bow- - -l yuw kæn- triy- zis- ti- mæn
you'll get bold you can't re - sist him and

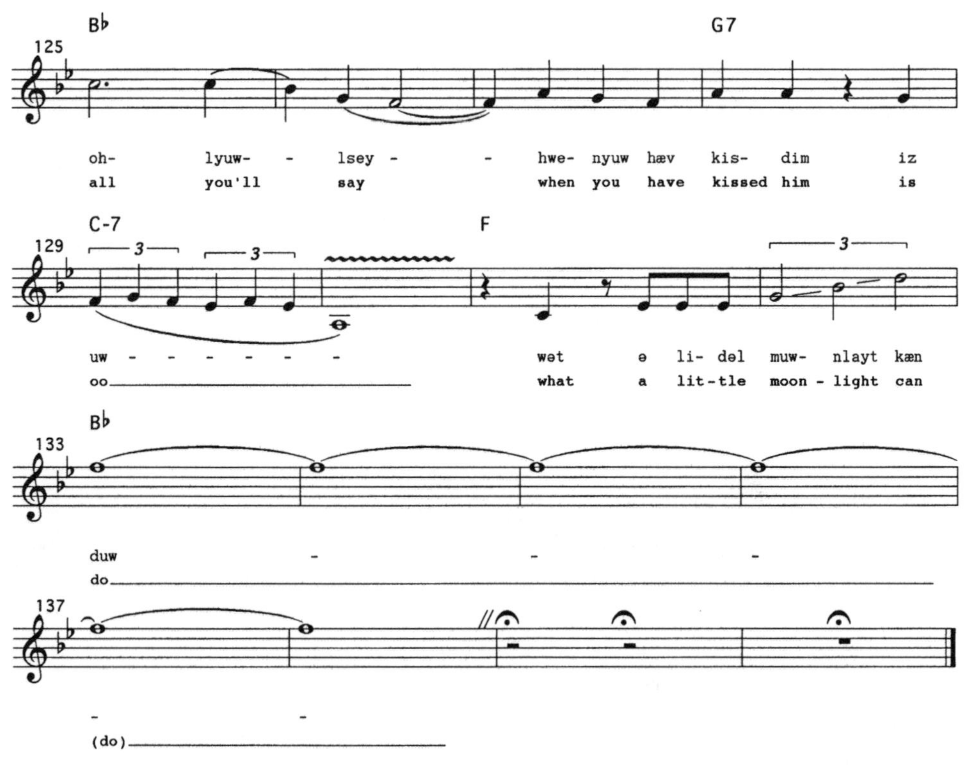
B♭ G7
125
oh- lyuw- - lsey - - hwe- nyuw hæv kis- dim iz
all you'll say when you have kissed him is
C-7 F
129
3 3 3
uw - - - - - - - wət ə li- dəl muw- nlayt kæn
oo what a lit-tle moon-light can
B♭
133
duw - - -
do
137
- -
(do)

The Good Life

ballad ♩= 56

freely *in tempo*

D♭△7 D♭△

ow ðə gu- dlay- - - - f fu- ləv fə- n siymz tuw biy - ðiy

Oh the good life full of fun seems to be the

3 C-7(♭5) F13 C-7(♭5) F7 B♭-

- ay diy - - --l ye- s ðə gu- lay- --f lets

i - deal yes the good life lets

6 B♭- G-9 C7 G-9 C7

yuw hay- - dohl - ðə sæd nes yuw - - fiy- - l yuw

you hide all the sad - ness you feel you

9 G♭△7 C♭13 D♭△7 E♭-7

wownt- riy liy - foh- lin lə- - v fohr yuw kænt tey- - k ðæ - čeh-

won't real - ly fall in love for you can't take the chance

12 D♭/A♭ C-7(♭5) B♭- B♭-(maj7) B♭-7 B♭-6

- ns sow - biy a ne- - st wi- θ yoh se- - lf down tray

so be hon - est with your self don't try

15 E♭-7/A♭ A♭7 E♭-7 A♭ D♭△7

tuw fey- k row - meh- - ns i- tsðə - gu- dlay - - f tuw biy

to fake ro - mance It's the good life to be

18
D♭△7
C-11(♭5)
F7♭9
friy - æn ek splohr - ðiy ən - - now- - - n lay
free and ex-plore the un - known like
21
B♭-
B♭-(maj7)
B♭-7
B♭-6
even
G-9
C7
k ðə har- tey- - ks hwe- nyuw lur- n yuw məs feys ðe mə low- - -
the heart aches when you learn you must face them a - lone
24
G-7
C7
G♭△7
C♭7
n pliy- - zriy mem bər - - ay s- til - wan- tyuw
please re - mem - ber I still want you
27
D♭△7
F-7(♭5)
B♭7
E♭-7
even
æn- din key- s yuw wə- - də - hway - - wel - jə- s wey- kə- - p ki-
and in case you won - der why well just wake up kiss
30
C7♭9
D♭
F-7(♭5)
B♭7
swing
s ðə gu- dlay- - f gud- bay - - wel jə
the good life good - bye well just
33
E♭-7
even
C7♭9
poco rit.
swing
D♭△
s wey- kə- - p ki- - - -s ðə gu- dlay- - f gud bay - - -
wake up kiss the good life good bye

Open the Door

1964

Bb7
Eb△
28
--z ke- --m ow - pin ðə dohr -
come o pen the door
Eb△
F-7
31
- - dih -
dear
ænd ðe-
and then
F-7
34
--n pə hæ- psyuwl fay- - n yuw- --v hæ--d
per haps you'll find you've had
Ab7
Bb△6
37
miy a- - --n yohr - may- - n
me on your mind
Bb△6
Eb△
40
now - mæ- - - tər -
no mat ter
Bb-7
B
Gb△6
43
hæw yuw tray - tuw - - - ə voy-
how you try to a void

G♭△6
46
--d miy - - yuw kæn- t ge- də wey
me you can't get a way
E♭△6
49
E♭7
sow iy- z liy - -
sow eas' ly
E♭-7
52
G♭△6
- i- - --f yuw - -
if you
G♭△6
55
E♭△6
- wi- --l nat kəm tuw miy a- - - --l kə- -
will not come to me I'll come
E♭△6
58
B♭7(♯5)
--m tuw - yuw -
to you
C
E♭△
61
3
ow - pin ðə dohr - - - pliy- -
o pen the door please

E♭△ F-7
64
3
- z hway - mey- kmiy be- - --g ænd -
why make me beg and
F-7 A♭7
67
3
be- g hway - - tohr čər miy layk ði-
beg why tor ture me like this?
A♭7 B♭△6
70
- - s - kæ- --n- tyuw
can't you
A♭-6 G-
73
- siy - - - - ay- --v
see? I've
G♭7 F- E△6
76
gat lə- - - v plen tiy lə- - --v tuw gi-
got love plen ty love to give
E♭ A♭-6
79
v tuw yuw - ayv gat lə-
to you I've got love

82
Ab-6
G-
Gb7
- - - - - --v l- a- tse - v
lot's of
85
F-
E△6
Eb
le- - --v tuw gi- - v tuw yuw- -
love to give to you
88
Ab-6
- ay- v ga- - tle- -
I've got love
91
G-
Gb7
F-
- - --v
94
E△6
Eb△
vamp and fade

I Could Write a Book

1969

A- D7 G A-7 D7♭9
♩= 84 accel. ♩= 336 ♩= 84
ə- --v may pla- t iz jus tuw -
of my plot is just to
G6 E- G♯o A-7
♩= 168
tel ðem ðæ- tay lə- vyuw - - ə- - la-
tell them that I love you a lot
F♯-7(♭5) B7 E- E-(maj7) A-7 D7
rit. freely ♩= 168
t hæ- --nd ðə wur- --l di- - skə vez hæw -
and the world dis co vers how
D-7 G7 C△ F7 B-7 B♭7
rit. ♩= 84 ♩= 116
may - buk en- --dz ow - hæw - tuw - meyk tuw
my book ends oh, how to make two
A-7 D7
♩= 84 ♩= 264-276
lə- - - - vər- --z əv fre- -- --ndz
lov ers of friends
G6 E- A- A♭7 G E7♭9
if ðey æsd miy ay ku- dray- tə bu- - k
if they asked me I could write a book

A-7 D7 G E-7 G♯°7
36
ə bæwt æə wey yuw - woh- k æn wi- spə
a bout the way you walk and whis per
A-9 A-/G F♯-7(♭5) B7 E- E-(maj7)
39
3
- æ- --nd lu- - k ay ku- dray- -
and look I could write
A-7 D7 C♯-7(♭5) F♯7♭9 B- B♭o
42
də pre fi- s an hæw wiy me- --t ænd ðə wur-
a pre face on how we met and the world
B°7 E7 E- A7 A-
45
- --l wud ne- - və - foh
would ne ver for
D13(♭9) G E- A- D7
48
3 3
ge- t sim pə- --l sim pəl siy kri- tə-
get sim ple sim ple sec ret of
G E-7 A-7 D7♭9 G6
51
--v may pla- - t i- --z jus tuw te- - --l ðe- --m
my plot is just to tell them

E- G♯o A-7 A-7/G F♯-7(♭5) B7
54
ðæ- tay lə- - vyuw - ə - la- t hænd ðə
that I love you a lot and the
E- E-(maj7) A-7 D7 D-7 G7
57
wur- - --l di- skə- vurz æz may - - bu-
world dis cov ers as my book
C△ F7 B-7 B♭7 A-7 D7
60
3
kenz hæw - tuw mey - k tuw - lə - və- zəv
ends how to make two lov vers of
B-7 E7(♯9) A-9
63
frenz hæw - tuw mey - - k
friends how to make
D7 D♭-7(♭5) C- B- B♭-
66
accel.
𝅗𝅥 = 126 (tag)
tuw lə - vur- zəv fre- -
two lov ers of friends
A- A♭△ G△
69
- - - - - - --nz

I Can't Help It

1976

C△ A7 D7 sharp
19
3 3
ŋz ay fiy- lin say- - d biy liy - - - - --v miy
I feel in side be lieve me
G7 sharp C C
22
i- ts ə riy- --l diy lay - - - -
it's a real de light
B
E- E- C7
25
hæ- v yuw kən si - dər- d hwet it də- z tuw yohr
have you con sid ered what it does to your
B7 A-7 D7
28
3
sow- - - - l yə s- e- li- t hwen yuw pley sə- mə- - - ðə- z
soul you sell it when you play some o ther's
D-7 sharp G7 C D7
31
row- - - --l sow biy yə se- --lf dih-
role so be your self dear
G7 C△ A7 even
34
- z in wə- tyuw čuwz tuw biy down let ðem
in what you choose to be don't let them

D7 G7 G-7
37
swing
čeyn- jyuw - ðey niy- dyuw
change you they need you
C7 F△ F♯°7
40
3
kæn- - - ǯə siy - sow tray it ən may
can't you see so try it and may
C/E A7 D7
43
3
- biy yuw- lay- kit ke- za- - - kænt- hel
be you'll like it 'cause I can't help
G△ C C△ E-7(♭5) A7
46
- pit ðæ- ts ðə wey
it that's the way
D
D7 G7 C△
49
ðæ- day - æ- - -
that I am
C△ D7 G7
52
--m a- - - - eh - - - - -
I

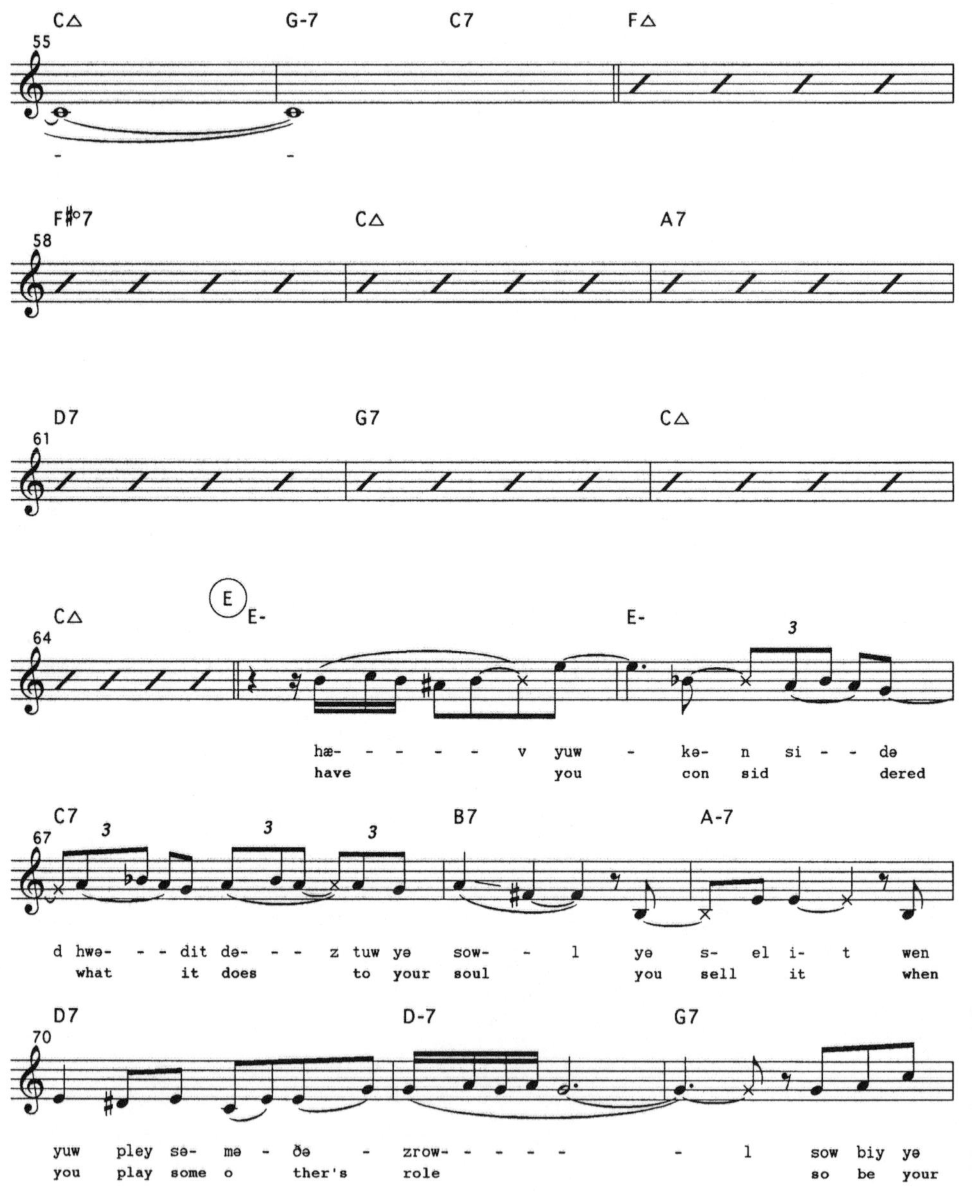
C△ G-7 C7 F△
55
F♯°7 C△ A7
58
D7 G7 C△
61
C△ E E- E-
64
3
hæ- - - - - - v yuw - kə- n si - - də
have you con sid dered
C7 B7 A-7
67
3 3 3
d hwə- - - dit də- - - z tuw yə sow- - l yə s- el i- t wen
what it does to your soul you sell it when
D7 D-7 G7
70
yuw pley sə- mə - ðə - zrow- - - - - - l sow biy yə
you play some o ther's role so be your

F
D7 G7 C△
73
sel- f dih- əz in hwət yuw čuw- z tə
self dear in what you choose to
A7 D7 G7
76
biy down let ðem čey- nj yuw - - - - - -
be don't let them change you
G-7 C7 F△
79
3 3
ðey niy- dyuw - - kæ- n- čə siy - sow tray - i-
they need you can't you see so try it
F♯o7 C/E A7
82
3
- t ən mey - biy - yuw- lay- kit kə za - -
and may be you'll like it 'cause I
D7 G7 C△
85
3
kæn- te- l pi- - t ðæ- ts ðə wey - - ðæ- tay
can't help it that's the way that I
E-7(♭5) A7 G D7 G7
88
tag
æ- m ay kæ he- --l- pi- - - t
am I can't help it

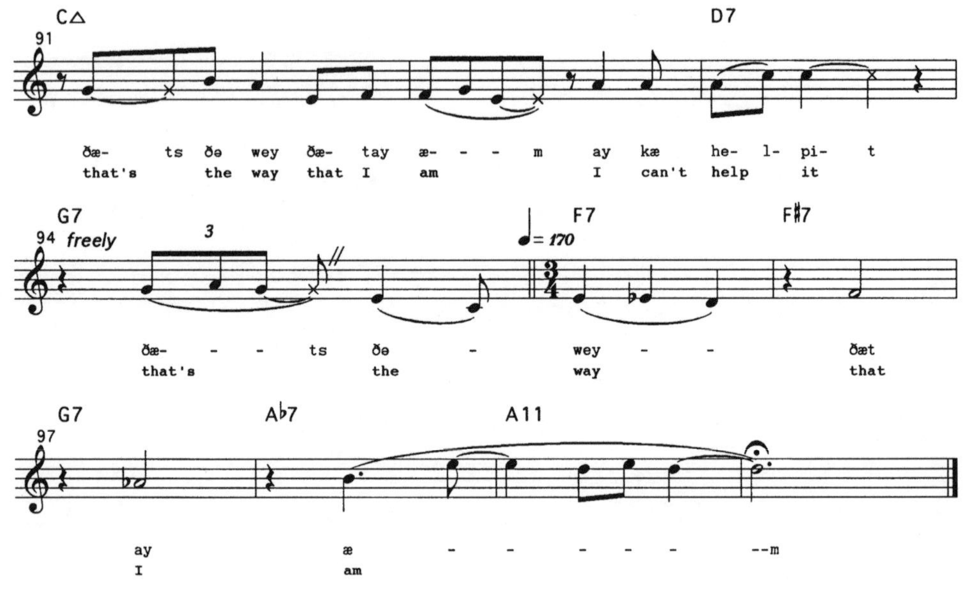
C△
91
ðæ- ts ðə wey ðæ- tay æ- - - m ay kæ he- l- pi- t
that's the way that I am I can't help it
D7
G7
94 freely
3
♩= 170
F7
F♯7
ðæ- - - ts ðə - wey - - ðæt
that's the way that
G7
97
A♭7
A11
ay æ - - - - - --m
I am

Open the Door

1976

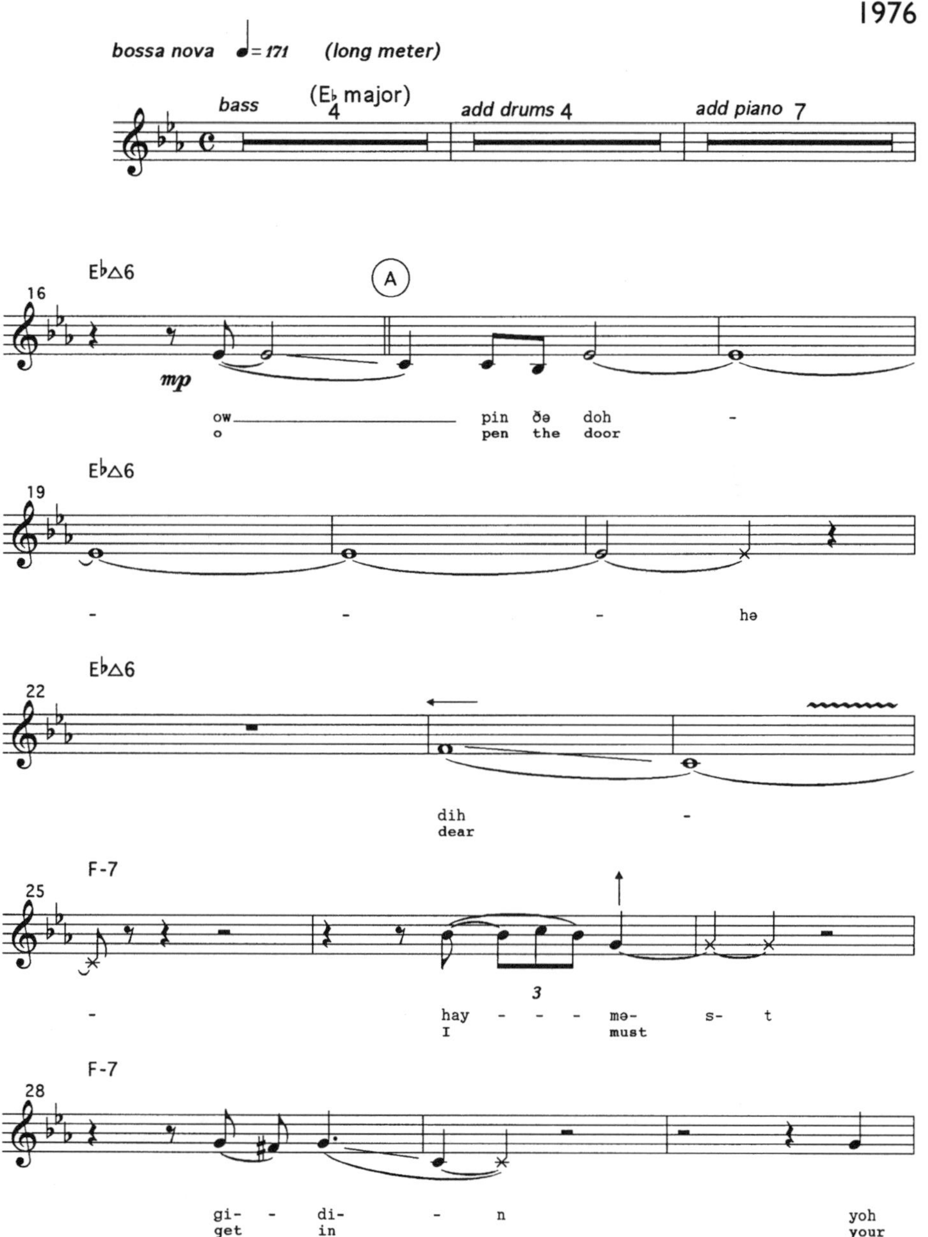

F-7
A♭7
31
3
ha- - - - - - t yoh- - - - -r mey- - ki- - - ŋ
heart you're mak ing
A♭7
34
3
it sow - - ha- - - - - - - d
it so hard
B♭6
37
B♭6
E♭△7
40
3
tuw - biy truw - - - -
to be true
E♭△7
B♭7
43
B♭7
46
3
sow pliy- - - - - - - - z ke- - - -
so please come

E♭△6
49
- m- - ow- - - pi-
o pen
E♭△6
52
--n ðə - doh - -
the door
E♭△6
F-7
55
--e may - - dih -
my dear
F-7
58
hæ- n- ðe- n pə - - - hæ-
and then per haps
3
F-7
61
p- s yuw - wi- --l fay- -
you will find
F-7
A♭7
64
nd ðæ- dyuw- wə mey - - - miy - - - a- n yoh - -
that you (have) me on your

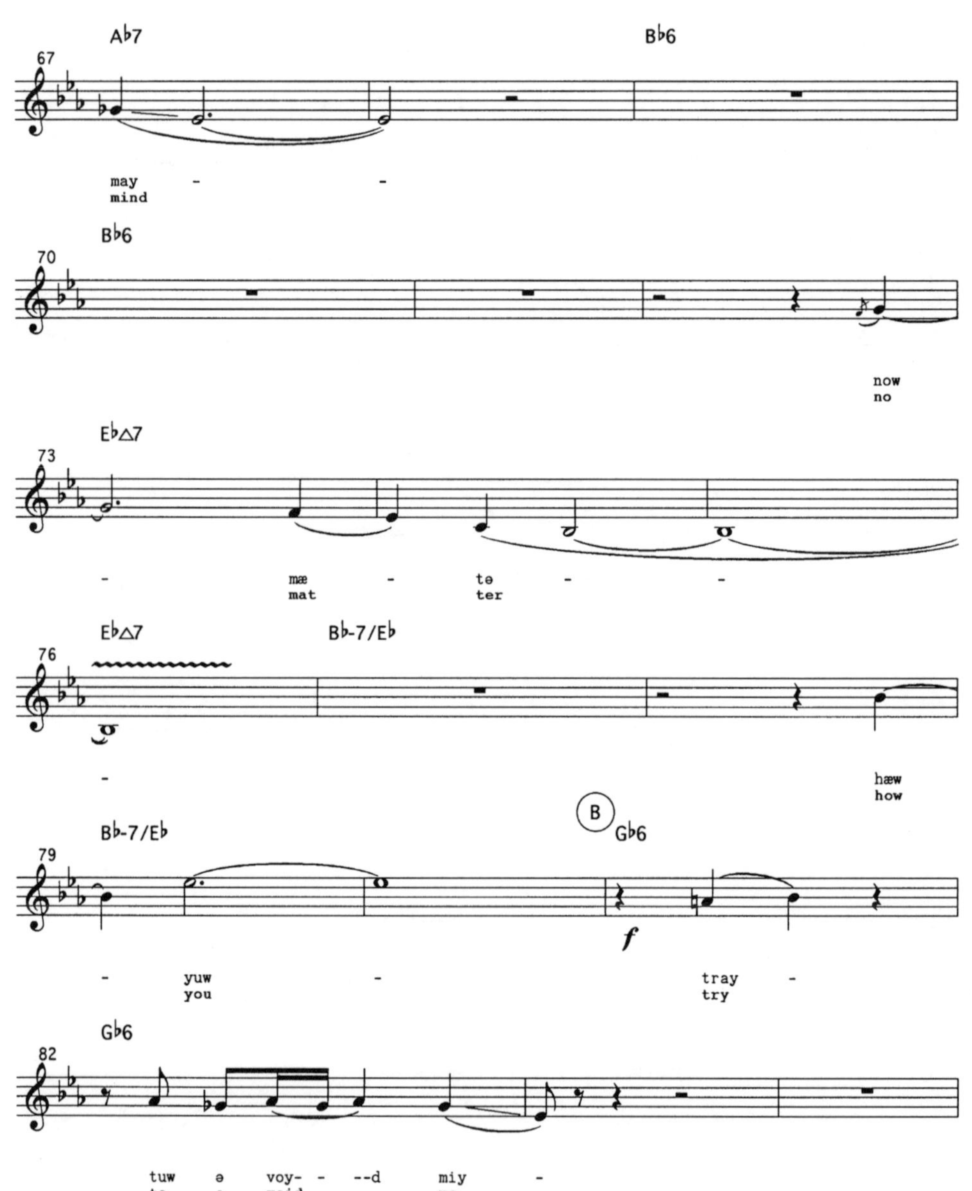
Ab7
Bb6
67
may - -
mind
Bb6
70
now
no
Eb△7
73
- mæ - tə - -
mat ter
Eb△7
Bb-7/Eb
76
-
hæw
how
B
Bb-7/Eb
Gb6
79
f
- yuw - tray -
you try
Gb6
82
tuw ə voy- - --d miy -
to a void me

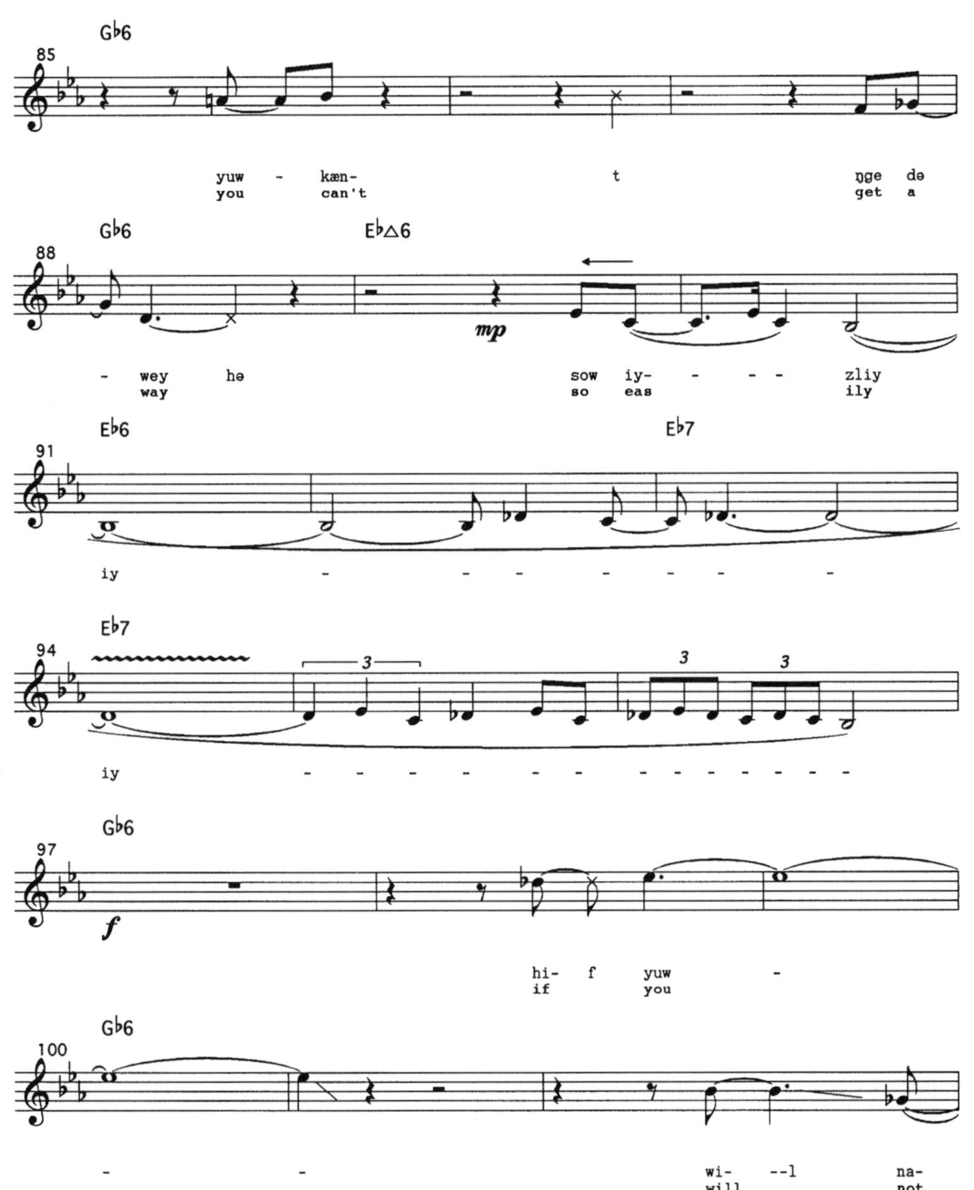
G♭6
85
yuw - kæn- t ŋge də
you can't get a
G♭6
E♭△6
88
mp
- wey hə sow iy- - - - zliy
way so eas ily
E♭6
E♭7
91
iy - - - - - - - -
E♭7
94
3
3
3
iy - - - - - - - - - - - - - - -
G♭6
97
f
hi- f yuw -
if you
G♭6
100
- - wi- --l na-
will not

Gb6
103
Eb△6
mp
- - t
kə- - m tə miy - - -
come to me
hay-
I'll
Eb△6
106
- el -
kə - - - m
come
Bb
109
3
tuw - - - yuw -
to you
C
Eb△6
112
ow -
o
Eb△6
115
pin ðə doh- hə
pen the door
Eb△6
118
pliy- - - - z
please

F-7
121
hway meyk miy be gən be gən be - gen be
why make me beg and beg and beg and beg
F-7
124
gən be gən be- g mbe- - -
and beg and beg beg
F-7
127
Ab7
g be- - - g way - - toh- r- cər miy
beg why tor ture me
Ab7
130
-
Bb6
133
3
3
hlay- --k ði- - - - - - - s
like this
136
Ab-6
(rubato)
kæ- n- tyuw - - - - siy - -
can't you see

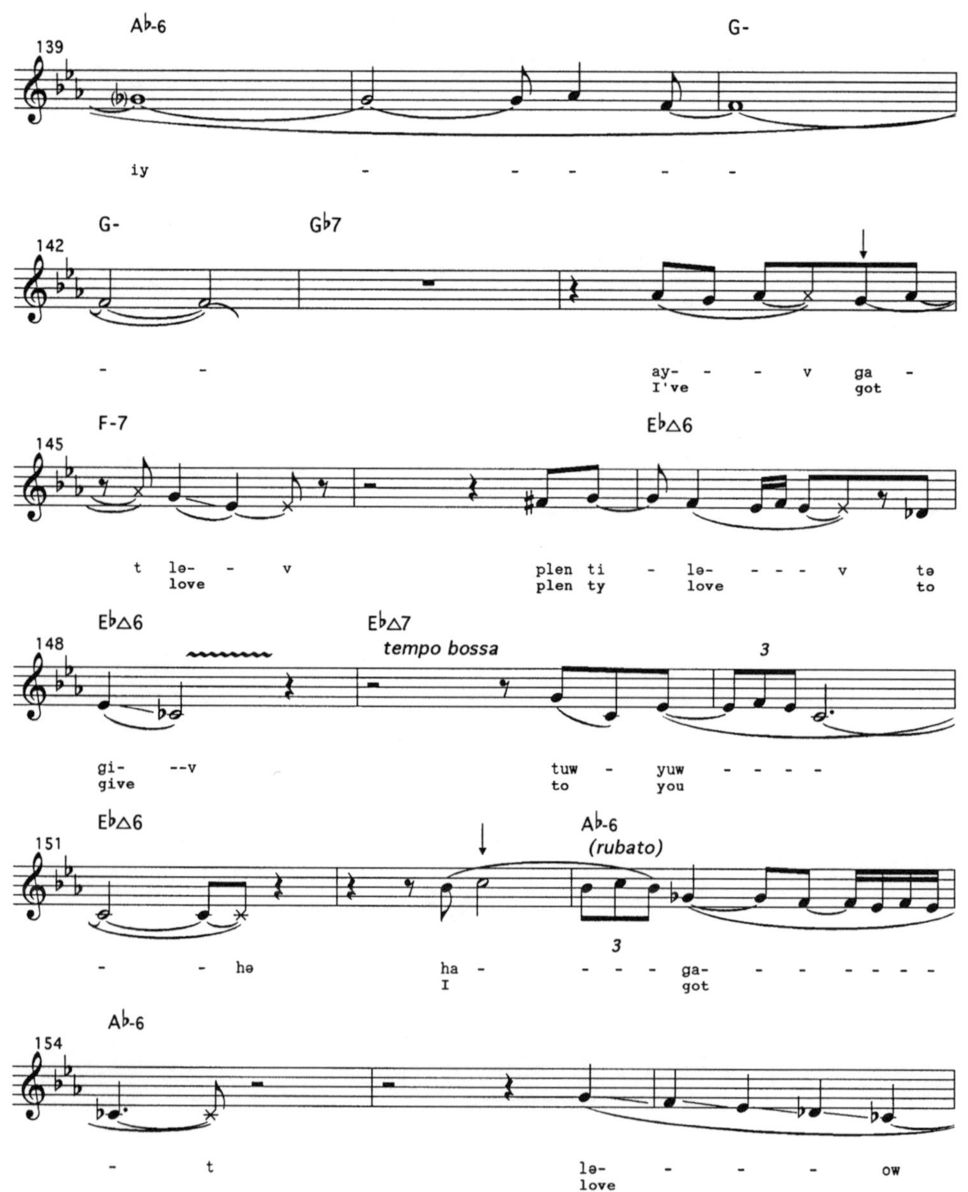
Ab-6
G-
139
iy - - - - - -
G-
Gb7
142
- -
ay- - - v ga -
I've got
F-7
Eb△6
145
t le- - v
love
plen ti - le- - - - v te
plen ty love to
Eb△6
Eb△7
tempo bossa
148
3
gi- --v
give
tuw - yuw - - - -
to you
Eb△6
Ab-6
(rubato)
151
3
- - he
ha - - - - - ga- - - - - - -
I got
Ab-6
154
- t
le- - - - ow
love

G-
Gb7
157
160
Gb7
F-
3
he - ow la- t- s e- - v le- - - - --v
o, lots of love
163
Eb△6
Eb△7
tempo bossa
tuw - gi- - --v tuw -
to give to
166
Eb△7
he
ay-
I've
169
Ab-6
(rubato)
--v ga - - -
got
172
Ab-6
G-
- - t le- - - -
love

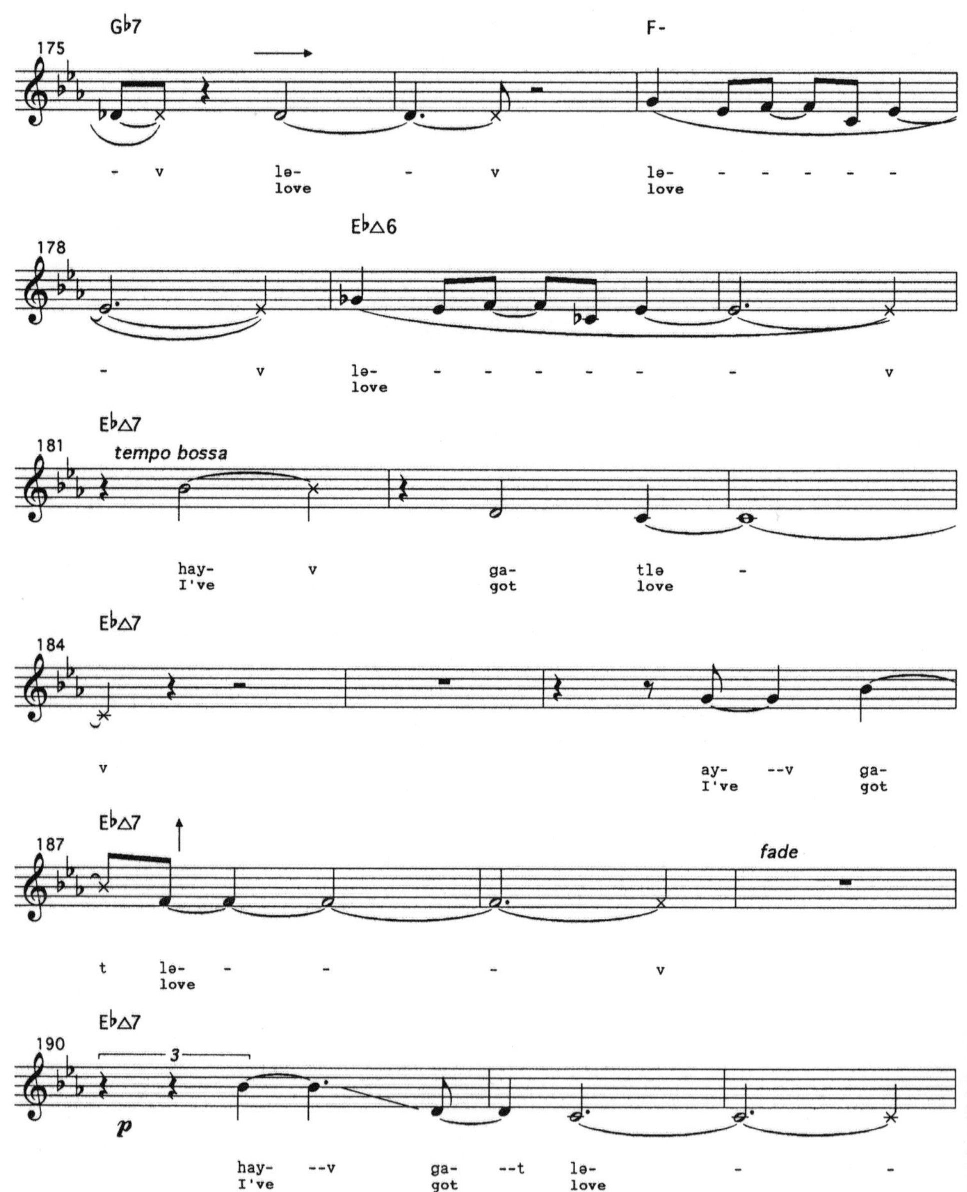

175
G♭7
F-
- v le- - v le- - - - - - -
love love
178
E♭△6
- v le- - - - - - - v
love
181
E♭△7
tempo bossa
hay- v ga- tle -
I've got love
184
E♭△7
v ay- --v ga-
I've got
187
E♭△7
fade
t le- - - - v
love
190
E♭△7
3
p
hay- --v ga- --t le- - -
I've got love

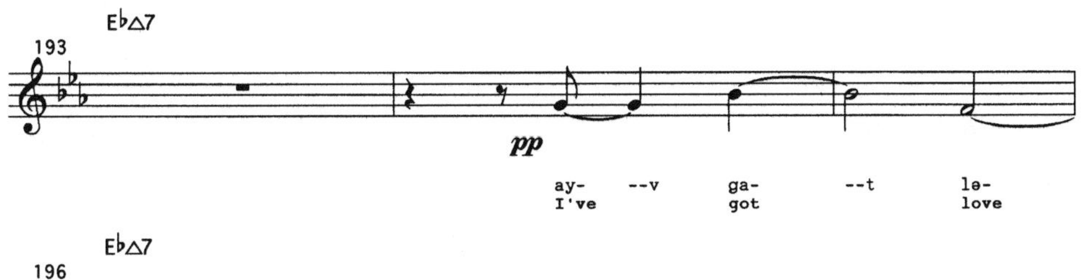
Eb△7
193
pp
ay- --v ga- --t lə-
I've got love

Eb△7
196
--v

Open the Door

1979

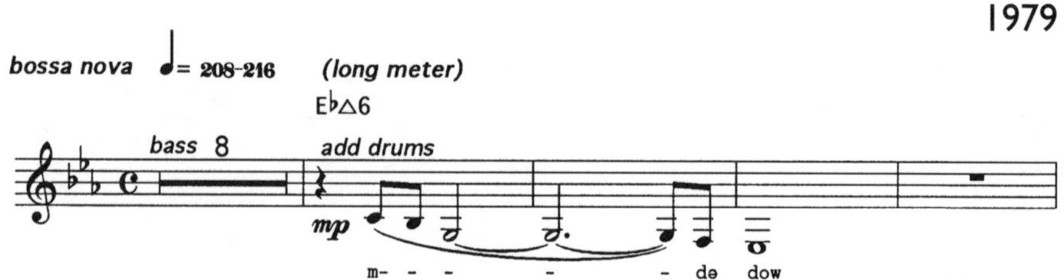

E♭△6
29
dey -
ow - pe-
o pen
mf
A
E♭△6
33
- n
ðə - doh- --r
the door
E♭△6
37
f
ma - - dih -
my dear
F-7
41
mp
hə
mf
ə
I
F-7
45
mə- s ge- di- n yə ha- - t
must get in your heart
A♭7
49
mp
yoh - mey
you're mak

B♭6
53
kiŋ it ha- - - - d
ing it hard
E♭△
57
yə m- ey- kiŋ it ha-
you're mak ing it hard
B♭
E7
61
d tuw biy truw - sə pliy-
to be true so please
E♭△6
65
- z ow - pe- -
o pen
E♭△6
69
n ðə - - doh - hə
the door
F-7
73
ma dih - hə æn ðe-
my dear and then

F-7
77
--n pə hæ- psyəl fayn
per haps you'll find
ə ðæ- tyuw hæ-
that you have
A♭7
81
- v hæ- - d miy - a- - n yoh
had me on your
B♭6
85
- may- - - nə
mind
E♭
89
now mæ tə hə
no mat ter
B♭-7
93
now - mæ- də - - how - yuw
no mat ter how you
B
G♭△6
97
- - - - t- ray - duw ə voy-
try to a void

G♭△6
101
dmiy
hyuw kæn- t
me
you can't
E♭
105
mp
3
ge- de wey -
sow iy- z- liy -
get a way
so eas ily
B♭-/E♭
B♭-(maj7)/E♭
B♭-7/E♭
E♭7
109
sow iy- - - z- liy - -
so eas ily
G♭△6
113
f
hi- fyuw -
if you
G♭△6
117
- -
wi- l n- a- t kə-
will not come
E♭△7
121
mp
m
tuw miy
to me

B♭
E9(♯11)
125
al ke- - m tuw yuw -
I'll come to you
C
E♭△6
129
- - - - - ow - pe-
o pen
E♭△6
133
- n ðə doh- - - r pliy-
the door please
F-7
137
- z- s- -
F-7
141
3
way meyk miy be- gən - be- gən be- - gən
why make me beg and beg and beg and
A♭7
145
be- gən - be- - gən be- - g
beg and beg and beg

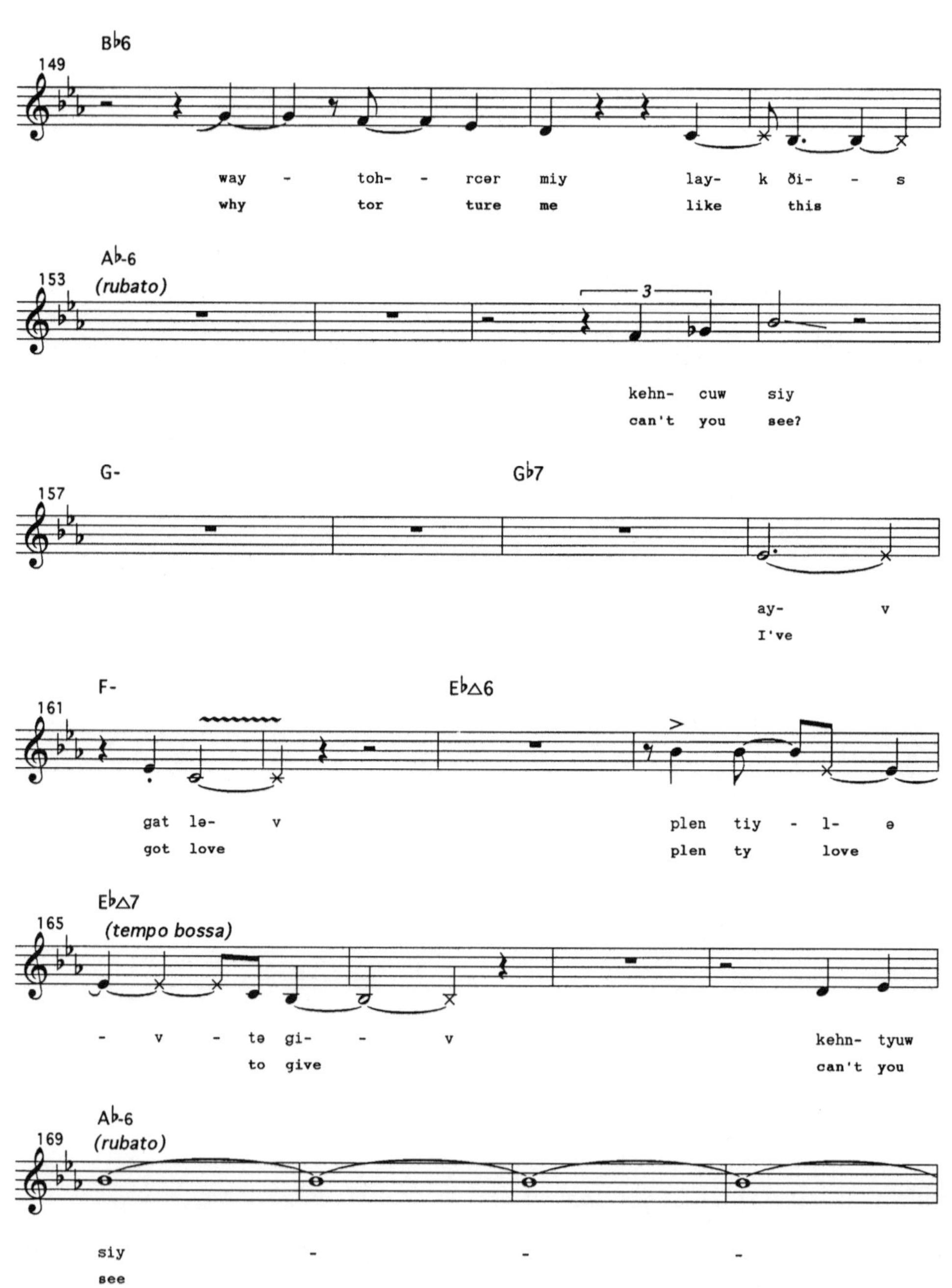
B♭6
149
way - toh- - rcer miy lay- k ði- - s
why tor ture me like this
A♭-6
153
(rubato)
3
kehn- cuw siy
can't you see?
G-
G♭7
157
ay- v
I've
F-
E♭△6
161
gat le- v plen tiy - l- e
got love plen ty love
E♭△7
165
(tempo bossa)
- v - te gi- - v kehn- tyuw
to give can't you
A♭-6
169
(rubato)
siy - - -
see

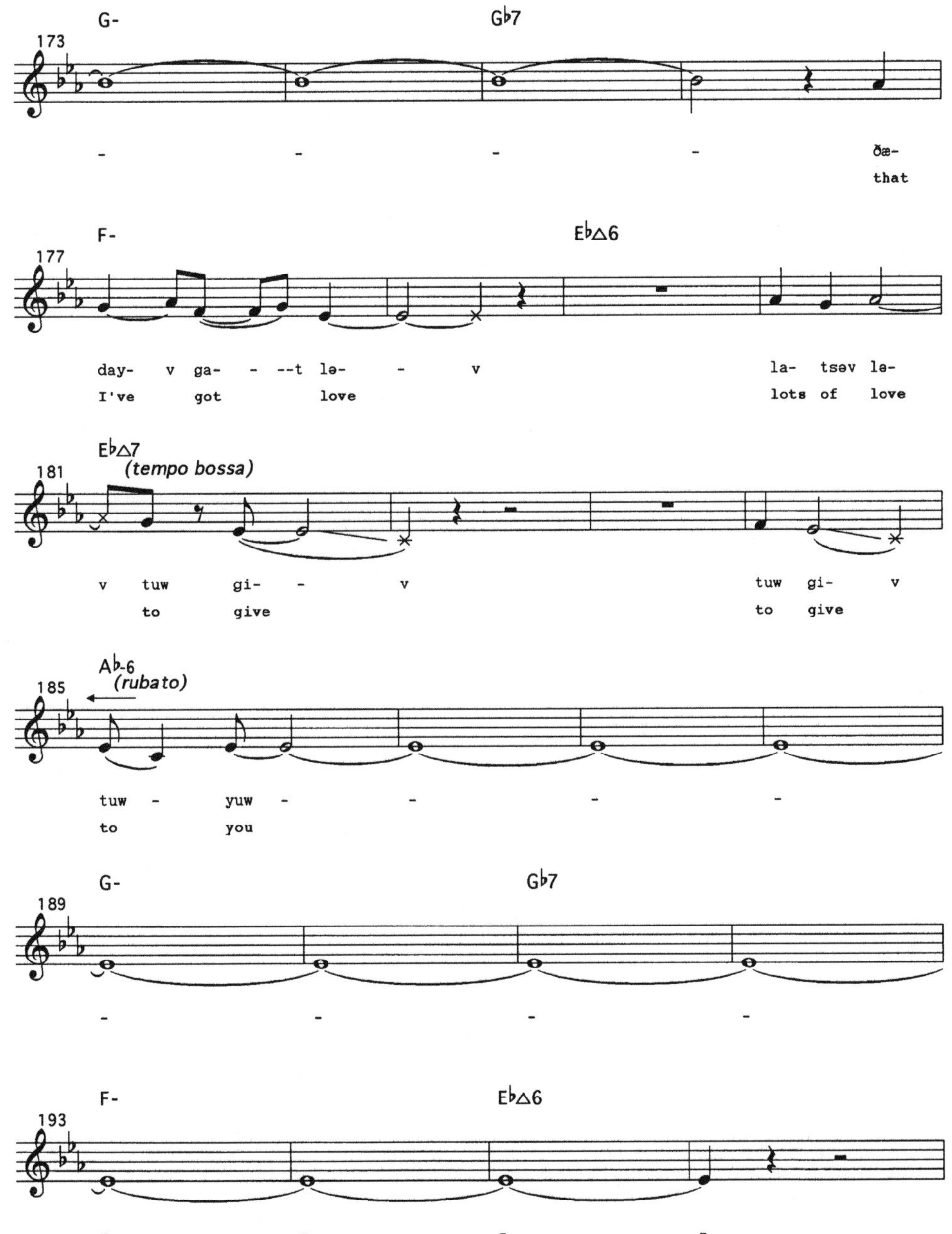
173
G-
G♭7
- - - - ðæ-
that
177
F-
E♭△6
day- v ga- - --t le- - v la- tsev le-
I've got love lots of love
181
E♭△7
(tempo bossa)
v tuw gi- - v tuw gi- v
to give to give
185
A♭-6
(rubato)
tuw - yuw - - - -
to you
189
G-
G♭7
- - - -
193
F-
E♭△6
- - - -

E♭△7
197 (tempo bossa)
ləv tuw giv tuw yuw - - - - - -
love to give to you
E♭△7
201
(rim)
hay - ga- t lə- v
I've got love
E♭△7
205
tə gi- v tə yuw - hə
to give to you
E♭△7
209
ay- v ga- t le- - - v tuw gi- - v
I've got love to give
E♭△7
213
tuw - yuw - hay-
to you I've
E♭△7
217
- v gat le- - v
got love

E♭△7
221
tə gi- - v
to give
E♭△7
225
diminuendo
tə gi- - v
to give
tuw
to
E♭△7
229
yuw - - -
you
E♭△7
233
- - - - - -
E♭△7
237
p
- - - -
E♭△7
241

I Could Write a Book

19
G△ E-7 A-7 D7 G△
3
low dow dow dow - le de
22
E- G♯°7 A-7 A-7/G F♯-7(♭5) B7
dow dey bow də bay ow bow ba ye
25
E- E-(maj7) A-7 D7 D-7 G7
doh dət day doh diŋ e kur dis lən diy yow
Cur-tis Lun-dy
28
C△ F7 B- B♭7 A-7 D7
la lə low la liyŋ
31
B- E7 A-7 D7 G△ E-
ley u dey u ley kə ba də
34
A-7 D7 G E- A-7 D7
dæ də da də dow də down ba

G△ E-7 G♯°7 A-7 A-7/G
37
liy nuw diy nuw diy liy nuw diy nuw duw duw duw duw - dey
F♯-7(♭5) B7 E- E-(maj7) A-7 D7
40
dey---m bow dey---m bow dey m bey
C♯-7(♭5) F♯7♭9 B- B♭7 B-7(♭5) E7
43
be dow be be be be be dow be be be bep be be be be bow bey be bow be bey
E-7 A7 A-7 D7
46
be be duw le low leyŋ le la low lay lay ley liy le luw le ley - le low lay lay le low
G△ E- A-7 D7 G△ E-
49
le ley ley ley le ley dey dow le dow bow bow bow dow le bey bey
A-7 D7 G△ E- G♯°7
52
- bey bey jan hi - ks
John - Hicks

A-7 A-7/G F♯-7(♭5) B7 E- E-(maj7)
55
mf
ba pla de
A-7 D7 D-7 G7 C△ F7
58
la low la dla dla dow daw - ə
B- B♭7 A-7 D7 B- E-
61
lə dlow - lə dow dow m bl yə dey
A-7 D7 G△ E- A-7 D7
64
mbu lyə dey i- --f ðey æ - s miy
If they ask me
G△ E- A-7 D7 G△
67
- a ku- dray də buk
I could write a book
E- G♯°7 A-7 A-7/G F♯-7(♭5) B7
70
ə bæwt ðə wey yuw woh- --k hæn- dwi- spə rænd lu- k
a - bout the way you walk and whis - per and look

E- E-(maj7) A-7 D7 C♯-7(♭5) F♯7(♭9)
73
ay - - ku- dra- - də pre fis an hæw -
I could write a pre - face on how
B- B♭7 B-7(♭5) E7 E-7 A7
76
- wiy - me - - - t ðen ðə wurld wud ne - - və
we met and the world would ne - ver
A- D7 G△ E-
79
fohr ge- t
for - get
A-7 D7 G△ E- A-7 D7
82
ðə sim pə- --l siy kri- təv may pla- - - t
the sim - ple se - cret of my plot
G- E-7 G♯°7 A-7 A-7/G
85
even
i- z jə- --s tuw te- --l ðe- --m ðæ- tay
is just to tell them that I
F♯-7(♭5) B7 E- E-(maj7) A-7 D7
88
even
swing
lə- - vyuw ə la- - - - - - - t
love you a lot

D-7 G7 C△ F7 B- B♭7
91
3
n ðə wur- - --l di- skə - və- z æ- z ma - - bu- - k
and the world dis - co - vers as may book
A-7 D7 B-7 E7
94
e- - n z hæ də mey- kit
ends (how to make it)
A-7 B-7 C△ D7 D♭-7(♭5) C-
97
hæw tuw mey - k tuwlə vur- -
how to make twdo-vers
B- B♭- A- A♭△ G△7
100
- - z əv fre- -
of friends
G△7
103
- --nz

What a Little Moonlight Can Do

1982

C9
25
s tə də
stut-ter
kə- zye təŋ -
'cause your tongue
C-7/F
7
F7
C-7/F
F7
29
jə- swil nat /e tə də we - dz
ay lə- vyuw -
just will not ut-ter the words
I love you
B♭△7
E♭7
3
D-7
G7(♯9)
33
uw - -
uw - - -
wə- də li-
oo
oo
what a lit -
C-9
C-7
F7
D♭7
37
- dəl muw- --n lay t
kæn duw - - -
tle moon light
can do
C-9
F7
A-7(♭5)
even
D7
41
wey- - də way - --l
ti- lə li- dəl muwn biy- -
wait a whi-le
til a lit-tle moon beam
G-9(11)
G♭7
F-7
swing
3
B♭7
45
m
kəm piy pin θruw - - - -
comes peep - ing through

E♭△7
A♭7
49
yə git bow - l- d yə kæn-
you get bold you can't
B♭△7
E♭7
D-7
G7
53
triy zis- ti m noh- - l yuwl sey - wen yə
re - sist him in all you'll say when you
C-9
C-7/F
F7
57
pp
mp
ki- st hi- - m i- zuw - -
kissed him is, oo
A♭7(alt)
61
mf
freely
wə- də li- dəl muwn layt kæn duw - uw - - uw - - - - -
what a lit-tle moon light can do oo oo
A
A♭7
G7
65
moderate swing ♩= 200-208
f
bə duw biy duw biy duw biyŋ lə də bə də bə ə
C-7
F7
69
mf
wət ðæt muwn kæn duw tuw yuw -
what that moon can do to you

C-7
F7
73
uw- -
oo
we- - də li- dəl muwn layt
what a lit-tle moon-light
F7
F-7/B♭
B♭7
77
kæn duw tuw yuw
can do to you
E♭△7
A♭7
81
yə- rin ləv
you're in love
yə ha- - tsə flə də rin- -
your hearts a flut-ter-ing
B♭△7
E♭7
D-7
G7
85
ohl- - dey - lohŋ -
all day long
yuw oh nliy stə də
you on-ly stut-ter
C7
89
bə koh- zyə təŋ
be-cause your tongue
jə- swil nat ə- tə -
just will not ut-ter
C-7/F
F7
C-7/F
F7
93
ðə wu- - dz
the words
ay lə- vyuw
I love you

A♭7
G7
97
f
ba bə duw bə biy biŋ bæw - duw biy yuw biy diyŋ
C-9
F7
101
mf
wət ðæt muwn kæn duw tuw yuw -
what that moon can do to you
C-9
F7
A-7(♭5)
D7
105
3
3
wey- də wa- --l ti- lə li- dəl muwn
wait a while 'til a lit-tle moon
G-9
G-9
G♭7
F-7
B♭7
109
biy- m kəm piy pin θruw - -
beam come peep - ing through
E♭△7
E♭-6
113
yə get bowld yə kæ- --nt riy zis- ti- m
you get bold you can't re - sist him
B♭△7
E♭7
D-7
G7
117
æ- nohl yuwl sey wen yuw hæv kis- dim i-
and all you'll say when you have kissed him is

C-9 C-7/F F7
121
zuw - ə - wət ðə muwn kæn
oo ah what the - moon can
B♭△7 G-7 C-7 F7
125
duw - he liŋ gə mu yə
do
D
B♭△7 E♭7 D-7 G7
129
low bey de duw biy - diyŋ də diŋ diŋ diŋ
C-7 C-9 F7 G7
133
biy uw də bey dn bey dn bey dn bey bow - diy ow də bow - bey
C-9 C-7 C-7 F7
137
biy d- lə buw də diŋ diy bə luw ba - liy k ley də bow
B♭△7 C-7 F7 B△7 F7 B♭7
141
- dey ə luw beh - liy ə loh bey bæw

E♭△7
E♭-6
145
- diy də diy də diyŋ ba lə bə biy ə biy ə buw
B♭△7
E♭7
D-7
G7
149
even
swing
ley dlow ley ha luw mba - liy - liy dow bow liy ow
C9
C9
153
bey ə m bey m bey m bey l- ow m bey m bey m bey bə bey
C-7/F
F7
C-7
F7
157
biy l duw də liyŋ də dohŋ də bohn də diŋ da lə buw bə
B♭△7
E♭7
D-7
G7
161
un diŋ hey dlow dlə bə bə bə bə bə lə luw bə
C-9
F7
165
luw lə dey bə lə m ə bə bey m low bə bey m low

C-7 F7 A-7(♭5) D7
169
ba yuw m ba la dow diŋ
G-9 (G♭7) F-7 B♭7
173
hə liy me biy ə biy ə uw ba - diy - diy hə luw bə diy dleh lə lə duw ba lan n down
E♭△7 E♭-6
177
- da n doh n dow n dow ə lə be bey n də də də də eh lad
B♭△7 E♭7 D-7 G7
181
luw de guw biy m də yuw bə ba iy n diy ba yuwm
C-9 C-7/F F7
185
ba low be dow bow bow be duw low bow m bow ba dey
B♭△7 G7 C-7 F7
189
ə weh - dlow dlow - dlə dle dle dlow dow diy d lə diy də

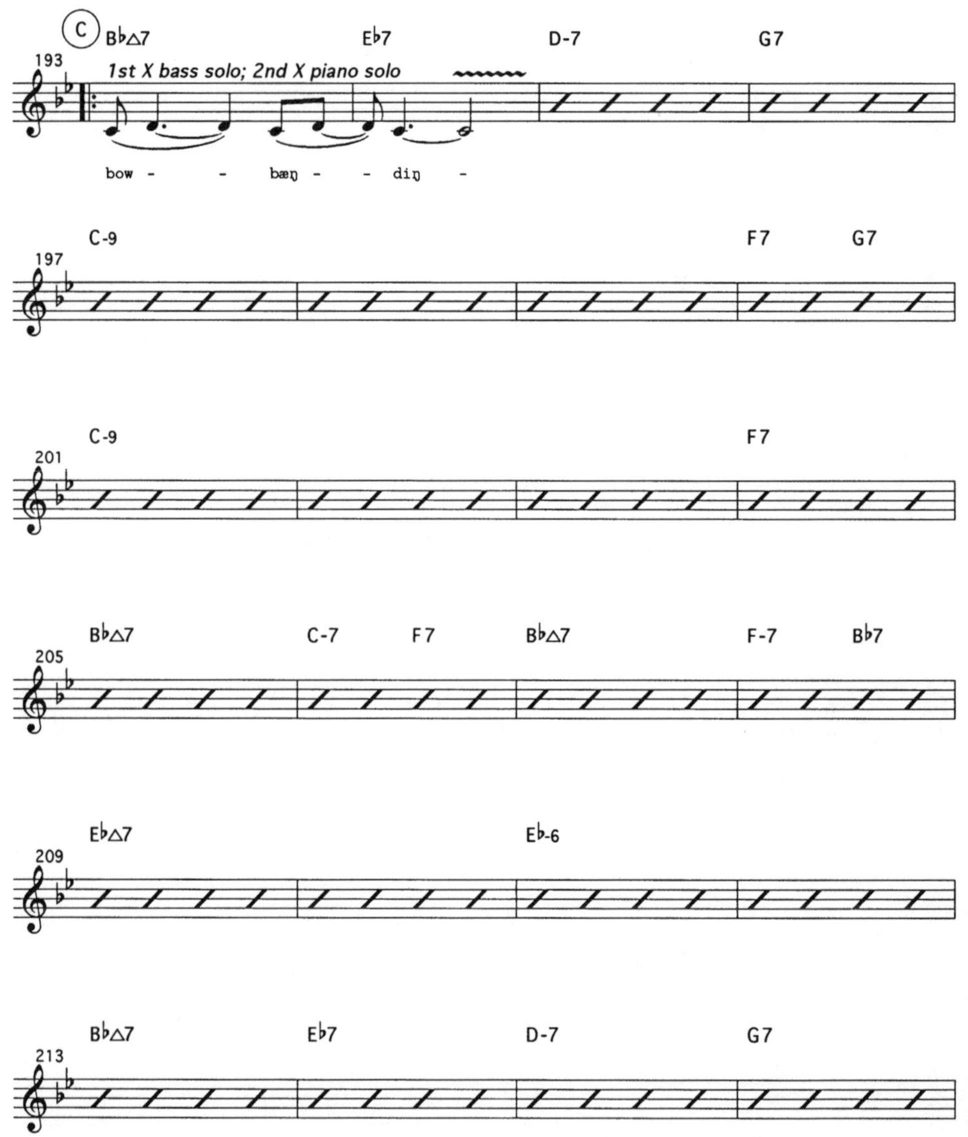
C
193
B♭△7
E♭7
D-7
G7
1st X bass solo; 2nd X piano solo
bow - - bæŋ - - diŋ -
197
C-9
F7
G7
201
C-9
F7
205
B♭△7
C-7
F7
B♭△7
F-7
B♭7
209
E♭△7
E♭-6
213
B♭△7
E♭7
D-7
G7

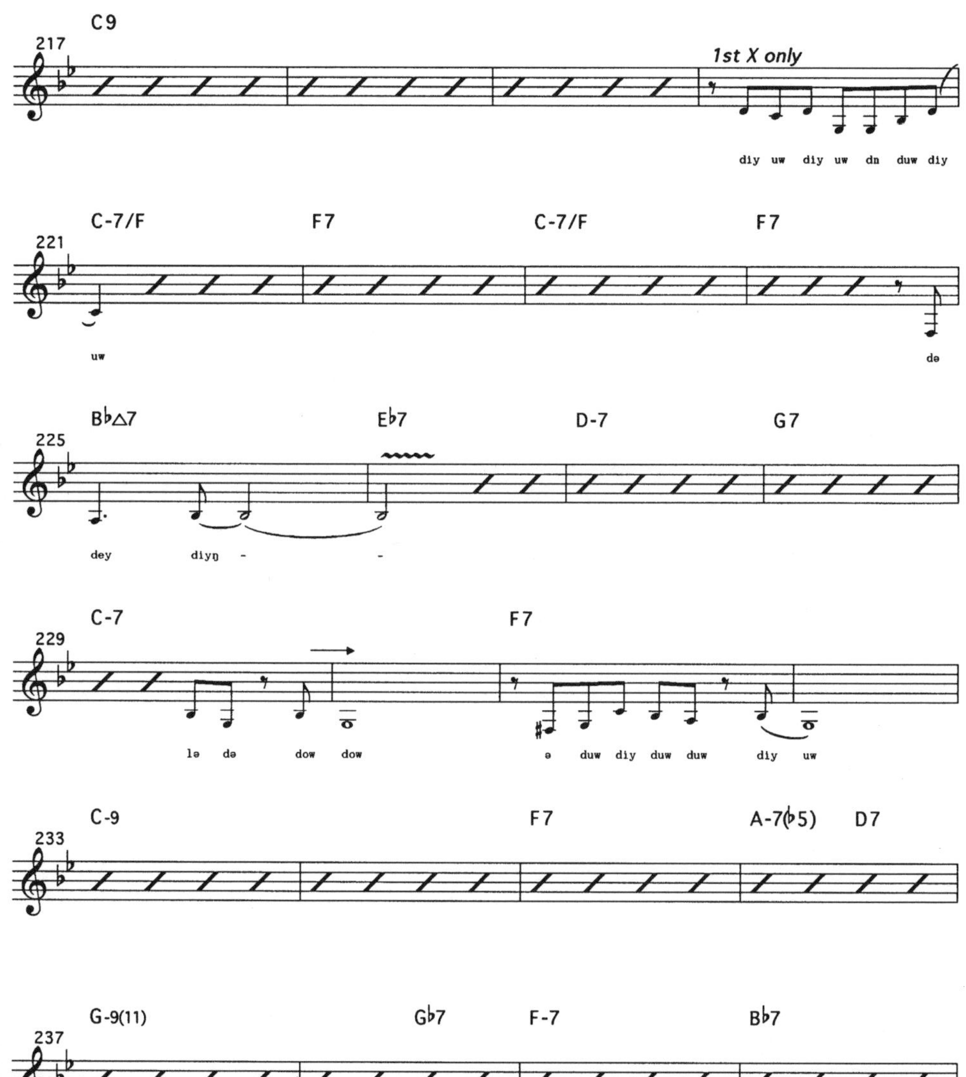

C9
217
1st X only
diy uw diy uw dn duw diy
C-7/F
F7
C-7/F
F7
221
uw
də
B♭△7
E♭7
D-7
G7
225
dey diyŋ - -
C-7
F7
229
lə də dow dow
ə duw diy duw duw diy uw
C-9
F7
A-7(♭5)
D7
233
G-9(11)
G♭7
F-7
B♭7
237

241
E♭△7
E♭-6
245
B♭△7
E♭7
D-7
G7
249
C-9
C-7/F
m diŋ dm də biy biy biy bow
253
B♭△7
G7
C-7
F7
bey - bey - kur dis - lən diy
D
double time ♩= 380
no chord throughout
257
drum solo
uw - - - - wət li- dəl muwn lay- t kæn
oo what lit - tle moon - light can
261
duw - - - -
do

265
uw - - - - wə- də li- dl muwn - lay- t kæn
oo what a lit - tle moon light can
269
duw - tuw - yuw - -
do to you
273
yə- rin lə- --v yə ha- sə flə tə rin
you're in love your hearts a flut - ter - ing
277
ohl - dey - loŋ yuw ohn liy stə- də biy
all day long you on - ly stut - ter be
281
koh - zyə teŋ - jə- swil nat ə tə - ðə
cause your tongue just will not ut - ter the
285
- wur - dz ay lə- vyuw
words I love you

289
3
uw we- də lə muwn layt kæn
oo what a (little) moon-light can
293
duw - -
do
297
wey- də wayl - ti- - lə li- dl muwn biym
wait a while till a lit-tle moon-beam
301
kəm piy pin θruw -
comes peep - ing through
305
yuw get bow- --l yuw kæn- triy zis- tim ə-
you get bold you can't re - sist him and
309
noh- --l yuw- --l sey wen yuw hæv kis- dim i-
all you'll say when you have kissed him is

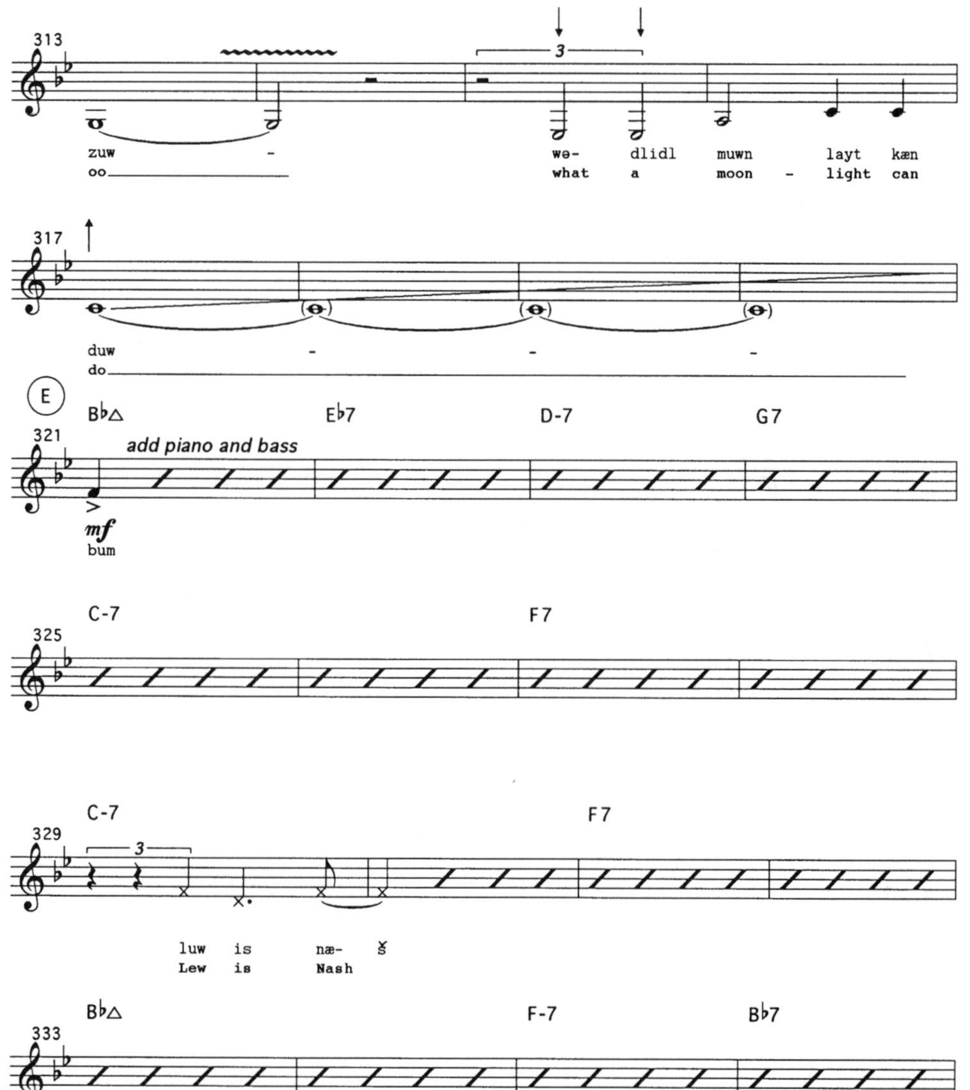
313
zuw -
oo
3
wə- dlidl muwn layt kæn
what a moon - light can
317
duw - - -
do
E
B♭△
E♭7
D-7
G7
321
add piano and bass
mf
bum
C-7
F7
325
C-7
F7
329
3
luw is næ- š
Lew is Nash
B♭△
F-7
B♭7
333

E♭△7
E♭-6
337
3
3
yoh- rin lə - v ye ha- tsə f- lə də rin
you're in love your hearts a flut - ter - ing
B♭△
D-7
G7
341
3
oh- --l dey - lohŋ yuw own liy stə də - biy
all day long you on - ly stut - ter be -
C9
345
koh- zyə tə - ŋ jə- swil na- tə tə - ðə
cause your tongue just will not ut - ter the
C-7/F
F7
349
- wu - dz hay lə- - vyuw -
words I love you
F
A♭7 moderate swing ♩= 192
G7
353
f
3
m ba luw biy uw biy biy - duw - biy wiy dow bwiy liy diŋ - di li bæŋ - di
C-9
F7
357
biy wət ðæt muwn kæn duw də yuw -
what that moon can do to you

C-9
F7
A-7(♭5)
D7
361
ley uw ba ba
G-7
G-9
G♭7
F-7
B♭7
365
he li dlde biyde biy dow buw le biy niy he liy de liy de low de low de low ley
E♭△7
E♭-6
369
le de bey de bey de ba de ba - de he doh de bey luw duw diy ba duw ba duw bey
B♭△
E♭7
D-7
G7
373
diy diy le duw ba - li di ba
G
C-7
F7
C-9
C♭7
377
be luw biy be duw bey be duw bey
B♭△
E♭7
D-7
G7
381
dow duw

C-9
F7
C-9
F7
385
le be ba be duw ba be duw bey

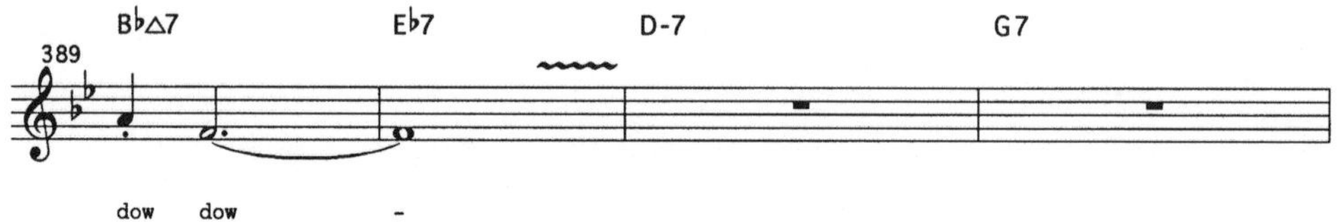
B♭△7
E♭7
D-7
G7
389
dow dow -

C-9
F7
C-9
F7
393
le le ba be luw ba be luw bey

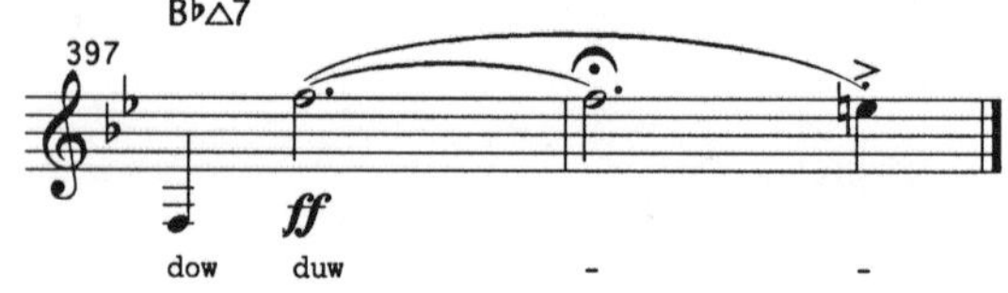
B♭△7
397
ff
dow duw - -

The Good Life

1988

16
C7
G♭△7
G♭△7
l- e- - ts yuw hay- - -
lets you hide - - - - - - -
19
C♭7
D♭9
3
- d ohl ðə sæ- --d ne- - -
all the sad - ness
22
E♭
A♭
D♭△7
C-7(♭5)
F7
s yuw - fiy- - --l
you feel
25
B♭-
B♭-7
yuw wow- --n- triy - liy - foh- - - - lin
you won't real - ly fall in
28
B♭-7
E♭-7
A7
- lə- --v yuw
love you
31
E♭-7
D7
D♭△7
- kehn- t teyk ðə čeh - - ns down- n tray
can't take the chance don't try

34
D♭△7
D♭△7
D♭△7
tuw fey- krow meh- - ns its ðə gu- dlay
to fake ro - mance its the good life
37
C-7(♭5)
F7
C-7(♭5)
- f tuw - - - biy friy -
to be free
40
F7
B♭-
æn- dek- sploh- - --r ðiy ə- n now- -
and ex - plore the un - known
43
B♭-7
G-7(♭5)
- n lay- --k ðə ha- --r dey- -
like the heart - aches
46
C7
G-7(♭5)
C7
- k- s - we- - nyuw lur- -
when you learn
49
G♭△7
G♭△7
C♭7
- n

52
C♭7
D♭9
D♭9
yuw mə- --s fey- s ðe- - --m ə
you must face them a -
55
F-7(♭5)/C♭
B♭7
E♭-9
- low- - - n
lone
58
E♭-
C♭7
C♭7
riy mem bə - ray wa- --n tyuw -
re - mem - ber I want you
61
D♭△7
A♭-6
æn- din key- s -
and in case
64
B♭7
E♭-7
E♭-7
C♭7
yuw - - wə - - də - - way -
you won - der why
67
C♭7
D♭△7
wey- - kə- - pæn- --d ki- - - s
wake up and kiss

70
D♭△7
E♭-7
A♭7♭9
f
hn ðə - gu- - dlay- - f gud
the good life good -
piano solo
73 fast bossa nova
D♭△7
= 296
bay - - -
bye
77
D♭△7
81
C-7(♭5)
F7
85
C-7(♭5)
F7
89
B♭-7
(B-7/B♭)
B♭-7
(A-7/B♭)

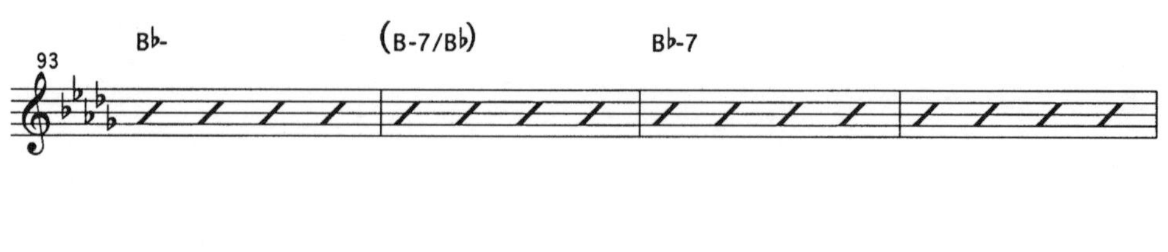
93
B♭-
(B-7/B♭)
B♭-7

97
G-7
C7

101
G-7
C7

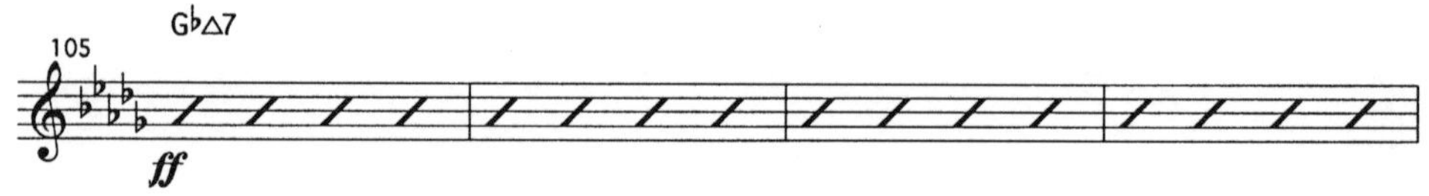
105
G♭△7
ff

109
C♭7

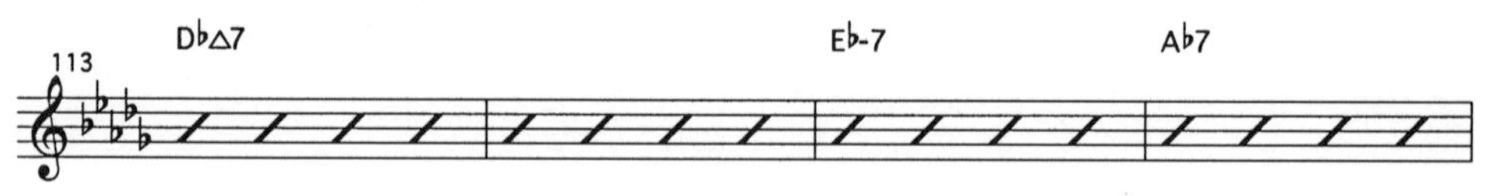
113
D♭△7
E♭-7
A♭7

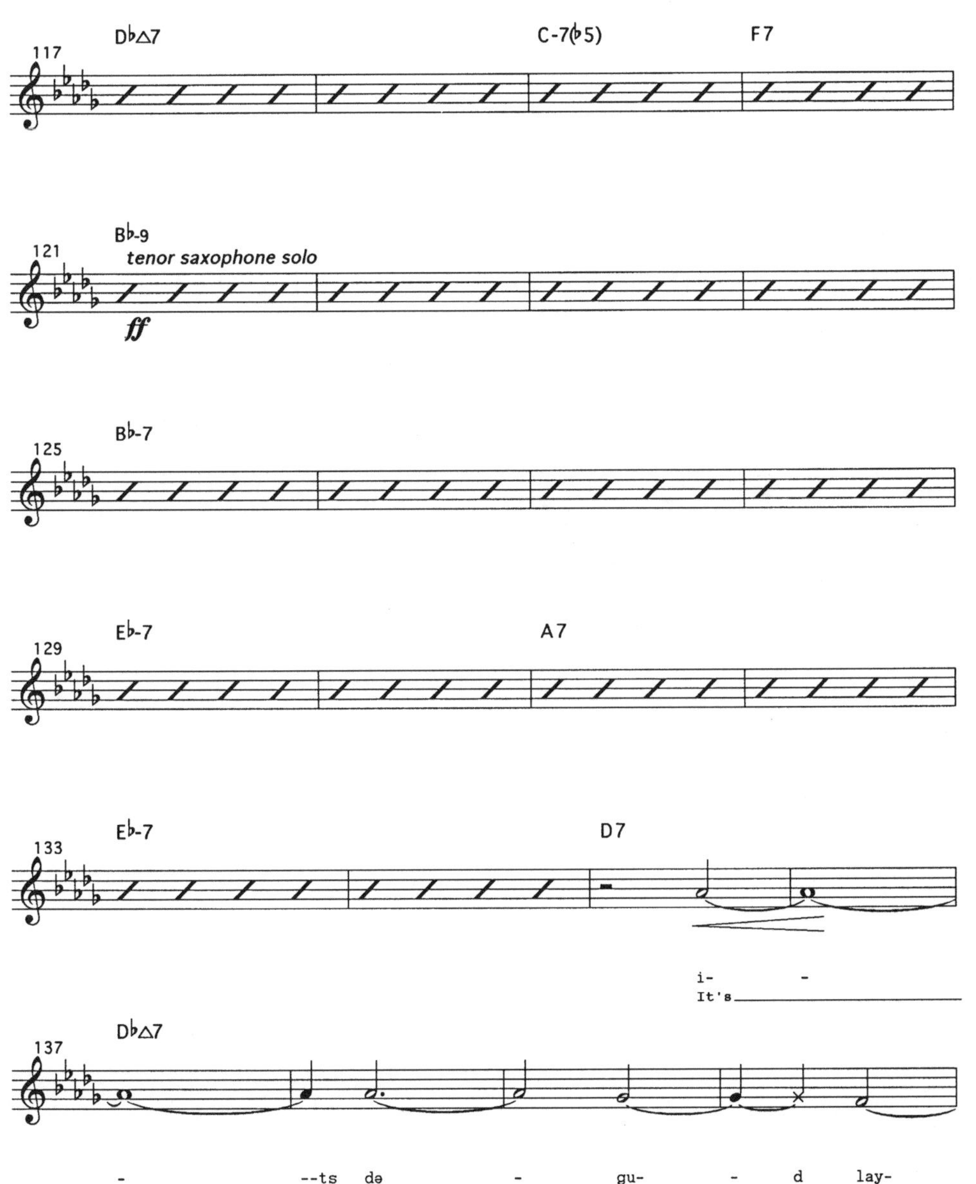
117
D♭△7
C-7(♭5)
F7
121
B♭-9
tenor saxophone solo
ff
125
B♭-7
129
E♭-7
A7
133
E♭-7
D7
i- -
It's
137
D♭△7
- --ts də - gu- - d lay-
the good life

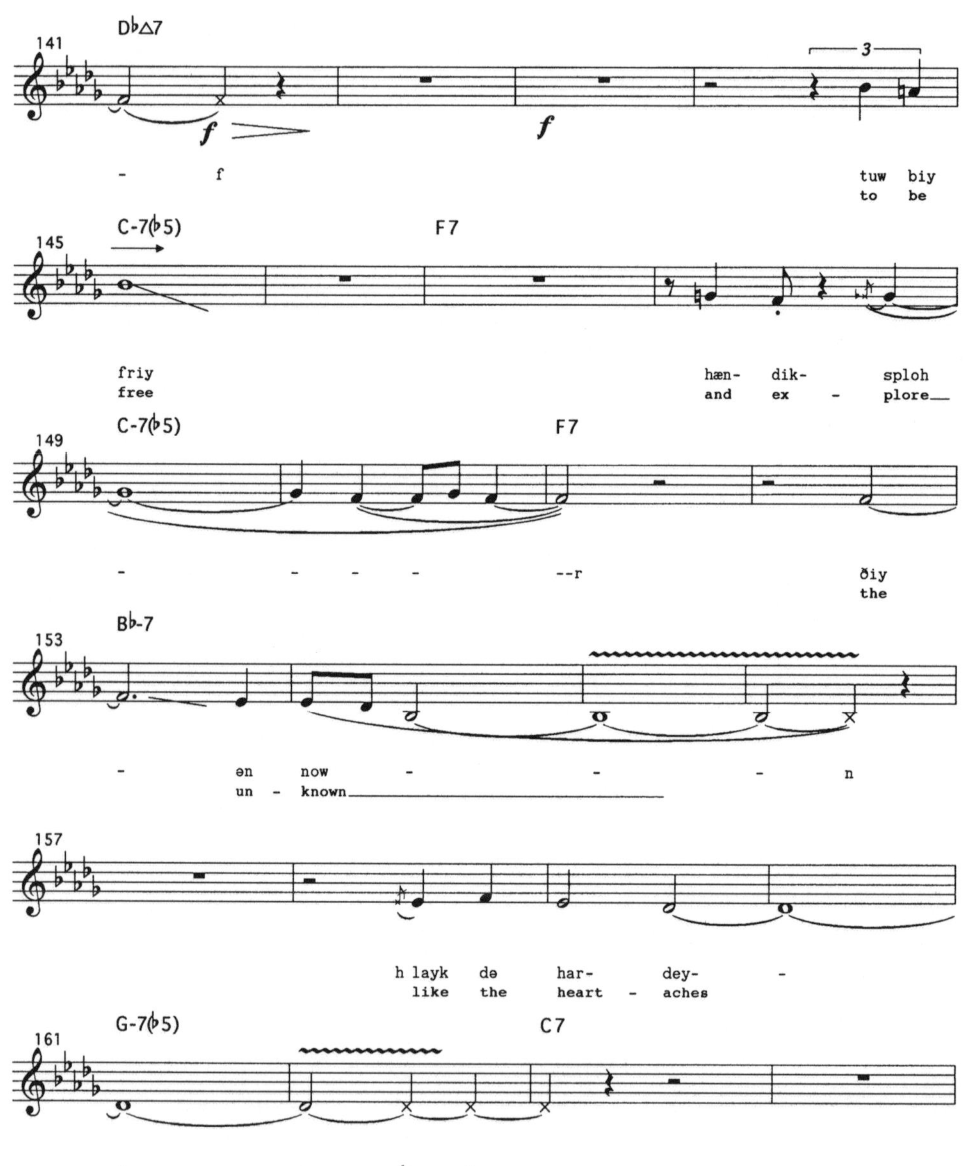
141
D♭△7
3
f
f
- f tuw biy
to be
145
C-7(♭5)
F7
friy hæn- dik- sploh
free and ex - plore
149
C-7(♭5)
F7
- - - - --r ðiy
the
153
B♭-7
- ən now - - - n
un - known
157
h layk də har- dey- -
like the heart - aches
161
G-7(♭5)
C7
- - k- s -

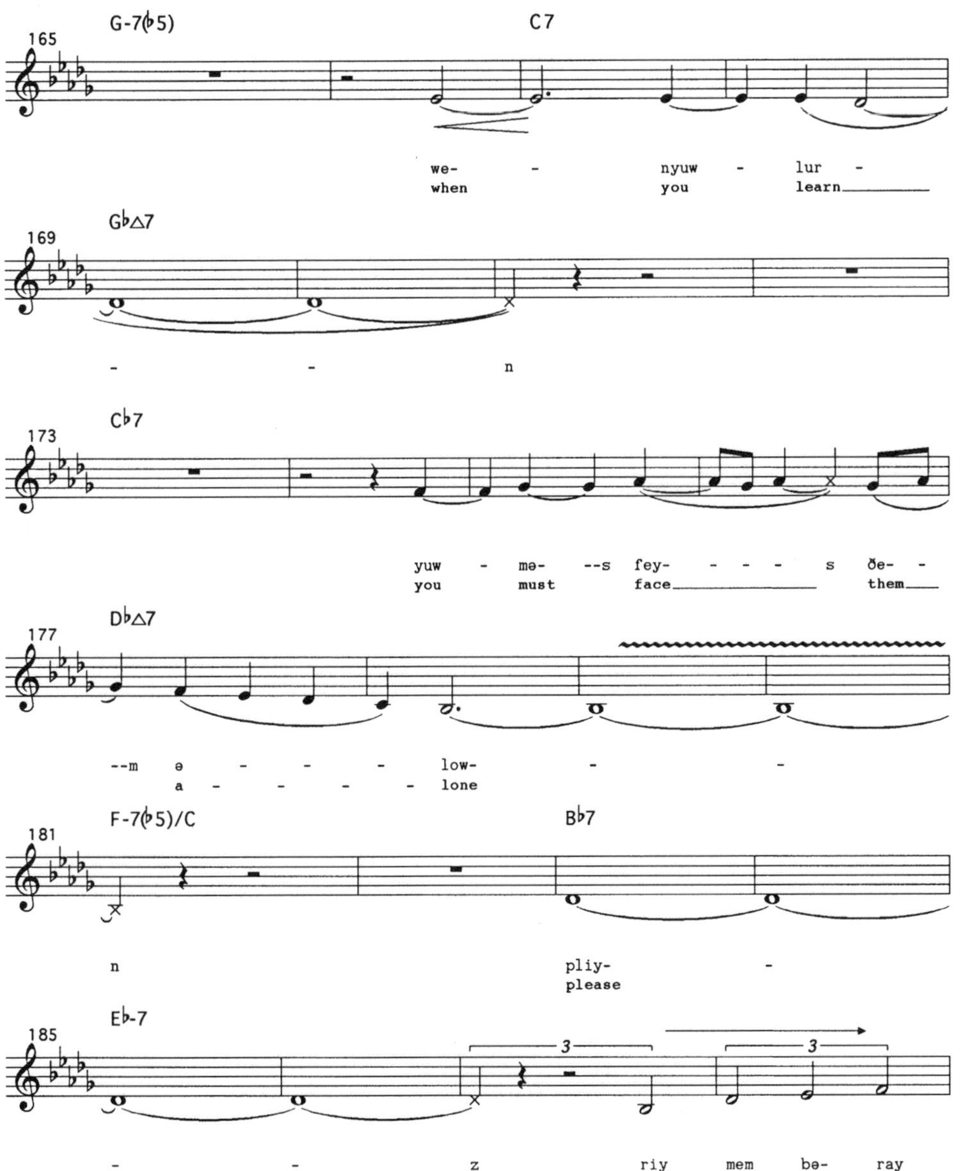
165
G-7(♭5)
C7
we- - nyuw - lur -
when you learn
169
G♭△7
- - n
173
C♭7
yuw - mə- --s fey- - - - s ðe- -
you must face them
177
D♭△7
--m ə - - - - low- - -
a - - - - lone
181
F-7(♭5)/C
B♭7
n pliy- -
please
185
E♭-7
3
3
- - z riy mem bə- ray
re - mem - ber I

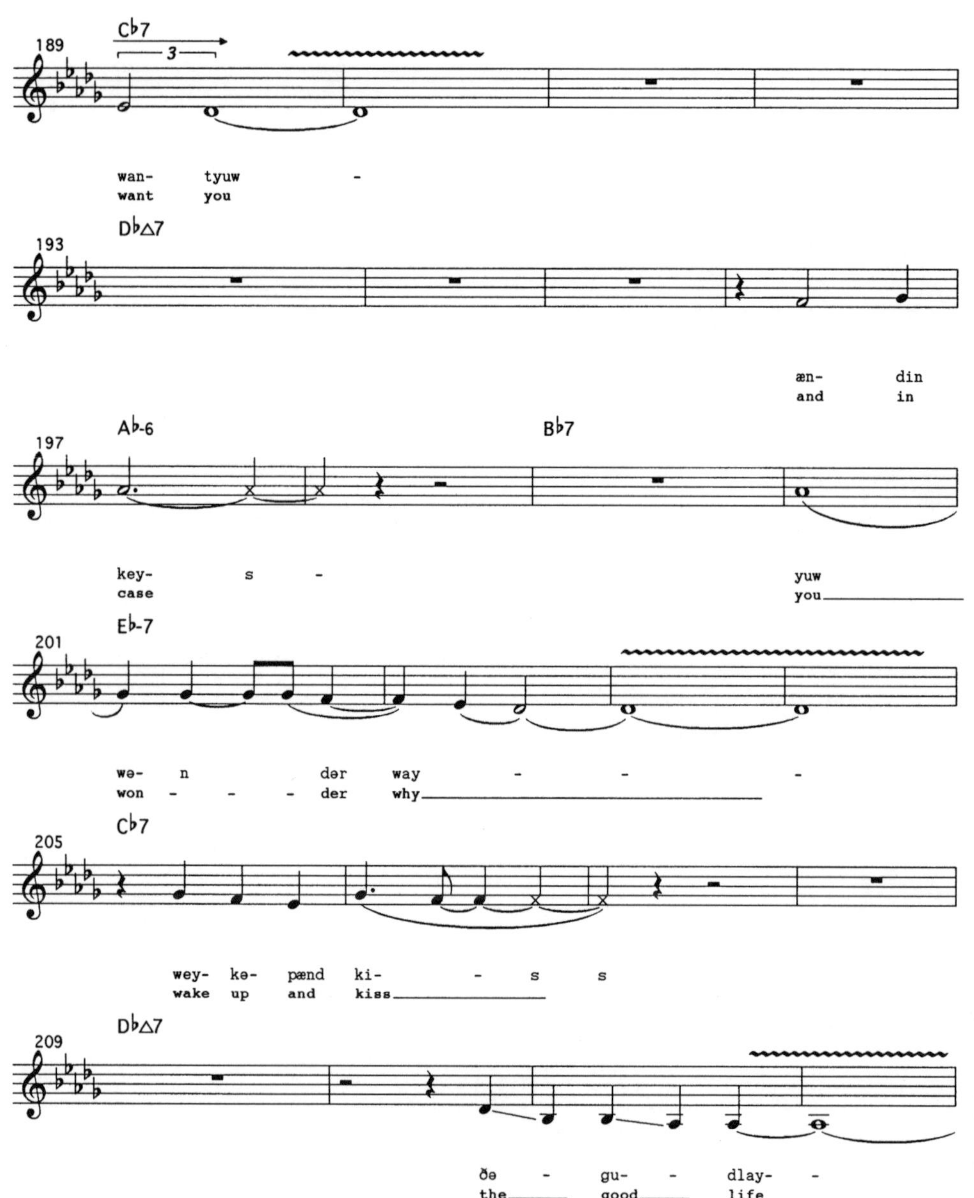
189
C♭7
3
wan- tyuw -
want you
193
D♭△7
æn- din
and in
197
A♭-6
B♭7
key- s -
case
yuw
you
201
E♭-7
wə- n dər way - - -
won - - - der why
205
C♭7
wey- kə- pænd ki- - s s
wake up and kiss
209
D♭△7
ðə - gu- - dlay- -
the good life

213
F-7(♭5)
B♭7
f
217
E♭-7
wey- kə- pænd ki- - s
wake up and kiss
221
C♭7
ðə gu- d lay- -
the good life
225
D♭
f
gu d bay -
good - bye
229
F-7(♭5)
B♭7
- - - -
233
E♭-7
wey- kə pænd ki- - s
wake up and kiss
ðə
the

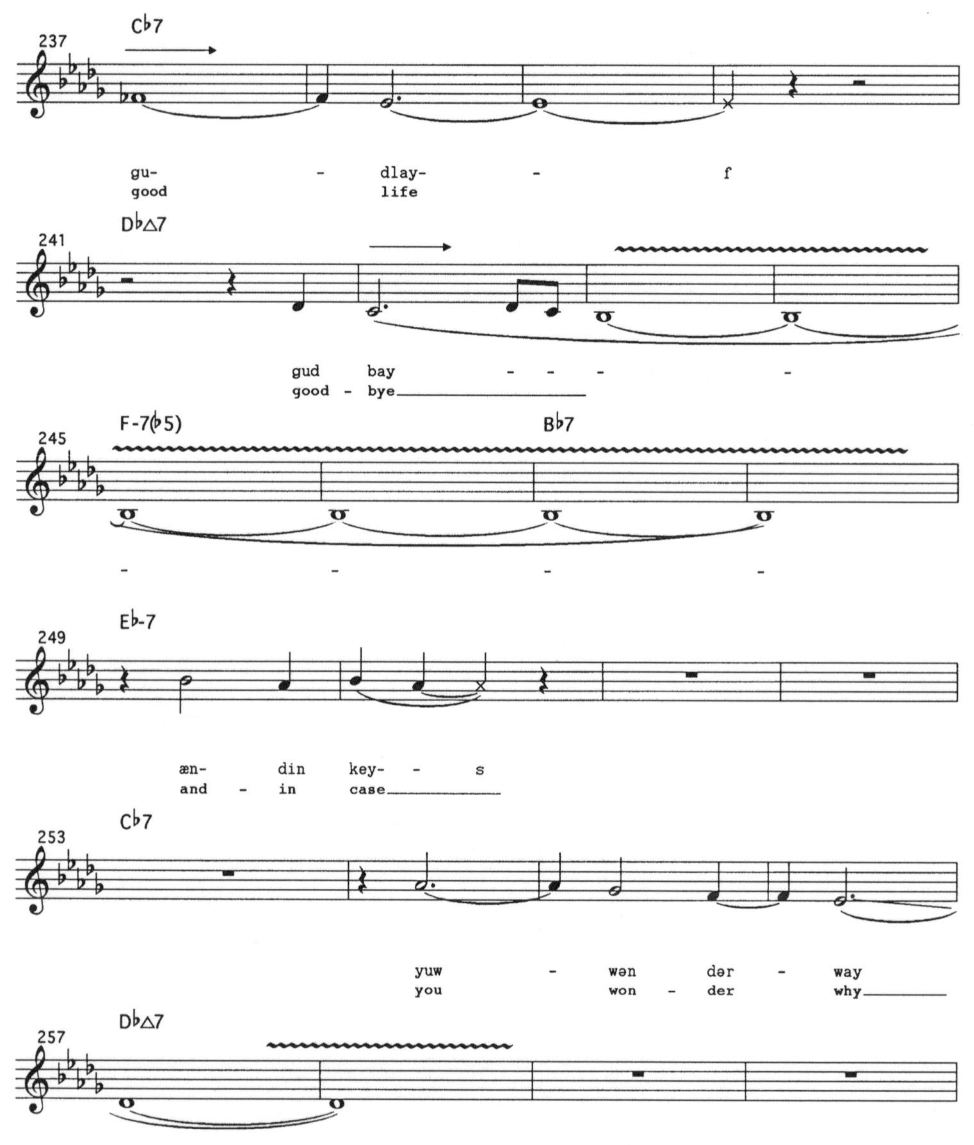
237
C♭7
gu- - dlay- - f
good life
241
D♭△7
gud bay - - - -
good - bye
245
F-7(♭5)
B♭7
- - - -
249
E♭-7
æn- din key- - s
and - in case
253
C♭7
yuw - wən dər - way
you won - der why
257
D♭△7
- -

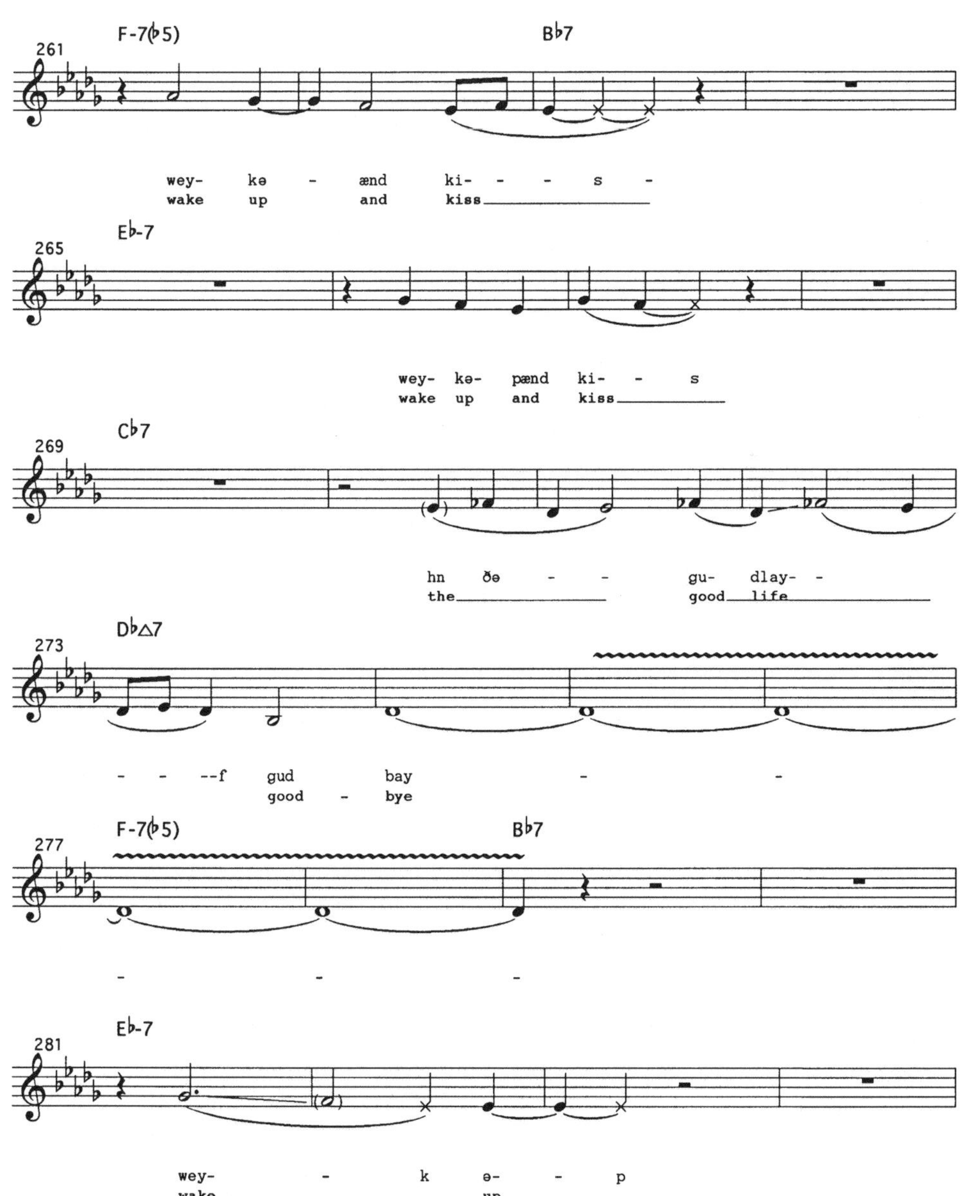
261
F-7(♭5)
B♭7
wey- kə - ænd ki- - - s -
wake up and kiss
265
E♭-7
wey- kə- pænd ki- - s
wake up and kiss
269
C♭7
hn ðə - - gu- dlay- -
the good life
273
D♭△7
- - --f gud bay - -
good - bye
277
F-7(♭5)
B♭7
- - -
281
E♭-7
wey- - k ə- - p
wake up

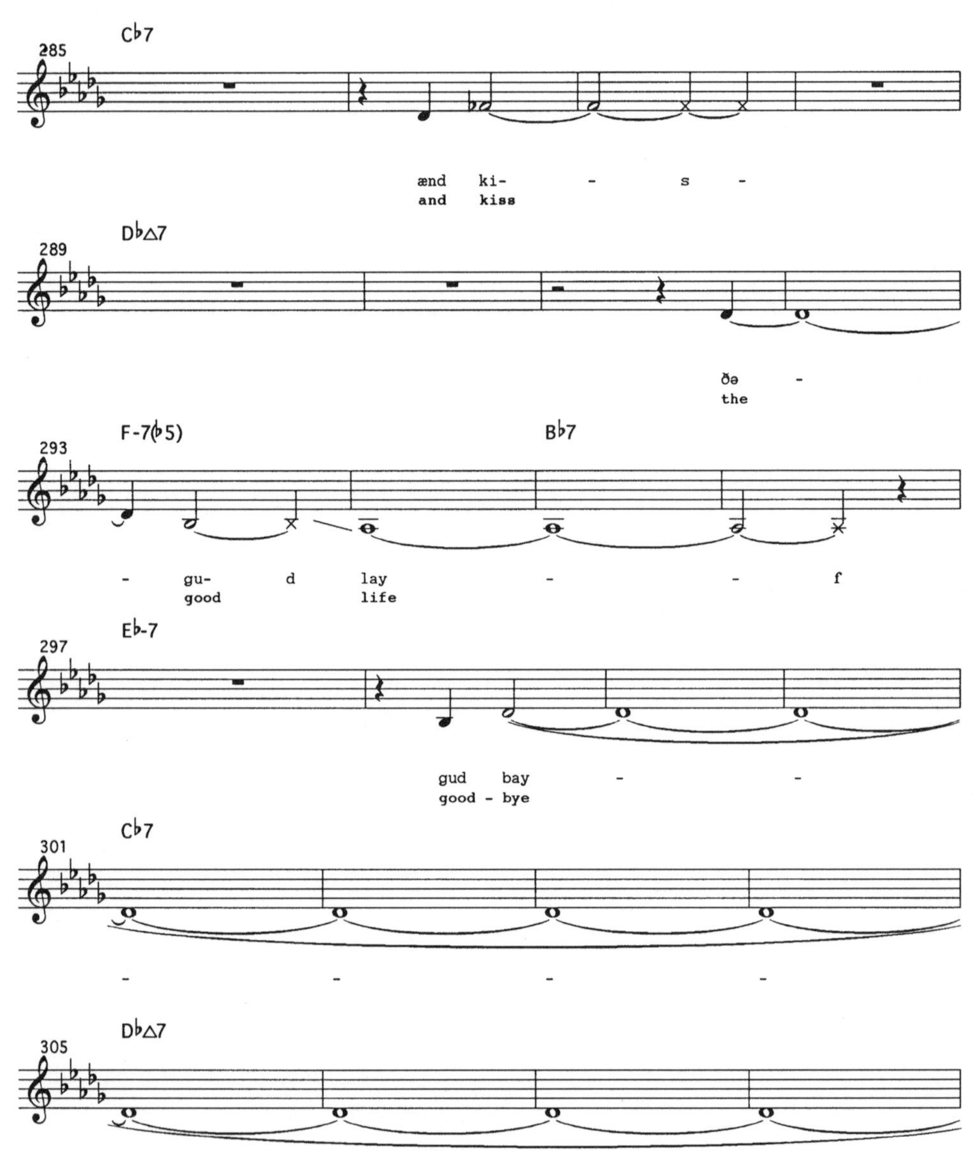

Cb7
285
ænd ki- - s -
and kiss
Db△7
289
ðə -
the
F-7(b5)
Bb7
293
- gu- d lay - - f
good life
Eb-7
297
gud bay - -
good - bye
Cb7
301
- - - -
Db△7
305
- - - -

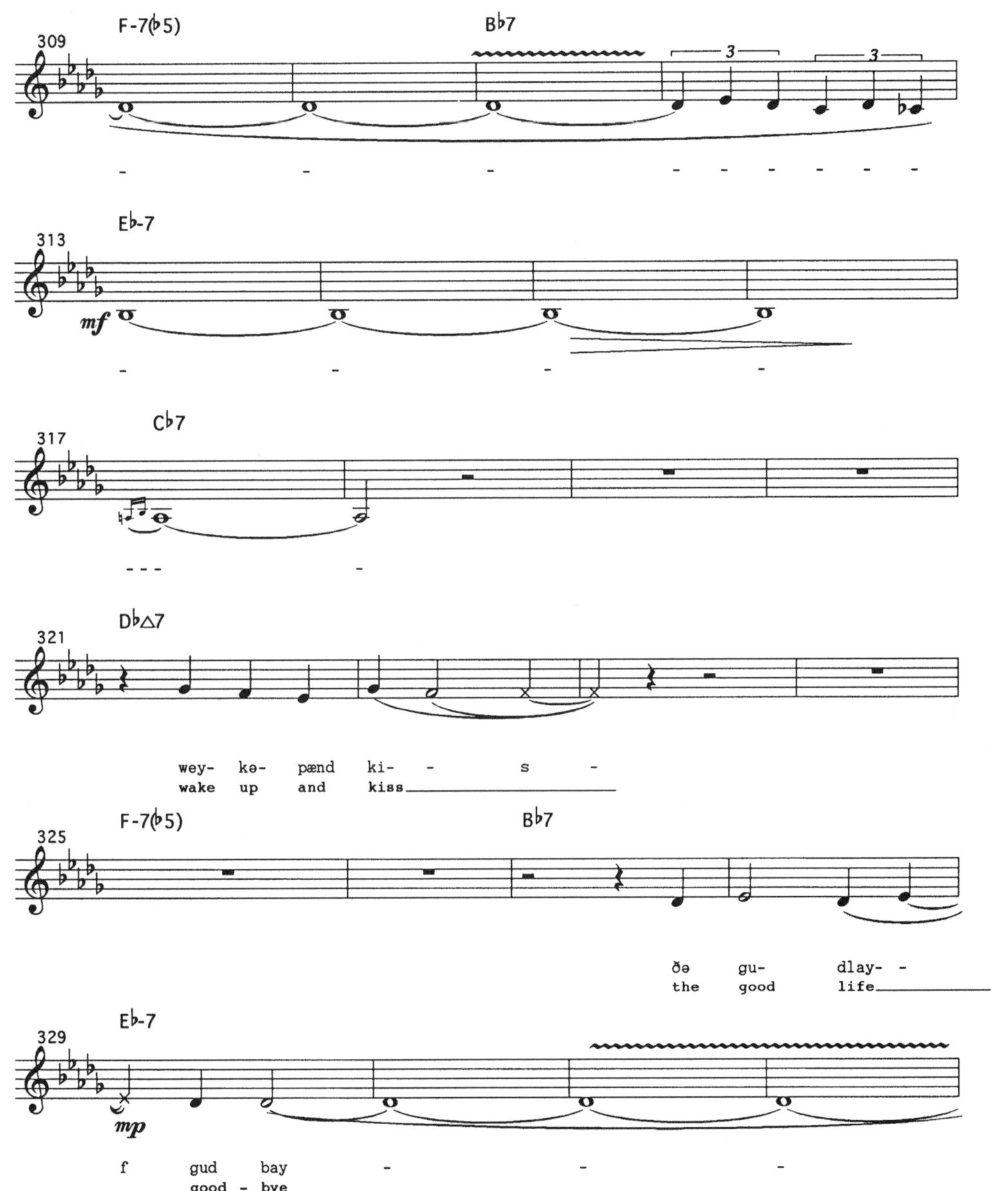
309
F-7(♭5)
B♭7
313
E♭-7
317
C♭7
321
D♭△7
wey- kə- pænd ki- - s -
wake up and kiss
325
F-7(♭5)
B♭7
ðə gu- dlay- -
the good life
329
E♭-7
f gud bay - - -
good - bye

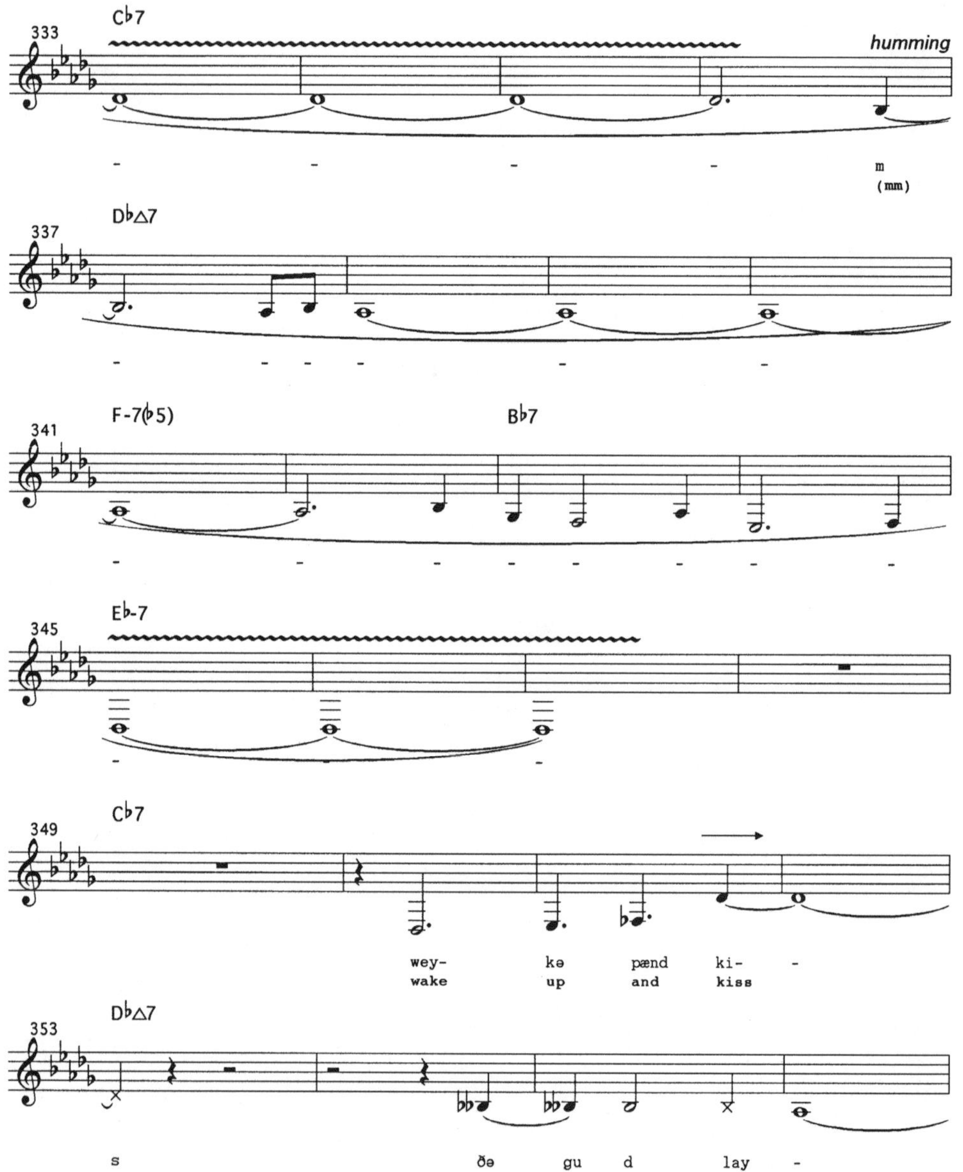

333
C♭7
humming
m
(mm)
337
D♭△7
341
F-7(♭5)
B♭7
345
E♭-7
349
C♭7
wey- kə pænd ki-
wake up and kiss
353
D♭△7
s ðə gu d lay
the good life

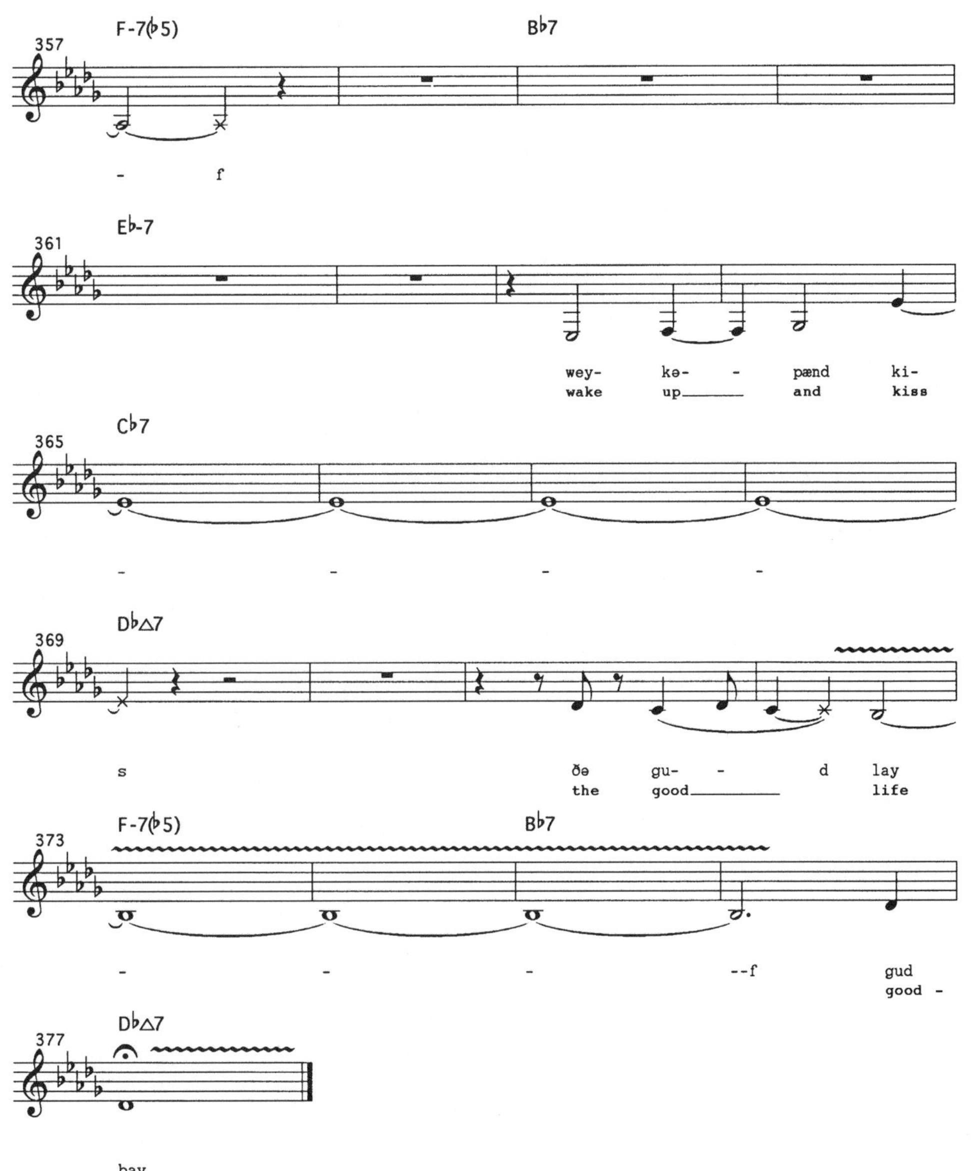
F-7(♭5)
B♭7
357
-
f
E♭-7
361
wey-
kə-
-
pænd
ki-
wake
up
and
kiss
C♭7
365
-
-
-
-
D♭△7
369
s
ðə
gu-
-
d
lay
the
good
life
F-7(♭5)
B♭7
373
-
-
-
--f
gud
good -
D♭△7
377
bay
bye.

Notes

Preface

1. Stanley Crouch, "Betty Carter: A Sure Enough Jazz Singer," *Village Voice,* 31 December–6 January, 1981, 30.

2. See James T. Jones IV, "Betty Carter: Look What We Got," *Down Beat,* August 1989, 24.

3. Curtis Wenzel, "Jazz, Scat, and Betty Bebop," *City Pages* (Minneapolis–St. Paul), Arts Pages, 11 May 1983, 11. Singer Pat Smythe told Kitty Grime, "I think someone like Betty Carter *is* a jazz musician." See *Jazz Voices* (London: Quartet Books, 1983), 172.

4. Ira Coleman, interview by the author, 12 January 1999.

5. Norman Provizer, "Youth and Energy from Betty Bebop," *Jazziz,* October–November 1990, 83.

6. As an example of this, David Amram quoted a comment Dizzy Gillespie made during a rehearsal, that "if you can sing it, you can play it" (interview by the author, 21 December 1998). See also Paul Berliner, *Thinking in Jazz: The Infinite Art of Improvisation* (Chicago: University of Chicago Press, 1994), 109, 140, 179, 180–81, and 187.

7. Betty Carter, interview by Arthur Taylor, 12 December 1972, in Taylor's *Notes and Tones* (New York: Perigee Books, 1977), 271.

8. Betty Carter, interview by Art Roberts, WERS-FM (Boston), 21 October 1983.

9. A handful of articles that include transcriptions of jazz vocals may be found in academic journals, but this book is the first about a singer to use transcriptions. The appendix clarifies how the phonetic symbols are used.

10. This approach is consistent with Carter's own way of thinking. Discussing how the feeling of a tune changes when you alter its tempo, Carter told Art Roberts, "I've got a fast version of 'Tight' that's about a minute and thirty seconds long, then I have a new version of it in the '79 album [*The Audience*], which is a slower. If you

ever wanna compare the two . . . feelings, if you get on a show and you say The Old and The New, the old one was lightning speed, the new one was . . . bouncy."

11. Joe Ferla, interview by the author, 2 November 1998.

12. "An Interview with Betty Carter," by Leothee Miller, 28 February 1972, *Black Creation* 3, no. 4 (1972): 36.

13. Johnathon Abbott, "Queen Betty and the Pirates," *Jazz on CD,* November 1994, 14.

14. David Amram, interview by the author, 28 December 1998.

15. Harvey Siders, "Quotet: Is There Such a Thing as a Jazz Singer. . . ?" *Down Beat,* 12 November 1970, 13.

16. Siders, "Quotet." In the same piece, singer Irene Reid echoed a sentiment shared by many: "Betty Carter is my idea of a jazz singer."

17. Carter, "Jazz Talk," videotaped interview by Chris White, 14 April 1976, Institute of Jazz Studies, Rutgers University, Newark.

18. For those who follow the reruns, this was the episode where Carey Weaver took on John Carter as a tenant.

Introduction

1. Sometimes spelled *Lorraine.* Carter pronounced it /loh*riyn*/.

2. Lionel Hampton with James Haskins, *Hamp: An Autobiography* (New York: Warner Books, 1989), 94; and *Baltimore African American,* 12 June 1948. Owned by Sunnie Wilson and located at 700 East Forest, the club was also known as the Forest Social Club.

3. Joel Dreyfuss, "Betty 'Slow Pop' Carter Speeds Up," *Rolling Stone,* October 1976, 18.

4. Michelle Parkerson, *but then . . . she's Betty Carter,* Eye of the Storm Productions, 1980.

5. Gil Noble, "Special Moments with Betty Carter," *Like It Is* 900, WABC-TV, 4 July 1993, transcript, (Denver, Colo.: Journal Graphics, 1993), 4.

6. Noble, "Special Moments," 4.

7. Matthew Yaple, transcript of interview with Betty Carter in Brooklyn, 1980. This and all subsequent Yaple citations come from the research he did for his master's thesis, Department of Radio-Television-Film, Temple University, which culminated in an unreleased videotape entitled *Jazz Is Betty Carter.* The transcripts, provided by Yaple, include all unedited interview footage.

8. Dreyfuss, "Betty 'Slow Pop' Carter," 18.

9. Parkerson, *but then . . . she's Betty Carter.*

10. Bill McLarney, "Betty Carter: The 'in' Singer," *Down Beat,* 28 July 1966, 19.

11. Carter, interview by Yaple, Brooklyn, 1980; Carter, "Jazz Talk"; Parkerson, *but then . . . she's Betty Carter;* John S. Wilson, "Betty Carter Sings Jazz on Broadway," *New York Times,* 24 November 1978; Noble, "Special Moments," 4; and Hampton and Haskins, *Hamp,* 94.

12. Hampton and Haskins, *Hamp,* 70.

13. Hampton and Haskins, *Hamp,* 199f., discography.

14. See Milt Hinton's comments in Dizzy Gillespie with Al Fraser, *To Be or Not to Bop: Memoir* (1979; rpt., New York: Da Capo, 1985), 104–6.

15. Leonard Feather, *Inside Jazz* (New York: J. J. Robbins, 1949 as *The Roots of Jazz;* rpt. New York: Da Capo, 1977), 39–40.

16. Jelly Roll Morton, interview by Alan Lomax, 1938, Library of Congress, 1657-B.

17. Gunther Schuller claims that while "the whole jazz orchestral world was going bebop crazy" in 1949, Hampton had begun a retrenchment from his bebop explorations. See *The Swing Era* (New York: Oxford University Press, 1989), 401. This conclusion may be based on Hampton's commercially recorded output, which did not reflect his live repertoire. Judging from AFRS Jubilee Broadcasts made during this time, Hampton's performances included bebop-oriented numbers that featured whole sections of the band playing solos transcribed from bebop recordings. Many of the tunes Carter sang with Hampton have a modern sound, and Hampton continued to perform tunes with such titles as "Rebop" and "Hamp's Bopology" at least until the early 1950s.

18. Hampton and Haskins, *Hamp,* 94. Hampton similarly claimed he had come up with the stage name "Dinah Washington" for Ruth Jones when she joined his band in December 1942 (*Hamp,* 85–86), but in that case other versions conflict with his. See also Wilson, "Betty Carter Sings Jazz." Lewis Porter has suggested that this may have been a reference to the cartoon character Betty Boop. See Lewis Porter and Michael Ullman, *Jazz: From Its Origins to the Present* (Englewood Cliffs, N.J.: Prentice-Hall, 1993), 434.

19. Taylor, *Notes and Tones,* 271, 274.

20. Michael Ullman, "Michael Ullman on Jazz: Betty Carter," *New Republic,* 27 May 1978, 24, reprinted in *Jazz Lives: Portraits in Words and Pictures* (Washington, D.C.: New Republic Books, 1980).

21. Carter, interview by Yaple, Brooklyn, 1980.

22. Michael James, *Kings of Jazz: Dizzy Gillespie* (London: Cassell, 1959), 28.

23. Barbara van Rooyen and Pawel Brodowski, "Betty's Groove," *Jazz Forum,* international edition, 57 (1979): 30.

24. Ullman, "On Jazz: Betty Carter," 24.

25. Ullman, "On Jazz: Betty Carter," 24.

26. Bob Blumenthal, "Betty Carter Sets Her Own Records," *Boston Phoenix,* 26 August 1975, sec. 2.4.

27. Van Rooyen and Brodowski, "Betty's Groove," 30.

28. Throughout her life, Betty Carter continued to use the name Lillie Mae Jones or variants of it. On her children's birth records she gave the name Betty Jones, as well as Lillie Mae Redding and Betty Redding, in connection with her sons' father's name, James Redding.

Chapter 1

1. Carter, interview by Yaple, Brooklyn, 1980.
2. Carter, "Jazz Talk."

3. Carter, "Jazz Talk."
4. Carter, interview by Yaple, Brooklyn, 1980.
5. James T. Jones III, interview by the author, 20 November 1998.
6. Carter, interview by Yaple, Brooklyn, 1980.
7. Jones, interview.
8. Jones, interview.
9. Carter, "Jazz Talk."
10. Carter, interview by Yaple, Brooklyn, 1980.
11. Information on Carter's paternal lineage comes from James T. Jones IV, "Roots: The Jones Version," *Detroit News,* 15 February, 1987, sec. B.1, 6, 8.
12. Documents are not definitive with regard to dates. On Elmira's death certificate, her daughter, Maude Sanders—who was living with her at the time of her death—gave 18 November 1885 as her mother's birth date. But in the 1920 census, Elmira claimed she was forty-three, which would place the year of her birth closer to 1875, the year James Jones IV proposed in his article.
13. According to dates given on their death certificates, they would have been sixteen when they started their family—on James Jones I's death certificate Elmira gave his birth date as 25 October 1885. In the 1920 census, however, his age was given as forty-four, which would place his birth nine years earlier.
14. C. G. Hall, ed., *Arkansas: A Guide to the State* (Arkansas Writer's Project sponsored by the Arkansas State Planning Board, 1941), 279.
15. According to the family history, which mentions no formal marriage, Elmira and James Sr. went on to have six more children, three daughters and three sons: Alberta, 1902; W.T., 1904; O.E., 1906; Booker T., ca. 1908; Maude, and Irene. The 1920 census lists only five children: Alberta, seventeen; T.T., fifteen; Booker T., ten; Cleophus, eight; and Irene, who was born on 12 January 1915, five.
16. Hall, *Arkansas,* 189–95, 267–68.
17. Estimated figures give us some idea of the black population's rate of expansion: in 1910 it had been close to 5,000; by 1920 it had risen to roughly 40,000, and during the following decade it would increase to about 120,000.
18. A birth record for Lillie May [*sic*] Jones filed in Genesee County on 16 July 1929 by James T. Jones and Bertha Cox gives her date of birth as 19 May, but family members insist that Carter was indeed born on the sixteenth. On similar lines, Carter spun confusion about her year of birth by telling some people that it was 1930 and others that it was 1929. She spelled her given name *Lillie Mae* but it also appears as *Lillie May* and *Lilly Mae* in various documents. She was sometimes known simply as Lillie, or Lilly, Jones.
19. Carter, interview by Miller, 36.
20. Thomas J. Sugrue, *The Origins of the Urban Crisis: Race and Inequality in Postwar Detroit* (Princeton, N.J.: Princeton University Press, 1996), 19.
21. Jones, "Roots," 8.
22. Similarly, Elmira had not provided her mother-in-law's name on James I's death certificate, but by the time Elmira met her husband-to-be his mother was out of the picture.
23. Jones, "Roots," 8.

24. It is not surprising, then, that when Carter's son Myles provided information for his mother's death certificate, the line for his grandmother's name is left blank.

25. Betty Carter, interview by the author, 24 October 1994.

26. Carter, interview by the author; and Carter, "Jazz Talk."

27. Carter, interview by the author.

28. Carter, interview by the author.

29. Irene Jones Meadows-Blanding, interview by the author, 8 June 1999. Irene said that Carter's half sister Louise and she were the family historians, but both limited the information they gave me. It seems Carter shared little about the family tree with her sons. As a result, gaps remain in our understanding of her genealogy.

30. Jones, "Roots," 8.

31. Meadows-Blanding, interview.

32. Jones, interview.

33. Meadows-Blanding, interview.

34. James T. Jones IV, "Betty Bebop Is Back in Town," *Michigan: The Magazine of the Detroit News,* 5 May 1985, 15.

35. Jones, interview.

36. Jones, interview.

37. Carter, interview by Yaple, Brooklyn, 1980.

38. Carter, interview by the author.

39. Carter, interview by the author.

40. Carter, interview by Yaple, Brooklyn, 1980.

41. Carter, interview by the author.

42. Carter, interview by Miller, 36.

43. Carter, interview by the author.

44. Carter, interview by Yaple, Brooklyn, 1980; and Dreyfuss, "Betty 'Slow Pop' Carter."

45. Carter, interview by the author.

46. For more detail about the church's role in other musicians' artistic development, see Berliner, *Thinking in Jazz,* 29.

47. Carter, "Jazz Talk." It seems unlikely that Carter did her first arranging in church, as Will Friedwald has suggested in *Jazz Singing: America's Great Voices from Bessie Smith to Bebop and Beyond* (New York: Charles Scribner's Sons, 1990), 403.

48. Carter, "Jazz Talk."

49. Jones, interview.

50. Carter, "Jazz Talk."

51. Accounts disagree about her age, but the split would have taken place around 1940–41. As bold as it seems, this act is not unheard of within the African American community.

52. Carter, interview by the author.

53. Harold McKinney, interview by the author, 4 December 1998.

54. Carter, interview by the author.

55. Carter, interview by the author.

56. "Rev. Charles A. Hill," a biographical sketch included in historical papers

from the Hartford Memorial Baptist Church. Many thanks to church historian, Charles Estus, for this literature.

57. Robert H. Mast, *Detroit Lives* (Philadelphia: Temple University Press, 1994), 248.

58. Van Rooyen and Brodowski, "Betty's Groove," 30.

59. Carter, interview by Yaple, Brooklyn, 1980.

60. Betty Carter, interview by Christopher Kuhl, 1982, *Cadence,* February 1985, 7.

61. Carter, interview by the author.

62. Carter, interview by the author.

63. Carter, interview by the author.

64. Carter, interview by the author.

65. Carter, interview by Yaple, Brooklyn, 1980.

66. Carter, interview by the author.

67. Carter, interview by the author.

68. Decca 23425.

69. Carter, interview by the author.

70. Alyn Shipton, *Groovin High: The Life of Dizzy Gillespie* (New York: Oxford University Press, 1999), 110–13.

71. *Michigan Chronicle,* 1 March 1947, 17.

72. Carter, interview by Miller, 36.

73. Van Rooyen and Brodowski, "Betty's Groove," 30.

74. Herb Nolan, "Betty Carter's Declaration of Independence," *Down Beat,* 12 August 1976, 24.

75. Carter, interview by Kuhl, 7.

76. Nolan, "Declaration of Independence," 24.

77. Carter, interview by Kuhl, 7.

78. Carter, interview by Kuhl, 7.

79. Carter, interview by Kuhl, 7.

80. Carter, interview by Kuhl, 7.

81. Van Rooyen and Brodowski, "Betty's Groove," 30.

82. Carter, interview by Miller, 36.

83. The WestSiders, *Remembering Detroit's Old West Side: 1920–1950 (A Pictorial History of the Westsiders)* (Detroit: WestSiders, 1997), 85, 99. Many thanks to Harold McKinney for informing me of this book. See also Mast, *Detroit Lives,* 78; and Sugrue, *Origins of Urban Crisis,* 21.

84. The WestSiders, *Detroit's Old West Side,* 59.

85. Carter, interview by Yaple, Brooklyn, 1980. In 1939 black students constituted about one-fifth of the school's student body of four thousand.

86. The WestSiders, *Detroit's Old West Side,* 61.

87. Sugrue, *Origins of Urban Crisis,* 21.

88. The National Guard had to intervene to prevent an outbreak of the riot in the West Side, at Northwestern High School's graduation ceremony. Two books effectively chronicle the events of one of the worst race riots in the history of the country: Alfred McClung Lee and Norman D. Humphrey, *Race Riot: Detroit, 1943* (1943; New

York: Octagon Books, 1968); and Robert Shogun and Tom Craig, *The Detroit Race Riot: A Study in Violence* (Philadelphia: Chilton Books, 1964).

89. Berliner, *Thinking in Jazz,* 774 n. 18.
90. Carter, interview by the author.
91. Carter, interview by the author.
92. Carter, interview by the author. Carter has described Wagner as the director of both the a capella choir and the Northwestern High School Choir. Her tenure may have been before Straucy Edwards became the director of the latter group. See The WestSiders, *Detroit's Old West Side,* 74.
93. Carter, interview by Yaple, Brooklyn, 1980.
94. Carter, interview by the author.
95. Carter, interview by the author.
96. Carter, interview by Yaple, Brooklyn, 1980.
97. Carter, interview by the author.
98. The WestSiders, *Detroit's Old West Side,* 80, 240.
99. Carter, interview by the author.
100. Carter, interview by Yaple, Brooklyn, 1980.
101. Jones, "Betty Bebop Is Back," 18.
102. Carter, interview by Yaple, Brooklyn, 1980.
103. Santoro, "Look What We Got," *Pulse!* September 1988, 62.
104. Carter, interview by Yaple, Brooklyn, 1980.
105. Carter, interview by Yaple, Brooklyn, 1980.
106. Carter, interview by Yaple, Brooklyn, 1980.
107. George Benson, interview by the author, 18 December 1998.
108. Ullman, "On Jazz: Betty Carter," 24.
109. Carter, interview by Yaple, Brooklyn, 1980. On two separate occasions Carter recalled the event taking place on a Wednesday night. Perhaps she was confusing this with the Frolic Show Bar's Wednesday night amateur hour, which began on 5 March 1947. See Larry Chism, "Swinging with Nitelifers," *Michigan Chronicle,* 22 February 1947, 19.
110. Carter, interview by the author.
111. "Detroiters Saw, Heard Much Talent," *Michigan Chronicle,* 4 January 1947, 13.
112. Carter, interview by Yaple, Brooklyn, 1980. In a later retelling of this story, Carter implicated her sister Vivian in her Tuesday night escape. See Gottleib Guntern, ed., *Risk-Taking and Creative Leadership* (London: Shepheard-Walwyn, 1998), 45–46.
113. Van Rooyen and Brodowski, "Betty's Groove," 30.
114. Taylor, *Notes and Tones,* 272. Carter presented conflicting descriptions of the event's aftermath. She either gave the fifty-dollar prize to her mother—"I tried to impress her, but she took the money and kept on stepping" (see Jones, "Betty Bebop Is Back," 15)—or split it with her younger sister (see Guntern, *Risk-Taking,* 46).
115. Carter, interview by Yaple, Brooklyn, 1980.
116. Carter, interview by Yaple, Brooklyn, 1980.
117. Guntern, *Risk-Taking,* 46.

118. Larry Chism, “Radio, Screen Stars Thrilled Detroiters,” *Michigan Chronicle,* 5 January 1946, 14.

119. Chism, “Radio, Screen Stars.”

120. Larry Chism, “Swinging with Nitelifers,” *Michigan Chronicle,* 5 January 1946, 14.

121. Chism, “Swinging with Nitelifers,” *Michigan Chronicle,* 5 January 1946, 14.

122. Sunnie Wilson, *Toast of the Town* (Detroit: Wayne State University Press, 1998), 63–64. Many thanks to Lois Sheely for alerting me to this book.

123. Russ J. Cowans, “I Cover the Town,” *Michigan Chronicle,* 25 May 1946, 22.

124. Carter, interview by the author.

Chapter 2

1. David Meltzer, *Reading Jazz* (San Francisco: Mercury House, 1993).

2. Weldon Kees, in *Reviews and Essays, 1936–55,* ed. James Reidel (Ann Arbor: University of Michigan Press, 1988), 194–98; reprinted in Meltzer, *Reading Jazz,* 204–5.

3. Dave Brubeck, “Jazz Perspectives [1951],” in *Perspectives U.S.A.* 15 (spring 1956): 22–28; reprinted in Meltzer, *Reading Jazz,* 239.

4. Other African American styles loosely labeled “rhythm & blues” came to support social dancing.

5. Scott DeVeaux, “Introduction: Stylistic Evolution or Social Revolution,” in *The Birth of Bebop: A Social and Musical History* (Berkeley and Los Angeles: University of California Press, 1997), 1–31. This book is required reading for anyone who wants to make sense of the conflicting musical, social, and economic forces that gave rise to bebop.

6. Talk given by Betty Carter at Laney Community College, Oakland, Calif., December 1979. Transcript provided by Matthew Yaple.

7. Carter, interview by Yaple, Brooklyn, 1980. Two provocative discussions of hipness may be found in Ingrid Monson, “The Problem of White Hipness: Race, Gender, and Cultural Conceptions in Jazz Historical Discourse,” *Journal of the American Musicological Society* 85, no. 3 (1995): 396–422; and Andrew Ross, “Hip and the Long Front of Color,” in *No Respect: Intellectuals and Popular Culture* (New York: Routledge, 1989), 65–101. Monson emphasizes that hipness was largely a male phenomenon, making Carter’s attainment of it all the more striking. Many thanks to Krin Gabbard for directing me to the latter source.

8. McLarney, “Betty Carter: The ‘in’ Singer,” 19.

9. Carter, interview by the author.

10. Lars Björn, “From Hastings St. to the Bluebird: The Blues and Jazz Tradition in Detroit,” *Michigan Quarterly Review* 25, no. 2 (1986): 257–68.

11. Björn, “From Hastings St.”

12. Carter, interview by the author. Black Bottom—specifically the area near Hastings Street and Antoine—was razed in order to build the Edsel Ford and Chrysler Freeways. These and other freeways enabled the predominantly white middle class to reside beyond the city limits while continuing to work within them.

13. Carter, interview by the author. Carter claimed that the forged birth certificate did not play a role in the confusion about her birth year, mentioned earlier.

14. Berliner, *Thinking in Jazz,* 23.

15. Daniel M. Faulk, "Barry Harris, Master Bebop Pianist: A Preliminary Study of His Life, Music, and Teaching Methods," M.A. thesis, Rutgers University, Newark, 1999.

16. "Nightclubs: Detroit," *The New Grove Dictionary of Jazz* (New York: St. Martin's Press, 1988), 874–75.

17. Ullman, "On Jazz: Betty Carter," 72.

18. In 1960 Greenlee acknowledged his Detroit roots by naming a composition "El Sino," after the bar of the same name (Slide Hampton, *Somethin' Sanctified,* Atlantic 1362).

19. Carter, "Jazz Talk."

20. Faulk, "Barry Harris."

21. Talk given by Betty Carter at the Great American Music Hall, San Francisco, during the first week of December 1979. Transcript provided by Matthew Yaple.

22. Barry Harris, conversation with the author, 16 July 1999.

23. Carter, interview by Yaple, Brooklyn, 1980.

24. Ullman, "On Jazz: Betty Carter," 74.

25. David Stowe, *Swing Changes: Big-Band Jazz in New Deal America* (Cambridge: Harvard University Press, 1994), 173–74.

26. Leonard Feather, "Singing: 6. New Singers and Styles of the 1940s and 1950s," in *New Grove Dictionary of Jazz,* 1127. Feather later cites Joe "Bebop" Carroll's presence in Gillespie's band as an exception to this statement, strangely neglecting to mention Gillespie's own contribution in the vocal department.

27. See Bret Primack, "Profile: Walter Davis, Jr.," *Down Beat,* 15 May 1978, 32.

28. The importance of timbre to the jazz aesthetic has links to African music, in which acoustically complex timbres such as raspy, buzzing, or scratchy noises are used to relate musical sounds to those of everyday life. The formulation of a cultural sound image, like that of a language, entails an "editing" process in which certain sonic possibilities acquire more aesthetic, or semiotic, value than others. For example, western European musicians' simplification of timbre, which allowed a tone's fundamental to resonate clearly, allowed them to explore the pitch relationships that led to tonal harmony. Similarly, timbral complexity in West African music enabled musicians to differentiate several levels of rhythmic activity in the music's intricate textures.

29. Perhaps because this sound (sometimes known as white, or pink, noise) hinders the pitch fundamental's audibility, it can detract from a musician's tone. In Carter's case, it may have contributed to the perception that she sometimes sang out of tune.

30. For the origins of this usage in earlier jazz styles, see Andre Hodeir, *Jazz: Its Evolution and Essence,* translated by David Noakes (New York: Grove Press, 1956), 67. Hodeir's translator coined the unfortunate expression *terminal vibrato*—it sounds like a fatal illness—to describe this phenomenon. The device serves as a way

to vitalize sustained pitches, which often occur at phrase endings, and thus continue the rhythmic momentum so essential to swing.

31. Betty Carter, interview by Leonard Lyons, 27 September 1975, archived at the Institute of Jazz Studies, Rutgers University, Newark.

32. Carter, interview by Lyons.

33. Carter, interview by Lyons.

34. Carter, interview by Lyons.

35. Carter, talk at Great American Music Hall, 1979.

36. Carter, interview by Yaple, Brooklyn, 1980.

37. Taylor, *Notes and Tones,* 272.

38. Feather, *Inside Jazz,* 41. Dave Usher, Gillespie's business partner at Dee Gee Records, recalled that he heard him at a "Dixieland" jazz concert at the Paradise Theater in 1945, perhaps when Gillespie and Parker were on the road together en route to California (Gillespie and Fraser, *To Be or Not to Bop,* 372).

39. *Michigan Chronicle,* 16 November 1946, 17.

40. "Detroiters Saw, Heard Much Talent," 13.

41. *Baltimore African American,* 15 February 1947, 3; *New York Amsterdam News,* 22 February 1947, 27.

42. *Michigan Chronicle,* 15 February 1947, 16.

43. Feather, *Inside Jazz,* 41.

44. Gillespie and Fraser, *To Be or Not to Bop,* 269.

45. "Hot Music Stirs Re-Bop Disciples into a Near Riot," *Michigan Chronicle,* 22 February 1947, 18.

46. Barry McRae, *Dizzy Gillespie: His Life and Time* (New York: Universe Books, 1988), 44.

47. Larry Chism, "Swinging with Nitelifers," *Michigan Chronicle,* 19 April 1947, 16. Also see Ross Russell, *Bird Lives: The High Life and Hard Times of Charlie "Yardbird" Parker* (New York: Charterhouse, 1973), 242.

48. "Be It Ever So Modernistic, There's No One Quite as Dizzy as Gillespie," *Michigan Chronicle,* 7 June 1947, 16. See also *New York Amsterdam News,* 29 June 1947, 25; and Taylor, *Notes and Tones,* 272. A one-paragraph syndicated item announced, after the fact, that Gillespie had performed a two-week run with his big band at El Sino ending on 2 May. Given the splash he had made in February, it is surprising the paper did not devote more ink to this appearance. See "Dizzy Plays Detroit Club," *Detroit Chronicle,* 3 May 1947, 16.

49. Taylor, *Notes and Tones,* 272; Carter, interview by Miller, 72; and Carter, "Jazz Talk."

50. Carter, interview by Yaple, Brooklyn, 1980; and Roy W. Stephens, "'The Real Thing' Is Here with Gillespie," *Michigan Chronicle,* 14 June 1947, 17. The recording *Dizzy Gillespie: The Complete RCA Victor Recordings* (reissued in 1995 on CD; Bluebird 07863–66528–2) gives us an idea of what listeners heard that night.

51. Carter, talk at Great American Music Hall, 1979.

52. Gillespie and Fraser, *To Be or Not to Bop,* 350–51.

53. This explains why Carter mistakenly attributed Gillespie's not having hired

her to a preference for male vocalists. See Linda Prince, "Betty Carter: Bebopper Breathes Fire," *Down Beat,* 3 May 1979, 13.

54. McRae, *Dizzy Gillespie,* 44.

55. Shipton, *Groovin' High,* 157.

56. For a transcription of Ella Fitzgerald's first scat chorus on "Oh, Lady Be Good," recorded on 18 March 1947, see Porter and Ullman, *Jazz,* 426.

57. McRae, *Dizzy Gillespie,* 44.

58. Bobby McFerrin, "Take the A Train," on *The Voice* (Elektra/Musician 60366, 7559–60366–2 [CD]).

59. Nolan, "Declaration of Independence," 24.

60. Guntern, *Risk-Taking,* 46.

61. Noble, "Special Moments," 1.

62. Noble, "Special Moments," 3.

63. Taylor, *Notes and Tones,* 272.

64. Carter, interview by Yaple, Brooklyn, 1980.

65. Santoro, "Look What We Got," 62.

66. Carter, interview by Yaple, Brooklyn, 1980. While members of his band were known to use drugs, Gillespie disapproved, and he was known to fire musicians if drug use impaired their performance.

67. Russell, *Bird Lives,* 252. See also Phil Schaap, *The Complete Dean Benedetti Recordings of Charlie Parker* (Mosaic Records, MD7–129 [August 1990]). Schaap's discography for this boxed set documents a 21 December club date that Parker's quintet played at El Sino.

68. "Stemmin' with Steve," *Michigan Chronicle,* 27 December 1947, 13; and "Bebop Clique Pays Homage," *Michigan Chronicle,* 3 January 1948, 11. The often repeated story of Bird's broken engagement in November seems apocryphal given that the press made no mention at all of his appearance. The less than enthusiastic writing on Parker may have resulted from the change in the paper's editorial staff—the previous entertainment writers had heartily supported the direction jazz was taking.

69. Ken Vail, *Bird's Diary: The Life of Charlie Parker, 1945–1955* (Surrey: Castle, 1996), 34.

70. Carter, interview by Yaple, Brooklyn, 1980.

71. Taylor, *Notes and Tones,* 273.

72. Ullman, "On Jazz: Betty Carter," 72.

73. Brian Priestley, *Charlie Parker* (Tunbridge Wells, England: Spellmount, 1984), 57.

74. Taylor, *Notes and Tones,* 273 and Carter, interview by Yaple, Brooklyn, 1980. Carter recalled skipping school to attend this rehearsal, but presumably she would have graduated the preceding June.

75. Noble, "Special Moments," 3.

76. Interview of Carter conducted on KJAZ radio during the first week of December 1979, transcribed by Matthew Yaple. See also Taylor, *Notes and Tones,* 273.

77. Taylor, *Notes and Tones,* 273.

78. Carter, "Jazz Talk."
79. Carter, "Jazz Talk."
80. Carter, interview by Yaple, Brooklyn, 1980.
81. Yusef A. Saleem, "Spotlight On: Betty Carter," *Journal and Guide* (Norfolk, Va.), 23 September 1981, 17.
82. Carter, "Jazz Talk."

Chapter 3

1. See Stowe, *Swing Changes,* 174, for more about singers in big bands.
2. It was significant to Malcolm X that so prominent an African American as Lionel Hampton stood up for black pride by not having his hair straightened, or "conked." Alex Haley and Malcolm X, *The Autobiography of Malcolm X: As Told to Alex Haley* (1964; rpt. New York: Ballantine, 1999), 57, 113–14.
3. Graciela Rava, "Betty Carter a Contrechant," *Jazz Magazine,* (February 1980): 40–43, 64; translated by Danielle Walker.
4. Decca 24248.
5. Noble, "Special Moments," 4. Brown's name appears incorrectly as "Winnie" in the transcript of this and other interviews.
6. Carter, interview by Yaple, Brooklyn, 1980.
7. Carter, interview by Yaple, Brooklyn, 1980.
8. Carter, interview by Yaple, Brooklyn, 1980. See also Hampton and Haskins, *Hamp,* 94.
9. Noble, "Special Moments," 3. Charlie Fowlkes went on to manage Wini Brown, who would have a minor hit on Billboard's R&B chart called "Be Anything (but Be Mine)," released in May 1952 on the Mercury label.
10. Carter, interview by Yaple, Brooklyn, 1980.
11. See Rainer E. Lotz and Ulrich Neuert, *The AFRS "Jubilee" Transcription Programs: An Exploratory Discography* (Frankfurt am Main: Ruecker, 1985). Many thanks to Lewis Porter for alerting me to Carter's presence on these AFRS broadcasts, the first recorded examples of her work, and for making them available to me.
12. Noble, "Special Moments," 3–4.
13. Noble, "Special Moments," 3–4.
14. Hampton and Haskins, *Hamp,* 94.
15. Hampton and Haskins, *Hamp,* 78.
16. Hampton and Haskins, *Hamp,* 79.
17. Carter, interview on KJAZ, 1979.
18. David Hinckley, "Betty Carter, Real Live," *Daily News Magazine,* 24 January 1988, 12.
19. Peter Vacher, "Buckner, Milt(on Brent)," *New Grove Dictionary of Jazz,* 166.
20. Other players Carter mentioned (in interview by Yaple, Brooklyn, 1980) who did not achieve prominence include Johnny Boyd, Walter Williams on trumpet, and the Japanese trombone player Paul Higaki, whom she claimed to have discovered for Hampton.
21. Noble, "Special Moments," 5; Paris's nickname, "Skylark," came from a tune

with the same name that he recorded in his first session as a leader in 1945 . Sonny Parker also recorded with Wes Montgomery around the time they were both with Hampton.

22. Pat Harris, "Hamp Packs Reopened Regal," *Down Beat,* 25 March 1949, 3.
23. Hampton and Haskins, *Hamp,* 94.
24. Carter, interview by Yaple, Brooklyn, 1980.
25. Carter, "Jazz Talk."
26. Bryant Mason, "Mom Is a Chanteuse," *Daily News,* 8 September 1975.
27. Taylor, *Notes and Tones,* 274.
28. Carter, talk at Laney Community College, Oakland, 1979.
29. Bill Crow, *Jazz Anecdotes* (New York: Oxford University Press, 1990), 294, 296; Ira Gitler, *Swing to Bop: An Oral History of The Transition in Jazz in the 1940s,* (New York: Oxford University Press, 1985), 88.
30. Taylor, *Notes and Tones,* 271. See also Prince, "Betty Carter: Bebopper Breathes Fire," 13.
31. Carter, interview by the author.
32. Carter, interview by Yaple, Brooklyn, 1980.
33. Crow, *Jazz Anecdotes,* 63.
34. Howard McGhee lasted a only few weeks (Gitler, *Swing to Bop,* 14, 87, 217).
35. Hampton and Haskins, *Hamp,* 93.
36. Hampton and Haskins, *Hamp,* 79. Malcolm X held Gladys's business ability in high regard, citing this incident as an example. See Haley, *Autobiography of Malcolm X,* 119, 113–14.
37. Prince, "Betty Carter: Bebopper Breathes Fire," 13.
38. Hampton and Haskins, *Hamp,* 93.
39. Santoro, "Look What We Got," 62.
40. Hampton and Haskins, *Hamp,* 93.
41. Mason, "Mom Is a Chanteuse."
42. Hampton and Haskins, *Hamp,* 93.
43. Stowe, *Swing Changes,* 174.
44. Hampton and Haskins, *Hamp,* 87.
45. Carter, interview by Yaple, Brooklyn, 1980.
46. Santoro, "Look What We Got," 62.
47. Carter, talk at Laney Community College, Oakland, 1979. See also Carter, interview by Yaple, Brooklyn, 1980.
48. Hampton and Haskins, *Hamp,* 94. See also Carter, interview by Yaple, Brooklyn, 1980.
49. Gladys received composer and lyricist credit for certain tunes, but this was a common ploy used by publishers to retain more of the revenue from a song's copyright, in the event that, for example, another band covered it. She may even have sung on a rare number or two, but aside from this she really had no musical connection to the band's activities.
50. Carter, interview by Yaple, Brooklyn, 1980.
51. Nolan, "Declaration of Independence," 24.
52. Nolan, "Declaration of Independence," 24. See also Carter, "Jazz Talk."

53. Taylor, *Notes and Tones,* 271.

54. Carter, talk at Laney Community College, Oakland, 1979.

55. See Hampton and Haskins, *Hamp,* 82, 203. Herbie Fields, whom Bobby Plater replaced, was with the band until at least May 1945, while Plater does not appear in Hampton's discography until the end of 1945. See also Chris Sheridan, "Plater, Bobby," in *New Grove Dictionary of Jazz,* 989.

56. Prince, "Betty Carter: Bebopper Breathes Fire," 13. See also Carter, interview by Yaple, Brooklyn, 1980.

57. Taylor, *Notes and Tones,* 271.

58. Prince, "Betty Carter: Bebopper Breathes Fire," 13.

59. Prince, "Betty Carter: Bebopper Breathes Fire," 13.

60. Capitol 1184.

61. Taylor, *Notes and Tones,* 271.

62. Taylor, *Notes and Tones,* 271.

63. Janet Thurlow, interview by the author, 2 December 1998.

64. Prince, "Betty Carter: Bebopper Breathes Fire," 13.

65. Hinckley, "Betty Carter, Real Live," 12.

66. As Will Friedwald (*Jazz Singing,* 404) has observed, for such singers as Dinah Washington (with whom Hampton recorded on one session, in New York, on 29 December 1943, accompanied by a sextet), Jackie Paris, Joe Williams, and Jimmy Scott, little recorded evidence exists of their time with the band.

67. Jubilee no. 307, which Lotz and Neuert, *AFRS "Jubilee" Transcription Programs,* date as circa October 1948.

68. Jubilee no. 321, approximately December 1948 (by which time the band had returned to the East Coast). Jubilee Broadcast no. 319, presumably from approximately January 1949, contains the same performance of "I'll Dance at Your Wedding." While Lotz and Neuert, *AFRS "Jubilee" Transcription Programs,* give it a distinct reference number, from the discography it is clear that the broadcasts were put together by assembling selections from different performances.

69. Hampton and Haskins, *Hamp,* discography.

70. Lotz and Neuert, *AFRS "Jubilee" Transcription Programs,* claim this was recorded in Hollywood around February 1949, which seems unlikely, given the band's touring schedule.

71. Savoy SJL2232.

72. Hampton was especially fond of Johnson's solo, having quoted its opening measures in a version of "Cobb's Idea."

73. A drummer himself, Hampton liked this style of drumming. Jack Tracy writing in *Down Beat* (30 December 1949, 4) complained that "you have to overlook the fact that Ellis Bartee is told to play two-beat drums. Hardly inspiring."

74. While the connection between rhythmic value and vowel length may seem tautological, composers and lyricists do not always correlate the law of agogics to prosody.

75. Leslie Gourse, *Louis' Children: American Jazz Singers* (New York: William Morrow, 1984).

76. Gourse, *Louis' Children,* 145. In this passage Terry goes on to observe,

"We've found that the most successful way to teach improvisation and phrasing with an instrument is to make the kids sing first. . . . Maybe knowing how to articulate, manipulate and attack on instruments, is an ally for scatting."

77. Jubilee Broadcast no. 327, ca. February 1949.

78. Savoy 683 (also issued as Savoy 799, 1143, and 1557). See Joel Whitburn, *Top R&B Singles, 1942–1988* (Menomonee Falls, Wis.: Record Research, 1988), 447.

79. Specialty 328 (Whitburn, *Top R&B Singles,* 293).

80. Hampton and Haskins, *Hamp,* 94.

81. Carter, "Jazz Talk."

82. Whitburn, *Top R&B Singles,* 180.

83. Roger Kinkle, *The Complete Encyclopedia of Popular Music and Jazz, 1900–1950* (New Rochelle: Arlington House, 1974).

84. Carter, interview by the author. See also "The High Mark of the Lionel Hamptons," *Color,* January–February 1951, 32.

85. "Cobb's Idea" was first recorded in 31 January on MCA but never issued, and recorded again on 9 September 1946 but not issued until much later (on *Hamp: The Legendary Decca Recordings of Lionel Hampton,* GRD 2–652). Another version in the Hampton discography occurs after Carter left the band in September 1951 (LP: Camay CA 3019; New World, NW 5019).

86. Data concerning one other possible recording by Carter in this period suggest that she participated in a recording session for the Bullet label in 1950, in Memphis (Walter Bruyninckx, "Betty Carter," in *60 Years of Recorded Jazz* [Mechelen, Belgium: Bruyninckx, 1979]). The fact that Carter's mentor, Bobby Plater, led the session increases the likelihood of her involvement. Carter's role in the session remains unclear, however, and she had no recollection of having participated in it.

87. Ted Hallock, "Hamp's Digging New Sounds: 'Bi-Noral,' Girl Tenorist, Etc.," *Down Beat,* 17 December 1953, 10.

Chapter 4

1. Carter, interview by Kuhl, 7–8.
2. Carter, interview by Yaple, Brooklyn, 1980.
3. Carter, "Jazz Talk."
4. Ullman, "On Jazz: Betty Carter," 23–25.
5. Carter, "Jazz Talk."
6. Carter, talk at Great American Music Hall, 1979. The expression "you do your thing" in this quote echoes the lyrics to a song from *The Audience with Betty Carter,* "Sounds (Movin' On)," which evokes the bustle and excitement of urban living.
7. Carter, interview by Yaple, Brooklyn, 1980.
8. Miles Davis and Quincy Troupe, *Miles: The Autobiography* (New York: Simon and Schuster, 1989), 145.
9. Carter, interview by Yaple, Brooklyn, 1980.
10. Carter, interview by Yaple, Brooklyn, 1980.
11. A term supposedly invented by Jerry Wexler for *Billboard* magazine in 1949.

12. Ullman, "On Jazz: Betty Carter."

13. Gourse, *Louis' Children,* 331.

14. Gourse, *Louis' Children,* 331.

15. Ullman, "On Jazz: Betty Carter," 75. See also Whitburn, *Top R&B Singles,* 31.

16. Grime, *Jazz Voices,* 166.

17. Carter, "Jazz Talk."

18. Carter, interview by Yaple, Brooklyn, 1980.

19. Carter, interview by Yaple, Brooklyn, 1980; Ullman, "On Jazz: Betty Carter"; and *New York Amsterdam News,* 3 May 1952, 11.

20. Primack, "Profile: Walter Davis, Jr."

21. Carter, interview by Yaple, Brooklyn, 1980.

22. Carter, "Jazz Talk."

23. Jose, "Betty Carter," *Variety,* 1 October 1952. The reviewer refers to the venue only as "Apollo, N.Y.," but Carter's first solo appearance at the Apollo Theater did not come until early in 1953.

24. Taylor, *Notes and Tones,* 278.

25. Dale Fitzgerald, *George "Big Nick" Nicholas,* Jazz Oral History Project (Newark, N.J.: Institute of Jazz Studies, 1980), 31. Many thanks to Lewis Porter for drawing this passage to my attention.

26. Carter, "Jazz Talk."

27. Carter, interview by Yaple, Brooklyn, 1980.

28. Max Jones, *Talking Jazz* (New York: W. W. Norton, 1987), 258–59.

29. Carter, "Jazz Talk."

30. Ullman, "On Jazz: Betty Carter."

31. Tina Pratt, "A Dancer on the Road," *Jazz Spotlite News: African-American Classical Music/Jazz,* fall–winter 1981, spring–summer 1982, 24. Thanks to editor Jim Harrison for giving me a copy of this hard-to-find newspaper.

32. Gourse, *Louis' Children,* 330.

33. Carter, interview by Yaple, Brooklyn, 1980.

34. *New York Amsterdam News,* 10 August 1955, 19. Many thanks to Lewis Porter for making available to me this and numerous other press notices.

35. Carter, interview by Yaple, Brooklyn, 1980.

36. Gourse, *Louis' Children,* 330; See also Ullman, "On Jazz: Betty Carter."

37. Mason, "Mom Is a Chanteuse."

38. Leonard Feather, "Betty Carter Be-Bops to the White House," *Los Angeles Times,* 23 August 1981, 68.

39. Sam Dockery, interview by the author, 4 February 1999.

40. Carter, talk at Laney Community College, Oakland, 1979.

41. Although the trombonist played in Lionel Hampton's band around 1956, the two musicians are not related to one another.

42. Carter, talk at Laney Community College, Oakland, 1979.

43. Carter, talk at Laney Community College, Oakland, 1979.

44. Carter, talk at Laney Community College, Oakland, 1979.

45. Carter, talk at Great American Music Hall, 1979.

46. Carter, "Jazz Talk."

47. Carter, interview by Yaple, Brooklyn, 1980.

48. Charlie "Little Jazz" Ferguson is also given as a leader of the session, even though the record came out under King Pleasure's name.

49. Carter, interview on KJAZ, 1979.

50. Carter, interview by Yaple, Brooklyn, 1980.

51. "'Red Top' Bows Out; All-Girl Group at Sino," *Michigan Chronicle,* 11 October 1947, 18.

52. For more on vocalese, see Friedwald, *Jazz Singing,* 233f. In *Lost Chords: White Musicians and Their Contribution to Jazz, 1915–1945.* (New York: Oxford University Press, 1999), 456–57, 806, Richard M. Sudhalter identifies early instances of this practice by Bee Palmer in 1928 and Marion Harris in 1934. Betty Carter claimed that when Annie Ross left the group, Jon Hendricks approached her about a Lambert, Hendricks, and Carter collaboration.

53. Carter, interview by Yaple, Brooklyn, 1980.

54. Will Friedwald erroneously claims that Carter replaced a piano part originally played by Blossom Dearie, but Dearie did not sing on either Ammons's or Pleasure's version of "Red Top." Ira Gitler may have the key to this confusion: On "one of Pleasure's several remakes of 'I'm in the Mood for Love,' . . . the vocal group [takes] the role played by Blossom Dearie on the Prestige recording that started it all" (liner notes to *Moody's Mood for Love,* Blue Note CDP 7 84463 2.) Carter claimed that King Pleasure had originally planned to use Blossom Dearie on "Red Top" but offers no explanation for why he chose her instead (interview by the author, 25 October 1994).

55. This tessitura forced Carter to take certain pitches either at the top of her chest voice and risk cracking a note, or low in her head voice, which had a thin sound at this stage in her career.

56. Carter, interview on KJAZ, 1979.

57. Carter, interview by Yaple, Brooklyn, 1980.

58. Ullman, "On Jazz: Betty Carter."

59. Ted Fox, *Showtime at the Apollo* (1983; rpt. New York: Da Capo, 1993), 269.

60. Grime, *Jazz Voices,* 82.

61. Carter, interview by Yaple, Brooklyn, 1980. See also *New York Amsterdam News,* 14 February 1953, 26. Almost a year later to the day she would perform there on the same bill as Lionel Hampton (*New York Amsterdam News,* 13 February 1954, 8).

62. Prince, "Betty Carter: Bebopper Breathes Fire," 43.

63. Hinckley, "Betty Carter, Real Live," 12. See also Carter, interview on KJAZ, 1979.

64. Van Rooyen and Brodowski, "Betty's Groove," 28–33. Also see Prince, "Betty Carter: Bebopper Breathes Fire," 13–14.

65. Santoro, "Look What We Got."

66. Carter, talk at Great American Music Hall, 1979.

67. Carter, talk at Laney Community College, Oakland, 1979.

68. Santoro, "Look What We Got."

69. Hinckley, "Betty Carter, Real Live," 12.

70. Santoro, "Look What We Got."

71. Chester Rentie had been her booking agent. A manager typically plays a more active role than an agent in guiding an artist's career.

72. Carter, interview by the author.

73. Carter, interview by the author.

74. Carter, interview by Yaple, Brooklyn, 1980; and Tadd Dameron, *The Clifford Brown Memorial Album,* Prestige LP7055.

75. *Meet Betty Carter and Ray Bryant,* Columbia/Legacy CK 64936, was reissued in 1996 with previously unissued material.

76. Feather, "Betty Carter Be-Bops."

77. "Betty Carter–Ray Bryant," in *Down Beat: Jazz Record Reviews, 1956,* ed. Jack Tracy (Chicago: Maher, 1957), 48.

78. "Betty Carter–Ray Bryant," 48.

79. "Betty Carter–Ray Bryant," 48.

80. Carter, "Jazz Talk."

81. Hinckley, "Betty Carter, Real Live," 13.

82. Carter, "Jazz Talk."

Chapter 5

1. Carter, interview by the author.

2. Gryce formed the two separate publishing companies to deal with the two major collection agencies, Broadcast Music Incorporated (BMI) and the Association for Composers, Authors and Publishers (ASCAP). Melotone was a BMI company, Totem an ASCAP one.

3. Many thanks to Noal Cohen for sharing his original research into Gryce's life and work, in a conversation with the author, 2 March 1999. Cohen is currently preparing a biography of Gryce with coauthor Michael Fitzgerald.

4. The composer credit is under Gryce's Muslim name, Basheer Qusim. Gryce was apparently not affiliated with the Nation of Islam. See Noal Cohen and Michael Fitzgerald, "Emotional Eloquence: An Historical Overview of Gigi Gryce," *Coda,* January–February 1999, 26–28.

5. Columbia Records did not release this date until 1980, with the reissue of Carter's sessions with Ray Bryant under the title *Betty Carter–Social Call,* Columbia 64936; reissued in 1990 as CBS Special Products A 36425. Official Records released the material (unofficially) as *The Bebop Girl.*

6. Carter, interview by Yaple, Brooklyn, 1980.

7. Michael Cuscuna, liner notes, *Meet Betty Carter and Ray Bryant.*

8. Andy Bey, interview by the author, 11 January 1999; Grachan Moncur III, interview by the author, 3 April 1999.

9. Moncur, interview.

10. Galen Gart and Roy C. Ames, *Duke/Peacock Records: An Illustrated History with Discography* (Milford, N.H.: Nickel, 1990), 199.

11. Gart and Ames, *Duke/Peacock Records,* 8.

12. Gart and Ames, *Duke/Peacock Records,* 37. The release of Willie Mae Thornton's "Hound Dog" (Peacock 1612) in 1953 established Peacock as a major independent label and laid the groundwork for Elvis Presley's 1956 hit (ibid., 53–56).

13. Gart and Ames, *Duke/Peacock Records,* 58.

14. McLarney, "Betty Carter: The 'in' Singer." According to Gart and Ames, *Duke/Peacock Records,* Dave Rolnick was Eastern promotions manager and A&R chief at this time, but Carter could have been referring to Robey, Al Grey, or even Gigi Gryce, whom Tommy Gryce described as the date's A&R man. Carter included Grey as one of the musicians involved in the date (interview by Yaple, Brooklyn, 1980), although he is not listed in the discographies.

15. In an interview with radio host Phil Schaap, WKCR-FM (New York), 2 July 1997, Gryce's brother Tommy suggested that the discographic data for these sessions are incomplete and that the entire recording used a full horn section. Thanks to Noal Cohen for bringing this interview to my attention. Tommy Gryce (misspelled Bryce on the liner notes) provided the chart for "The Blue Bird of Happiness" (Tommy Gryce, interview by the author, 11 January 1999).

16. Danny Bank, interview by the author, 11 January 1999.

17. Gary Giddins, "Betty Carter Sings Like a Woman," *Village Voice,* 1 November 1976. The USSR launched the first sputnik on 4 October 1957.

18. Gart and Ames, *Duke/Peacock Records,* 162.

19. McLarney, "Betty Carter: The 'in' Singer," 19.

20. Carter, "Jazz Talk."

21. Carter, interview by Lyons.

22. Ullman, "On Jazz: Betty Carter," 72. See also Davis and Troupe, *Miles,* 105–6.

23. Davis and Troupe, *Miles,* 133.

24. Carter, interview by Yaple, Brooklyn, 1980.

25. Carter, talk at Laney Community College, Oakland, 1979.

26. Davis and Troupe, *Miles,* 131. Speaking in 1989, Davis was partly reacting to Carter's open denunciation of his conversion to fusion in the 1970s. Even in her criticism of him, however, her respect for his musicianship shone through.

27. Davis and Troupe, *Miles,* 173–74.

28. Carter, interview by the author.

29. Carter, talk at Laney Community College, Oakland, 1979. See also Ken Vail, *Miles' Diary: The Life of Miles Davis, 1947–1961* (Surrey: Castle, 1997), 131; *Village Voice,* 11 March 1959, 9; *Chicago Defender,* 26 December 1959, 12; and *New York Amsterdam News,* 30 July 1960, 17. Carter also recalled performing at the Royal Theater in Baltimore.

30. Fox, *Showtime at the Apollo,* 268–70.

31. Barbara J. Kukla, *Swing City: Newark Nightlife, 1925–50* (Philadelphia: Temple University Press, 1991), 240.

32. Kukla, *Swing City,* 236.

33. James Romeo Redding, interview by the author, 7 June 1999.

34. Ray Charles with David Ritz, *Brother Ray: Ray Charles' Own Story* (1978; rpt. New York: Da Capo, 1992), 168, 221–22. Charles recalled this taking place in 1957, long after she had left Hampton.

35. Carter, interview by Yaple, Oakland, 1979. See also Santoro, "Look What We Got."

36. See Lewis Porter, *John Coltrane: His Life and Music* (Ann Arbor: University of Michigan Press, 1998), 140; and Michael Lydon, *Ray Charles: Man and Music* (New York: Riverhead Books, 1998), 164f.

37. Fox, *Showtime at the Apollo*, 246–47.

38. Lydon, *Ray Charles*, 165–68.

39. Robert Palmer, *New York Times*, 21 November, 1980.

40. Lydon, *Ray Charles*, 165–68. See also Charles, *Brother Ray*, 197.

41. Lydon, *Ray Charles*, 178.

42. Lydon, *Ray Charles*, 181. Quincy Jones was doing some arranging for Charles then (they had known each other years before in Seattle) and may have provided another bridge between Carter and Charles.

43. Jack Bradley and Jeann Failows, "New York," *Coda*, June 1960, 16–17.

44. *New York Amsterdam News*, 30 July 1960, 17. See also Carter, talk at Laney Community College, Oakland, 1979.

45. Recorded on 18, 19, and 30 August and released as ABC-Paramount S 363. Later reissued with the Peacock material in 1976 under the title *What a Little Moonlight Can Do* on Impulse! A (S) 9321, and again in 1992 by MCA Records as *Betty Carter: I Can't Help It* (GRD-114).

46. Sid Feller, interview by the author, 31 January 1999.

47. Feller could not recall specific instances, but the tag at the end of "Remember" (built on the standard turnaround changes: $iii^7(\flat 5)–V^7/ii–ii^7–V^7$) or the tempo change at the end of "At Sundown" [2:23] would likely have been decided upon in the routining, as well as the key change at the end of "Stormy Weather." In addition, the insertion of the metric disruption toward the end of "Jazz (Ain't Nothin' but Soul)" [1:34–1:39], which goes from one measure of 2/4 to three of 3/4 to one of 1/4, probably originated in Carter's planning with Feller.

48. Feller, interview.

49. Incidentally, Gryce's Melotone Publishing held the song's copyright. Thanks to Noal Cohen for drawing this to my attention.

50. The session was taped on a two-track machine with the signal from Carter's microphone recorded on both tracks. On playback, her voice would therefore sound "in the middle," exploiting the benefits of stereo sound. In contrast, the brass was recorded on one track and the saxes on the other. When the listener hears the resulting recording, brass and saxes play off one another antiphonally while the voice, in both speakers, takes center stage.

51. Released as *The Genius of Ray Charles*, Atlantic LP1312. See also, Lydon, *Ray Charles*, 158.

52. Bob Porter, liner notes to *Betty Carter: I Can't Help It*, Impulse! GRD 114, 5.

53. Friedwald, *Jazz Singing*, 404.

54. Carter, interview by Yaple, Brooklyn, 1980. See also Nolan, "Declaration of Independence," 54.

55. David Ritz, liner notes to *Ray Charles: Genius + Soul (The 50th Anniversary Collection)*, Rhino R272859, 22.

56. Ritz, liner notes to *Ray Charles: Genius + Soul,* 22.

57. While straddling the abyss that increasingly separated jazz and pop, Charles retained the respect of jazz musicians and critics partly by promoting jazz at a time when it was becoming less and less profitable to do so.

58. Ralph Gleason, "Caught: Ray Charles Orchestra," *Down Beat,* 16 March 1961, 36–37.

59. *New York Amsterdam News,* 1 October 1960, 16.

60. Lydon, *Ray Charles,* 184–85.

61. McLarney, "Betty Carter: The 'in' Singer."

62. Nolan, "Declaration of Independence," 23. See also Carter, talk at Laney Community College, Oakland, 1979.

Chapter 6

1. Santoro, "Look What We Got."

2. Nolan, "Declaration of Independence," 23.

3. James Redding, interview.

4. Lydon, *Ray Charles,* 193.

5. Lydon, *Ray Charles,* 196, 197.

6. John S. Wilson, "Two Concerts Given by Ray Charles: Singer-Musician Brings Big Troupe to Carnegie Hall," *New York Times,* 1 May 1961; and George T. Simon, "Ray Charles Sings Seven Tunes in Concert at Carnegie Hall," *New York Herald Tribune,* 1 May 1961.

7. Wilson, "Two Concerts Given."

8. Simon, "Charles Sings Seven Tunes."

9. Santoro, "Look What We Got." See also Graham Lock, "In Her Own Sweet Way: The Great Jazz Singer: Energy, Adventure, and Aggression," *Wire,* February 1986, 33.

10. Santoro, "Look What We Got."

11. Sid Feller, liner notes to *Ray Charles and Betty Carter,* DCC Compact Classics, DZS-039.

12. Feller, interview.

13. Van Rooyen and Brodowski, "Betty's Groove," 32. Charles had no special reason to keep the arrangements after they made the record, so he gave them to Carter. This gift amounted to a considerable savings for her.

14. Feller, liner notes to *Ray Charles and Betty Carter.*

15. Lydon, *Ray Charles,* 199.

16. Recorded on a two-track machine, the tape required no mix-down; volume levels were therefore adjusted during the performances. Feller followed the score during the taping and warned the engineer right before a particular passage—a solo, for example—needed to be boosted. Feller, interview.

17. McLarney, "Betty Carter: The 'in' Singer."

18. Capitol 567.

19. Decca 24644.

20. Betty T. Miles, *The Miles Chart Display,* vol. 1: *Top 100—1955–1970* (Boul-

der, Colo.: Convex Industries, 1971), 400. See also Ullman, "On Jazz: Betty Carter," 71.

21. Dreyfuss, "Betty 'Slow Pop' Carter," 18.

22. *New York Amsterdam News,* 17 June 1961, 19. Originally a one-week engagement, it was extended because Charles was drawing such huge crowds (Lydon, *Ray Charles,* 199).

23. Charles would go on to record Scott on his newly formed Tangerine Label in the following year. The record, *Falling in Love Is Wonderful*—which had a big influence on Carter—would ultimately be withdrawn due to Scott's contractual obligations to Savoy Records.

24. Henry Kahn, "I Could Sing as Soon as I Could Walk: I Live to Sing, Says Ray Charles," *Melody Maker,* 28 October 1961, 13.

25. *New York Amsterdam News,* 2 September 1961, 17.

26. Alfred T. Hendricks, "A Singer's Credo: He Voices the Troubles He's Known," *New York Post,* 4 January 1962, 40.

27. Edward Kosner, "Singer Ray Charles Held on Drug Charge," *New York Post,* 4 November 1961.

28. "Drop One of Three Charges against Ray Charles," *New York Post,* 13 November 1961.

29. At one time they were stored in the MCA vault, but according to record producer Michael Cuscuna, who oversaw the reissue of *The Modern Sound,* the masters have been lost (interview by the author, 18 December 1998). See also *Betty Carter: I Can't Help It,* Impulse, GRD-114, liner notes. Carter would record "I Cry Alone" again in 1982.

30. *New York Amsterdam News,* 10 February 1962, 17.

31. Lydon, *Ray Charles,* 218.

32. Carter, interview by the author. On Saturday, 24 February, Monte Kay presented Carter at the Kaufman Concert Hall with the John Coltrane Quintet and Clara Ward (*New York Amsterdam News,* 17 February 1962, 17).

33. Carter, "Jazz Talk."

34. Van Rooyen and Brodowski, "Betty's Groove," 31.

35. Ted Joans, "Betty Carter," *Coda,* March 1976, 10–11.

36. Carter, "Jazz Talk."

37. Bob Weinberg, "The Days of Bags and Betty Bebop," *Miami New Times,* 20 October 1994.

38. Charles, *Brother Ray,* 36–37.

39. Charles, *Brother Ray,* 221–22.

40. Charles, *Brother Ray,* 221–22.

41. Lydon, *Ray Charles,* 168–69.

42. Joel Dorn, interview by the author, 3 December 1998.

43. Nolan, "Declaration of Independence," 23.

44. Atco 6254.

45. These recordings, which were later lost in a fire at Atlantic's warehouse, were renditions of songs Carter recorded on other occasions, for different labels. The version of "You're a Sweetheart" that she cut two and a half years later for United Artists,

for example, initially went unissued as well, but finally appeared on a 1993 Capitol reissue. She recorded "What's New" in 1969 and then again in 1987 as a duet with Carmen McRae. The unissued Atco session also included another version of "Moonlight in Vermont."

46. Mark Jacobson, "Betty Carter Is Alive in Bed-Stuy," *Village Voice,* 18 August 1975, 100.

47. Kenny Washington, interview by the author, 12 January 1999; and JoAnne Jimenez, interview by the author, 10 June 1999.

48. Carter, interview by Yaple, Brooklyn, 1980.

49. Recalling the beginning of her ballad "I Can't Help It," the song's a capella opening may have been her idea as well.

50. Carter, interview by the author.

51. Carter, interview on KJAZ, 1979.

52. Nolan, "Declaration of Independence," 23.

53. Oliver Nelson, *Blues and the Absolute Truth,* New York: MCA/Impulse! MCAD-5659/JVC 468, 23 February 1961, liner notes.

54. Nolan, "Declaration of Independence," 23.

55. Carter, interview on KJAZ, 1979.

56. McLarney, "Betty Carter: The 'in' Singer."

57. Carter, "Jazz Talk."

58. James Redding, interview.

59. Dockery, interview.

60. Larry Ridley, interview by the author, 2 February 1999.

61. "Sonny Rollins Meets the Japanese Press," *Down Beat,* 19 December 1963, 16.

62. "Sonny Rollins Meets Press."

63. "Sonny Rollins Meets Press."

64. McLarney, "Betty Carter: The 'in' Singer," 19.

65. Many thanks to Lewis Porter for making this tape available to me.

66. Carter, interview by Yaple, Brooklyn, 1980. The transcriber of this interview mistook Billy Hart for Billy Harper.

Chapter 7

1. Fredric Dannen, *Hit Men: Power Brokers and Fast Money inside the Music Business* (New York: Vintage, 1990), 44–47.

2. Joel Dorn, interview by the author, 6 January 1995. Also mentioned in the liner notes to *'Round Midnight,* Atco CD7 80453–2.

3. Dreyfuss, "Betty 'Slow Pop' Carter," 18.

4. Louis Armstrong took pride in topping the Beatles on the charts with "Hello Dolly," and Ella Fitzgerald continued to enjoy success during the 1960s, but both performers did so by adding pop songs to their books. Such well-established singers, who did not have to make a choice between pop stardom and loyalty to jazz, enjoyed a loyal mainstream following that buffered them somewhat from jazz's loss of market share.

5. McLarney, “Betty Carter: The ‘in’ Singer,” 38.

6. Atlantic 1289. Thanks to David Kagan for bringing this record to my attention.

7. Carter, “Jazz Talk.”

8. Tom Schultheiss, *A Day in the Life: The Beatles Day by Day, 1960–1970* (Ann Arbor: Pierian Press, 1980), 81.

9. Schultheiss, *Day in the Life,* 111.

10. Carter, “Jazz Talk.”

11. Carter, talk at Great American Music Hall, 1979.

12. Ullman, “On Jazz: Betty Carter.”

13. In *Ebony* magazine, Sinatra stated unequivocally that “it was Billie Holiday whom I first heard in 52nd Street clubs in the early ’30s who was and still remains the greatest single musical influence on me” (this quote appears, edited, in Donald Clarke, *Wishing on the Moon* (New York: Penguin, 1994), 96. See also Stuart Nicholson, *Billie Holiday* (Boston: Northeastern University Press, 1995), 134.

14. Leslie Gourse, *Sassy: The Life of Sarah Vaughan* (New York: Da Capo, 1994), 87.

15. Gourse, *Louis’ Children,* 331.

16. Carter, talk at Great American Music Hall, 1979.

17. Clement Price, “Talkin’ ’bout a Crisis: The History of Black Newark,” *Blue Newark Culture,* December 1989, 28–45.

18. C. Vann Woodward, *The Strange Career of Jim Crow* (New York: Oxford University Press, 1974), vii–viii.

19. Carter, talk at Laney Community College, Oakland, 1979.

20. According to discographer Walter Bruyninckx, Carter performed at Annie’s Place, a club in London owned by Annie Ross, in 1964, but this date is not corroborated elsewhere. (In reference to a visit to Copenhagen, see Ullman, “On Jazz: Betty Carter,” 71.)

21. Leroi Jones (Amiri Imamu Baraka), *Black Music* (1968; rpt. New York: William Morrow, 1998), 117–18. This passage first appeared in *Wild Dog* or *Down Beat.*

22. Bruyninckx claims that Carter recorded the first seven sides in June 1964, but data provided on the reissue’s liner notes give April. On this reissue for United Artists there is previously unreleased material—not produced by Alan Douglas—that was recorded on 4 March and 26 May 1965 at Regent Sound, where Carter would record again nearly a decade later.

23. Michael Cuscuna, who produced the reissue, has surmised that Kenny Burrell played guitar on another session from that same time, but the other musicians who were there have not been identified. Incidentally, Burrell and Bob Cranshaw were among several musicians on the bill when Carter performed in “A Tribute to the Memory of Charlie Parker” on Sunday, 14 March 1965 at the Cafe Au Go Go.

24. Carter, “Jazz Talk.”

25. Van Rooyen and Brodowski, “Betty’s Groove,” 33; Carter, interview by Yaple, Brooklyn, 1980.

26. Ullman, “On Jazz: Betty Carter,” 77–78.

27. Carter, interview by Yaple, Brooklyn, 1980.

28. His full name, Mark Kagle Jason Redding, gave him the same initials as his brother, Myles Kevin James.

29. According to data provided in the Kerner Report, "In four suburban cities—Bloomfield, Harrison, Irvington, and Maplewood—forming an arc around Newark, out of a total population of 150,000, only 1,000 were Negroes." *Report of the National Advisory Commission on Civil Disorders,* Otto Kerner, chairman (Washington, D.C.: National Advisory Commission on Civil Disorders, 1968), 38.

30. *The New Wave in Jazz,* Impulse A 90; McLarney, "Betty Carter: The 'in' Singer." Also mentioned in *Village Voice,* 25 March 1965, 14. Cecil Taylor was billed in the advance press but did not appear.

31. Reprinted in Jones, *Black Music,* 175.

32. Carter, interview by Roberts.

33. Friedwald, *Jazz Singing,* 400.

34. Carter, interview by Yaple, Brooklyn, 1980.

35. McLarney, "Betty Carter: The 'in' Singer."

36. Carter, interview by Yaple, Brooklyn, 1980.

37. *Daily News,* 7 July 1966.

38. *Village Voice,* May 1966, 12; 21 July 1966, 10; 11 August 1966, 16; 3 November 1966, 34; 24 November 1966, 33.

39. Carter, "Jazz Talk."

40. Joel Herson, "Profile: John Hicks," *Down Beat,* 7 June 1979, 32. Also, Hicks's interview with Arnold Jay Smith in "Jazz Insights," 17 November 1998, New School for Social Research.

41. John Hicks, interview by the author, 23 November 1998.

42. Nat Hentoff, "Raising Waxing Criteria," *Down Beat,* 20 October 1966, 10. Many thanks to Lewis Porter for alerting me to this piece.

43. McLarney, "Betty Carter: The 'in' Singer," 38.

44. McLarney, "Betty Carter: The 'in' Singer," 38.

45. McLarney, "Betty Carter: The 'in' Singer," 38.

46. McLarney, "Betty Carter: The 'in' Singer," 38.

47. McLarney, "Betty Carter: The 'in' Singer," 38.

48. McLarney, "Betty Carter: The 'in' Singer," 19.

49. Gourse, *Louis' Children,* 334.

50. Carter, interview by Miller, 37.

51. Mike Hennessey, "Caught in the Act: Antibes Jazz Festival," *Down Beat,* 3 October 1968, 29.

52. Ted Joans, "Votez Carter (Betty)" *Jazz Magazine,* November 1976. The title, "Vote for Carter," is a reference to the presidential election in the States, where Jimmy Carter was running for office against Gerald Ford.

53. James Redding, interview. In this interview Redding expressed regret for having pressured his wife to pursue a hit record, feeling that this pressure contributed to the marriage's dissolution.

54. Myles Redding, interview by the author, 31 March 1999.

55. Carter, talk at Great American Music Hall, 1979.

Chapter 8

1. Taylor, *Notes and Tones,* 277.
2. Taylor, *Notes and Tones,* 277.
3. Van Rooyen and Brodowski, "Betty's Groove," 32.
4. Carter, interview by Yaple, Brooklyn, 1980.
5. Jim Harrison, interview by the author, 2 February 1999.
6. Harrison, interview.
7. Others included, at various times, Arthur Bailey, Hilly Saunders, Bill Mabron, Neil Hamilton, and Sonny Harrison.
8. Harrison named "Big George" from Brooklyn and Aziz Atiz as others who arranged work for Carter then.
9. Harrison, interview.
10. Carter, interview by Yaple, Brooklyn, 1980.
11. Carter, interview by Yaple, Brooklyn, 1980.
12. McRae made a live recording on the Mainstream label (56065) at the Village Gate in 1965, about a month before Carter performed at a benefit concert there for WBAI-FM.
13. Mark Gardner, "Norman Simmons Talks to Mark Gardner: Concluded," *Jazz Monthly,* January 1971, 6.
14. Gardner, "Norman Simmons Talks."
15. Carter, interview by Yaple, Brooklyn, 1980. See also Carter, interview by Kuhl, 9.
16. Stuart Nicholson, liner notes to *Finally—Betty Carter,* Roulette CDP 795332. Simmons and Carter may have started working together while she was still in California.
17. Carter, talk at Laney Community College, Oakland, 1979. Carter has also mentioned Academy Hall as the venue, and there are conflicting discographic data about the site(s) of the live recording, with Bruyninckx's earlier edition identifying only Club Ruby.
18. Nicholson, liner notes to *Finally—Betty Carter.*
19. Tam Fiofori, "Betty Carter: Judson Hall, New York City, New York," *Down Beat,* 30 April 1970, 32. The recordings were made available in 1991 on CD as reissues distributed by EMI. The discussion in the text of the music from this date refers to these CDs, particularly *Finally—Betty Carter* (Roulette CDP 7953332).
20. Fiofori, "Betty Carter: Judson Hall." John Wilson's review in the *New York Times* on 8 December 1969, p. 61—"Jazz Songs Given by Betty Carter: She Links Her Judson Hall Recital to Billie Holiday"—was ambivalent.
21. Fiofori, "Betty Carter: Judson Hall." In his discography Bruyninckx mentions only the last of these three tunes, so the remainder of the medley apparently did not make it onto the tapes that evening.
22. Carter, talk at Laney Community College, Oakland, 1979.
23. Carter, interview by Lyons. Jimmy Scott insisted that he never sang any other way: "I was so long in singing the words that people would say: 'Are you counting?'" (interview by the author, 9 June 1999).

24. Arnold J. Smith, interview by the author, 9 November 1998. By boosting the signal from her microphone when she lowered her volume, or fading down when she sang loud, the sound engineer would only flatten the musical effect she wanted.

25. This was not an unusual technique for an instrumentalist to use. In his version of Cole Porter's "All of You" from his 1964 Philharmonic Hall concert, for example, Miles Davis had similarly used the turnaround.

26. The reviewer reported that Carter "choreographed" the performance "with appropriate gestures to emphasize the mood, pace and intent of the songs," but her movements were largely unplanned. Fiofori, "Betty Carter: Judson Hall."

27. Reaching out to the entire house was so important to Carter that, later in her career, she refused to perform in certain spaces, such as Iridium in Manhattan, because they would limit her impact on the audience. The stage at Iridium, located at the end of a long narrow room, gives the performer direct access only to the front rows of listeners.

28. Carter, "Jazz Talk." In this same interview she also compared her approach to a tennis stroke, saying, "When I play tennis that's one of the things I learned. I can hit the ball low and straight. And then it goes in."

29. Van Rooyen and Brodowski, "Betty's Groove," 30.

30. Carter, interview by Roberts.

31. Singer Tanya Reed, who would later receive coaching from Carter, described how, in rehearsals, the older singer helped her and her sisters develop their own interpretations of a song by getting them to speak the lyrics (interview by the author, 20 August 1999).

32. Carter, interview by Roberts.

33. James Redding, interview.

34. Michael Cuscuna recalled that Randy Weston was also burned by Orville O'Brien when something of Weston's showed up on the Springboard label, which Cuscuna termed "a questionable operation."

35. Carter, interview by the author.

36. Carter, "Jazz Talk."

37. Carter, interview by Yaple, Brooklyn, 1980.

38. James Redding, interview.

39. Carter, "Jazz Talk."

40. A.O., "Betty Carter," *Coda,* July–August 1972, 21.

41. Jim Harrison circulated a flier that reads, "You are cordially invited to attend a special birthday party and celebration for Betty Carter."

42. Carter, interview by Yaple, Brooklyn, 1980. The bleeding she was referring to resulted from inadequate separation in the recorded tracks, with, typically, the drum sounds spilling into microphones intended to pick up he vocal, piano, or bass alone. Such bleeding makes it almost impossible to "fix the mix" by controlling the levels of each track when they are condensed into a stereo format.

43. Carter, interview by Kuhl, 9.

44. Carter, interview on KJAZ, 1979.

45. Carter, interview by Miller.

46. Taylor, *Notes and Tones,* 282.

47. Carter, interview on KJAZ, 1979.

48. Bob Blumenthal, liner notes to the reissue *Betty Carter at the Village Vanguard,* Verve 314-519–851–2, July 1993.

49. Carter, interview on KJAZ, 1979.

50. John Wilson, "Betty Carter Calls Miss Holiday to Mind," *New York Times,* 29 March 1971. There is no record of any tapes that may have been made of this concert.

51. Daniel Mixon, interview by the author, 1 December 1999.

52. A graphic from Harold X. Connolly's *A Ghetto Grows in Brooklyn* (New York: New York University Press, 1977), 133, indicates that in 1970 the population of some locations in Fort Greene was 35–59 percent African American, but in other places as high as 80 percent.

53. Rita Seiden Miller, *Brooklyn, U.S.A.: Fourth Largest City in America* (New York: Brooklyn College Press, 1979), 263, 266. Aside from a small segment of the area's population that lived around Pratt Institute, the residents earned about half the nation's median income level of ten thousand dollars per year, and between 25 and 40 percent of families in the neighborhood were living below the poverty level.

54. "By 1970 over half the borough's 310 schools were . . . more than 75 percent minority . . . and by 1973 whites constituted only 29 percent of the nearly 300,000 total enrollment" (with blacks constituting 43 percent) (Connolly, *Ghetto Grows in Brooklyn,* 221).

55. Barbara Habenstreit, *Fort Greene, U.S.A.* (Indianapolis: Bobbs-Merrill, 1974), 5.

56. Mixon, interview.

57. Jim Sleeper, *The Closest of Strangers: Liberalism and the Politics of Race in New York* (New York: W. W. Norton, 1990), 212. Thanks to Isaac Bauer for pointing this passage out to me.

58. Carter, interview by Yaple, Brooklyn, 1980.

59. Mixon, interview.

60. Carter, interview by Miller, 38.

61. Herb Nolan, "Betty Carter: Unabashed Jazz Singer," *Down Beat,* 7 December 1972, 28.

62. Nolan, "Betty Carter: Unabashed Jazz Singer," 28.

63. Nolan, "Betty Carter: Unabashed Jazz Singer," 28.

64. Nolan, "Betty Carter: Unabashed Jazz Singer," 28.

65. Mixon, interview.

66. Nolan, "Betty Carter: Unabashed Jazz Singer," 28.

67. Nolan, "Betty Carter: Unabashed Jazz Singer," 28.

68. Carter, interview by Miller, 37.

69. Taylor, *Notes and Tones,* 276.

70. Arnie Cheatum, "Magic Moment: Betty Carter," *East West Journal* (Boston), March 1973, 26–27.

71. Carter, "Jazz Talk."

72. Taylor, *Notes and Tones,* 276.

73. Taylor, *Notes and Tones,* 282.

74. Taylor, *Notes and Tones,* 280–81.

75. Bill McLarney, "Boston Digs Betty Carter," *Journal of New England,* November 1975, 24–25.

76. Cheatum, "Magic Moment," 27.

77. Cheatum, "Magic Moment," 26–27.

78. *Coda,* September–October 1973, 24–25.

79. J. R. Taylor, "Riffs: Getting What She Deserves," *Village Voice,* 30 May 1974, 60. She had been planning a second record for her label—in addition to the children's record—as early as February 1972 (see Carter, interview by Miller), but there is no evidence that she took action on these plans until later.

80. Carter, interview by Kuhl, 55.

81. Ferla, interview.

82. She also structured the track assignments of "Children Learn What They Live" so that Mixon could play an introduction on celesta and proceed to play the rest of the tune on piano without a pause or edit (Mixon, interview).

83. Ferla, interview.

84. Carter, interview by Kuhl, 55.

Chapter 9

1. Blumenthal, "Betty Carter Sets Her Own Records," 4.

2. Feather, "Betty Carter Be-Bops." See also *Billboard,* 25 October 1975.

3. Arnold J. Smith, "Jazz Insights," a panel discussion with John Hicks, Kenny Washington, and Curtis Lundy at the New School, 17 November 1998.

4. Carter, interview by Lyons.

5. Carter, interview by Lyons.

6. Ted Joans, "Betty Carter," 10–11. See also McLarney, "Boston Digs Betty Carter," 24–25.

7. Joans, "Betty Carter," 11.

8. McLarney, "Boston Digs Betty Carter," 24.

9. Jacobson, "Alive in Bed-Stuy," 100.

10. Jacobson, "Alive in Bed-Stuy."

11. Blumenthal, "Carter Sets Her Own Records," 4. Also see McLarney, "Boston Digs Betty Carter," 25.

12. Jacobson, "Alive in Bed-Stuy," 100.

13. McLarney, "Boston Digs Betty Carter," 25.

14. Blumenthal, "Carter Sets Her Own Records," 4.

15. Feather, "Betty Carter Be-Bops."

16. Feather, "Betty Carter Be-Bops"; and Carter, interview by Lyons.

17. Carter, interview by Lyons.

18. Mixon, interview. Also J. R. Taylor, "Getting What She Deserves"; and "Daniel Mixon" in *New Grove Dictionary of Jazz,* 783–84.

19. Gourse, *Louis' Children,* 335.

20. Hicks, interview.

21. McLarney, "Boston Digs Betty Carter," 25.

22. Carter, interview by Lyons.

23. Carter, interview by Lyons.

24. Carter, interview by Lyons.

25. Joel Dorn, interview by the author, 8 October 1999.

26. Carter, interview by Lyons.

27. Carter, interview by Lyons.

28. Conrad Silvert, "Betty Carter: Keystone Korner," *Billboard*, 25 October 1975.

29. Todd Barkan of the Keystone Korner also had a role in the deal. He received a percentage point of the royalties for Kirk's signing with Warner Brothers, as he did for other artists he brought to Krasnow, and he appeared as a percussionist on Kirk's first record for that label. Todd Barkan, interview by the author, 8 October 1999.

30. Carter, interview by Lyons.

31. Dorn, interview, 8 October 1999.

32. Carter, interview by Lyons.

33. Mason, "Mom Is a Chanteuse." See also Joans, "Betty Carter," 11.

34. Hicks, interview.

35. Hicks, interview.

36. Hicks, interview.

37. Max Gordon, *Live at the Vanguard* (1978; rpt. New York: Da Capo, 1980) 57.

38. Joans, "Betty Carter," 11.

39. Van Rooyen and Brodowski, "Betty's Groove," 32.

40. Carter, interview by Lyons.

41. Silvert, "Betty Carter: Keystone Korner."

42. Blumenthal, "Carter Sets Her Own Records"; also Silvert, "Betty Carter: Keystone Korner."

43. Carter, "Jazz Talk."

44. Dannen, *Hit Men*, 36.

45. Dannen, *Hit Men*, 31–57.

46. Dannen, *Hit Men*, 41.

47. Dannen, *Hit Men*, 38.

48. William Knoedelseder, *Stiffed: A True Story of MCA, the Music Business, and the Mafia* (New York: HarperCollins, 1993), 12–13.

49. Carter, "Jazz Talk."

50. Carter, "Jazz Talk."

51. Carter, "Jazz Talk."

52. Nolan, "Declaration of Independence," 23–24; also Carter, interview by Lyons.

53. Nolan, "Declaration of Independence," 23.

54. Nolan, "Declaration of Independence," 23–24.

55. Carter, interview by Yaple, Brooklyn, 1980.

56. Carter, interview by Yaple, Brooklyn, 1980.

57. Carter, "Jazz Talk."

58. *Newsweek*, 8 August 1977.

59. Tony Schwartz, "The Jazz Singer," *Newsweek*, 10 July 1978, 78.

60. John Wilson, "Jazz: The Songs of Betty Carter," *New York Times*, 28 November 1978.

61. Owen McNally, "Jazz Singer Brings Magic to the Park," *Hartford Courant,* 29 July 1979, sec. G.1.

62. Clifford Barbaro, interview by the author, 22 January 1999.

63. Nolan, "Declaration of Independence," 24.

64. Van Rooyen and Brodowski, "Betty's Groove," 32.

65. Carter, interview on KJAZ, 1979.

66. Giddins, "Sings Like a Woman," 73.

67. See the following *Cadence* issues from 1976: April, 32–33; May, 28–29; June, 34; and November, 18; and *Coda,* March 1976, 11.

68. Hicks, interview.

69. Carter, talk at Laney Community College, Oakland, 1979.

70. Betty Carter, press kit, unpublished biography.

71. John Wilson, "Jazz: Betty Carter, Song Stylist," *New York Times,* 24 December 1976.

72. Barbaro, interview.

73. Carter, "Jazz Talk."

74. Don Nelsen, "Carter at Schubert," *Daily News,* 23 November 1978.

75. Dreyfuss, "Betty 'Slow Pop' Carter," 18.

76. Steve Bloom, "Betty Bops Jazz-Rock," *Soho Weekly News,* 18 April 1978.

77. She was filling in for Carmen McRae, who had to back out at the last minute. See Ernie Santosuosso, "Dizzy's Disciples," *Boston Globe,* 24 April 1977, B1, B6. Thanks to Tom Everett and Lewis Porter for this information.

78. Dreyfuss, "Betty 'Slow Pop' Carter," 18.

79. John Wilson, "Superb Singing by Betty Carter Overshadows Three Jones Brothers," *New York Times,* 27 June 1977.

80. Robert Kantor, interview by the author, 8 June 1999. See also "Betty Tapes for TV," *Down Beat,* 15 June 1978, 11.

81. Kantor, interview.

82. Many thanks to Danny Michael and Steve Horelick for preserving this remarkable performance and for granting me a hearing of it.

83. Robert Palmer, "Betty Carter with Roach and Gordon," *New York Times,* Tuesday, 27 June 1978.

84. Schwartz, "The Jazz Singer," 78.

85. Smith, interview. See also Ullman, "On Jazz: Betty Carter," 25.

86. Washington, interview. See also van Rooyen and Brodowski, "Betty's Groove," 32.

87. Cameron Brown, interview by the author, 11 January 1999; Washington, interview.

88. Nelson, "Carter at Schubert." See also Wilson, "Betty Carter Sings Jazz on Broadway" and "Jazz: The Songs of Betty Carter." This show was my first exposure to Betty Carter in performance.

89. Brown, interview.

90. Christopher Petkanes, "Betty Carter Can Still Look Back," *Villager,* 25 December 1978; Giddins, "Betty Carter Reaches Out," *Village Voice,* 8 January 1979, 45.

91. Brown, interview.

92. Alan Kellogg, "Betty Carter Is Remarkable," *Edmonton Journal,* 21 February 1979; Tom Elsworthy, "Scatting at the Palms," *Edmonton Journal,* 23 February 1979. See also Randy Hutton, *Calgary Herald,* 26 February 1979, D9.

93. Washington, interview. See Curt Davis, "Palling around with Carter," *New York Post,* 25 June 1979, 33. See also W. A. Brower, "Betty Carter: Carnegie Hall," *Down Beat,* 6 September 1979, 47.

94. Schwartz, "The Jazz Singer," 78.

95. McNally, "Jazz Singer Brings Magic," G1.

96. Carter, talk at Laney Community College, Oakland, 1979.

97. Carter, interview on KJAZ, 1979.

98. Carter, talk at Great American Music Hall, 1979.

99. Carter, interview by Yaple, Brooklyn, 1980.

100. Carter, interview on KJAZ, 1979. By the end of 1984 Yaple's editing was nearing completion, and shortly thereafter he submitted the video to the Department of Radio-Television-Film at Temple University in partial fulfillment of the requirements for his masters degree. See Francis Davis, "In Jazz, Her Power Is Touching with Words," *Philadelphia Inquirer,* 21 December 1984. I owe many thanks to Francis Davis for putting me in touch with Matthew Yaple.

101. Carter dismissed the resemblance "Sounds (Movin' On)" bears to the beginning of Beethoven's Waldstein Sonata, crediting her inspiration to one of her children's banging on the piano.

102. For this reason I do not believe the Schenkerian approach—a method of analysis developed for European classical music that has been applied to jazz by Henry Martin (to Charlie Parker), Steve Larsen (to Bill Evans), and others—would unearth significant relationships in her music.

103. Critics sometimes attributed key changes to her as well; however, while she often used secondary dominants to tonicize new tonal areas, she rarely modulated in her charts.

104. Carter, interview by Yaple, Brooklyn, 1980.

105. Carter, interview by Yaple, Brooklyn, 1980.

106. Hinckley, "Betty Carter, Real Live."

107. Carter, interview on KJAZ, 1979.

Chapter 10

1. Benny Green, interview by the author, 25 June 1999.

2. Carter, interview by Yaple, Brooklyn, 1980.

3. Carter, interview by Roberts.

4. Wenzel, "Jazz, Scat, and Betty Bebop," 11.

5. Coleman, interview.

6. Dwayne Burno, interview by the author, 20 November 1998.

7. Crouch, "Betty Carter: A Sure Enough Jazz Singer," 30.

8. Carter, interview by Yaple, Brooklyn, 1980. Also Burno, interview, and Brown, interview.

9. Willard Jenkins, "Forever Young," *City Pages*, 22 February 1989.

10. Coleman, interview. Research by Princeton neuroscientist Dr. Jonathan Cohen on the anterior cingulate—whose role it is to register conflict, which, in turn, leads a person to pay more attention to his surroundings—suggests that there may be a scientific basis for Carter's methods. Sandra Blakeslee, "Just What's Going on Inside That Head of Yours," *New York Times*, 14 March 2000.

11. Khalid Moss, interview by the author, 9 February 1999.

12. Lewis Nash, interview by the author, 30 June 1999.

13. Smith, "Jazz Insights."

14. Smith, "Jazz Insights."

15. Crouch, "Betty Carter: A Sure Enough Jazz Singer," 30.

16. Smith, "Jazz Insights."

17. W. Kim Heron, "Betty Carter Still Scats, and Still Works," *Detroit Free Press*, 27 March 1980.

18. Carter, interview on KJAZ, 1979.

19. Della Green and Tom Nutile, "Betty Carter's Livingston College Concert Gives Student Audience Something to Learn," *Courier-News*, 14 March 1980.

20. W. Royal Stokes, "Jazz at Howard," *Washington Post*, 30 March 1979.

21. Gourse, *Louis' Children*, 326–34; Feather, "Betty Carter Be-Bops."

22. Feather, "Betty Carter Be-Bops."

23. Tracey L. Smith, "Salute to Black Women," *Hilltop* (Howard University), 15 October 1982.

24. Junnette A. Pinkney, "All That Jazz," *Washington Post*, 24 October 1980.

25. Theresa Haynie, "Betty Carter on Film," in *Plexus*, September, 1981, 16; Michael Anthony, "Betty Carter Sings Songs of a Survivor," *Minneapolis Tribune*, 14 March 1982, 14G; Veronica L. Banks, "Black Filmmaker on Location," *St. Louis Argus*, 5 November 1981, sec. 1.9.

26. Cuscuna, interview.

27. Moss, interview.

28. Carter, interview by Yaple, Brooklyn, 1980.

29. Elaine Guregian, "Record Reviews: Betty Carter," *Down Beat*, October 1980; and W. Kim Heron, "Jazz Records: Betty Carter at Her Best," *Detroit Free Press*, 19 November 1980.

30. Moss, interview.

31. Crouch, "Betty Carter: A Sure Enough Jazz Singer," 30.

32. Jimenez, interview, 10 June 1999.

33. Elaine Guregian, *Down Beat*, March 1981, 30; and Bill Shoemaker, *Coda*, 1 February 1981, 21.

34. Richard Harrington, "Jazz Maverick Betty Carter," *Washington Post*, 4 June 1981.

35. Amram, interview, 21 December 1998.

36. Amram, interview, 21 December 1998.

37. Mixon, interview.

38. Myles Redding, interview.

39. Jimenez, interview, 10 June 1999. See Haynie, "Betty Carter on Film," 16.

40. For an in-depth discussion of this phenomenon, see Katharine Cartwright, "Quotation and Reference in Jazz Performance: Ella Fitzgerald's 'St. Louis Blues,' 1957–1979," Ph.D. diss., CUNY Graduate School, 1998.

41. Amram, interview, 21 December 1998.

42. Amram, interview, 21 December 1998

43. Feather, "Betty Carter Be-Bops." Also mentioned in Gourse, *Louis' Children*, 327.

44. Gourse, *Louis' Children*, 327.

45. Carter, interview on KJAZ, 1979.

46. Amram, interview, 28 December 1998.

47. Amram, interview, 21 December 1998.

48. Amram, interview, 21 December 1998.

49. Carter, interview by Roberts.

50. This analysis is based not on any performance, but on the chord chart. Many thanks to pianist Bruce Flowers for providing copies of several charts from Carter's book.

51. Amram, interviews.

52. Amram, interview, 28 December 1998.

53. Amram, interview, 21 December 1998.

54. Amram, interview, 21 December 1998; also Carter, interview by Roberts.

55. Nash, interview; also Carter, interview by Roberts.

56. Jesse Hamlin, "Betty Carter and Strings Flying High," *San Francisco Chronicle*, date unknown. Based upon the personnel for the date, it took place sometime between October 1982 and May 1983.

57. Amram, interview, 28 December 1998.

58. The singer was known to shout at waiters and scowl at audience members who were disrupting her show by being too loud.

59. Gourse, *Louis' Children*, 327. Gourse mistakenly placed this concert around Christmas, but Carter performed at Fat Tuesday's then, not the Bottom Line, and there were no strings at that event.

60. Gourse, *Louis' Children*, 333.

61. Once used as Benny Goodman's closing theme, this song is incorrectly attributed to Cole Porter in the liner notes.

62. Benny Green, interview by Alwyn Lewis and Laurie Lewis, *Cadence*, February 1995, 12.

63. Grime, *Jazz Voices*, 21.

64. Carter, interview by Yaple, Brooklyn, 1980.

65. In this performance the song "Goodbye" is presented in complete form in contrast to the truncated version done by Ray Charles.

66. Carter, interview by Roberts.

67. Stephen Holden, "Jazz Songs: Betty Carter," *New York Times*, 31 March 1982, sec. 6, 48–49; Gourse, *Louis' Children*, 335.

68. Selections from this date were hastily released as a bootleg called *Jazz Büne Berlin*, and then just as suddenly withdrawn from the shelves. Thanks to Vincent Pelote for making this recording available to me.

69. Moss, interview. Ironically, this meant that certain errors Hicks made in those performances, such as his introduction to "Fake," were replicated in later trios' versions (Washington, interview).

70. Gene Seymour, "Feeding the Fire: With a New Album and a Concert Run That Begins Tonight, Betty Carter Brings It All Back Home," *Newsday,* 15 November 1994, B4.

71. Bob Protzman, "A Balladeer with Love in Her Heart," *Knight-Ridder Newspapers,* ca. 30 June 1983.

72. Whitney Balliett, "Jazz: Betty Bebop," *New Yorker,* 20 September 1982, 110f.

73. Mike Butler, "Scat Queen Bebops onto BAM Stage," *New York News World,* 19 November 1982.

74. Clarence Atkins, "Betty Carter in Benefit for Young Musicians," *Jazz Spotlite News,* fall–winter 1981 and spring–summer 1982, 14, 15. Many thanks to Jim Harrison for sharing this information with me.

75. George Edward Tait, "Betty Carter and Jazz Ensemble Perform at Benefit Concert," *New York Amsterdam News,* 5 June 1982, 52.

76. Jeff Edwards, "Betty Carter Happy to Bring Classic Jazz to the South," *Jackson Daily News,* 29 April 1983.

77. Smith, "Salute to Black Women." Carter's bio from her then current press kit mentioned this award among several she received between 1979 and 1983, including a Black Music Association Award in 1982.

78. Jimenez, interview, 10 June 1999.

79. JoAnne Jimenez, interview by the author, 12 January 1999.

80. Butler, "Scat Queen Bebops." See also unpublished factsheet to accompany press releases, "Betty Carter Biography," Bet-Car Productions (possibly from 1983). In the sheet's discography Carter mentions her association with Broadcast Music International (BMI), which collects income from broadcasts and distributes it to artists.

81. Jimenez, interview, 12 January 1999.

82. Betty Carter, "Current Biography," for Liljay Productions, March 1982, 3.

83. Moss, interview. Moss recalled that Bandy had gotten the boot during a stint at Rising Sun in Montreal because he sparred with the boss verbally one too many times.

84. Green (interview by the author) remembered playing with her in April, perhaps recalling when he was called about the job, but according to press from this time Moss was in the trio until the beginning of May.

85. Gourse, *Louis' Children,* 335; Grime, *Jazz Voices,* 145.

86. Kagle Redding, conversation with the author, 18 March 2000.

87. Gourse, *Louis' Children,* 336.

88. Grime, *Jazz Voices,* 144.

89. Fred Bouchard, "Betty Carter Strings Out Beantown," *Down Beat,* February 1984, 12.

90. Bouchard, "Betty Carter Strings Out Beantown."

91. Bouchard, "Betty Carter Strings Out Beantown."

92. Carter, interview by Roberts.

93. According to Jimenez, interview, 10 June 1999, she originally conceived of the agency as a joint venture with Carter but had decided to run it herself shortly before the singer dismissed her from Liljay.

Chapter 11

1. Nolan, "Declaration of Independence," 24. When Carter finished only one vote ahead of Joni Mitchell for fourth place in the *Down Beat* reader's poll of 1978, with Flora Purim finishing first, she was so incensed that she suggested the poll had been fixed. She had placed second in the critic's polls in 1977 and 1978. See Prince, "Betty Carter: Bebopper Breathes Fire," 12–13.

2. Steve Bloom, "An Intimate Conversation with Linda Ronstadt," *Down Beat,* July 1985, 17.

3. Leonard Feather, "Jazz: Sophisticated Ladies," *Los Angeles Times,* 23 March 1986, 81; Stephen Holden, "Our Perennial Songbirds," *New York Times Magazine,* 15 November 1987.

4. Taylor, *Notes and Tones,* 275.

5. Robert Palmer, "Black Uhuru, Reggae Ambassadors to the World," *New York Times,* 17 July 1981.

6. Jennifer Dunning, "Pop-Jazz: Sweet Honey in the Rock, a Celebration at Town Hall," *New York Times,* 2 December 1983.

7. Stephen Holden, "Pop-Funk: Chaka Kahn and Mtume," *New York Times,* 17 July 1983.

8. Richard Harrington, "Singing the Blues about Jazz," *Washington Post,* 22 April 1983.

9. Richard Weis, "Jazzing and Jiving," *Daily Targum,* 16 March 1989, 3.

10. As James T Jones IV observed, Anita Baker's physical gestures recalled those of Carter ("Betty Carter," 26). A singer named Lady B.J. would record "Tight" in 1988 accompanied by a group led by Ellis Marsalis. Thanks to Evan Spring for locating this recording for me.

11. Gourse, *Louis' Children,* 335.

12. Cassandra Wilson, "What Betty Taught Me," *Jazziz,* January 1999, 43.

13. Wilson, "What Betty Taught Me."

14. Amram, interview, 21 December 1998.

15. Nolan, "Declaration of Independence," 23.

16. Nolan, "Declaration of Independence," 23.

17. Ben Sidran, *Talking Jazz,* 2d ed. (New York: Da Capo, 1995), 115.

18. Carter, interview by Lyons.

19. Barbara Barrow-Murray, "An Evening with Betty Carter," aired on WGBH Boston's television program *Say Brother,* October 1983.

20. Carter, interview by Roberts.

21. Carter, interview by Roberts.

22. Lee Jeske, "On Jazz," *Cash Box,* 13 February 1988.

23. Jones, "Betty Carter."

24. Don Braden, interview by the author, 8 October 1988.

25. Lock, "Her Own Sweet Way," 33. In a studio, musicians are typically separated from one another so the sound levels of their individual tracks can be balanced when they are mixed onto two tracks.

26. Clarence Atkins, liner notes *The Carmen McRae–Betty Carter Duets,* 1996 reissue, Verve 314–529–579–2.

27. Jimenez, interview, 12 January 1999.

28. Great American Music Hall 2706. See *Washington Post,* 7 August 1987.

29. Bo Emerson, "Betty Carter's Style Is Distinctively Her Own," *Atlanta Journal and Constitution,* 24 April 1987, 3P.

30. Stephen Holden, "Jazz: Betty Carter Sings," *New York Times,* 5 August 1987.

31. Mary Campbell, "Records: Betty Carter Sings Educational Jazz," *Associated Press News Feature,* 3 August 1987.

32. Lock, "Her Own Sweet Way," 33.

33. Holden, "Our Perennial Songbirds."

34. Steven Radwell, "Betty Carter: A Jazz Survivor, Thanks to Her Own Record Company," *Chicago Tribune,* 12 November 1987, 37N; released from Reuters on 4 November 1987.

35. Jeske, "On Jazz."

36. David Hinckley, "The Betty Carter Songbook," *Daily News Magazine,* 24 January 1988.

37. Holden, "Our Perennial Songbirds."

38. Green, interview by the author.

39. Radwell, "Betty Carter: A Jazz Survivor."

40. Holden, "Our Perennial Songbirds."

41. Typically an artist's agency cannot directly book performances at a venue outside the States, but must go through a third party.

42. Kai El'Zabar, "Betty Carter: Black, a Woman, and Independent," *Jam Sessions,* March 1988, 10.

43. "Polygram Jazz Newsletter," *Jazz News,* June 1988.

44. Thanks to Luann Dragone for making this performance available to me.

45. Thanks to Lewis Porter for making this performance available to me.

46. Braden, interview; and Green, interview by the author.

47. Ferla, interview.

48. Peter Watrous, "The Voices You Hear Are Inimitably Their Own," *New York Times,* 3 July 1988. Also in *San Diego Union-Tribune, Boston Phoenix, Washington Post, Christian Science Monitor,* and *Down Beat.*

49. Ken Franckling, "Betty Bebop Likes It at the Top," *Jazz Times,* November 1990, 25.

50. Michael Bourne, "On the Set of Cosby's Show, Betty Carter Adds Some Jazz," *Target: The Sunday Herald Times,* 20 November 1988.

51. Coleman, interview.

52. Jones, "Betty Carter."

53. Anthony J. Tortici, Coca-Cola press release later reproduced by PR Newswire

Association (Atlanta) as "Bill Cosby, Betty Carter Fuse Jazz Talents for New Coca-Cola Classic Advertising," August 1989.

54. Jenkins, "Forever Young"; Jones, "Betty Carter," 25.

55. Jones, "Betty Carter," 24.

56. Bob Protzman, "Jazz Singer Betty Carter Hotter Than Ever: She's Worked Steadily, and She's Done It Her Way," *St. Paul Pioneer Press Dispatch,* 26 February 1989.

57. Betsy Pisik, "Carter and Charles Reunited in Song," *Washington Times,* 26 October 1989.

58. Jones, "Betty Carter," 26.

59. Jenkins, "Forever Young."

60. Jim Miller, "Bringing It All Back Home," *Newsweek,* 28 August 1989.

61. Weis, "Jazzing and Jiving," 3.

62. Jenkins, "Forever Young."

63. Burno, interview.

64. Pascal Kober, "Jazz Au Feminin: Betty Carter," *Jazz Hot,* January 1992, 20–21, translation by Danielle Walker.

65. Betty Carter, Polygram press kit, September 1990. This tune is never mentioned in reviews of Carter's gigs, nor do any of the unissued tapes of her work include it, so it seems unlikely that she taught it to her trios before this record.

66. Polygram press kit.

67. Craig Handy, interview by the author, 5 October 1998.

68. Kober, "Jazz Au Feminin," 20–21.

69. Handy, interview.

70. Handy, interview.

71. Burno, interview.

72. Polygram press kit for *Droppin' Things.*

73. Burno, interview; and Mike Joyce, "Betty Carter," *Washington Post,* 19 November 1990.

74. Burno, interview.

Chapter 12

1. James T. Jones IV, "Carmen McRae: Cut the Crap," *Down Beat,* June 1991, 24.

2. Sound track to *mo' better blues,* Columbia CK46792.

3. Black Star (Mos Def and Talib Kweli), "Respiration: Remix," and Saul Williams, "Twice the First Time." Rap artist Common attended the memorial concert for Betty Carter at BAM in June 1999. Thanks to Conrad and Isaac Bauer for this information.

4. 4/4 Productions and Bernie Drayton.

5. Burno, interview.

6. Burno, interview.

7. Sonja Williams, producer, *Jazz Profile,* narrated by Nancy Wilson.

8. Wayne K. Self, "American Jazz Masters Fellowship Award 1992," *Jazz Educators Journal* 24, no. 2 (1992): 30.

9. John Ephland and Frank Alkyer, "IAJE's Tropical Teachings," *Down Beat,* April 1992, 11.

10. Leonard Feather, "Variety Provides Spice at Educators Fest," *Los Angeles Times,* 14 January 1992.

11. Bob Young, "Tradition: Histories of Leaders and Followers," *Jazziz,* January 1994, 126.

12. Peter Watrous, "A World Written, and Rewritten, by Betty Carter," *New York Times,* 28 August, 1992.

13. For an extensive elaboration of the elements of this language and how one acquires it, see Paul Berliner's *Thinking in Jazz.*

14. Gene Santoro, "Challenging 'Em to Bebop All They Can Be," *Daily News,* 16 August 1994.

15. Self, "Jazz Masters Fellowship," 29.

16. Self, "Jazz Masters Fellowship," 29.

17. Wayne K. Self, "Betty Carter: American Jazz Diva," *Jazz Educators Journal* vol. 24, no. 3 (1992): 73.

18. Watrous, "World Written, and Rewritten."

19. Self, "Betty Carter: American Jazz Diva," 29.

20. Self, "Betty Carter: American Jazz Diva," 29.

21. Willard Jenkins, "Betty Carter: What She's About," *Jazz Times,* December 1992, 40–41.

22. Peter Watrous, "A Jazz Singing Legend Guides a New Generation," *New York Times,* 15 April 1993.

23. Kevin Whitehead, "Behind Every Singer Is a Piano Player: Betty Carter and John Hicks," *Down Beat,* December 1992, 36.

24. Watrous, "Jazz Singing Legend."

25. Zoe Anglesey, "Not Just the Melody: Betty Carter Finds New Freedom in Old Standards," *San Francisco Examiner,* 23 October 1994, 34.

26. Self, "Betty Carter: American Jazz Diva," 27–29, 73.

27. George Kanzler, "Trio Suits Betty Carter as Singer Stumbles with Big Band," *Star-Ledger,* Newark, N.J., 1 March 1992.

28. Concert program.

29. Karen Carrillo, "Betty Carter Follows Footsteps of Jazz Greats Ella, Sarah Vaughan," *New York Amsterdam News,* 31 July 1993, 31.

30. Whitehead, "Behind Every Singer," 36.

31. Watrous, "World Written, and Rewritten."

32. Jenkins, "Betty Carter: What She's About."

33. Chip Deffaa, "Just No Slowing Betty's Singing," *New York Post,* 29 August 1992.

34. Jenkins, "Betty Carter: What She's About."

35. Press release. See also Anglesey, "Not Just the Melody," 12.

36. Jenkins, "Betty Carter: What She's About."

37. Robert Tanzillo, "Expect the Unexpected: Betty Carter Knows How to Take Charge of a Song," *Milwaukee Sentinel,* 1 October 1993, 16D.

38. Tanzillo, "Expect the Unexpected."

39. Jenkins, "Betty Carter: What She's About." Watts had played on the sound

track to *mo' better blues* with Branford Marsalis and Terence Blanchard, released in 1990, and in the *Tonight Show* band.

40. Handy, interview.

41. Net sales (profits) were $17,974 for CDs and $5,459 for cassettes, totaling $23,433. These figures come from Verve's marketing plan for Carter's next record, assembled in a memo from Ben Moody, product manager, dated 23 June 1994.

42. Marie Elsie St. Leger, "Educating Betty," *Jazziz,* February 1997, 54.

43. John Anderson, "BAM's One Hundred Years of Jazz and Blues Festival Salutes Our Musical Heritage," *Newsday,* 3 April 1992.

44. Raphael Sugarman, "The Street Beat: Betty Carter Rides Ft. Green's Rhythms," *Newsday,* 21 February, 1993, 3.

45. Watrous, "Jazz Singing Legend."

46. Whitehead, "Behind Every Singer," 36.

47. Playthell Benjamin, "School for Cats," *London Times,* 25 April 1993.

48. Carrillo, "Betty Carter Follows Footsteps."

49. Javon Jackson, *When the Time Is Right,* Blue Note, CDP 0777 7 89678 2 8.

50. Jimenez, interview, 10 June 1999.

51. St. Leger, "Educating Betty," 53.

52. Javon Jackson, interview by the author, 6 August 1999.

53. Michael Bourne, "It's Not about Teaching, It's about Doing," *Down Beat,* December 1994, 21; and Richard Cook's liner notes to *Feed the Fire,* Verve 314 523 600–2. In the press release announcing the CD's release in October 1994, Holland was quoted as saying, "You never feel that you're backing a singer with Betty, you're right in the thick of a creative experience with her."

54. Anglesey, "Not Just the Melody," 12.

55. Bourne, "It's Not about Teaching," 21.

56. Tanzillo, "Expect the Unexpected."

57. The $\flat VII^7(13)$ here continues the circle-of-fifths movement begun by the preceding I^7 to IV^7 move, as though leading to C major, that is, a $V^7/\flat III$ harmonic function. The following $V^7(\sharp 9)$ sounds like a dominant in A minor coming from the preceding chord.

58. Carter's treatment of "Lover Man" brings to mind a passage from Charles Rosen's *The Classical Style* (New York: W. W. Norton, 1972), 83, in which he describes how Haydn expands a twenty-measure theme into a larger work. Comparisons between jazz and classical music bring certain risks. The well-intentioned efforts of some scholars who needlessly use such comparisons to show that jazz is "just as good" as European classical music have often had an unintended patronizing tone. But because Carter herself expressed an interest in classical music, it seems likely that for some of her work, "Jumps" and "Sounds (Movin' On)" for example, she drew upon this tradition for inspiration in her treatment of large dimension growth.

59. Geri Allen included this tune and "Feed the Fire" on her 1994 Blue Note issue, *Twenty One,* CDP 7243 8 30028 2 5.

60. Bourne, "It's Not about Teaching," 21.

61. Memo from Andrew Lewis at PolyGram to Charles Shidell at BBC, 16 June 1994.

62. On that occasion bassist Michael Bowie, who had worked with Carter eight years before, and Alvester Garnett, who had finished a short stint with Carter at the end of 1993, backed Lincoln. Either directly or indirectly, it would seem that working with Carter led to other jobs.

63. Marketing plan in a memo from Ben Moody, product manager at Verve, 23 June 1994.

64. Misha Berson, "Carter Puts Her Signature on Old and New Tunes," *Seattle Times*, 14 September 1994.

65. Javon Jackson recalled that Carter had been so eager to secure a commitment from Terrasson earlier in the fall that, when she came to the second session for *When the Time Is Right*, she brought a retainer check.

66. Aside from Geri Allen, Carter never hired a woman for her working trio.

Chapter 13

1. In her interview with Zoe Anglesey ("Not Just the Melody," 12), for example, she mentioned Tony Bennett's appearance on MTV.

2. Ria A. Niccoli, "Either Get with TV, or Video Will Create Own Bands: Hamp," *Down Beat*, 2 November 1951, 2.

3. Seymour, "Feeding the Fire," B4.

4. Sheila Rule, "The Pop Life: An Answer for Jazz," *New York Times*, 25 August 1993.

5. Betty Carter, interview by Evan Spring, WKCR-FM (New York), 13 May 1993.

6. Rule, "The Pop Life."

7. Frederic M. Biddle, "Television: 'A World of Different Music' Brings Together Diverse Talents," *Boston Globe*, 31 January 1994.

8. Brian D. Johnson, "Rhombus Makes Films That Resonate the World Over," *McLeans*, 21 February 1994.

9. Johnson, "Rhombus Makes Films."

10. Geoffrey Himes, "Wholly Wonderful (If Not Whole) Jazz," *Washington Post*, 18 February 1994.

11. Stephen J. Dubner, "The Next Miles Davis May Be on This Page," *New York Times Magazine*, 25 June 1995, 38.

12. Ella Fitzgerald died on 15 June 1996.

13. Verve 314–523150–2.

14. On the invitation, entitled *A 651 Gala Celebration*. From the clipping files at the Institute of Jazz Studies, Rutgers University, Newark.

15. Michael Bourne, "Betty Carter Definitive," *Cognac Hennessy Jazz Notes*, winter 1994, 3. Although Carter was specifically speaking of her trio here, her remarks seem broadly applicable to what she was accomplishing with the Jazz Ahead program as well.

16. Bourne, "Betty Carter Definitive."

17. Club owners from Bradley's (Wendy Cunningham), Village Vanguard (Lorraine Gordon), and the Blue Note (Sal Haries) also had signed onto the committee.

18. Verve press release, undated.

19. Richard Gehr, "More Than the Melody," *Brooklyn Bridge,* August 1996, 53.

20. Dubner, "Next Miles Davis," 38.

21. Dubner, "Next Miles Davis," 38.

22. Dubner, "Next Miles Davis," 38–39. In conjunction with the Jazz Ahead program in 1995, John Hicks accompanied Carter at a workshop conducted at BAM. She would do this again in the following years, even after Jazz Ahead moved to Washington.

23. Undated memo to Verve from Chazz Bryant of P-Funk Video Promotions, ca. spring 1997.

24. Derek Gordon, interview by the author, 14 April 2000.

25. Undated press release.

26. Over the following years, Carter would continue her association with the Clintons. In addition to performing at a private party given by the Clintons, she would be in Washington in August 1996 to participate in the president's birthday celebration, which was beamed by satellite link to Radio City Music Hall.

27. Guntern, *Risk-Taking.*

28. Geri Allen recalled Carter's using this approach as far back as the 1980s when she had Carter come do a clinic at Howard University where Allen was teaching (Bourne, "It's Not about Teaching," 21).

29. Press kit for the program.

30. Carl Atkins, *Harman: How to Listen,* Harman International Expanded in-School Curriculum, 1997.

31. Verve itinerary. The run was from 23–28 September, and the children's performance took place that Sunday afternoon at 3:00 P.M.

32. John Schreiber, interview by the author, 8 November 1998.

33. Gail Goldstein, interview by the author, 8 November 1998. Newark WBGO-FM radio host Monifa Carson accompanied the singer on some of these excursions.

34. David Zaworski, "Carter's Listening Lesson Lets Young People Sing," *Down Beat,* January 1998, 66.

35. Zaworski, "Carter's Listening Lesson."

36. Goldstein, interview.

37. Zaworski, "Carter's Listening Lesson."

38. Goldstein, interview.

39. David Lionel Smith, e-mail correspondence, 6 October 1998. Dean Smith wrote the letter of nomination.

40. The medal is normally awarded to twelve individuals, but Adrienne Rich declined hers that year in protest of the Clinton administration's "cynical politics" and the increasing disparity between the rich and the poor. See Dinitia Smith, "Clinton Awards Medals in Arts and Humanities," *New York Times,* 26 September 1997.

41. The bootleg from East Berlin in 1985, *Jazz Bühne Berlin,* captures Carter on such a night.

42. Coleman, interview.

43. Jimenez, interview, 10 June 1999.

44. Several web sites, including those of the American Cancer Society (www.cancer.org), the National Cancer Institute (www.cancerlinkusa.com), and Univer-

sity of Pennsylvania (oncolink.upenn.ecu), concur about these aspects of the illness. There is a general consensus among researchers that, while the incidence of pancreatic cancer is only slightly more frequent in African Americans than European Americans, mortality rates among black people who develop this disease have been increasing since 1970. Among all cancer cases, the illness only strikes about 2 to 3 percent of the general population, but because it is generally caught so late in its progress, it is the fourth most frequent cause of death. Its causes remain unclear.

45. James Redding, interview. Carter confirmed that she had been in touch with her former husband and that they had been spending some holidays together during the preceding few years. Betty Carter, conversation with the author, 9 July 1998, as well as in other conversations.

46. He added that "she knew exactly what she was doing" (James Redding, interview).

47. James Redding, interview.

48. Shortly after Betty Carter was cremated, a closed service was held.

49. Coleman, interview.

50. Willard Jenkins, "The True Meaning of Betty Carter: 1929–1998," *Down Beat,* December 1998, 67–68.

51. "A Tribute to Betty Carter," with contributions from Cassandra Wilson, Howard Mandel, and Clarence Atkins, *Jazziz,* January 1999, 41–49.

52. Matthew McCann Fenton, "Betty Carter," *Entertainment Weekly: '99 Yearbook,* January 1999, 134.

53. Richard Harrington, "For a Jazz Great, Great Jazz," *Washington Post,* 15 April 1999.

54. Marc Fischer, "Jazzed for Betty Carter's Legacy," *Washington Post,* 10 April 1999. Thanks to Marshall Hornblower for providing me with these last two references.

55. Kevin Struthers, director of jazz programs at the Kennedy Center, conversation with the author, 31 March 2000.

56. <http://kennedy-center.org/programs/jazz/jazzahead/press.html>. The release goes on to describe the program as "an annual part of the John F. Kennedy Center for the Performing Arts Jazz Programs," suggesting that it will be around for a long time to come.

57. Gordon, interview.

58. Andrew Gilbert, "The Vocal Jazz Explosion," *Down Beat,* October 1999, 36.

Appendix

1. Carter, interview by Lyons.

2. Henry Lee Smith Jr., "Dialects of English," *The American Heritage Dictionary of the English Language,* ed. William Morris (Boston: Houghton Mifflin Company, 1979), xxv–xxx, l.

Selected References

Published Sources

Anglesey, Zoe. "Not Just the Melody: Betty Carter Finds New Freedom in Old Standards." *San Francisco Examiner,* 23 October 1994, 12, 34.

Berliner, Paul. *Thinking in Jazz: The Infinite Art of Improvisation.* Chicago: University of Chicago Press, 1994.

Björn, Lars. "From Hastings St. to the Bluebird: The Blues and Jazz Tradition in Detroit." *Michigan Quarterly Review* 25, no. 2 (1986): 257–68.

Blumenthal, Bob. "Betty Carter Sets Her Own Records." *Boston Phoenix,* 26 August 1975, sec. 2, p. 4.

Bourne, Michael. "Betty Carter Definitive." *Cognac Hennessy Jazz Notes,* winter 1994, 3.

———. "It's Not about Teaching, It's about Doing." *Down Beat,* December 1994, 21.

Bruyninckx, Walter. "Betty Carter." *Sixty Years of Recorded Jazz.* Mechelen, Belgium: Bruyninckx, 1979.

Carrillo, Karen. "Betty Carter Follows Footsteps of Jazz Greats Ella, Sarah Vaughan." *New York Amsterdam News,* 31 July 1993, 31.

Carter, Betty. "Betty Carter." Interview by Christopher Kuhl, 1982. *Cadence,* February 1985, 5.

———. "An Interview with Betty Carter." Interview by Leothee Miller, 28 February 1972. *Black Creation* 3, no. 4 (1972): 36.

———. Interview by Arthur Taylor, 12 December 1972. *Notes and Tones.* New York: Perigee Books, 1977.

Cartwright, Katharine. "Quotation and Reference in Jazz Performance: Ella Fitzgerald's 'St. Louis Blues,' 1957–1979." Ph.D. diss., City University of New York, 1998.

Charles, Ray, with David Ritz. *Brother Ray: Ray Charles' Own Story.* 1978; rpt. New York: Da Capo, 1992.

Cheatum, Arnie. "Magic Moment: Betty Carter." *East West Journal* (Boston), March 1973, 26–27.

Cohen, Noal, and Michael Fitzgerald. "Emotional Eloquence: An Historical Overview of Gigi Gryce." *Coda,* January–February 1999, 26–28.

Crouch, Stanley. "Betty Carter: A Sure Enough Jazz Singer." *Village Voice,* 31 December–6 January, 1981, 30.

Crow, Bill. *Jazz Anecdotes.* New York: Oxford University Press, 1990.

Dannen, Fredric. *Hit Men: Power Brokers and Fast Money inside the Music Business.* 1990; rpt. New York: Vintage, 1991.

Davis, Francis. "In Jazz, Her Power Is Touching with Words." *Philadelphia Inquirer,* 21 December 1984, 1-C, 3-C.

Davis, Miles, and Quincy Troupe. *Miles: The Autobiography.* New York: Simon and Schuster, 1989.

DeVeaux, Scott. *The Birth of Bebop: A Social and Musical History.* Berkeley and Los Angeles: University of California Press, 1997.

Dreyfuss, Joel. "Betty 'Slow Pop' Carter Speeds Up." *Rolling Stone,* October 1976, 18.

Dubner, Stephen J. "The Next Miles Davis May Be on This Page." *New York Times Magazine,* 25 June 1995, 38.

Faulk, Daniel M. "Barry Harris, Master Bebop Pianist: A Preliminary Study of His Life, Music, and Teaching Methods." M.A. thesis, Rutgers University, Newark, 1999.

Feather, Leonard. "Betty Carter Be-bops to the White House." *Los Angeles Times: Calendar,* 23 August 1981, 1, 68, 70.

———. *Inside Jazz.* New York: J. J. Robbins, 1949, as *The Roots of Jazz;* rpt. New York: Da Capo, 1977.

Fiofori, Tam. "Betty Carter: Judson Hall, New York City, New York." *Down Beat,* 30 April 1970, 32.

Fox, Ted. *Showtime at the Apollo.* 1983; rpt. New York: Da Capo, 1993.

Friedwald, Will. *Jazz Singing: America's Great Voices from Bessie Smith to Bebop and Beyond.* New York: Charles Scribner's Sons, 1990.

Gardner, Mark. "Norman Simmons Talks to Mark Gardner: Concluded." *Jazz Monthly,* January 1971, 6.

Gart, Galen, and Roy C. Ames. *Duke/Peacock Records: An Illustrated History with Discography.* Milford, N.H.: Nickel, 1990.

Gillespie, Dizzy, with Al Fraser. *To Be or Not to Bop: Memoirs.* New York: Doubleday, 1979; rpt. New York: Da Capo, 1985.

Gourse, Leslie. *Louis' Children: American Jazz Singers.* New York: William Morrow, 1984.

———. *Sassy: The Life of Sarah Vaughan.* New York: Da Capo, 1994.

Grime, Kitty. *Jazz Voices.* London: Quartet, 1983.

Guntern, Gottlieb, ed. *Risk-Taking and Creative Leadership.* London: Shepheard-Walwyn, 1998.

Hall, C. G., ed. *Arkansas: A Guide to the State.* Arkansas Writer's Project sponsored by the Arkansas State Planning Board, 1941.

Hampton, Lionel, with James Haskins. *Hamp: An Autobiography.* New York: Warner Books, 1989.

Haynie, Theresa. "Betty Carter on Film." *Plexus,* September 1981, 16.

Hinckley, David. "Betty Carter, Real Live." *Daily News Magazine,* 24 January 1988, 12.

Hodeir, Andre. *Jazz: Its Evolution and Essence.* Trans. David Noakes. New York: Grove Press, 1956.

Holden, Stephen. "Our Perennial Songbirds." *New York Times Magazine,* 15 November 1987, Sec. 6, 47–49, 69–70, 72.

Jacobson, Mark. "Betty Carter Is Alive in Bed-Stuy." *Village Voice,* 18 August 1975, 100.

James, Michael. *Kings of Jazz: Dizzy Gillespie.* London: Cassell, 1959.

Jenkins, Willard. "Betty Carter: What She's About." *Jazz Times,* December 1992, 40–41.

Joans, Ted. "Betty Carter." *Coda,* March 1976, 10.

Jones IV, James T. "Betty Bebop Is Back in Town." *Michigan: The Magazine of the Detroit News,* 5 May 1985, 15.

———. "Roots: The Jones Version." *Detroit News,* 15 February, 1987, B.1, 6, 8.

———. "Betty Carter: Look What We Got." *Down Beat,* August 1989, 24.

Jones, Leroi (Amiri Imamu Baraka). *Black Music.* New York: William Morrow, 1968; rpt. New York: Da Capo, 1998.

Jones, Max. *Talking Jazz.* New York: W. W. Norton, 1987.

Kernfeld, Barry, ed. *The New Grove Dictionary of Jazz.* New York: St. Martin's Press, 1988.

Kober, Pascal. "Jazz au Feminin: Betty Carter." *Jazz Hot,* January 1992, 20–21.

Kukla, Barbara J. *Swing City: Newark Nightlife, 1925–50.* Philadelphia: Temple University Press, 1991.

Lee, Alfred McClung, and Norman D. Humphrey. *Race Riot: Detroit, 1943.* 1943; rpt. New York: Octagon, 1968.

Locke, Graham. "In Her Own Sweet Way: The Great Jazz Singer: Energy, Adventure, and Aggression." *Wire,* February 1986, 31.

Lotz, Rainer E., and Ulrich Neuert, *The AFRS "Jubilee" Transcription Programs: An Exploratory Discography.* Frankfort am Main: Ruecker, 1985.

Lydon, Michael. *Ray Charles: Man and Music.* New York: Riverhead, 1998.

Mason, Bryant. "Mom Is a Chanteuse." *New York Daily News,* 8 September 1975, 45.

Mast, Robert H. *Detroit Lives.* Philadelphia: Temple University Press, 1994.

McLarney, Bill. "Betty Carter: The 'in' Singer." *Down Beat,* 28 July 1966, 18.

———. "Boston Digs Betty Carter." *Journal of New England,* November, 1975, 24–25.

McNally, Owen. "Jazz Singer Brings Magic to the Park." *Hartford Courant,* 29 July 1979, G1.

McRae, Barry. *Dizzy Gillespie: His Life and Time.* New York: Universe Books, 1988.

Meltzer, David. *Reading Jazz.* San Francisco: Mercury House, 1993.

Nicholson, Stuart. *Billie Holiday.* Boston: Northeastern University Press, 1995.

———. *Ella Fitzgerald: A Biography of the First Lady of Jazz.* New York: Charles Scribner's Sons, 1994.

Nolan, Herb. "Betty Carter: Unabashed Jazz Singer." *Down Beat,* 7 December 1972, 28.

———. "Betty Carter's Declaration of Independence." *Down Beat,* 12 August 1976, 23.

Porter, Lewis. *John Coltrane: His Life and Music.* Ann Arbor: University of Michigan Press, 1998.

Porter, Lewis, and Michael Ullman. *Jazz: From Its Origins to the Present.* Englewood Cliffs, N.J.: Prentice-Hall, 1993.

Price, Clement. "Talkin' 'bout a Crisis: The History of Black Newark." *Blue Newark Culture,* December 1989, 28–45.

Priestley, Brian. *Charlie Parker.* Tunbridge Wells, England: Spellmount, 1984.

Primack, Bret. "Profile: Walter Davis, Jr." *Down Beat,* 15 May 1978, 32.

Prince, Linda. "Betty Carter: Bebopper Breathes Fire." *Down Beat,* 3 May 1979, 12.

Provizer, Norman. "Youth and Energy from Betty Bebop." *Jazziz,* October–November 1990, 83.

Radwell, Steven. "Betty Carter: A Jazz Survivor, Thanks to Her Own Record Company." *Chicago Tribune,* 12 November 1987, 13N.

Rava, Graciela. "Betty Carter a Contrechant." *Jazz Magazine,* February 1980, 40–43, 64.

Russell, Ross. *Bird Lives: The High Life and Hard Times of Charlie "Yardbird" Parker.* New York: Charterhouse, 1973.

Santoro, Gene. "Look What We Got." *Pulse!* September 1988, 62.

Schuller, Gunther. *The Swing Era.* New York: Oxford University Press, 1989.

Schwartz, Tony. "The Jazz Singer." *Newsweek,* 10 July 1978, 78.

Self, Wayne K. "American Jazz Masters Fellowship Award 1992." *Jazz Educators Journal* 24, no. 2 (1992): 30.

———. "Betty Carter: American Jazz Diva." *Jazz Educators Journal* 24, no. 3 (1992): 73.

Shipton, Alyn. *Groovin High: The Life of Dizzy Gillespie.* New York: Oxford University Press, 1999.

Shogun, Robert, and Tom Craig. *The Detroit Race Riot: A Study in Violence.* Philadelphia: Chilton, 1964.

Siders, Harvey. "Quotet: Is There Such a Thing as a Jazz Singer . . . ?" *Down Beat,* 12 November 1970, 13.

Silvert, Conrad. "Betty Carter: Keystone Korner." *Billboard,* 25 October 1975, 63.

"Sonny Rollins Meets the Japanese Press." *Down Beat,* 19 December 1963, 16.

Stowe, David. *Swing Changes: Big-Band Jazz in New Deal America.* Cambridge: Harvard University Press, 1994.

Sugrue, Thomas J. *The Origins of the Urban Crisis: Race and Inequality in Postwar Detroit.* Princeton, N.J.: Princeton University Press, 1996.

Tanzillo, Robert. "Expect the Unexpected: Betty Carter Knows How to Take Charge of a Song." *Milwaukee Sentinel,* 1 October 1993, 16D.

Tracy, Jack, ed. *Down Beat: Jazz Record Reviews, 1956.* Chicago: Maher, 1957.

Ullman, Michael. *Jazz Lives: Portraits in Words and Pictures.* Washington, D.C.: New Republic Books, 1980.

———. "Michael Ullman on Jazz: Betty Carter." *New Republic,* 27 May 1978, 24.

Vail, Ken. *Bird's Diary: The Life of Charlie Parker, 1945–1955.* Surrey: Castle, 1996.

———. *Miles' Diary: The Life of Miles Davis, 1947–1961.* Surrey: Castle, 1997.

van Rooyen, Barbara, and Pawel Brodowski. "Betty's Groove." *Jazz Forum* (international edition), 57 (1979): 30.

Watrous, Peter. "A World Written, and Rewritten, by Betty Carter." *New York Times,* 28 August 1992, C3.

———. "A Jazz Singing Legend Guides a New Generation." *New York Times,* 15 April 1993, C15, C22.

Weis, Richard. "Jazzing and Jiving." *Daily Targum,* 16 March 1989, 3.

Wenzel, Curtis. "Jazz, Scat, and Betty Bebop." *City Pages,* Arts Pages Twin Cities, 11 May 1983, 11.

The West Siders. *Remembering Detroit's Old West Side: 1920–1950 (A Pictorial History of the Westsiders).* Detroit: The WestSiders, 1997.

Whitburn, Joel. *Top R&B Singles, 1942–1988.* Menomonee Falls, Wis.: Record Research, 1988.

Whitehead, Kevin. "Behind Every Singer Is a Piano Player: Betty Carter and John Hicks." *Down Beat,* December 1992, 36.

Wilson, John S. "Betty Carter Sings Jazz on Broadway." *New York Times,* 24 November 1978, C10.

Wilson, Sunnie. *Toast of the Town.* Detroit: Wayne State University Press, 1998.

Zaworski, David. "Carter's Listening Lesson Lets Young People Sing." *Down Beat,* January 1998, 66.

Unpublished Interviews and Talks

Betty Carter

Interview by Leonard Lyons, 27 September 1975. Audiotape. Institute of Jazz Studies, Rutgers University, Newark.

"Jazz Talk." Interview by Chris White, 14 April 1976. Videotape. Institute of Jazz Studies, Rutgers University, Newark.

Interview at the Newport Jazz Festival, 30 June–1 July 1979. Audiotape. Voice of America Music Library Collection, VOA 7 inch tape no. 1053. (Held at Library of Congress.)

Talk at Laney Community College, Oakland, Calif, December 1979. Transcript by Matthew Yaple.

Talk at the Great American Music Hall, San Francisco, December 1979. Transcript by Matthew Yaple.

Interviewer unknown, December 1979. KJAZ-FM (San Francisco). Transcript by Matthew Yaple.

Interview by Matthew Yaple, at Carter's home in Brooklyn, early 1980. Transcript by Matthew Yaple.

Interview by Art Roberts, 21 October 1983. WERS-FM (Boston).

The *Nature of Music* programs 1, 3, 4, and 6. Karl Signell, producer. Guildford, CT: Audio Forum of Jeffrey Norton Publishers, 1987.

Interview by Terry Gross, ca. 1990 *Fresh Air,* National Public Radio.

Interview by Evan Spring, 13 May 1993. WKCR-FM (New York).
"Special Moments with Betty Carter." Interview by Gil Noble, 4 July 1993. Transcript of broadcast on *Like It Is* 900, WABC-TV (New York). Denver, Colo.: Journal Graphics 1993.
Interviews by the author at Carter's home in Brooklyn, NY, 24 October 1994 and 9 July 1998. Audiotape.

Others

Unless otherwise indicated, interviews are by the author.

Amram, David. 21 and 28 December 1998.
Bank, Danny. 11 January 1999.
Barbaro, Clifford. 22 January 1999.
Barkan, Todd. 8 October 1999.
Benson, George. 18 December 1998.
Bey, Andy. 11 January 1999.
Braden, Don. 8 October 1999.
Brown, Cameron. 11 January 1999.
Burno, Dwayne. 20 November 1998.
Chestnut, Cyrus, Louis Nash, Curtis Lundy, and others. *Jazz Profile: Betty Carter.* National Public Radio. Sonja Williams, producer.
Cohen, Noal. 2 March 1999.
Coleman, Ira. 12 January 1999.
Cuscuna, Michael. 18 December 1998.
Dockery, Sam. 4 February, 1999.
Dorn, Joel. 6 January 1995, 3 December 1998, and 8 October 1999.
Feller, Sid. 31 January 1999.
Ferla, Joe. 2 November 1998.
Goldstein, Gail. 8 November 1998.
Gordon, Derek. 14 April 2000.
Green, Benny. 25 June 1999.
Gryce, Tommy. Interview by Phil Schaap. New York: WKCR-FM, 2 July 1997.
———. 11 January 1999.
Handy, Craig. 5 October 1998.
Harris, Barry. 16 July 1999.
Harrison, Jim. 2 February 1999.
Hicks, John. 23 November 1998.
Hicks, John, Curtis Lundy, and Kenny Washington. "Jazz Insights." Interview by Arnold Jay Smith. 17 November 1998. New York: New School of Social Research.
Jackson, Javon. 6 August 1999.
Jimenez, JoAnne. 12 January and 10 June 1999.
Jones III, James T. 20 November 1998.
Kantor, Robert. 8 June 1999.

McBee, Cecil. 6 February 1999.
McKinney, Harold. 4 December 1998.
Meadows-Blanding, Irene Jones. 8 June 1999.
Mixon, Daniel. 1 December 1999.
Moncur III, Grachan. 3 April 1999.
Morton, Jelly Roll. Interview by Alan Lomax, 1938. Library of Congress 1657-B.
Moss, Khalid. 9 February 1999.
Nash, Lewis. 30 June 1999.
Nicholas, George "Big Nick." Interview by Dale Fitzgerald, 1980. Jazz Oral History Project. Institute of Jazz Studies, Rutgers University, Newark.
Redding, James Romeo. 7 June 1999.
Redding, Kagle. 18 March 2000.
Redding, Myles. 31 March 1999.
Reed, Tanya. 20 August 1999.
Ridley, Larry. 2 February 1999.
Schreiber, John. 8 November 1998.
Scott, Jimmy. 9 June 1999.
Smith, Arnold J. 9 November 1998.
Smith, David Lionel. 6 October 1998.
Struthers, Kevin. 31 March 2000.
Thurlow, Janet. 2 December 1998.
Washington, Kenny. 12 January, 1999.

Discography

This discography includes private recordings from a variety of sources as well as commercially issued material. Commercial releases that contain only a few Betty Carter items are identified by song. Private recordings are identified by venue, location, and date whenever possible. Information about unissued material from commercial sessions is available from published discographies such as Bruyninckx.

"Confess." With the Hamptones and Lionel Hampton. On *AFRS Transcription: Jubilee Broadcast No. 307,* possibly recorded ca. October 1948 (unissued).

"I'll Dance at Your Wedding." With the Hamptones and Lionel Hampton. On *AFRS Transcription: Jubilee Broadcast No. 321,* possibly recorded ca. December 1948 (unissued).

"Jay Bird." On *Lionel Hampton and His 1948 Orchestra in Concerts,* WK Records 12–1, and *Lionel Hampton and His Orchestra 1948,* Alamac QSR 2419 (ca. late 1948). Also on a two-volume compilation of Lionel Hampton's work from 1948 on MCA-Coral 82018–2.

"Benson's Boogie." On *Lionel Hampton 4: Seeds of Swing (1945–1949),* MCA (F) 510–112 24 January 1949.

"I'll Dance at Your Wedding" and "Nothing in View." With the Hamptones and Lionel Hampton. On *AFRS Transcription: Jubilee Broadcast No. 319,* possibly recorded ca. January 1949 (unissued).

"Gladys's Idea." With Lionel Hampton. On *AFRS Transcription: Jubilee Broadcast No. 327,* possibly recorded ca. February 1949 (unissued).

"The Hucklebuck." On *Hamp: The Legendary Decca Recordings of Lionel Hampton,* GRD2–652 10 May 1949. Also on *Lionel Hampton,* Chicago: Time-Life Music, 1986. Time Life STBB-24.

Betty Carter may have participated in a session with Bobby Plater, Memphis, 1950, Bullet 327.

"Red Top." With King Pleasure. On *The Source*, Prestige PR-24017 (1952). Listed as Prestige 821 in Bruyninckx. Also on Charlie "Little Jazz" Ferguson session listed as Prestige 855.

Meet Betty Carter and Ray Bryant. Epic LN-3202 (1955).

Betty: Betty Carter—Social Call. Col JC-36425. CBS Special Products, CBS A 36425 (1990). Includes Epic 3202 and previously unissued material recorded with Gigi Gryce on 25 April 1956.

Out There. Peacock Progressive Jazz 90 (1958).

The Modern Sound of Betty Carter. ABC-Paramount 363 (1960).

What a Little Moonlight Can Do. Impulse! ASD-9321 (1976). Reissue of Progressive Jazz 90 and ABC-Paramount 363, above.

I Can't Help It. Reissue of Impulse! ASD-9321 on CD, GRD-114 (1992).

Ray Charles and Betty Carter. ABC-Paramount 385 (1961). Reissued by Dunhill Compact Classics, DZL-039 (1988).

'Round Midnight. Atco 6239 (1962). Atco-33–152. Reissued by Atco on CD 7 80453–2.

Venue unknown. Tokyo, with Sonny Rollins (19 September 1963; unissued).

Inside Betty Carter. UAS-5639 (1964). Later catalogued by Bet-Car as MK-1000. Reissued by Capitol Jazz CDP 0777 7 89702 2 4 with previously unreleased material from sessions in 1965.

Finally Betty Carter. Roulette SR-5000 (1969). Produced by Bush records. Released by Roulette in 1975. Reissued by Roulette on CD, CDP 7953332 (1991).

Round Midnight. Roulette SR-5001. (1969). Released by Roulette in 1975. Reissued by Roulette on CD, CDP 7 95999 2 (1991).

Betty Carter: At the Village Vanguard. Bet-Car MK-1001 (1970). Reissued by Verve, 314 519 851–2 (1993).

The Betty Carter Album. Bet-Car MK-1002 (1976). Reissued by Verve, 835 682–2 (1988). Recorded before 1975.

Keystone Korner. San Francisco (1975; unissued).

Public Theater Cabaret. New York (April 1975; unissued).

Now It's My Turn. Roulette SR-5005 (1976). Also released as RA-20243 (1976).

Venue unknown. Arhus, Sweden (1978; unissued).

The Audience with Betty Carter. Bet-Car MK-1003 (1979). Reissued by Verve, 835–684–2 (1988).

I Didn't Know What Time It Was. Jazz Door CD 1261. Released in 1993; recorded sometime between 1975 and 1979. Copy held at the Library of Congress.

Whatever Happened to Love? Bet-Car MK-1004 (1982). Reissued by Verve, 835–683–2 (1988).

Fat Tuesday's. New York. *Jazz Alive* (31 December 1982; unissued).

Greek Theater. San Francisco (May 1984; unissued).

Jazz Bühne Berlin '85. Repertoire 4901-CC (1985; released in 1990).

Tufts University. Boston (6 February 1986; unissued).

Carmen McRae–Betty Carter Duets. Great American Music Hall Records 2706 (1988). Reissued by Verve, 314–529–579–2 (1996).

Look What I Got. Verve 835–661 (1988).

Music cruise. (22 August 1987; unissued).

"I'm Wishing." On *Stay Awake: Music From Disney Films.* A&M Records CD 3918 DX003644 (1988).

Droppin' Things. Polygram 843–991 (1990).

SUNY Purchase. Harrison, N.Y. (11 October 1991; unissued).

Fat Tuesday's. New York (28 December 1991; unissued).

It's Not about the Melody. Polygram 314–513870–2 (1992).

"The Music Never Stops." Alice Tully Hall, New York (28 March 1992; selections broadcast on WBGO and WNYC, 12 September 1994; unissued).

"You're Mine You." *Jazz at Lincoln Center Presents: The Fire of the Fundamentals.* Sony.

Montreux/Detroit Festival. Detroit (7 September 1992; unissued).

International Association of Jazz Educators. Houston (9 January 1993; unissued).

Feed the Fire. Polygram 314–523–600–2 (1993).

"How High the Moon" and on "Now's the Time." *Carnegie Hall Salutes the Jazz Masters.* Verve 314 523 150–2 (1994).

Yoshi's. Seattle (31 December 1994; unissued).

Robert Treat Hotel. Newark, N.J. (14 May 1995; unissued).

I'm Yours, You're Mine. Verve 314 533 182–2 (1996).

"Let It Snow" and "Home for the Holidays." On *Verve Christmas Album: Jazz for Joy.* Verve 314 531 960–2 (1996).

"Lonely House." On *September Songs: The Music of Kurt Weill.* Sony SK63046 (1997).

Chicago Jazz Festival. Chicago (31 August 1997; unissued).

Kennedy Center. Washington, D.C. "Jazz Set." National Public Radio. Selections from *Jazz Ahead*'s fifth year (15 April 1998; unissued).

Videography

Saturday Night Live. 13 March 1976.

Kansas City Jazz Festival. 1978.

Newport Jazz Festival. Saratoga Springs, N.Y. 1979.

Yaple, Matthew. *Jazz Is Betty Carter: Is She the Last Jazz Singer?* With footage of performance at the Great American Music Hall, San Francisco, December 1979. Master's thesis, Temple University, 1982.

Parkerson, Michelle. *but then . . . she's Betty Carter.* With footage of a performance at Howard University in 1980. Eye of the Storm Productions, 1980. Distributed by Women Make Movies.

Montreux/Detroit Jazz Festival. July 1980.

The Hague. July 1980.

Call Me Betty Carter. 1981. CBS Cable, New York. Michael Cuscuna, producer.

Montreal Jazz Festival. 1981 or 1982.

"An Evening with Betty Carter." Filmed at Symphony Hall, Boston. *Say Brother,* WGBH (Boston), October 1983.

Hamburg, Germany. 1984.

CBS Sunday Morning, Urban Update segment. With footage from Tufts University from 6 February 1985. CBS, 2 May 1986.

Jazz in Exile. Chuck France with Kathleen Lattarelli, producer. Rhapsody Films, 1982.

DOC International Show. November 1987.

ZDF Club. Germany. 1987.

Trumpets, Montclair, N.J. 4 December 1988.

Leverkusen Jazz Festival. Leverkusen, Germany. 1988.

Sunday Today: Michelob Presents Night Music. NBC, 12 March 1989.

Cosby Show. NBC, November 1988.

Hit Hotel. Perugia, Italy. 15 April 1990.

CBS Sunday Morning. 3 August 1993.

Verve Fiftieth Anniversary Tribute at Carnegie Hall. 6 April 1994. Richard Seidel and Don Sickler, producers.

Cyrus Chesnut profile. *CBS Sunday Morning,* 10 June 1996.

CBS Sunday Morning. 24 November 1996; aired again on 1 December 1996.

"I'm Yours, You're Mine." Verve Records, music video. 6 May 1997.

CBS Sunday Morning. 30 September 1997.

CBS Sunday Morning. Includes footage of Jazz Ahead, 15 April 1998. 4 October 1998.

Betty Carter: A Complete Original. BET on Jazz, Black Entertainment Television, fall 1998. Includes footage of St. Lucia Jazz Festival and Carter's visit to Beijing. More footage exists.

Over Easy. PBS, San Francisco. Date unknown.

Index